The Thomas Merton Letters Series

Witness to Freedom

Books by Thomas Merton

The Ascent to Truth*

The Asian Journal of Thomas Merton

The Collected Poems of Thomas Merton

Conjectures of a Guilty Bystander

Contemplation in a World of Action

The Courage for Truth: Letters to Writers*

Disputed Questions*

Gandhi on Non-Violence

The Hidden Ground of Love:
Letters on Religious Experience and Social Concerns*

The Last of the Fathers*

The Literary Essays of Thomas Merton

Love and Living*

My Argument with the Gestapo

No Man Is an Island*

The Road to Joy: Letters to New and Old Friends*

The School of Charity:
Letters on Religious Renewal and Spiritual Direction*

The Secular Journal of Thomas Merton

Seeds of Destruction

The Seven Storey Mountain*

The Sign of Jonas*

The Silent Life

Thoughts in Solitude

Vow of Conversation

The Waters of Siloe*

The Way of Chuang Tzu

Witness to Freedom: Letters in Times of Crisis*

*Available in a Harvest paperback edition from
Harcourt Brace & Company

WITNESS TO FREEDOM

The Letters of
THOMAS MERTON
in Times of Crisis
Selected and edited by
William H. Shannon

A Harvest Book
Harcourt Brace & Company
SAN DIEGO   NEW YORK   LONDON

Library of Congress Cataloging-in-Publication Data
Merton, Thomas, 1915–1968.
Witness to freedom: the letters of Thomas Merton in times of crisis/
selected and edited by William H. Shannon.—1st Harvest ed.
p.   cm.—(A Harvest book)
Originally published: New York: Farrar, Straus, Giroux, 1994.
Includes index.
ISBN 0-15-600274-4
1. Merton, Thomas, 1915–1968—Correspondence.   2. Trappists—
United States—Correspondence.   I. Shannon, William Henry,
1917–   .
II. Title.
[BX4705.M542A4   1995b]
271'.12502—dc20   95-22488
[B]

Designed by Cynthia Krupat

Printed in the United States of America

First Harvest edition 1995

A B C D E

Contents

IV. Religious Thought and Dialogue

Introduction

*To defend one's faith is to defend one's freedom, and at
least implicitly the freedom of everyone else.*
CONJECTURES OF A GUILTY BYSTANDER

*Only in the Lord's service is there true freedom, as the
prophets would tell us. This is still the clear experience
of the Jews, as it ought to be of the Christians, except
that we were too sure of our freedom and too sure we
could never alienate it. Alas, for hundreds of years we
have disregarded the fact that we are the children of
God and now the whole world is reaping the consequences. If only Christians had valued the freedom of
the children of God that was given them. They preferred
safety and the Grand Inquisitor.*
TO ERICH FROMM

Truth is the solid foundation of freedom, and truth only.
TO ARTHUR HAYS SULZBERGER

There is a sense of joy and relief in bringing to a close the publication of
the five volumes of the Letters of Thomas Merton. There has been the
joy of being in touch with Merton's many correspondents, at times through
personal contact and at others through the intimate sharing that comes
from reading so many warmly personal letters. There was joy in experiencing the friendships that Merton made and added joy in making some
of those friendships mine also. The task of acting as general editor—
editing the first volume myself and then being closely involved in the
editing of the next three—has been a deeply enriching experience and
a source of personal growth for me.

It all started on July 14, 1982, at a luncheon meeting with Robert
Giroux, James Laughlin, and Anne McCormick at the Chelsea Place
Restaurant on Eighth Avenue in New York. They asked me, on behalf of
all the members of the Merton Legacy Trust, to take on the job of general
editor of the Letters of Thomas Merton. We had no idea at that point
how many volumes would result. I am grateful to Dr. Robert E. Daggy,
Brother Patrick Hart, and Dr. Christine M. Bochen (who edited Volumes

II, III, and IV, respectively) for their excellent help in moving this project toward completion. At the same time there is a sense of wholesome relief that, after more than ten years of work on the letters, the project is reaching a successful and fruitful outcome.

I have entitled this volume *Witness to Freedom*. I believe it to be an appropriate title—one way of summing up Merton's life. He knew the importance of freedom; he knew also, perhaps most particularly in himself, the barriers that prevent freedom from being a living reality in a person's life. Merton's notion of what freedom meant underwent radical change. Roughly, I would designate three stages in the story of his growth to freedom. For the first half of his life, it meant largely the removal of restraints that prevented him from doing what he wanted to do (though it should perhaps be added that during this period of his life he was never quite sure what he wanted to do).

At the midpoint of his life—specifically the evening in 1941 when he arrived at the Abbey of Our Lady of Gethsemani in Kentucky to begin life as a monk—he reached stage two in his journey to freedom. When he was received by the brother at the gatehouse, he tells us: "Brother Matthew locked the gate behind me and I was enclosed in the four walls of my new freedom" (*SSM*, p. 372). A curious way of looking at freedom: a locked gate and a four-wall enclosure! At this stage Merton seemed to look outwardly for freedom—that is, he looked to the monastic rule and to the decisions of his superiors as a mediated way of exercising his freedom. Perhaps this was a necessary stage for him as he first entered the monastery. He had experienced in his own life the disaster that unrestrained freedom could bring, and he now saw the need of discipline and asceticism. Following the rule and obeying the directives of his superiors opened the way to a freedom much more real than the unbridled freedom of his youth.

But Thomas Merton's life was anything but static. As he grew in the monastic life and in the living of the contemplative life, his understanding of freedom underwent drastic modifications. At this third stage he saw freedom as an inner reality, guided much more from within than from without. In this stage the will of God presses down on one's freedom with an immediacy that at times can be frightening. Encountering God can mean the discovery of our deepest freedom. Merton writes: "Our encounter with God, our response to God's word is the drawing forth and calling out of our deepest freedom, our true identity" (*CWA*, p. 344). To be free and to experience one's true identity means to rid one's life of the illusions and fictions we so often live by: living in the real world and not in a world constructed by our own fantasies or expectations. It means taking responsibility for one's own life: standing on one's own feet, making one's own decisions of conscience. This was the kind of freedom that Merton came to see as the only authentic way of living the monastic life and, indeed, the Christian life. To what degree he achieved it is something difficult, perhaps impossible, for us to judge. But that he never ceased to strive for it is, to my mind, the chief biographical fact about Thomas Merton.

If the content of these letters is about freedom, the context in which he wrote them was one of struggle. The times called for critique and reappraisal. The institutional structures of monastic life, Roman Catholicism, and American life were coming under close scrutiny. The Western world saw its identity being threatened by the cultural inroads of the great civilizations of the East.

Merton was facing his own struggles too. To give but one example, an ongoing struggle of his life was dealing with the question: How does one balance an authentic understanding of freedom with a monk's commitment to obedience? Part III of this volume includes letters I have labeled "Vocation Crisis: 1959–1960." These letters tell the story of an important phase of the freedom-obedience struggle in Merton's life. They witness to the delicate balance he was generally able—though not always without personal anguish—to achieve in his life's journey to the place of perfect freedom.

This fact—that Merton lived in an era of struggle, both personal and societal—suggested the subtitle of this book, "Letters in Times of Crisis." Merton readers will remember that in *Seeds of Destruction* he used a similar (though not identical) title for a group of letters he published in that volume, describing them as "Letters in a Time of Crisis." These were the very first letters of Merton's to be published commercially. That the last volume of his published letters should recall that title seems to be singularly appropriate.

It should be clear that Thomas Merton was not content simply to seek freedom in his own life. As the monastic walls began to move out and he found himself in contact with more and more people outside those walls, he accepted the responsibility of helping others to move along the way of true freedom. He chose to place his own freedom at the service of the freedom of others. He became freedom's witness.

From his monastic vantage point, he could see a good deal of unfreedom in the world and yet at the same time wondrous resources of good will and generous love. In an article written in 1966 for *Commonweal*, he describes himself:

This is simply the voice of a self-questioning human person who, like all his brothers [and sisters] struggles to cope with turbulent, mysterious, demanding, exciting, frustrating, confused existence, in which almost nothing is really predictable, in which most definitions, explanations and justifications become incredible even before they are uttered, in which people suffer together and are sometimes utterly beautiful, at other times impossibly pathetic. In which there is much that is frightening, in which almost everything public is patently phony, and in which there is at

*the same time an immense ground of personal authenticity that is right
there and so obvious that no one can talk about it and most cannot even
believe that it is there.* [CWA, p. 160.]

"In which almost everything public is patently phony"—this meant
many things to Merton. It meant the world of communication and advertising—communication which regularly slanted the truth or distorted
it, advertising that created false needs in people and prevented them
from seeing clearly what was for their good. It meant technology which,
however much good it might do for people (and he readily acknowledged
that good), was all too frequently soiled by the all-consuming push for
profit and efficiency, achieved so often at the expense of people's true
humanity. It meant the military-industrial complex that sought profit in
producing arms and was able to live with an attitude of callous indifference
toward the destruction of human lives which their products were meant
to accomplish.

One of the manifestations of unfreedom that haunted Merton much
of his life, but especially in the 1960s, was the terrible specter of war.
War destroys the freedom of its victims and blinds the freedom of its
"victors." Merton wrote a great deal about the evils of war and the obligation of all people of good will to do everything possible to make war
a thing of the past. He wrote articles in such journals as *The Catholic
Worker, Commonweal, Jubilee*, and *Blackfriars*. In April 1962 he was
forbidden by the highest authority in the Cistercian Order to publish on
the topic of war and peace. He obeyed the prohibition against *publishing*,
but continued circulating mimeographed articles through his wide net-
work of friends. The most famous of these mimeographs was, without a
doubt, a selection he made of his own letters and issued under the title
The Cold War Letters. These letters form a major part of this volume.

It may seem an anachronism, now that the Berlin Wall is down and
the Soviet Union no longer exists, to publish Merton's Cold War Letters.
After all, the "Cold War," as the term was first used by Walter Lippmann
in 1947, meant the confrontation between the two superpowers: the
U.S.A. and the U.S.S.R. Yet even though that confrontation is a thing
of the past, it would be wrong to say that our present state is one of peace.
The threat of war continues, even though the protagonists, and also the
issues, are less clearly defined. Nuclear missiles still exist in abundance
and new types of "conventional" weapons with terribly destructive power
have been produced and their destructiveness was demonstrated in the
Persian Gulf War. National rivalries, economic factors, ethnic and religious antagonisms have produced a worldwide instability that could at
any moment break into hot war (something, for instance, that at this
writing is going on in what was once Yugoslavia). Hence, though the term
may have taken on a different meaning, our world is still in a situation,
not of true peace, but of Cold War. Many of the things Merton had to

say in the 1960s are equally applicable to the world situation that now exists. That is why I believe that Merton's Cold War Letters still say important things that we need to hear.

For Thomas Merton freedom was grounded in his religious faith. "To defend one's faith is to defend one's freedom, and at least implicitly the freedom of everyone else" (*CGB*, p. 88). And what did that freedom amount to? It is a freedom from all those forces from the outside that would try to prevent anyone from saying his or her own "yes" or "no." This ability to say a personal "yes" or "no"—that does not echo the "yes" or "no" of state, party, corporation, institution, or system—is the bedrock of authentic freedom. Merton believed that it was this kind of freedom that helped to define true art and authentic writing. It was this kind of freedom that was the goal of all major religions. His own Church, he felt, was meant to be a center of freedom. All her laws and all the various ways in which she exercised her authority must be subordinate to the Holy Spirit and the freedom which is the Spirit's gift to all. He recognized that the Church does not look like that to many who are outside her. They believe that the Church acts on the principle of authority, not of freedom. But it is in Christ and in His Spirit that true freedom is found; and the Church is, first and foremost, not simply an institution, but Christ's Body, His people living by His Spirit. (See *CGB*, p. 89.)

Among the letters in this volume are many to well-known persons, such as the artist and printer Victor Hammer; the ecologist Rachel Carson; his dear friend and literary agent Naomi Burton Stone; his fellow poet and teacher Mark Van Doren; his Abbot, Dom James Fox; the fellow Trappist writer who was his contemporary at Gethsemani, Fr. Raymond Flanagan; the distinguished French Arabic scholar Louis Massignon; the Canadian philosopher Leslie Dewart; and a host of others. There is even an open letter to the American hierarchy on the issue of war.

But there are also quite a number of letters to little-known persons, even some unidentified. The inclusion of these letters would, I think, have pleased Thomas Merton. He very much believed in the importance of ordinary people.

In terms of the issues discussed, the letters have been arranged around the following categories (though with the realization that Merton's letters are like a river frequently overflowing its banks, which is to say that few of them can be restricted to a single issue): art and freedom; war and freedom; Merton's life and works; Merton's thoughts about some aspects of religion and religious dialogue. These groupings make up the four parts of this book. The leaven that informs them all, implicitly or explicitly, is always freedom. Thus, for instance, in reference to Part IV, one cannot understand Judaism, Islam, Eastern religions, and Christianity in its various manifestations except in terms of their being, at an ultimate level (which unhappily they do not always reach), guarantors of human freedom.

Merton's life was a struggle for freedom and his writings were an articulation of that struggle. It was chiefly in the way he lived and in what he wrote that he was a living witness to freedom, perhaps one of the great witnesses of our century.

W ILLIAM H. S HANNON
Editor

I.
Art and Freedom

*It is the greatest glory of Christian art that it expresses
the freedom of the children of God.*
PREFACE TO WILLIAM CONGDON'S
In My Disc of Gold

Copy of a woodcut by Victor Hammer, used as an
illustration in the second limited edition of Hagia Sophia.
Printed with the permission of Carolyn Reading Hammer

To Victor Hammer

Born in Vienna on December 9, 1882, Victor Hammer was brought up in the old quarter of the city among modest artisans. At the age of sixteen he entered the Vienna Academy of Fine Arts and learned to support himself by drawing and painting. An inveterate traveler, he visited many places in Europe and before he had reached the age of forty had gone twice to the United States. He became famous as a typographer who formulated principles that others were to follow; he was also adept in bookbinding and calligraphy.

With Hitler's rise to power and the spread of Nazism to Austria, Hammer gave up his position as professor of art at the Academy of Fine Arts in Vienna and came to the United States. In 1939 he accepted the position of professor of art at Wells College in Aurora-on-Cayuga, New York, where he taught lettering, drawing, and painting and, with his son Jacob, founded the Wells College Press and the Hammer Press. In 1948 he retired from Wells College to become artist-in-residence at Transylvania College in Lexington, Kentucky. He and his wife, Carolyn, whom he married in 1955, lived in a historical residence in Gratz Park in Lexington. One of his presses was brought from Florence and became the King Library Press. Under the imprint he had used in Italy, Stamperia del Santuccio, he printed special limited editions of several of Merton's books. On one of his visits to the Hammers, Merton saw a triptych that Victor had painted. The central panel showed a woman and a young boy standing in front of her; the woman was putting a crown on the child's head and Merton asked who the woman was. Hammer answered that he had begun to paint a madonna and child, but it had not turned out as he expected and he no longer knew who the woman was. Merton said, "I know who she is. I have always known her. She is Hagia Sophia."

On May 2, 1959, Hammer wrote to Merton asking him to come bless the triptych and also to explain in more detail what he had said about Hagia Sophia. Merton did so in the following letter. The contents of this letter later grew into the text of his long poem, "Hagia Sophia," printed by Hammer in a limited edition; it was also published in Emblems of a Season of Fury *and appears in* Collected Poems.

May 14, 1959

I have not rushed to reply to your letter—first, because I have been a little busy, and second, because it is most difficult to write anything that really makes sense about this most mysterious reality in the mystery of God—Hagia Sophia [Holy Wisdom].

The first thing to be said, of course, is that Hagia Sophia is God Himself. God is not only a Father but a Mother. He is both at the same time, and it is the "feminine aspect" or "feminine principle" in the divinity that is the Hagia Sophia. But of course as soon as you say this the whole thing becomes misleading: a division of an "abstract" divinity into two abstract principles. Nevertheless, to ignore this distinction is to lose touch with the fullness of God. This is a very ancient intuition of reality which goes back to the oldest Oriental thought. (There is something about it in Carolyn's wonderful book *Peaks and Lamas* [written by Marco Pallis], incidentally.) For the "masculine-feminine" relationship is basic in *all* reality—simply because all reality mirrors the reality of God.

In its most primitive aspect, Hagia Sophia is the dark, nameless *Ousia* [Being] of the Father, the Son, and the Holy Ghost, the incomprehensible, "primordial" darkness which is infinite light. The Three Divine Persons, each at the same time, are Sophia and manifest her. But where the Sophia of your picture comes in is this: the wisdom of God, "reaching from end to end mightily" is also the Tao, the nameless pivot of all being and nature, the center and meaning of all, that which is the smallest and poorest and most humble in all: the "feminine child" playing before God the Creator in His universe, "playing before Him at all times, playing in the world" (Proverbs 8). (This is the Epistle of the Feast of the Immaculate Conception.) This feminine principle in the universe is the inexhaustible source of creative realizations of the Father's glory in the world and is in fact the manifestation of His glory. Pushing it further, Sophia in ourselves is the *mercy* of God, the tenderness which by the infinitely mysterious power of pardon turns the darkness of our sins into the light of God's love.

Hence, Sophia is the feminine, dark, yielding, tender counterpart of the power, justice, creative dynamism of the Father.

Now the Blessed Virgin is the one created being who in herself realizes perfectly all that is hidden in Sophia. She is a kind of personal manifestation of Sophia. She crowns the Second Person of the Trinity with His human nature (with what is weak, able to suffer, able to be defeated) and sends Him forth with His mission of inexpressible mercy, to die for man on the Cross, and this death, followed by the Resurrection, is the greatest expression of the "manifold wisdom of God" which unites us all in the mystery of Christ—the Church. Finally, it is the Church herself, properly understood as the great manifestation of the mercy of God, who is the revelation of Sophia in the sight of the angels.

The key to the whole thing is, of course, *mercy and love*. In the sense that God is Love, is Mercy, is Humility, is Hiddenness, He shows Himself to us within ourselves as our own poverty, our own nothingness (which Christ took upon Himself, ordained for this by the Incarnation in the womb of the Virgin) (the crowning in your picture), and if we receive the humility of God into our hearts, we become able to accept and embrace and love this very poverty, which is Himself and His Sophia. And then the darkness of Wisdom becomes to us inexpressible light. We pass through the center of our own nothingness into the light of God.

I wrote that first page without keeping a carbon, but I am getting someone to copy it because I am going to want to know what I said. I say these things and forget them, and then someone refers to them again and I can no longer remember what is being talked about. I cannot remember what it was I said when I was there in Lexington and we were looking at the triptych.

The beauty of all creation is a reflection of Sophia living and hidden in creation. But it is only our reflection. And the misleading thing about beauty, created beauty, is that we expect Sophia to be simply a more intense and more perfect and more brilliant, unspoiled, spiritual revelation of the same beauty. Whereas to arrive at her beauty we must pass through an apparent negation of created beauty, and to reach her light we must realize that in comparison with created light it is a darkness. But this is only because created beauty and light are ugliness and darkness compared with her. Again the whole thing is in the question of mercy, which cuts across the divisions and passes beyond every philosophical and religious ideal. For Sophia is not an ideal, not an abstraction, but the highest reality, and the highest reality must manifest herself to us not only in power but also in poverty, otherwise we never see it. Sophia is the Lady Poverty to whom St. Francis was married. And of course she dwelt with the Desert Fathers in their solitude, for it was she who brought them there and she whom they knew there. It was with her that they conversed all the time in their silence.

I wish I had a fuller remembrance of your pictures. I just remember the general idea. The story you tell of its growth is very interesting and revealing and I am sure Hagia Sophia herself was guiding you in the process, for it is she who guides all true artists, and without her they are nothing.

When [Ad] Reinhardt [the painter, Merton's classmate] was here he was discussing art too. His approach is very austere and ascetic. It is a kind of exaggerated reticence, a kind of fear of self expression. All his paintings are very formal and black. I certainly do not think he is a quack like so many others; on the contrary, he is in strong reaction against them.

I think you and he would be in fundamental agreement. It is a pity he was not able to get over there. He is certainly not a brilliant success (like so many of the others who are making fortunes with their stuff).

Now J. Laughlin, whom you know, is coming down in June. He wants very much to see you, and will write to you about it. My novice, who was in the hospital, came out but is going back, and it is possible that perhaps it might be necessary for me to make one trip more. I do not know what the future will bring, but until I know more about it let us wait and expect the possibility at any rate. If nothing comes up, then we could plan on you both coming over here later in June. I could write about that. I think often of the Desert Fathers, and the work [is] progressing. And how is the broadside? Maybe we could make a little broadsheet on Sophia, with the material begun here???

I am really enjoying *Peaks and Lamas*, and also the Athos book has been very fine—and the Hesiod. When you have thought about this material on Sophia, perhaps we could make a further step toward thinking of a title. I am so happy to be involved in what is clearly a very significant work, spiritually as well as artistically.

Thank you for the photostats from the [Catholic] Encyclopedia [on Wisdom]. I looked them over, and they just begin to touch on the mysterious doctrine. Carolyn should try to get for the Library a book by Sergius Bolgakov, called *The Wisdom of God*, published in London in the thirties. It would cover very well the Sophia theme. I have notes on it, but the book is very technical in its way.

On January 21, 1962, Hammer wrote to Merton and asked him what he thought "brainwashing" meant. How, he asked, can we escape it with all the newspapers and other means of communication?

[*Cold War Letter 24b*]   c. January 25, 1962

As for brainwashing, the term is used very loosely about almost anything. Strict technical brainwashing is an artificially induced "conversion," brought about by completely isolating a person emotionally and spiritually, undermining his whole sense of identity, and then "rescuing" him from this state of near-collapse by drawing him over into a new sense of community with his persecutors, now his rescuers, who "restore" his identity by admitting [him] into their midst as an approved and docile instrument. Henceforth he does what they want him to do and likes it, indeed finds a certain satisfaction in this, and even regards his old life as shameful and inferior.

In the loose sense, any mass man is a "brainwashed" man. He has lost his identity or never had one in the first place, and he seeks security, hope, a sense of identity in his immersion in the pressures and prejudices of a majority, speaking through TV, newspapers, etc. Having no real power or meaning in himself, he seeks all in identification with a presumably all-powerful all-wise collectivity. Whatever the collectivity does is right, infallible, perfect. Anything approved by it becomes legitimate and even noble. The worst crimes are virtues when backed up by the all-powerful collectivity. All that matters is to be part of the great, loud mass.

It seems to me that the great effort of conscience that remains for modern man is to resist this kind of annihilating pressure, this defection, in every possible way. The temptation comes unfortunately from very many angles, even seemingly good sources. The Cold War is the deadly influence that is leading Western man to brainwash himself.

When the process is completed there will be nothing left but the hot war or the decline into totalitarian blindness and inertia, which also spells hot war in the end. The prospects are very dark, aren't they? Yet I think that perhaps some providential accident may happen that will wake everyone up. Some kind of plague of radiation, perhaps, something unexpected and unforeseen that will force people to their senses. But can we say we have done anything to deserve this? I hardly think so. Fortunately, if we only get what we deserved, we would never have very much of anything good. God is not simply just, He is also and above all merciful. I wish that this had not been so thoroughly forgotten . . .

The French situation is very disturbing indeed. Much evil can come of this. Everyone expects De Gaulle to get it this year sometime, and I wonder how long he can survive. He has been a good man in many ways, yet perhaps mistakenly messianic too. But what could any reasonable human being [have] done with Algeria? If he goes, then France goes too. And this may be the spark that will finally ignite everything. The next few months will tell us a thing or two. And the next three years, or four: well, to call them fateful is putting it so mildly as to be ridiculous.

I wonder if there is going to be much left of the Western world by 1984 to fulfill George Orwell's prophecies.

Meanwhile, we have only to be what we are and to retain the spirit and civilization which we were blessed with, and to keep as human as we can.

[*Cold War Letter 71*]   May 1962

More and more I see that it is not the moral principles which are at stake but, more radically, the whole outlook of modern man, at least in America, and the basic assumptions which tend to guide his thought, if it can be called thought. We are living in an absurd dream, and a very bad one. And it is the fruit of all sorts of things we ought not to have done. But the whole world is in turmoil, spiritually, morally, socially. We are sitting on a thin crust above an immense lake of molten lava that is stirring and getting ready to erupt. Nothing will stop this eruption. But at least we can refrain from setting off bombs that will start it in some far worse way than it normally would.

November 9, 1963

I shudder at the thought of attempting a long didactic poem on art. Yet who knows, someday it may happen. I generally end up doing what I never expected to do, and I suppose that is a very good thing. However, I am firmly resolved to do anything but this at the moment.

Of course, one could approach the subject of art as a way of "knowing" and seeing. You sometimes cannot see a thing at all unless you take pains to make something like it. And yet not like it. Nothing gets to be known without being changed in the process.

As to saying "What is art?," well, I don't think there is much chance of making any sense out of the question if one is looking for a pure essence. On the other hand, the question is not without *meaning*. It is a matter of communication, not of discovery: not of defining the thing and getting command over it, but of clarifying one's own concepts and conveying what one means, or does not mean.

After all, one has to be able to say that abstract expressionism is *not* art, and I think that clarifies most of what needs to be said about it, both for and against. That is precisely what is "for" it: that it is not art, though it seems to be. I know this statement is scandalous, and I think the ambiguities are bad ones in the long run (it should not pretend to be art, which in fact it does). I do not think that throwing paint on canvas and saying "This is art" merits twenty thousand dollars. It is too obvious. However, even the obvious has its place.

If I write a long didactic poem on art it will certainly not be about this.

December 18, 1963

Thanks for your good letter: I find you much more scrupulous about the treatment of religious subjects than most artists would be. In fact, the use of the "vexillum" or cross-flag in the iconography of the Resurrection [Hammer had done a painting of the Resurrection] is not common these days. I suppose it is a late-medieval motif, suggested by the Crusades. In any event, there is no reason on earth why you should even give it a second thought. The flag is simply a sign of victory, and I suppose it means that the artist wants you to recognize the Resurrection, in case the tomb does not look sufficiently like a tomb. There are certainly other ways of doing this.

Today is a bright, snowy morning, and it helps make one ready for Christmas. I hope that January will bring us some nice days. The middle of the month is out of the question for me (from the 18th to the 26th) because then we are on retreat and incommunicado. But in any case, things will work out and we will be able to get together in due time.

I like Pascal, and of course he was a fervent devotee of Port Royal, where they took the spiritual life seriously. I wonder if I sent you the meditation on Julien Green? I enclose one, it may have something in it of a sardonic comment on that background, but on the other hand I have no notion of saints being dull. It is only the pseudo-saints that are oppressive. The real ones, from what I have read, are exceedingly lively. Of course, canonization manages to wash all the liveliness out of them and reduce them to safe limits, so that the *bien pensants* will not be disturbed.

August 5, 1964

It is good to see your handwriting again. This is a sign that things are going well and that you are recovering after your operation. But I am sorry to hear there is another one on the way. However, if it will be of some help, then that is good. I hope it, too, will be successful.

Will you be ready to come over on the 22nd? If so that would be a fine date for me . . . We are now on our summer schedule, which means that though still on Eastern Standard Time, we do everything an hour later. Thus while I can easily meet you at 11:15 in the winter, it will have to be about 12:15 in this season. In any case, unless I hear otherwise from you or Caroline, I will look forward to seeing you at 12:15 on the 22nd.

Please thank Carolyn (this time I have spelled it properly) for sending the two reprints ["Pleasant Hill: A Shaker Village in Kentucky," published in *Jubilee*]. I think I could use half a dozen more, if they can be spared. I believe the Shaker Foundation at Pittsfield wants to get reprints too. If anyone corresponds with them, they can be advised to apply to *Jubilee*. It is perfectly all right, as far as I am concerned, if any number of reprints are made.

Your Latin project sounds interesting and mysterious. For my part I am working on Celtic monks. They have some wonderful poetry, not, of course, that I can translate Gaelic but I read it in English when I can get it.

August 12, 1964

Perhaps your hernia operation is all over by now. I hope so, and hope that it has been successful. May you have a good rest and rebound in happy strength. After that I will look forward to seeing you and Carolyn here sometime soon. I will be eager to hear when it may be possible.

Your letter and the letter from Lexi [Grunellius] reached me. Actually, the book that I sent [through John Howard Griffin] to Clyde Kennard was a copy of your [limited edition] *Hagia Sophia*, and I know he was very glad to have it. He was then dying in a hospital in Chicago, of cancer. He had been "framed" by the Mississippi police for trying to register at Miss. State University, and had been put on a chain gang and very badly treated though he already had cancer. The story, as I hear it, was simply that he had been very pleased with the book and that it had given him some joy in his last days. It seems the story is becoming a bit amplified now. But still, it is good that we are both able to think we have helped such a person and brought something meaningful into a tragic life, which, however, was full of meaning because of his own dedication.

I hear that Jacques Maritain continues in good health, and I am glad of it. I have not heard from him for some time.

Please let me know when you will be well enough to come over.

November 3, 1964

I was so pleased to hear from you and to know that you are at least fairly well, that though I am no Latin poet I immediately attempted a poem. Here it is. I do not know if it scans. All I can say is that I think it does. The lines are supposed to be hexameters. If you hear a strange noise it is the whole choir of Latin poets turning in their graves. [The poem is called "A Prayer of Thanksgiving Written for Victor Hammer."]

O Tu, Pater Splendoris Dator luminis
Ad Te gaudens precor restituto lumine
Da quaesumus mihi servulo tecum perpetuam
· Nox ubi non contristet corda vel umbra diem.

O thou Father of Splendor, Giver of Light,
To Thee I pray in joy, with light restored
Grant, I beg, to me Thy servant everlasting
Day in which no night makes sad the heart and no shadow [*the day*].

[*CP*, p. 1005]

It is certainly good to know that your eyes are serving you well again and that you are working along as usual, or more or less so. I can well understand that things might be tiring to you and I hope you will not attempt a trip over here until you are sure that it will not be a burden. Meanwhile, perhaps something else might offer itself. We shall see. But we can be patient and look forward to our next meeting whenever and wherever God wills it to be.

My hands are still afflicted with skin trouble though I can use them all right. But it is a nuisance. I suppose I will finally have to take some tests and find out precisely what the trouble is and what is to be done. My assumption is still that poison ivy started it all, but I never heard of it going on as long as this.

If you should hear news of my exhibiting strange blobs of ink in Louisville, ignore the information: it is not worthy of your notice. As always, my feelings about it are very mixed, but it was something that presented itself in such a way that I thought I could do it without harm to anyone. I think I have made plain to all concerned that I do not regard it as "art" and that they are not supposed to either . . .

Today I did not vote for Goldwater . . .

December 4, 1964

Yesterday I asked Father Abbot if I could perhaps have an exceptional permission to get over to Lexington to see you. He said that someone is driving over to the doctor on December 16th and that he would let me go with them and have lunch with you, if this were possible. So I am writing to ask if that would be a good day for me to come over for lunch. It is Wednesday. I think that if that day is impossible for you, if you can suggest another thereabouts I might be able to get a ride. But in any case I hope I can see you and Carolyn and have lunch in your fine studio, as monastic as any monastery, and in fact more.

For my part things are going quite well. There is every likelihood now that I will be able to live at the hermitage continuously. In fact, I am already sleeping there and coming down for some of the offices and for my work in the novitiate, which still takes up quite a bit of time, but anyway in the night hours and in the afternoon at least I am in the woods and it certainly agrees with me. It seems to me that this is really what I came here for, at last, and that the community life has been somehow provisional and preparatory. However, we shall see what develops. Part of the agreement may end up by being a cutting off of contacts with visitors, perhaps almost completely. But as I say, we shall see. I will do my part and leave the rest up to Superiors with their concept of how things ought to be.

Meanwhile, I look forward to the joy of seeing you.

Very best wishes to both you and Carolyn. Yesterday I sent a copy of the new book [*Seeds of Destruction*], which is not like the others in many respects. God bless you. Is it really five years since I was last in Lexington?

January 9, 1965

Thanks for your letter. I am glad that you liked the "Pilgrimage" piece [see "From Pilgrimage to Crusade" in *Mystics and Zen Masters*] and I think you are right about the title. I will have to give it some thought. A more complete text with footnotes, etc., was published by a magazine called *Cithara* at St. Bonaventure University, New York. I had not thought about the title problem at that time, however. Marco Pallis also asked me to let him submit it to some magazine in England for which he himself writes. Incidentally, I have been trying to get the Columbia Record people interested in recording some of the works of Marco Pallis' group called "The English Consort of Viols." They must play a lot of things I would like to hear, especially settings of sixteenth- and seventeenth-century songs. Does the university library have a record collection from which one can borrow? Perhaps not. I would be interested in some of the original settings of songs by Edmund Waller, etc., if they exist and are there. But I suppose this is rather a complex and difficult request. You can suggest it to Carolyn, but probably nothing can be done.

Certainly I would be delighted to write some notes on your religious paintings for a booklet of reproductions. I think it is an excellent idea. I would have to look more at the paintings to get my thoughts in order. We shall see what comes of the project. But I am certainly willing to get into it, though of course I cannot right at this instant. I still have a couple of prefaces and reviews hanging over my head.

Here are the best pictures I took, or rather two of them Carolyn took. They are not as bad as all that, in fact in every case I was disobeying the advice of the camera. So that just shows that one must not always bow to technology. In fact I am sure that if I did what the camera wanted and took the pictures with a flash, they would have been very stupid and insipid. As it is, they seem to me to have a little character.

It was very good to see you, and it is good to hear from you. Your writing is as firm and regular as ever, and I am sure that working on the "Resurrection" [painting, which he never completed] will keep your hand in trim. It is a pity you can't print "Pilgrimage." It is something I would love to have in a booklet from the Stamperia.

March 24, 1965

Thanks for your letter. I was glad to get it because I had been thinking about you and wondering how you were. I am happy to hear that things are going better.

The note of Maritain is splendid and I am delighted that he sent it. Your translation, as far as I can see, leaves nothing to be desired. You are correct in your rendering of "roman" and you need have no misgivings about it. I am returning Lexi's letter and the copy of the Maritain note.

I have been pretty busy, and have had the usual series of slight mishaps, trouble with an eye which was accidentally injured and so on. There is a fair amount of flu about in the monastery and I seem to be getting a bit of it. But that is all quite usual at this time of year. Later, after Easter, I am hoping that J. will be down.

Did I send you the notes on the eremitical life I put out recently? I think you might be interested. In any case, I enclose a copy, as I have plenty of them. Naturally this is the kind of thing I am most interested in at present . . .

June 23, 1965

Here is an uncorrected carbon copy of the complete Chuang Tzu ms. I will need it back before too long, so what I suggest is this: that you look through it and pick out the pieces you want, which you can copy, and if you like I will proof and read the copy to make sure it is all right. I do not mean to rush you, and certainly you can take a reasonable time, but I would like to have the ms. back, say, about the middle of August. Would that be all right? I hope you find it fairly legible.

Things were quite unpleasant in the hospital but they found out that the trouble was, as I thought, an infection. They gave me some antibiotics, which have cleared it up quite efficiently. So I am grateful for that.

I have very much enjoyed *The Tao of Painting*, which I will send back soon. Duveen is priceless. But I am afraid it has almost fallen apart. Could I borrow your copy of Eric Gill on *Clothes*?

Carolyn, I have here a copy of Giles's *Confucianism and Its Rivals*, which you sent me. I have never been clear if this was a loan or an extra that you wanted to get rid of. Could you please let me know.

July 11, 1966

Everything is going all right with me, do not worry about me; except for details like bursitis and now a sprained ankle, I imagine I will survive and go on to other follies, and I am not disturbed.

When do you suppose you will be able to come back this way again? Should we plan something for August? It is a bit hot now, though we had a fine wild storm here last night.

Carolyn, thanks for the books. I would like to look at the two books you do have of Jean Grenier since he is important for Camus.

August 29, 1966

Many thanks for your note and for Lexi's good letter, which I return herewith. Yes, I knew that Maritain was coming and I am delighted that he will be able to. I hope nothing gets in the way, as I look forward very much to being with him for a little while.

As to you, yes, by all means let us plan on something in September. The first Saturday is bad for me. The 10th, 17th, and 24th are all right, and maybe the 17th would be the best. However, any of those three will do. Just drop me a line when, and I will expect to meet you at the usual time.

Have we ever spoken of Thomas Mann? I do not recall. I have never really been able to get into him, but I see that I must quite probably read *Doktor Faustus*. Do you know it? It is apparently a horrifying indictment of modern art and culture and probably a hair-raising book to read. I wonder if Carolyn could get it for me. If you want to look at it before she sends it on, fine. Or perhaps you would prefer to look it over in German.

Does she perhaps have in the library any poems of Miguel Hernández? A modern Spanish poet who died in one of Franco's jails. I am very impressed by him. Not to be confused with Menéndez, a Peruvian.

December 24, 1966

Thanks very much for your two notes. I was very glad to hear from you and to know you were out of the hospital. I agree with you, a hospital is an awful place, and sometimes that is good only for getting out of. I hope everything will go well at home, and that you will get the necessary rest and make a quick recovery.

Any Saturday in January will be all right. Can we plan on the 7th or 14th? Those would both be good. In fact if it seemed we were going to have nice weather on the 31st and you felt like coming over then, just call me the day before, in the morning. But make sure I get the message. In any event, drop me a note when you hope to come.

April 24, 1967

Thanks for your letter of the other day. I was very pleased to hear from you and to receive a letter in your own handwriting, which shows you are better. The papers are going off to Friedrich Georg Juenger but I have not been able to find exactly the ones you asked for. However, the material I am sending is roughly equivalent—including, for example, the article that was recently in the *Saturday Review*, which has a bearing on technology, at least indirectly.

In such lovely weather as we have now, I wish I could spend a few hours quietly picnicking with you and Carolyn. The spring has been perfect. However, I shall probably have to be content with the hope of dropping in on you again in Lexington next time some friend of mine comes down with a car. I have been rather overvisited lately—largely for business reasons—and that has held up both work and correspondence.

The other day I sent the new book, and I want also to send you the little book (Cassiodorus) which they printed at Stanbrook. I like it in its splendor, but I prefer the simplicity of the Stamperia del Santuccio. But the nuns went to immense trouble to get paper and so on.

June 16, 1967

It was very good to hear from you again. Yes, I would very much like to come and see you and see the book too. I am not sure what I can plan just now, but I have a friend coming to visit and he will have a car. Perhaps then we will be able to drive over to Lexington. I am not sure when he will be coming. Perhaps next week. If he comes and I can get permission I will try to call you, but will come over to Lexington anyway . . .

It is rather hot now, and I suppose that is uncomfortable for you: it certainly is for me, as I do not get all the breeze in my cottage. However, I can go out into a cool place in the woods. I am reading [Lewis] Mumford's new book, which the publisher sent me as a reward for writing that letter to the *Times*, more or less.

Father Juenger sent me a nice letter and I must reply sometime. As to the Herrigel book on Zen: actually there are two, one of which is quite good—*Zen in the Art of Archery*.

Yes, you are right about "getting old." I have more aches than I used to have and the machinery runs less well from year to year. Not having found the secret of arresting the process, I must accept it as you also do. Let us rejoice that things are not worse and go on as happily as we can. I hope to see you soon, if I possibly can. I will let you know as soon as I have more definite plans.

On July 10, 1967, Hammer died in Lexington, Kentucky.

II.
War and Freedom

*I just cannot in conscience, as a priest and as a writer
who has a hearing with a lot of people, devote myself
exclusively to questions of devotion, the life of prayer,
or monastic history, and act as if we were not in the
middle of the most serious crisis in Christian history.*

TO JOSIAH G. CHATHAM

1. The Cold War Letters

In my biography of Thomas Merton (Silent Lamp), I have referred to a period in Merton's life which I call "The Year of the Cold War Letters." Not a calendar year, it is a period in his life that extends from October 1961 to October 1962. His first published article on war and peace, entitled "The Root of War Is Fear," appeared in the October 1961 issue of The Catholic Worker. *From then till the end of April 1962, he wrote a flurry of articles, as well as one book, about the Christian's responsibility to work for peace and for the outlawing of war. On April 26, 1962, he was informed by his abbot, Dom James Fox, that the Abbot General of the Cistercian Order, Dom Gabriel Sortais, had sent orders that he was no longer to publish books or articles on the issues of war and peace.*

Merton obeyed the prohibition against publishing anything on war and peace. Nevertheless, he continued to write articles, which, while unpublished, were privately circulated in mimeographed form among his friends. He even ventured two articles in 1963 in The Catholic Worker *under pen names—Benedict Monk and Benedict Moore. The prohibition was eased somewhat after Pope John XXIII issued his encyclical* Pacem in Terris *in April 1963 and Merton did write some articles following the publication of the encyclical. But it is still a fact that the period from October 1961 to October 1962 was the most vigorous, concentrated, and productive period of Merton's writings on war and peace.*

I have called this period "The Year of the Cold War Letters" because during this time Merton's many articles on war and peace were interlaced with a constant stream of letters to his friends in which he discussed the same topics. In the fall of 1961 Merton conceived the plan of putting together a book that would comprise selected letters of his own, written to a wide variety of people, and linked by the common themes of war and peace. Not only did he conceive the book, he also decided on a title—The Cold War Letters. It was a cleverly conceived plan, a way in which Merton could express his ideas without very much publicity coming his way. The letters would get to people who would be inclined to agree with his position and do something to implement it; at the same time there would be a minimal risk of their getting into the hands of those most opposed to his views.

I have no information as to the precise time of Merton's decision but I believe it may well have been about the same time as his Catholic Worker *article appeared. One indication is that the letters he selected began with October 1961 and ceased with October 1962; a second may be found in the letter he wrote on December 21, 1961, to Dr. Wilbur H. ("Ping") Ferry of the Santa Barbara Center for the Study of Democratic Institutions. He asked Ferry if he would be willing to circulate some of his material in mimeographed form. "I am having a bit of censorship trouble," he remarked casually and he made clear that getting his "stuff" around in this way would not require prior censorship. He then mentioned the Cold War Letters for the first time, as an example of material that could be circulated in this private fashion. "I have, for instance, some copies of letters to people—to make up a book called* Cold War Letters. *Very unlikely to be published (!)." At that time Merton would have had only eleven such letters, yet the collection of Cold War Letters finally mimeographed consisted of forty-nine letters in its early edition (circulated in the late spring of 1962) and 111 in a collection circulated in January 1963, the latter including a preface by Thomas Merton.*

What I am suggesting is that the Cold War Letters were not, as many have believed, an afterthought that came to Merton in the wake of the prohibition to publish on the topic of war and peace. Quite the contrary, the idea was a part of his thinking almost from the moment he decided to enter the "war on war." This may well suggest that the letters that eventually became part of this collection were written at least with some eye to their possible inclusion in The Cold War Letters.

"The Year of the Cold War Letters" needs to be singled out as a unique year in the life of Thomas Merton. Articles on war and peace are interwoven with Cold War Letters to form a literary fabric out of which emerges a fairly clear image of Thomas Merton the peacemaker. The Cold War Letters were mimeographed and put together with a spiral binding. The letters are arranged in chronological order, and he identified his correspondents only by initials and place. After a good bit of detective work, I have been able to identify by name all the correspondents except one—Letter 50 to W. D., Oyster Bay, Long Island. Some of the Cold War Letters have appeared in previous volumes of the Merton correspondence: thirty-seven are in The Hidden Ground of Love, *ten are in* The Road to Joy, *one is in* The School of Charity, *and five are in* The Courage for Truth. *These are listed in their proper order, though their texts are not reprinted here.*

There is a richness to the Cold War Letters that goes beyond their specific topic. Merton often branches off into other areas that have nothing to do with war and peace. To the expanded version of The Cold War Letters, *he added the preface which follows.*

The Cold War Letters: Preface

These copies of letters written over a period of little more than one year preceding the Cuban Crisis of 1962 [the confrontation between Kennedy and Khrushchev over the deployment of missiles in Cuba] have been made for friends who might be expected to understand something of the writer's viewpoint, even when they might not agree with all he has said, still less with all that he may have unconsciously implied.

As a matter of fact, the letters themselves have been copied practically without change, except that the more irrelevant parts have been cut out. There have been none of the careful corrections, qualifications, and omissions which would be required before such a book could possibly be considered for general circulation, or even for any but the most limited and private reading. As it stands, it lies open to all kinds of misinterpretation, and malevolence will not find it difficult to read into these pages the most sinister of attitudes. A few words in a preface may then serve to deny in advance the possible allegations of witch hunters.

There is no witch here, no treason and no subversion. The letters form part of no plot. They incite to no riot, they suggest no disloyalty to government, they are not pandering to destructive machinations of revolutionaries or foreign foes. They are nothing more than the expression of loyal but unpopular opinion, of democratic opposition to what seem to be irresponsible trends. Without such voices raised in opposition to grim policies and majority compulsions, democracy would be without meaning. The writer is then confident that the values of free speech and free opinion traditional in the Western world are still not so far subverted by totalitarian thinking as to make these letters, even in their carelessness, and at times in their confusion, totally unacceptable.

There are certainly statements made in these pages which the writer no longer holds just as they stand. There is much that might have been modified since the letters were written or copied. There are many expressions that the writer would be ready to withdraw or soften without more ado. The letters were written, as most letters are, in haste, in the heat of the moment, and the moments of that year were often unusually fraught with excitement. The perspectives of these letters are then often distorted by indignation or by vehement protest. It is hoped that this may not cause them to be too grossly misinterpreted. Perhaps it is not out of place that those readers for whom these letters are not intended and of whose business they are none, may be asked politely to withhold their judgment. The author is not, never was, and never will be a Communist. The author in fact detests every type of totalitarian coercion, under whatever form, palliated by whatever high-sounding and humanitarian excuse. These letters are, indeed, biased by a frank hatred of power politics and by an uninhibited contempt for those who use power to distort the truth or to silence it altogether. The somewhat belligerent tone—usually more bel-

ligerent than the writer himself would like it to be—should be heard
against this background of easily aroused indignation which the writer
generally hopes is righteous. But of course such indignation is not always,
in the event, as justified as one might hope.

What is the ground for the general protest uttered in these pages?
It is the conviction that the United States, in the Cold War, are in grave
danger of ceasing to be what they claim to be: the home of liberty, where
justice is defended with free speech, where truth is accessible to everybody, where everybody is alike responsible, enlightened, and concerned,
and where responsibility is sustained by a deep foundation of ethics. In
actual fact it would seem that during the Cold War, if not during World
War II, this country has become frankly a warfare state built on affluence,
a power structure in which the interests of big business, the obsessions
of the military, and the phobias of political extremists both dominate and
dictate our national policy. It also seems that the people of the country
are by and large reduced to passivity, confusion, resentment, frustration,
thoughtlessness and ignorance, so that they blindly follow any line that
is unraveled for them by the mass media.

There has been above all a tendency to insulation behind a thick
layer of misinformation and misinterpretation, so that the majority opinion
in the United States is now a highly oversimplified and mythical view of
the world divided into two camps: that of darkness (our enemies) and that
of light (ourselves). The enemy is totally malevolent and totally dedicated
to evil. We are totally innocent and committed, by our very nature, to
truth, goodness, and light. In consequence of this, everything the enemy
does is diabolical and everything we do is angelic. His H-bombs are from
hell and ours are the instruments of divine justice. It follows that we have
a divinely given mission to destroy this hellish monster and any steps we
take to do so are innocent and even holy.

Now, there is no question of the evil of Communism, but the evil
is more complex and more variable than we are willing to think. And
furthermore our own economic and political system is not always either
just or ideal . . .

It is a curious fact that those who insist that the only way to peace
is the hard-nosed and stiff-necked way of missile rattling and nuclear
threats, are developing a mentality that is insensitive to the realities of
nuclear war, and indifferent to the missiles and menaces of the enemy.
Indeed it is counted bravery and patriotism to ignore the realities of the
situation or to shrug them off with a few platitudes about the number of
megacorpses we are ready to tolerate. Such thinking seems to be more
prevalent in the United States than anywhere else except perhaps Soviet
China, and obviously fanaticism of this type is able to dispose of the
rationality which, it is assumed, will be "deterred" by H-bombs from rash
and suicidal actions.

The protest in these letters is not, however, merely against the
danger or the horror of war. It is not dictated by the fear that few lives

might be lost, or that property might be destroyed, or even that millions of lives might be lost and civilization itself destroyed. The protest is not merely against physical destruction, still less against physical danger, but against a suicidal moral evil and a total lack of ethics and rationality with which international policies tend to be conducted. True, President Kennedy is a shrewd and sometimes adventurous leader. He means well and has the highest motives, and he is, without doubt, in a position sometimes so impossible as to be absurd. The same can be said of any national leader. I would not judge that any of the great ones today—even Khrushchev or Mao Tse-tung—are unexampled crooks or psychotics like Hitler.

Unfortunately there seems to me to be a general air of insanity about the whole conduct of public life today, even though the leaders are well-intentioned and "well-adjusted" men, and this is what makes it morally impossible for most people *even to consider objectively* the fact that war might no longer be a rational way of settling international differences. *It is taken for granted* that the mere idea of questioning recourse to war as a valid, rational, and ethical means of settling problems is not only absurd but may even be treasonable. There are not lacking moralists, Catholic theologians, who can argue that there exists a *moral obligation* to threaten Russia with nuclear destruction! In the opinion of the present writer such opinions are not only disgraceful, scandalous, and unchristian, but also plainly idiotic. They make far less sense than the measured mumblings of the theological experts who, in Galileo's day, did not want the earth to turn about the sun.

The writer is a Catholic, devoted to his Church, to his faith and to his vocation. He does not believe that in differing from theologians like these, even when they may perhaps be bishops, he is turning against Christ or the Church. On the contrary he believes himself obliged in conscience to follow the line of thought which has been made quite clear by the modern Popes, particularly Pius XII and John XXIII, who have repeatedly pleaded for rational and peaceful ways of settling disputes, and who have forcefully declared that the uninhibited recourse to destructive violence in total war, nuclear or conventional, is "a sin, an offense and an outrage" (Pius XII).

The protest in these letters is then the same as the protest of Pope Pius XII, who said that total and indiscriminate nuclear war would be "a crime worthy of the most severe national and international sanctions" (to World Medical Congress, 1954).

The appeal of these letters is the same as the appeal of Pope John XXIII repeatedly urging national leaders to "shun all thought of force."

It is the same as the appeal of Cardinal Meyer of Chicago in his Lenten pastoral of 1962, where he said, "We are overcome by evil not only if we allow Communism to take over the world but if we allow the methods and standards of Communism to influence our own. If we adopt a policy of hatred, of liquidation of those who oppose us, of unrestrained use of total war, of a spirit of fear and panic, of exaggerated propaganda, of unconditional surrender, or pure nationalism, we have already been overcome by the evil."

To hold that nuclear war is an evil to be avoided at all costs is not the same as holding that one must make "peace at any price." Those who cling, with an almost psychotic obsessiveness, to the "red or dead" alternative, as if no other choice could be possible, are simply admitting their incapacity to face the problems of our time in an adult and rational way. The greatest tragedy of our time is not the mere existence of nuclear weapons but the apparent incapacity of men to think in terms that will enable them to deal with the problem of these weapons effectively.

It is certainly true that international cooperation must finally bring about the control and even the abolition of war, if the human race is to survive. It is of course equally true that this effort must proceed in such a way that it does not capsize in a sudden seizure of power by one of the great antagonists. How this is to be done, nobody can yet clearly see. But until really honest efforts are made surely nobody is even going to look at the problems squarely. We are living in a condition where we are afraid to see the total immorality and absurdity of total war. One reason for this incapacity is the fact that the whole nation is fattening on the profits of the war industries and on the production of fantastically expensive and complex weapons that are obsolete almost before they are produced.

The burden of protest in these letters is simply that such a state of affairs is pure madness, that to accept it without question as right and reasonable is criminally insane and that in the presence of such fantastically absurd and suicidal iniquity the Christian conscience cannot keep silent.

Merton's first article on war and peace appeared in the Catholic Worker *issue of October 1961. The first Cold War Letters were written that same month. The complete list follows.*

1. *To E.G. (Etta Gullick), Oxford, c. October 25, 1961 (HGL, p. 346).*

2. *To John C. Heidbrink, Nyack, N.Y., October 30, 1961 (HGL, p. 402).*

3. *To Paulo Alceu Amoroso Lima, Rio de Janeiro, November 1961 (CT, pp. 164–66).*

In November 1961, Merton's article "Shelter Ethics" was published in The Catholic Worker *(in response to an article by L. C. McHugh, S.J., in the September 30, 1961, issue of* America*).*

4. *To M.S. (Maynard Shelly, editor of* The Mennonite*), Newton, Kan., December 1961.*

Thank you for your kind letter of November 14. I am looking forward to receipt of the copy of *The Mennonite* which contains my poem about the extermination camps. I am happy that you saw fit to use it and I am proud to appear in your magazine.

Certainly it is most necessary for all to realize that the terrible situation in the world today is a vivid sign in which the mercy of God seeks to spell out the truth of our sins and win us to repentance. The agonizing thing is to see how inexorably all mankind, even with the best and most honest of intentions, remain blind and indifferent to the light which is offered them. If we only knew how to read the "signs of the times." It seems that even the faithful who have sincerely clung to the Gospel truth, and are not just Christians for social reasons and for prestige, have lost their sensitivity to these things . . .

Surely we ought to see now that repentance means something far deeper than we have suspected: it can no longer be a matter of setting things right according to the norms of our own small group, the immediate society in which we live. We have to open our hearts to a universal and all-embracing love that knows no limits and no obstacles, a love that is not scandalized by the sinner, a love that takes upon itself the sins of the world. There must be total love of all, even of the most distant, even of the most hostile. Without the gift of the Holy Spirit this is mere idealism, mere dreaming. But the Spirit who knows all things and can do all things, He can be in us the power of love that heals, unites, and redeems, for thus the Blood of Jesus Christ reaches all men through us.

It is with these thoughts in mind that I tell you what respect and reverence I have for the Mennonite tradition of peaceful action and non-violence. Though not a total pacifist in theory myself, I certainly believe that every Christian should try to practice non-violence rather than violence and that some should bind themselves to follow only the way of peace as an example to the others. I myself as a monk do not believe it would be licit for me ever to kill another human being even in self-defense and I would certainly never attempt to do so. There are much greater and truer ways than this. Killing achieves nothing. Finally, though as I said in theory I would still admit some persons might licitly wage war to defend themselves (for instance the Hungarians in 1956), yet I think that nuclear war is out of the question, it is beyond all doubt murder and sin, and it must be banned forever. Since in practice any small war is likely to lead to nuclear war, I therefore believe in practice that war must be absolutely banned and abolished today as a method of settling international disputes.

5. *To E.F. (Erich Fromm), Mexico City, December 1961 (HGL, pp. 317–19).*

6. *To J.T.E. (John Tracy Ellis), Washington, December 7, 1961 (HGL, pp. 174–75).*

7. *To L.F. (Lawrence Ferlinghetti), San Francisco, December 1961 (CT, pp. 270–72).*

8. *To B.S. (Bruno Schlesinger), Notre Dame, December 13, 1961 (HGL, pp. 541–43).*

9. *To J.R. (probably should be T.R., Archbishop Thomas Roberts, S.J.), London, December 1961.*

I do not have a totally clear picture of the situation, but clear enough to understand something of the essential problem, and to feel, with you, deep concern. For here, in this whole tormented problem in which we are all involved, and you more than most, it is not merely the rights of this or that person, but the honor and holiness of the Church as the guardian of truth and the minister of mercy and salvation to men. I have no hesitation in agreeing with you that I must expect a small amount of what has been visited on you. I think this is going to be the *only* visible fruit of most of our protests in favor of peace, honesty, truth, and fidelity to the Law of Christ. This is of course to me a shattering and totally disconcerting question, and I do not hesitate to admit to you that it reaches down into the very foundations of my life and, but for the grace of God, might shake them beyond repair.

Do you mind if I give you a little news of my own very small problems? As I may or may not have indicated, and as you certainly know very well: the situation in this country is extremely serious. It amounts in reality to a moral collapse, in which the policy of the nation is more or less frankly oriented toward a war of extermination. Everybody else claims not to "want" this, certainly. But step by step we come closer to it because the country commits itself more and more to policies which, but for a miracle, will make it inevitable.

This gradual process is accepted with fatalistic indifference or ignored in a spirit of irresponsibility and passivity. The most scandalous thing of all, and this has been stated very explicitly by some few sane people who are still pointing to the danger, is that the Church and her clergy have been almost completely silent. In some cases, statements that have been made have tended rather to promote an atmosphere of hatred and irresponsibility, like the famous Fr. McHugh, of your Society, with his advice to take a revolver into your shelter with you and kill anyone who tries to get in [see *America*, September 30, 1961]. Such is the climate in which we are now living in America.

In this situation I have felt that it would be a matter of fidelity to my vocation as a Christian and as a priest, and by no means in contradiction with my state as a monk, to try to show clearly that our gradual advance toward nuclear war is morally intolerable and even criminal and that we have to take the most serious possible steps to realize our condition and do something about it.

The question is, what does one do?

At present my feeling is that the most urgent thing is to say what has to be said and say it in any possible way. If it cannot be printed, then let it be mimeographed. If it cannot be mimeographed, then let it be written on the backs of envelopes, as long as it gets said. But then, of course, what is the purpose of saying things just for the sake of saying them, without hope of their having any effect? Am I not reduced to doing what they demand of me, to sit in silence and make no protest?

I realize, of course, that if I were a holier person, if I had been more faithful to God's will all along the line, if I were less undermined by my own contradictions, I would have much more of the needed strength and clarity. Perhaps the Lord wants me to keep silence lest by my writing I do more harm than good. I don't know. And it seems impossible to get a clear idea of what ought to be done . . .

10. To E.K. (Ethel Kennedy), Washington, December 1961 (HGL, pp. 444–46).

11. To D.D. (Dorothy Day), New York, December 20, 1961 (HGL, pp. 140–43).

12. To E.D. (Edward Deming Andrews), Pittsfield, Mass., December 21, 1961 (HGL, p. 36).

13. To J.C. (Josiah G. Chatham), Jackson, Miss., December 1961.
I think that in this awful issue of nuclear war there is involved much more than the danger of physical evil. The Lord knows that is enormous enough. What concerns me, perhaps this is pride, is the ghastly feeling that we are all on the brink of a spiritual defection and betrayal of Christ, which would consist in the complete acceptance of the values and the decisions of the callous men of war who think only in terms of megacorpses and megatons, and have not the slightest thought for man, the image of God.

I know the moral theologians are very wise in their circumspect avoidance of self-commitment to anything but very "safe" positions. But all of a sudden it seems to me that these safe positions yawn wide open and where they open is right into the depths of hell. That is not what I call safety. The German clergy, the German Catholic press, even the German bishops, some of them, got in there behind Hitler and said that his war was just. They urged all the faithful to give the Vaterland everything they had. This they did in order, in some measure, to try to keep peace with a tyrant who threatened to destroy the Church. Their action did nothing whatever to keep men like Fr. Metzger from being executed, or to save hundreds of priests and religious from Dachau . . .

I just cannot in conscience, as a priest and a writer who has a hearing with a lot of people, devote myself exclusively to questions of devotion, the life of prayer, or monastic history, and act as if we were not in the middle of the most serious crisis in Christian history. It is to me incomprehensible that so many other writers and theologians and whatnot simply ignore this question or, if they treat it, do so in a manner that encourages people to line up with a frankly godless and pragmatic power bloc, the immense wealth and technical capacity of which is directed entirely to nuclear annihilation of entire nations, without distinction between civilians and combatants.

14. *To E.G. (Etta Gullick), Oxford, December 22, 1961 (HGL, pp. 348–50).*

15. *To J.B. (Jeanne Burdick), Topeka, December 26, 1961 (HGL, pp. 108–10).*

16. *To R.L. (Robert Lax), December 1961 (RJ, p. 173).*

17. *To C.L. (Clare Boothe Luce), New York, December 1961 or January 1962.*

What can I say about those three utterly magnificent books? Especially the Giotto. I cannot remember when I have seen anything so fine as this last, and yet we have lived in a time when marvelous things are produced. I remember most of the Giottos from Santa Croce, especially St. Francis before the soldan, which for some reason hit me very hard and has always stayed with me. Now that I am very interested in Moslems, and have contact with some, I think I understand the reason why. But what the book gives that nothing else can is the appreciation of all the marvelous detail. It is an unending pleasure for me and for the novices, and we are all still wondering at it.

Thank you, then, for having added to our Christmas this wonder. And it has been a marvelous Christmas for me. The darkest in my life and yet in many ways the clearest and most radiant. Dark of course because of the situation we are all in. And radiant because one comes to understand that darkness is there for a reason also. That the Light has come into darkness which has not understood it: this we have known long since. But we have not known all the implications. Nor have we understood the immense depth of the mystery which we nevertheless know by rote: that the Light not only shall and will triumph over the darkness, but already has. This is not a spiritual bromide, it is the heart of our Christian faith. Have you ever read the English mystic Julian (sometimes wrongly called Juliana) of Norwich? I will write to you about her sometime. She is a mighty theologian, in all her simplicity and love.

Though "all manner of things shall be well," we cannot help but be aware, on the threshold of 1962, that we have enormous responsibilities and tasks of which we are perhaps no longer capable. Our sudden, unbalanced, top-heavy rush into technological mastery has left us without the spiritual means to face our problems. Or rather, we have thrown the spiritual means away. Even the religious people have not been aware of the situation, not become aware until perhaps too late. And here we all stand as prisoners of our own scientific virtuosity, ruled by immense power that we ought to be ruling and cannot. Our weapons dictate what we are to do. They force us into awful corners. They give us our living, they sustain our economy, they bolster up our politicians, they sell our mass media, in short we live by them. But if they continue to rule us we will also most surely die by them . . .

It shows what comes of believing in science more than in God. The business about Pharaoh in Exodus is not so far out after all, is it? Bricks without straw, and more than that. Faith is the principle of the only real freedom we have. Yet history is full of the paradox that the liberation of the mind of man by Christianity did a great deal to make the development of science possible too. Yet you can't blame all this on the Bible or on the Greeks or on the Council of Nicaea (which brought into the spotlight the meaning of the Person). There was also too much underground that we didn't know about, I presume.

I don't want to waste your time philosophizing. But I do want to say this one thing. We are in an awfully serious hour for Christianity, for our own souls. We are faced with the necessity to be very faithful to the Law of Christ, and His truth. This means that we must do everything that we reasonably can to find our way peacefully through the mess we are in. Yet we remain responsible for doing the things that "are for our peace." ("Jerusalem, Jerusalem, if thou hadst known the things that are for thy peace . . . and now there shall not be left of thee a stone upon a stone.")

We have to be articulate and sane, and speak wisely on every occasion where we can speak, and to those who are willing to listen. That is why for one I speak to you. We have to try to some extent to preserve the sanity of this nation, and keep it from going berserk, which will be its destruction, and ours, and perhaps also the destruction of Christendom.

I wanted to say these few things, as we enter the New Year. For it is going to be a crucial year, and in it we are going to have to walk sanely, and in faith, and with great sacrifice, and with an almost impossible hope . . .

18. *To W.S. (Walter Stein), Leeds, England, December 1961 or January 1962.*

I have your letter of the 12th and am glad to hear from you. As I said in the letter to the people of the Merlin Press, I found the book edited by you [*Nuclear Weapons and the Christian Conscience*, 1961] very impressive. What struck me most was the fact that the level was high, the thinking was energetic and uncompromising, and I was stimulated by the absence of the familiar clichés, or by worn-out mannerisms which have served us all in the evasion of real issues. For example (without applying these criticisms to any other book in particular), I was very struck by the superiority of your book over *Morals and Missiles*, which nevertheless had some good things in it. But *Morals and Missiles* had that chatty informality which the Englishman of Chesterton's generation thought he had to adopt as a protection whenever he tried to speak his mind on anything serious. Thank God you have thrown that off, because it emasculates a lot of very good thought.

At the moment, the publisher [James Laughlin] here is hesitating a bit because he finds your book "hard," but I am going to give him the business on that. It is necessary that for once a book be a little hard. We are submerged in all kinds of confused journalism on this awful issue, and there is very little thought. I do hope, however, to get some very good things. Lewis Mumford has said some of the clearest and most pointed moral judgments on nuclear warfare that have been uttered in this country and I hope for at least one—possibly two—fine essays of his. Erich Fromm is a psychiatrist whom you may or may not know. He is a leftist and is outspoken, appearing in all sorts of places, and operating from Mexico. He has a good book out called *May Man Prevail*. I'll send you a copy because I think I can dig up an extra one somewhere. There are several essays the publisher especially wants, about the effects of bombs and the uselessness of civil defense measures. Most of the material at this end is about the psychology of the present nuclear crisis in this country, not that I want it to be this way. And I am hoping to get something constructive about a way toward peace. The title of the book is provisionally *The Human Way Out* [the final title was *Breakthrough to Peace*] though I am afraid there is not yet a great deal about the way out, except for the moral principles in your collection. I am of course going to hold out for the inclusion of your whole book in this anthology, and I think the publisher will see the point of it. He ought to come down here in a couple of weeks and we will come to our conclusions then.

Many of us here feel that 1962 is going to be awfully critical. Humanly speaking, the mentality of this country, as I now understand it, is about as bad as it could be. Utterly sinister, desperate, belligerent, illogical . . . The one hope is that a lot of people who have more sense are protesting and there is a real communication going on among them which is quite heartening. But one wonders just what can be done, when the country is in the grip of the business-military complex that lives on the weapons and is dominated by them . . .

I am seriously wondering if the efforts some of us are making (a belated formation of an American Pax group, etc.) can have more than symbolic value. This may sound pessimistic, and of course it is. But it is not so pessimistic that it excludes the dimensions of a real hope: a hope that is not seen. What is seen seems to me to be more or less hopeless, at the moment. The debacle is at hand, and it is a question of helping to save what God wills to save, not of preserving present structures that seem to me to be doomed. For the very effort to preserve them is what is bringing on the disaster. However, I do not pretend to weigh and measure things on such an enormous scale. I think our first duty is to preserve the human measure and to stay on the level where judgment is pertinent and does not become pure hubris. That is what the essays in your book and their judgments seem to me to affirm clearly and sanely: the human and the Christian measure . . .

19. *To J.G.M. (Jean Goss-Mayr), Vienna, January 1, 1962 (HGL, pp. 325–26).*

20. *To S.T. (Sister Thérèse Lentfoehr), Wisconsin, January 11, 1962 (RJ, p. 239).*

21. *To G.Z. (Gordon Zahn), Chicago, January 11, 1962 (HGL, pp. 649–51).*

22. *To S.E. (Sister Emmanuel de Souza y Silva, O.S.B.), Petrópolis, Brazil, January 16, 1962 (HGL, pp. 186–88).*

23. *To J.F. (John Ford, S.J.), Washington, January 1962.*
     You may see an article of mine in *Commonweal* these days [February 9]. This too, I regret to say, is a bit sweeping and shows something of the lack of perspective from which I necessarily suffer to some extent. It was written before I got in touch with you and I have not had an opportunity to make changes, expecting it to appear from issue to issue. Since it is in *Commonweal*, however, I think the readers will know how to qualify the statements to some extent. If not, well, they will find people to tell them, I am sure!
     I suffer from my limitations, and I wish I were more of a professional, because an increased sophistication and a deeper experience of the problems and methods would help me serve the truth much better: and of course that is what I want to do. But I must say this: I am very deeply concerned with what seems to me to be the extreme reticence and hesitation on the part of Catholics who might take a position for peace, or for a more positive and constructive approach to world problems, when there seem to be quite a few irresponsible voices, which have great influence on some of the faithful, giving the impression that the Church needs and even wants a kind of nuclear crusade against the godless Communists. I do not claim to be an expert in world affairs, but the superficial knowledge that I have of the arms race and of present-day military policies and the power involved in them, shows me that there is not much chance of the things we want to defend actually surviving a nuclear war—even a "limited" one, which would necessarily affect at least some cities.
     It is for that reason that I believe that I am obliged, out of fidelity to Our Lord and to my priestly and religious vocation, to state very definitely some alternative to this awful passivity and lotus-eating irresponsibility which, in the end, delivers us all over bound hand and foot into the power of political forces that know nothing of God or morality,

whether natural or divine. Sure, the theologians are divided, and the bishops rely on the theologians. But can't the theologians and the bishops say something? Can't there be some constructive and courageous discussion? Can't there be some show of genuine concern? Father, my heart is very sick with the feeling that we don't give the impression of caring at all what happens to man, the image of God. We seem to be concerned more with abstractions. Of course I know we are all warmly devoted to those around us and to our students, penitents, and whatnot. But as other Christs we should have universal horizons and we should not be limited by any dividing line whatever. We should be just as concerned about man in Russia and man in China as about man in America. How is it possible that we should, with equanimity, toss around statistics and estimates of deaths running into the millions and then proceed to justify these deaths, and even justify them on the basis of our Christian faith and loyalty to the Church? I know you agree with me that there is something terribly wrong somewhere . . .

But of one thing I am convinced: the vital importance of a forceful and articulate Catholic position, in this country, in favor of peace, rather than the permissive and silent attitude that seems to prevail at the moment. We seem to be able to get excited over everything but the important problem. We are deeply involved in a movement toward a war of annihilation which certainly promises to be criminal, and the Pope certainly seems to fear this.

Father, I am trying your patience. But I do so knowing that you are interested not only for my own sake but for the sake of the Church. And I know you will have wise advice to give me. I do need opportunities for some kind of dialogue. One cannot develop correct views of issues like this in a vacuum. So I trust your charity to bear with me.

24. To M.B. (Mary Childs Black), Williamsburg, c. January 24, 1962.
I need not tell you how I would love to be there on February 2nd. There are few earthly desires I cherish more than the desire to see the Shaker spiritual drawings in the original. I am still hoping that the collection may find its way out here. It is with great regret that I must decline your kind invitation. I never obtain permission to travel that far or indeed to travel at all merely for a "social" occasion. This would be called a social occasion, I suppose. Though to me it would be more.

Recently, though, I did have the happiness to get to the old Pleasant Hill Shaker Community near here, and even took some photographs which came out quite well and I hope I will be able to use them in a little photo essay on the place and on the Shakers. The ideas have not crystallized out yet, and one must give them time. I know Edward Andrews will be interested, though.

This much I can do: share with you all a few thoughts that are at work in my mind about the Shakers and their deep significance, which manifests itself in a hidden and archetypal way in their art, craftsmanship and in all their works. Their spirit is perhaps the most authentic expression of the primitive American "mystery" or "myth": the paradise myth. The New World, the world of renewal, of return to simplicity, to the innocence of Adam, the recovery of the primeval cosmic simplicity, the reduction of divisions, the restoration of unity. But not just a return to the beginning, it is also an anticipation of the end. The anticipation of eschatological fulfillment, of completion, the New World was an earnest and a type of the New Spiritual Creation.

In the secular realm this consciousness was of course very pronounced, the consciousness of the pioneer and later of the businessman who thought that America could literally be the earthly paradise. The belief that there was nothing impossible, that all goodness and all happiness was there for the asking. And in the poor of other lands, America existed as the place where they thought gold could be picked up on the streets.

For the Shakers, it was a different consciousness, for at the same time they saw the deceptiveness of the secular hope, and their eyes were open, in childlike innocence, to the evil, the violence, the unscrupulousness that too often underlay the secular vision of the earthly paradise. It was a paradise in which the Indian had been slaughtered and the Negro was enslaved. In which the immigrant was treated as an inferior being, and in which he had to work very hard for the "gold" that was to be "picked up in the streets."

The Shakers realized that to enter into a genuine contact with the reality of the "paradise spirit" which existed in the wonderful new world, they had to undergo a special kind of conversion. And their conversion had this special, unique, wonderful quality in that it, more than any other "spirit," grasped the unique substance of the American paradise myth, and embodied it in a wonderful expression. For myths are realities, and they themselves open into deeper realms. The Shakers apprehended something totally original about the spirit and the vocation of America. This has remained hidden to everyone else. The sobering thing is that their vision was eschatological! And they themselves ended.

24 (number repeated). To V.H. (Victor Hammer), c. January 25, 1962 (see this volume, pp. 6–7).

25. To J.F. (James H. Forest), January 29, 1962 (HGL, pp. 261–63).

26. To W.H.F. (Wilbur H. Ferry), Santa Barbara, January 30, 1962 (HGL, pp. 205–8).

27. To E.A.S. (Evora Arca de Sardinia), January 31, 1962 (see this volume, p. 78).

28. *To E.E. (Elsa Englander), Linz, Austria, February 4, 1962.*

I was happy to hear from you again and have very much enjoyed the beautiful book of Austrian churches, *Glanz des Ewigen*. Like you, I feel many pangs of nostalgia over the wonderful unappreciated grace of the civilization that is inexorably perishing all around us. Austria has been such a wonderful rich and living source of this European Christian culture. Mozart represents for me all the purest and best in the Austrian and Christian genius, and those unabashed excesses of baroque attempt to keep up with his inexhaustible imagination. They do not of course succeed, but they have their charm and their boldness. I admire especially the daring of baroque that was not afraid to risk terrible lapses of taste, and yet managed almost always to come off with some marvels of ingenuity and playfulness. In former days I found it hard to take seriously but now I think nevertheless its significance grows on me. I suppose it is terribly out of fashion. As for the older Austrian churches, especially the earliest of all, they are simply enchanting. So your gift has given me great pleasure and made me secretly homesick for the Europe I shall never see again . . .

There is no question that we live in an age of revolutionary change, perhaps even of cataclysm. We cannot simply cling to the past, yet we must advance into the future while trying to preserve what is relevant and vital in the past, insofar as we can. It is of the greatest importance that we advance peacefully. If by miscalculation or accident, or even by the pride and fury of men, war breaks out again, then there is every danger that nothing at all will be left of what was valuable and great in Europe. And all the wonderful possibilities of North America will be destroyed. It is a shame that we have such great capabilities and so little wisdom.

I keep you in my masses and in my prayers. May the love of Christ protect your heart and may you rejoice in His peace. But in our time it is not possible to have a peace that is altogether without sorrow nor should we even desire it, for sorrow is salutary in such an age.

29. *To J.T.E. (John Tracy Ellis), Washington, February 4, 1962 (HGL, pp. 175–77).*

(There is no letter 30. There are, however, two letters numbered 24.)

31. *To J.F. (James Forest), New York, February 6, 1962 (HGL, pp. 263–64).*

32. *To J.F.S. (Frank J. Sheed?), New York, February 1962.*

It has taken me a little time to get around to answering your letter, because I did not want to just dash off a hasty note. Certainly it is important to explain this matter if it is causing comment and upsetting some people, hence I will try to do so.

I can see that the leaflet ["The Root of War"], being cheaply printed, and perhaps circulated in a random and irresponsible-seeming way, might cause suspicion in some minds. It is put out by a very poor group of Catholics who, however, number among them some quite saintly people. The leaflet consists largely of part of a chapter from a book [*New Seeds of Contemplation*], and doubtless those who read it in the context of the book will find it less surprising. Added to that are a few introductory paragraphs which were written in the heat of the moment when I was shocked by the highly regrettable public statement of a Jesuit Father [L. C. McHugh] who seemed to be advising people to be completely ruthless and selfish and keep others out of their shelter, with a gun if necessary. There you have the background.

I know that this whole unpleasant issue of war is a delicate one to handle. I know too that people are very upset and excitable, and that it is difficult to keep a straight perspective when discussing such a critical problem. It is very unfortunate that many people think that the mere fact of hesitating to approve an all-out nuclear war makes a man by that very fact a Communist.

Now this is the real danger I am getting at. We have got to try to keep our heads and judge this war problem with traditional moral standards. We have got to remember that such standards still exist. Even some of our clergy are stretching things quite far. I personally believe it is my duty to explain and spread the clear teaching that has been given by the Popes for the last twenty years, and they have stated very forcefully what our duty is. Of course they have not condemned nuclear war formally, but they want us to be extremely careful and to try at all costs to find some other way of settling international problems.

It does not seem to me that this fact is clearly realized in America, and consequently I have felt obliged to state my opinion, and to call attention, where possible, to what the Popes have said. The most recent utterance is that of John XXIII, last Christmas, when he spoke in the most solemn terms, both pleading with and warning national leaders and publicists to shun all thought of force.

It is certainly true that Communism presents an immense danger. It is a terrible menace to the Church and to free society. But that does not mean that the only answer is nuclear war. We have a choice between the arduous and sacrificial path of negotiation and the insane course of destruction. Public opinion is still very important. As Christians we are bound to make our choice in the light of God's will as expressed by the teachings of the Church. It is true that there is a lot of loose talk and debate. A witless pacifism is no answer. There is no question of just giving up. We have to seek and find the sane middle path, to protect our faith and our freedom while at the same time keeping peace.

The February 9, 1962, issue of Commonweal *carried an article by Merton entitled "Nuclear War and Christian Responsibility." The article was criticized in* The

Catholic Standard *(the archdiocesan paper of Washington, D.C.) in an article probably written by Auxiliary Bishop Philip Hannan. It was also criticized in a letter to* Commonweal *(April 20, 1962) by Joseph G. Hill. Merton's reply was published in the same issue and became Cold War Letter 49. The* Commonweal *article Merton rewrote several times.*

33. *To E.R. (Edward Rice), New York, February 10, 1962 (RJ, p. 285).*

34. *To B.S. (Bruno P. Schlesinger), Notre Dame, February 10, 1962 (HGL, pp. 543–45).*

35. *To K.S. (Karl Stern), Montreal, February 1962.*

I was very happy to hear you had written something about peace. If possible, please send me a copy at once, as I might be able to include it in an anthology of such essays which we are putting out, my publisher and I. We have got a lot of very fine things, and I would like very much to have something of yours. There is a first-class little book that has just come out in England, *Nuclear Weapons and the Christian Conscience*, edited by Walter Stein, which you may know.

In the United States things are by no means hopeful and as you point out it is the Catholics who give evidence of the worst moral insensibility. In a collection of articles on nuclear war presumably from a "religious" point of view, the first breath of religious fresh air, after some fifty pages of pure secularism dressed up in clerical garb, was from a rabbi who finally spoke as if knowing something about the relation of ethics to the holiness of God . . .

I was pleased to hear about the memorial to Fr. Metzger and of your devotion to him. I hear that there has been a plea to Rome for his process to begin and that the plea comes from Jews.

I am reading Jeremias a lot and working on the Old Testament. And last summer I met a wonderful guy from Winnipeg, a Rabbi S. [Zalman Schachter], a fine great Hasid who has become a warm friend. I wish you knew him . . .

36. *To J.N. (James Roy Newman), Washington, mid-February 1962.*

Cordial thanks for your letter and for the clipping from *The Washington Post*. I think that was one of your best letters and enjoyed it immensely. In return I am sending a modest proposal of my own, which may or may not make the pages of the magazine to which it was sent.

The Rule of Folly contains some excellent things, and above all the dissection of Herman Kahn. Your title is all too literally correct. The way people are working their way up to the most fabulous of all decisions is nothing short of fantastic. It would be unbelievable if anyone wrote it in a novel, before it came to happen. This is to me a source of inexhaustible and disheartening meditations . . .

I am exercised about some of the things that are being said about "other worlds" sending us messages, a few beeps to teach us their language followed by "the equivalent of a volume of the encyclopedia." Mr. N.— please, for the love of God, tell me how to build a shelter that will protect me from these hurtling volumes of the Encyclopedia Martiana. I am not afraid of fallout, but I am a man of books and I dread of all things these huge volumes. I know how much concentrated frightfulness they can contain and indeed I have contributed to two of them recently. I fear that the Lord is about to punish me in a manner that fits my crime. I am planning an encyclopedia shelter, then, in the woods near here. But don't tell anyone.

I am also evolving a private theory that specially intelligent animals, like seals, dolphins, gorillas, etc., are really the remains of smart civilizations that blew themselves up before us. A few people had the brains to turn into dolphins. If you can tell me how one gets enrolled in the guild of the dolphins, or if you foresee that some new creature is lining up for the future and applications are acceptable . . . I am rather tired of being a human, and would enjoy being a nice, quiet, civilized fish, without political affiliations.

By the way, I got two copies of *The Rule of Folly*. I will pass the extra one along to someone who can profit by it, and am grateful for both.

37. To Z.S. (Rabbi Zalman Schachter), Winnipeg, February 15, 1962 (HGL, pp. 535–36).

38. To J.H. (John C. Heidbrink), February 15, 1962 (HGL, pp. 406–8).

39. To W.F. (Wilbur H. Ferry), February 17, 1962 (HGL, p. 208).

40. To R.L. (Robert Lax), New York, February 16–24, 1962 (RJ, p. 174).

41. To S.S. (Rabbi Steven Schwarzschild), Boston, February 24, 1962.
Thanks for your two very good letters. I am happy that Zalman sent you my texts on peace, for they have brought us into contact and have brought me your fine offprints, which I have very much enjoyed. The one on "Speech and Silence before God" is wonderful and very close to my own heart. Thank you for it.

As a matter of fact, I had also read your essay in *Worldview*, the collection of essays on nuclear war, gathered around the rather dubious witness of good Fr. [John Courtney] Murray. I felt that yours was the only voice that really spoke with a full and unequivocally religious note and really was loyal to the holiness of Him who is All Holy. It seemed to me that the others were not listening to His demands, and that from the book as a whole He was absent.

God's absence among religious people, among religious groups, His absence where it is claimed that He is worshipped, is something terrifying today. Or sad in the utter extreme, because it is not His wrath, exactly, it is His loneliness, His lostness among us. That He waits among us unknown and silent, patiently, for the moment when we will finally destroy Him utterly in His image . . . And leave Him alone again in the empty cosmos.

It is the terrible power that He has given to man, that man can isolate himself and blast himself irrevocably into an outer darkness where he is separated from Him Who is nevertheless everywhere. I cannot believe that this is designed to be irrevocable, but so we are told and so perhaps it is. How can it be? There are dimensions that we are not capable of investigating.

But at any rate let us finally have pity on Him, that we may return to ourselves and have pity on one another.

Certainly I think the unutterable pity of the fate of the Jews in our time is eschatological, and is a manifestation of the loneliness and dejection of God, that He should bring upon Himself so much sorrow and suffer it in His Beloved People. In this He is speaking to us who believe ourselves, in His mercy, to have been adopted into His Chosen People and given, without any merit, the salvation and the joy promised to the Sons of Abraham. But we on the other hand have been without understanding and without pity and have not known that we were only guests invited to the banquet at the last minute.

We have not lived up to our share in the promise and we have not been to Israel, as we were meant to have been, a consolation. It is terrible to see how little we have been that, so little that the irony is almost unbearable. Who notices this?

I am not worthy yet to write about the mystery of Judaism in our world. It is too vast a subject. I wish I could. Maybe someday. If there is anything I say en passant that happens to make sense to you, you can quote it if you like. The article will have to be a thing of the future, if God wills us to have a future on this earth. (I do not doubt that He does, but sometimes the chances are a little disconcerting.)

42. To M.A. (Mother Angela of the Eucharist, O.C.D.), Carmel in Louisville, February 1962.

The issues about civil defense concern not only you but the whole community, and since my opinion has been implicitly asked, I would like to clarify.

Certainly I would think it would be very important for everyone to take any *effective* steps to protect themselves against a nuclear attack and its effects. I suggest that if the Louisville Carmel wants to be protected effectively against nuclear war . . . well, you might move to New Zealand.

Look: the problem is this. An awful lot of poor well-meaning people have been simply "had" by this nonsense about fallout shelters. The ignorance and well-meaning mistakes that have occurred have been monumental. First of all, the estimates of nuclear radiation on which this whole program is based are purely a guess as to *the kind of attack* that would occur. The estimates of the dangerous radiation have been figured out in terms of a ridiculously small attack, with small bombs. A fallout shelter in Louisville might be of some use if the nearest target hit were, say, Chicago. Perhaps Cleveland. But if Louisville or Fort Knox got hit, then you and we have simply had it. No fallout shelter will be of any use whatever within twenty to fifty miles of a target hit by a big bomb. The H-bomb is an *incendiary* bomb. Fallout is the least of its effects. The fire caused by an H-bomb will not only burn out everything within a radius of twenty to fifty miles or more, depending on the size of the bomb, but will cause firestorms which devour all the oxygen, so that even in a deep fireproof shelter you would smother. If not bake. In Hamburg, in the last war, with ordinary incendiary bombs, people were roasted alive in shelters. This is the brutal truth, and we might as well face it.

Hence if the bomb were to hit anywhere near here a fallout shelter would be useless. The higher in the air the bomb explodes, the wider the range of the fire. If the bomb explodes on the ground then there is more fallout. There is no reason for exploding the bomb on the ground around Louisville (though maybe at Fort Knox). If they wanted to hurt Louisville they would just burn it out with one bomb exploded fairly high up.

An atomic scientist built himself a fallout shelter in California last summer, and what happened? An ordinary brush fire came through and destroyed his house, his garage, and his fallout shelter. Lots of shelters that have been built have caved in or filled with water, etc. I am not saying that a good shelter cannot be had, but the question to be asked is, is this a reasonable expense? A lot of people I know, rather than build shelters, are taking the cost of a shelter and giving it to a fund to build houses for poor people in underdeveloped countries. And so it goes. My own feeling is that it is absolutely against religious poverty to risk money on a thing like that. If it were something everyone could easily have and which could be very effective, then I would say by all means build one. But since it is so risky and precarious and might be totally useless, as well as absurd, I think the best thing is to trust God and wait until we find something that makes a little more sense. This is my opinion, anyway. I have no intention of taking shelter if anything happens. If I am still around after the bomb explodes, and am not blinded completely by it, I will try to help others. That, it seems to me, would be my serious obligation as a priest. Certainly if a nuclear attack takes place, there is going to be terrible confusion and suffering, and though there is every reason for people to take effective steps to survive and try to build up the country afterward, there is also every reason for those who don't give a hoot for survival to go about trying to help those who, like the majority, will be in need of some help in their last hours. This of course for a priest is not a matter of what he feels or thinks about survival, it is just his ordinary duty.

43. *To T.T. (Tashi Tshering), Seattle, February–March 1962 (RJ, p. 320).*

44. *To E.S. (Elbert R. Sisson), Maryland, February–March 1962.*

Friends have been keeping me supplied with information, and as a result I have seen *Visible Witness* and the King Hall pamphlet, which I have not yet read but which is here. I liked the Young pamphlet very much. I will look into the book you mentioned to which Jerome Wiesner has contributed. It is good to know about him. If I had been aware of him before, I would have asked him for a contribution to a collection of essays I have been getting together, to be published in a paperback by New Directions. Szilard I know of course. What about this organization Szilard is running, for peace?

I wonder if there ought not to be something done to get these various peace movements together in one solid bloc, so to speak.

Certainly it is very important that all the rational and clearheaded opinion which still exists in this country should become articulate and exert force. It would be a tragedy, when so much good has been accomplished and when so much can really be done with the amazing power of science, if the whole thing were to run away with us and if the crazy people were to take over completely. Unfortunately the lack of balance between technology and spiritual life is so enormous that there is every chance of failure and of accident . . .

45. *To A.R. (Ad Reinhardt), New York, February–March 1962 (RJ, p. 279).*

46. *To S.E. (Steve Eisner), Detroit, February–March 1962.*

Forgive me for waiting so long to acknowledge the book. As a matter of fact, I remember having some correspondence with Raymond Larsson several years ago and had kept track of him from a distance since then. I knew he was still writing, but I had no idea the poems he had done were so fine. It is a splendid book [*Book Like a Bow Curved*], and I congratulate you on it. And of course him also. I will have to get in touch with him, and send him something of my own.

Larsson has used traditional idioms with perfect integrity, and he is certainly a fine poet, underestimated and probably little known, for all I can tell. It is interesting that his sickness has given him a valid and a fruitful kind of distance, protecting him from movements and delusive fashions. More power to him. This is fine poetry, from a noble person.

Of course I knew Bro. Antoninus' book put out by your press [University of Detroit Press]. In fact I think the program of the press sounds very good, and can only encourage you with all my heart.

Of course too, I thank you for writing. I am not one who believes that a man has to show his religious party card before one can speak to him. And I am well aware that there are plenty of people who shy away from religion and its institutional aspect precisely because of a certain abuse of this kind of thing. God asks of us, first of all, sincerity and truth. Conformity is not the first requisite, or the second, or the tenth. I do not know where it may stand on the list, or whether it is on the list at all, since God has not shown me His list. But since He has made us for the truth, it stands to reason that we have to be true in order to know the truth.

47. *To J.G.L. (Justus George Lawler), Chicago, February–March* 1962.
   I am certainly glad that you wrote, for several reasons. It is heartening to get such a good response on such an important issue, and the response has been good all along. Since the shelter panic last summer people seem to have been waking up, and I think the Jesuit Father who commended the shotgun in the shelter has shocked Catholics, or some Catholics, into realizing how far we have descended. There is certainly a lot of more or less articulate concern. But as you say, one wonders gravely about the bishops and, I might add, the theologians.
   It does not seem to me that the gravity of the situation is sensed by the people who ought to sense it. They are hypnotized by Communism, which is certainly a real menace, but by no means the only menace. Nor is it perhaps the most urgent menace: on this I am perhaps not competent to judge. But the descent into secularism and the drift into irresponsibility have gone perhaps irreparably far. Do moralists realize to what extent the gravest of decisions are now being made not only by men who are frankly amoral and opportunistic, but by machines fed with their guesses and suppositions? Are the consciences of Christians in this crisis to be guided by the Church and by the Holy Spirit, or turned over by Churchmen to the blind guidance of computers? It is not a cheerful thought.

48. *To W.H.F. (Wilbur H. Ferry), Santa Barbara, March* 6, 1962 *(HGL, p.* 209*).*

49. *To the Editors of* Commonweal. *(Published in* Commonweal, *April* 20, 1962, *but obviously written earlier, probably in early March. It was written as a reply to Joseph G. Hill, who criticized his February* 9 *Commonweal article.)*
   I admit that living in a monastery, as I have done for many years now, I am not in an ideal position to obtain up-to-the-minute information about world events. But when your correspondent asserts that in the Berlin crisis "the use of nuclear force had not come up for consideration," I find his statement barely credible. Is he serious? What are fallout shelters supposed to be for? In my utter innocence, I have been supposing all this time that they had something to do with the by-products of a thermonuclear explosion. True, I am told that one atomic scientist built one that was destroyed by a brush fire.
   A moratorium on weapons? What is the budget expenditure for weap-

ons and related items this year? Are we spending more on armaments or less?

I do not accept the argument that "massive and indiscriminate destruction of targets is nothing new," and the implication that since it was done in the last war a precedent has been established and we can now do anything we like. Pope Pius XII declared at the very beginning of World War II that such methods "cry out to Heaven for vengeance." According to him, even with conventional weapons, these destructive acts were criminal. What will they be with fifty-megaton bombs?

I do not claim to be a "lone voice" in this matter of irresponsibility. The Joint Letter of the U.S. Bishops in 1960 deplored the growing moral irresponsibility of our people, and it has never been more evident than now. I would like to ask whether the ever increasing and ever more decisive role of the computer in reaching crucial judgments on the question of war is not a threat to human and moral responsibility. It certainly places an enormous burden upon the expert who uses these instruments and thus guides the judgments of strategy planners. I am glad to hear that Los Alamos is full of conscientious men who are doing a lot of "clear unemotional thinking" because they are going to have to do a great deal more of it in the future. The rest of us are not going to be in a position to make a positive contribution one way or the other. And that is why I brought up that unpleasant hypothesis. We may be rendered physically helpless by the consequences of judgments made in high places over which we have no control. But that does not mean we can or should give up our moral freedom and our responsibility. President Eisenhower said that if governments do not soon make peace they will "have to get out of the way and let the people make it." I am not so sure that there is any likelihood of this happening, but the individual retains the right and the duty to refuse participation in collective crime. Of course it must be evident that what he refuses to participate in is immoral. My hypothesis clearly supposed a situation that was beyond control, criminal and suicidal.

What basis do I have for contending that our foreign policy relies largely on deterrence? What is the ultimate sanction in our dealing with Russia if not the threat of nuclear destruction? What is Mr. Herman Kahn writing about all the time? What was the basis of the foreign policy of the late Mr. Dulles if not "brinkmanship" and the threat of "massive retaliation"? What is our policy shaping up to now if not to preemption? I do not say it has got that far, but can anyone assert that the idea of the preemptive first strike is not taken seriously in America today? Can anyone deny that such a strike might easily lead to a war of massively destructive proportions?

In an article on nuclear war an author is hardly expected to talk about the Marshall Plan and the Peace Corps. My thesis was not political but ethical. I wanted to make clear a point which cannot seriously be controverted, at least by a Christian: that *uncontrolled destruction* of entire populations and regions with nuclear weapons whose lethal effect may extend to neutrals and even affect future generations, is morally inadmissible. Whatever may be said about the feasibility of limited nuclear war, Pope John XXIII clearly told us in his Christmas message that heads of nations must do all in their power to avoid acts that might lead to disastrous consequences. What are the chances of our wars indefinitely staying "limited"?

Meditations on a dangerous book, the Bible, have convinced me that when the human race gets itself into a major crisis, it shows a strong tendency to abdicate moral responsibility and to commit sin on an enormous scale. That is the kind of situation we face now. Unless we realize the moral and spiritual roots of the problem, our best efforts to solve it in a positive and human way are bound to be meaningless. In my article I showed a mistrust of man's capacity to control nuclear power once it was unleashed in war. Your correspondent infers, quite gratuitously, that I am against nuclear energy as such. Where does he get that idea? Is he by any chance thinking emotionally?

To leave the plane of ethics and to draw a political conclusion: certainly I am in favor of every sane policy that can promote peace while preserving the spiritual, cultural, and social heritage of Christian civilization. I do not defend the thesis of peace at any price. But I do not believe that any policy in which individual nations can, on their own judgment, resort to nuclear force on a massive scale, is to be considered either reasonable or efficacious. I see no good results whatever coming from any such policy. I believe we are going to have to prepare ourselves for the difficult and patient task of outgrowing rigid and intransigent nationalism, and work slowly toward a world federation of peaceful nations. How will this be possible? Don't ask me. I don't know. But unless we develop a moral, spiritual, and political wisdom that is proportionate to our technological skill, our skill may end us.

The first edition of The Cold War Letters *ended with letter 49. The collection was sent out in mimeographed form sometime in late April or early May 1962. Later Merton added sixty-two more letters for the second edition.*

50. *To W.D., Oyster Bay, L.I. (not identified).*

I will, at this time, say at least the following: I agree with much of what you have sent, but I cannot agree with all of it, and if I write on these subjects I think I will take a position which diverges from that which some of these books adopt. But there is a certain variety in the works you have sent, and some come closer to my viewpoint than others. Here is what I think, in a few succinct points.

There is absolutely no question of the utter gravity and seriousness of the Communist menace. We must resist this movement which is explicitly and formally dedicated to the destruction of the kind of society and culture which we know, and in particular its religious and ethical code, its whole spirit, and all that it values. We know that Communism is out to destroy us by fair means or foul. You of the so-called radical right are thoroughly convinced of the possible emphasis on the *foul* means. In many respects you are right, at least in principle. The Communists themselves have declared that there are no holds barred, this is a struggle to the death, truth and agreements mean nothing except insofar as they are politically advantageous to the cause of their revolution. They have demonstrated time and again that they mean exactly what they say in this, and this is their way of operating.

This being the case, it is also true that they work by infiltration, by espionage, by the clever manipulation of "front" organizations, and by the exploitation of well-meaning persons in free society who, often without being aware of it, take positions which are highly advantageous to Communism and prepare the way for further Communist successes. This is a real danger, and where the danger really exists it must be unmasked.

In these matters of principle, there seems to me to be no objection and no argument. But where it comes to putting these principles into practice I tend to question a lot of the conclusions and procedures that have been adopted by the extreme conservatives.

1. First of all I think that the zeal in ferreting out "Communists" tends to be very sweeping and confused. The difference between the Communist and the liberal seems to be dangerously and systematically obliterated, and the term Communist comes to be applied to anyone and everyone who is not on the extreme right. For instance, President Eisenhower has been accused of being a "card-carrying Communist." I am sure almost everyone can see that this is a bit exaggerated . . . But I don't think enough are aware that it is a bit unrealistic to call J. M. Keynes a Communist. I say unrealistic. It harms your own cause, and it brings discredit upon the arguments advanced in favor of it. I see no reason why you should not be opposed to Keynesian economic theories if you want, but then I think they should be classified more accurately and their possible tendencies in a collectivist direction must be shown as tendencies and not as accomplished facts. Hence, it seems to me that too sweeping condemnations of one and all as "Communists" have caused the right-wing conservative youth to be regarded with suspicion as not fully responsible in their judgments.

2. You do yourselves a grave disservice if you get in the habit of automatically dismissing everything and everyone who does not agree with you on the grounds that he is a conspirator. In a word, I would say that the case of the extreme right needs to rest on a much more disciplined and objective use of available data, and on real proofs rather than on indistinct and general argumentation. Mark what I mean: the real proofs are there, but there is so much indiscriminate use of all kinds of material together that the true may be buried in a pile of much that is totally irrelevant. Much more work needs to be done in thinking really hard and clearly defining one's terms and goals, and stating exactly what one is trying to prove. I think some of the authors tend to take the shotgun

approach—that is to say, they spray pellets all around the target instead of aiming at the bull's-eye, and they are satisfied if they hit New Dealers and leftish Democrats, even Republicans, as long as they hit someone. And everyone who is hit becomes, by that very fact, a Communist.

3. My chief fear of the methods of the radical right is that this is just the sort of thing that Communists can use to great advantage. Remember, the Communist proceeds by dialectical thinking. His favorite way of preparing and softening up certain kinds of situation is to favor the extreme right wing, the dictator type, the autocracy which tends to discredit itself by its own extremism. In making an overemphatic case for one extreme we drive people to the other extreme, and prepare them to accept it.

What is needed is moderation, rationality, objective thought, and above all a firm continued reliance on the very things which are our strength: constitutional processes of government, respect for the rights we want to defend, rational discussion, freedom of opinion, and a deep loyalty to our inherited ideals. This requires mental and spiritual discipline, and we all owe it to our country and to our faith to develop this kind of discipline, along with objectivity, fairness, respect for rights. The fact that Communists do the opposite does not entitle us to take over all their methods, and I am afraid there is a tendency to learn from them and apply some of their techniques.

Do believe me sincerely grateful for your interest, and let me sum up my message as a plea for a more middle-of-the-road course and for attachment to our basic ideals of freedom and rationality and thought.

51. *To S.M.M. (Sister M. Madeleva), Notre Dame, early March 1962.*
The chief reason why Julian of Norwich and the other English mystics are not in the notes I sent is that I did not have time to treat them adequately, and in proportion to my love for them. I also left out the Cistercians, practically. But Julian is without doubt one of the most wonderful of all Christian voices. She gets greater and greater in my eyes as I grow older, and whereas in the old days I used to be crazy about St. John of the Cross, I would not exchange him now for Julian if you gave me the world and the Indies and all the Spanish mystics rolled up in one bundle. I think that Julian of Norwich is, with Newman, the greatest English theologian. She is really that. For she reasons from her experience of the substantial center of the great Christian mystery of Redemption. She gives her experience and her deductions clearly, separating the two. And the experience is of course nothing merely subjective. It is the objective mystery of Christ as apprehended by her, with the mind and formation of a fourteenth-century English woman. And that fourteenth-century England is to me and always has been a world of light, for I have almost lived in it. So many villages and churches of the time are still there practically without change, or were thirty years ago. One can still breathe the same air as Julian, with the admixture of a little smog and fallout, of course . . .

It was necessary that I bear witness to my love for the Lady Julian, and that is why I have written. But now that I am speaking to you, I know you will help me along with your prayers. I don't pretend to be a lone crusader for peace or anything romantic like that, but I do feel there is a job to be done that is not being done and that there is an awful silence on the part of the hierarchy and the clergy, especially in America, on this subject which is really crucial.

52. *To H.M. (Herbert Mason), Goreham, Mo. (should be Maine), March 9, 1962 (see this volume, pp. 271–72).*

53. *To J.T.E. (John Tracy Ellis), Washington, March 10, 1962 (HGL, pp. 177–78).*

54. *To G.L. (Gerald Landry), Glen Garden, N. J., mid-March 1962.*

It has been a long time since you sent me your letter and the leaflet and later on your pamphlet. I am very moved by your story of your pacifism in Canada as a Catholic, during the last war, and of the support you received from the Bishop of Valleyfield. The story haunts one, it is so mysterious and so significant.

How sad it is that we have reached this strange present situation in the Church. I feel that we are in the presence of a very great mystery which leaves us almost helpless: not only helpless to understand God's designs in allowing His Church to become so completely implicated in the motives and ideals of the secular world, and in its obsessions (some of which are pathological), but helpless to know what we should do about it ourselves. It is almost as if true conscience had been reduced to a level of total insignificance, as if what came from within man and presumably from the Holy Spirit were by that very fact automatically suspect, and as if external social controls were now at last the whole story, with no room left for anything else.

It is good to have your little leaflet and the booklet, which I shall treasure as a valued possession. That too is a moving document, when one notices how articulate so many priests were in favor of peace in those days. And now, how few voices speak. I am meeting with very stern and resolute opposition, I can assure you, and I have no guarantee that I will be heard very much longer. But while I have a voice I will try to use it as best I can, with honesty and I hope objectivity. Meanwhile your booklet with its mine of material is an inspiration to me and will certainly prove useful. And it is a historic document in its own way.

We must try to make sense out of this senseless situation, with God's grace. Certainly we must never give up striving for Christian peace. The problems are almost infinitely complex and strange. There is so much that is totally new. May God protect and preserve us. Above all may He defend us from our own folly.

55. *To J.T.E. (John Tracy Ellis), Washington, March 19, 1962 (HGL, pp. 179–80).*

In a letter of March 14, 1962, Czeslaw Milosz expressed his puzzlement over Merton's papers about the duties of a Christian regarding the issue of war.

56. *To C.M. (Czeslaw Milosz), Berkeley, March 1962 (CT, pp. 80–81).*

57. *To T.L. (Thomas J. Liang), Oakland, March 1962 (RJ, p. 321).*

58. *To F.S. (Frank J. Sheed), New York, March 1962.*
I have been reading Gordon Zahn's book [*German Catholics and Hitler's War*] which you published. It is a most important and very well-done job of work. It deserves far more than the obvious platitudes which spring to mind about any good new book. To say that it raises a vitally important issue is so far short of doing it justice that it is ridiculous. It raises an issue that most of us are frankly incapable of understanding or even thinking about intelligently. It goes terribly deep, and much too deep for the average Catholic, the average priest, the average bishop. Zahn is objective with scientific innocence. There is no guile in his approach. He just says what he says, and overstates nothing. Where the impact comes is in the delayed action after one has read a chapter or so. Then all of a sudden one comes to with a jolt and says to himself: "This really means that something very dreadful is happening and has been happening, and that the bottom is dropping out of what we have been accustomed to regard as a fully satisfactory and complete picture of Christianity, or Christian civilization. Perhaps it has already dropped . . ." That is a mixed metaphor no doubt. The bottom drops out of a bucket, not out of a picture. But perhaps one tends to feel that the picture itself has just dropped out of a frame.
Then the Hans Küng book, *The Council, Reform and Reunion*. This too is splendid. One's reaction is more hopeful and more positive. But the sense of urgency remains the same. This Council has got to fulfill great hopes or be a disaster. It is absolutely no use reaffirming the disciplinary and juridical positions that have been affirmed one way or another for a thousand years. This is not reform, not renewal. That is what comes out of those two books, with great force. This is not the world of Gregory VII or Innocent III or Pius V, or even Pius X. To be a perfect Christian, even a saint according to their pattern, is no longer enough. On the contrary, it is apt to be terribly dangerous, even fatal.

59. *To K.McD. (Kilian McDonnell), Trier, March 1962.*
I certainly envy you going to study under Küng at Tübingen. I am finishing his book now and it is really one of the most exciting books I have read in years, without exception of books intended to be exciting in the most obvious way. There is really a breath of new life about this book

and about his outlook. It is awake and frank and not wild, but objectively Catholic in the finest sense—not the sense of the poor good people who have been paralyzed for ages by rigidities and conventions. A book like this makes one realize many, many things. It enables one to judge and to accept many things that were felt heretofore in the conscience only as obscure and ambiguous gnawings. It is then quite true that we are right to feel so uncomfortable and so terribly beaten down by the old negative, falsely conservative, and authoritarian spirit that purely and simply clings to the status quo for its own sake. It is quite true that so many things that we have feared to call dead are really dead after all. "Why do you seek the dead among the living?" There is after all something to the spiritual and Churchly sense which remains uneasy and crippled under the burden of what have to be frankly admitted as "dead works." And evasions and even dishonesties, not perhaps fully conscious ones.

Realizing this does not make one proud and rebellious. It is a chastening and humbling experience. One sees that so many people, in good faith, and with subjectively good reasons, are clinging blindly to ways of life and ways of seeing life which lead to spiritual blindness and which almost choke the life out of the faithful. The priestly mentality that comes out of so many seminaries. The beaten-down bright subservience and cultivated stupidity of the Catholic layman. The official and managerial insolence and self-complacency of some in authority, so often. The diplomacies, the subterfuges, the wiles, the manipulations of the law to keep people "quiet and happy." And when one sees all this frankly, he realizes that he himself is likewise involved, likewise at fault . . . Obviously Christian humility is not purely the humility of the subject who is always wrong before the official who is always right, but something far deeper, nobler and more human: the humility of the member of Christ who realizes that he and all the other members are so unworthy of their Head in so many ways, and yet that they can help one another by honesty and humility to be more worthy of the Spirit Who is given to them all.

Thanks for the material on Una Sancta and Fr. Metzger's prison letters. I have not plunged into these yet, it will take time. I want to write a bit more about him and make him known: a great man, one of the *seven* who, out of so many thousands in the German peace movement, continued to stick to his principles after Hitler long enough and uncompromisingly enough to pay for them with his life. That too is terribly significant, a strangely meaningful chapter in the history of the Church.

60. To J.G.L. (*Justus George Lawler*), *Chicago, March 1962.*
Your article on the Bishops is very timely and I appreciate it fully having just finished Küng's remarkable book on the Council. How right you are. I am so afraid that the concept of "renewal" will turn out to be nothing more than a tightening of the screws on the poor rank-and-file religious, clergy, and layman who have been hog-tied for so long. This Council is going to have to be a proof that we are not just a monolithic

organization, because that is how such organizations renew themselves: by tightening their grip on the rank and file and reasserting the perpetual rightness of the managers. If that happens this time, so help us, it will be one of the most horrible scandals that ever took place. It will be a disaster. That, principally, is the object of my prayers: that it will be a real renewal, or a step toward it. But honestly, I am scared. I ought to have more faith, one might say. It is not exactly that. I am scared because in a way I think we have deserved to come out in our true light. We have deserved the fate of efficiency for good and all. But God is merciful. He can save us from an endless succession of Good Joe Bishops whose greatest concern is to keep up a perpetual flow of innocent Irish drolleries about Pat and Mike and never say a serious word about anything except that so-and-so's marriage case is hopeless.

I am most grateful for the books. Rahner's *Theology of Death* was the first thing I grabbed, and I finished it quickly. It is superb. Funnily enough, my reaction would shock him, but besides clarifying my Christian faith it threw immense light on the real nature of Buddhism. He would be horrified. But that is precisely the Buddhist approach: that death can and should be an act of complete liberation, a going forth, an *act* by which one freely and completely leaves behind all that is not definitive, and the affirmation of the meaning hidden in all one's other acts. He of course tries to dismiss Buddhism as a spiritual sin, and he may be right of certain aspects of it. But I have been studying it a bit, and I think this is the real meaning of nirvana, and it has absolutely nothing whatever to do with a quietist ecstasy. The other books came yesterday and I shall enjoy them, bit by bit.

61. *To J.F. (James H. Forest), Hart's Island (prison), March 28, 1962 (HGL, pp. 265–66).*

62. *To T.McD. (Thomas McDonnell), Boston, c. March 28, 1962.*
I owe you, once again, five or six letters. Thanks for the most recent one which did not strike me as "neverous." I was sorry to hear about Yevtushenko. Yes, he was bound to get it eventually. It is too bad that such courageous people in the Iron Curtain countries are exploited sensationally by the press on our side, for political and propaganda motives, and then get the ax as a result. It is the ambiguous position that one gets in by protesting and trying to be honest. Whatever you do, you can be used by one side or the other and in the end you are discredited by everybody and gain nothing: except the invisible and unknowable gain of having witnessed to what is incomprehensible and therefore useless.

Thanks above all for the [John Howard] Griffin book [*Black Like Me*]. I found it moving and important, and of course read it right through with unflagging interest. As someone has aptly said: what we have in the southern United States is not so much a Negro problem as a White problem. There is no question that there the real problem lies, and it is more than the race question. The problem of peace is involved too in the belligerency and obtuseness of the same types . . .

Oh, by the way: I never got around to writing to Steve Allen and I don't think I can write to Griffin right now. I have to be realistic. There is a drawer full of unanswered letters here, and I am not in a position to go looking for more trouble than I have already. I will pray for them instead, it is more effective anyway.

No more for present. It rains like mad, probably fallout coming down in every drop.

63. To E.G. (Etta Gullick), Oxford, March 30, 1962 (HGL, pp. 350–53).

64. To T.McD. (Thomas McDonnell), Boston, early April 1962.

Thanks for your good letter and the enclosures. And for the previous one, which I do not think I have answered. I have always liked Brecht a lot; the only thing I have wondered is how he managed to get along so long with the Communists. He is obviously not one of "theirs" any more than Picasso or Pablo Neruda, though Neruda manages to be a faithful and humble believer and as a result he turns out some awful trash.

I saw you reviewed the Julien Green book, and he sent me a copy. He is a friend of Fr. Danielou and has even expressed a desire to try translating some of my poems into French. I wish he would, but he is too modest about his own capacity to do so. The novel is curious, reads very well, but is much too intricate, I think. But he is absorbed in the problem of sin, and when it comes clear he does well. However, some of the more sinister and stock figures tend to obscure the main issue. I suppose you could say he was doing a kind of medieval morality. His basic ideas on sin, or rather his basic haunting preoccupation with it, is interesting and real. Though within a kind of Calvinistic framework that makes it too "logical." Actually he struggles against the logic, wisely and rightly, but never fully succeeds in overcoming it.

65. To A.F. (Allan Forbes, Jr.), Philadelphia, early April 1962.

Your good letters have been reaching me with their encouraging comments. I do indeed wish it were possible for the monks to come out on a walk for peace from here to Washington. Wouldn't that be something? But unfortunately, though I might like this idea and a few others might join me, I am sure the majority would not understand it. That would be in part because they have just never heard of such things. And then I do not think most of them have a very good idea of the kind of situation we are in and are not able to evaluate it.

Yet as you say, if there is anything of the prophetic spirit left in us, it can find something to do while we are here in silence. And I myself do not underestimate the power of silence either. I know that as a matter of fact I can do much more for peace here, in silence, than I can by coming out and showing my head aboveground so to speak.

This is just another way of saying that there are many, many unexplored aspects of resistance and of witness. But I have read Wilmer Young's pamphlet and found it deeply moving. I do hope we can all preserve the purity of heart and simplicity of spirit that must go into such a thing. It is certain that the Quakers and the Mennonites have retained an unassailable simplicity and sincerity in this dedication to peace and non-violence. There should be many, many more Catholics in it with you.

66. *To R.deG. (Roger de Ganck), Belgium, early April 1962.*

When Rev. Dom Edward was here I did indeed speak to him about my interest in the Beguines in the Low Countries and their relation both to the Cistercians on the one hand and to the Rhenish mystics on the other. He advised me to write to you, but as I had little or no time to pursue the study further, I failed to do so.

But now it is a great pleasure to receive your letter, which came several weeks ago, I regret to say—I am behind with all my correspondence—and then the splendid book of Fr. Mens on the Beguines. I have never tried reading a whole book in Flemish before and this will be a kind of challenge. But I am most grateful for your gift and deeply appreciate it . . .

Certainly I will be very glad to send all the books that may be desired by the Sisters from Nazareth in their new foundation in California. Please let me know when they arrive there and what their address will be. This foundation is very interesting, and I think it is fine that a foundation of Cistercian nuns should be made in America in the direct line of the great mystical communities of the Middle Ages in the Low Countries.

Will you be coming to this country with the Sisters? Perhaps I may have the joy of meeting and speaking with you here. In any case, I assure you of my prayers for the success of the new foundation. From what I hear of the site, it is very well chosen and will be most inspiring.

67. *To A.A. (Abdul Aziz), Pakistan, April 4, 1962 (HGL, pp. 51–52).*

68. *To L.S. (Leo Szilard), Washington, April 12, 1962.*

I have had the good fortune to receive and read a copy of the talk you gave in Washington last November. It was particularly welcome, since I am at the same time undergoing the disheartening experience of reading the book of Edward Teller [*The Legacy of Hiroshima*]. It was encouraging to hear the contrasting notes struck by a civilized voice, yours. Dr. Teller's book seems to me to be a systematic piece of amorality which will probably have serious and far-reaching effects. Hence my conviction that your proposals about a peace lobby are of the greatest importance. I wish to assure you of my desire to cooperate in any way possible with your plan.

One way which suggests itself to me is to devote a notable part of the royalties of a book I am currently writing, on peace, to your cause. Another part of the same royalties will go toward the formation of a Catholic peace group which I am sponsoring. I do not have a regular income, being a member of a monastic Order. I think my Superiors will grant me permission to use these royalties in the way I have outlined.

It would seem that one of the most urgent problems is the prevalence of absurd, inhuman, and utterly distorted assumptions that have become the basis of the thinking and decisions of the majority, including the majority of those in power. The constant articulate resistance of an atomic scientist group has been the most effective corrective to this kind of thinking. But with people like Dr. Teller throwing the weight of their authority in the scales against the saner and more restrained views, the situation becomes serious. I need not add that the fact that many of the Catholic clergy and theologians have compounded the evils of the situation by mistakenly taking the so-called realist position. In my view the situation is now extremely grave, and if we go on in the direction we have now taken, in this country, the United States is liable to start a nuclear war out of sheer confusion, obsession, and misinterpretation of international realities.

Yet certainly there is plenty of clear thinking and sane analysis going on. I think we must do all we can to get these saner views more widely disseminated. It is a pity I did not know of your talk sooner or I would have asked to include it in a collection of essays on peace [*Breakthrough to Peace*] which I am editing and which should appear this fall. If you are making any further statements of this nature, or writing any articles, I hope I can get to know of them.

One encouraging thing, though it does not amount to much. A Senator Kowalski asked me to write a prayer for peace, which he intends to read in Congress when testing is resumed. At least a symbolic gesture. But what we need is a really strong organization of all the different peace groups, and above all some way of making clear that this is not a question of oddball pacifism or radicalism of some spurious kind.

69. *To J.F. (James H. Forest), New York, April 29, 1962 (HGL, pp. 266–68).*

70. *To J.G.L. (Justus George Lawler), Chicago, April (end of) or May 1962.*

I am in trouble with my own book about peace. It appears that the Higher Superiors have suddenly decided that my writing about peace "falsifies the monastic message." Can you imagine that? I have appealed the case, though, and am hoping that they will at least relent enough to permit this book to be censored, though even then they may decide that it is scandalous, subversive, dissipated, and worldly. Offensive, in a word, to pious ears, which are of course first of all monastic ears. Let our ears not be contaminated with any news of what is happening. Let us go up in radioactive dust still blissfully imagining it is the twelfth century and that St. Bernard is roving up and down the highways and byways of old France preaching the crusade to troubadours and occasional jolly goliards, but not too jolly, it would falsify a message.

Monks must preach to the birds, for the birds, and only for the birds.

71. *To V.H. (Victor Hammer), Lexington, Ky., May 1962 (see this volume, p. 7).*

72. *To A.F. (Allan Forbes, Jr.), Cambridge, May 1962.*
It was a bit of a jolt to see that your letter was dated February 5th. I cannot remember answering it, and so apologies are in order.

By now you know that the anthology is coming along with your essay in it, or rather the part on the arms race itself, with, I believe, a short summary of your proposals. I am very glad to have it in the book and I think it will be a very good little collection.

Your paragraph about the possibility of a preemptive strike being seriously considered has been substantiated, I think, by developments. I am not able to keep track of everything here, but in any case I heard of the interview Kennedy gave to some writer for *The Saturday Evening Post* saying "we may have to take the initiative." That might mean anything. Of course, the initiative, he said, would be "limited."

On one level one sees that it is impossible and even a bit absurd for the common man (whatever that is) to make a moral judgment in this situation. Nobody knows enough to make any serious judgment, I suppose. And everything is kept hidden in a jungle of double-talk from beginning to end, so that one wonders if the people who think they are running things understand what they are trying to do themselves.

But on another level everything is plain as day in the obvious nonsense and ambiguities of the double-talk itself. One has only to put one cliché up against the next and see how they react on one another. "We will take the initiative but the initiative will be limited." That tells us all we need to know.

73. *To R.C. (Roger Caillos), Buenos Aires, May 1962.*
I wonder if there is anyone in the world of Western culture today who does not know Victoria Ocampo [see *The Courage for Truth*] and who has not come within the sphere of her radiance. She is one of those wonderful people, alas rapidly becoming less and less numerous, who includes in herself all the grace and wisdom of a universal culture at a given time. I advisedly refrain from using the word cosmopolitan, which in an age of tourism has been reduced to meaninglessness and vulgarity. In a sense she is a model for all of us in the breadth of her interests, her sympathies, and her capacity for sensitive understanding. She is, in our age of miraculous communications, miraculously a person who has something to communicate. The rest of us, perhaps, use our fantastic instru-

ments merely to echo one another's noise. And communication must always fulfill one essential condition if it is to exist at all: it must be human, it must have resonances that are deeper than formal statements, declarations, and manifestos. And yet at the same time one of the great things about Doña Victoria is that if an intelligent manifesto is still possible, somewhere, somehow, one is likely to see her name on it. I do not make this as a statement of accurate fact, as I am in no position to follow all the manifestos and declarations that are made: but simply as a kind of poetic truth about Doña Victoria. She is a symbol of the bright and articulate judgment of a cultured person. To me she symbolizes America in the broad sense, the only sense, in which I am proud to be numbered among Americans. I am honored and delighted to join all those who, in proclaiming their admiration and love for her, are thereby taking what may perhaps be one of the final opportunities left to men to declare themselves civilized.

74. To V.D. (Valerie Delacorte), New York, early June 1962.

Your letter was wonderful. It is a pity I have so little time to write decent letters promptly, this war business has brought me in touch with so many wonderful people. It is a grace, in that sense, I think the Lord is waking us all up to the real futility and absurdity of our society that thinks purely in terms of quantity.

I had heard a little about the Women Strike for Peace. It is good to hear from one of you directly, and to be able to tell you how deeply I share your conviction of the rightness and importance of your action. I do believe there is a deep, hidden spiritual meaning in woman's part in our crisis.

The crisis of the world is, for one thing, a crisis of falsity. The enormous lies by which we live have reached a point of such obvious contradiction with the truth that everything is contradiction and absurdity. But I think it can be said, at least I feel that this is worth saying: woman has been "used" shamelessly in our commercial society, and in this "misuse" has been deeply involved in falsity. Think, for instance, of advertising, in which woman is constantly used as bait. And along with that, the mentality that is created for woman, and forced on her complacently, by the commercial world. She becomes herself a commodity. In a way the symbol of all commodities. In the false image of woman, life itself is turned into a commodity in its very source. Woman too has been used to create a kind of spiritual smoke screen behind which the "reality" of the power struggle evolves. Give the soldiers enough pinup girls and they will go gladly into battle.

I won't philosophize longer. But the first and most basic affirmation of all, that you must all make, is to refuse any longer to be part of the image of woman that is created by the commercial world. I leave you to meditate on the implications of that. Your refusal to remain passive in the fantastic nonsense of the big campaign to sell shelters has been providential. You have reacted against one of the more ultimate commercial perversions of the sacred reality of the family (commercialism exploits the family all down the line, and in doing so undermines the proper formation of the child's mentality, etc.). These are realities of great seriousness, and if it is granted us to have time we must try to think about them. But the springs of thought have been poisoned. Thank you for trying to help purify them.

75. *To R.McD. (R.McG.?) (Robert McGregor, New Directions publishing house), New York, early June 1962.*

As to the Tibetan monks [who had established a monastery in New Jersey], if you have any influence with them please urge them from me (and I have plenty of experience and am well qualified to advise) that it is most important for them to protect themselves against all forms of indiscreet press and other publicity, and that they protect themselves against visitors. They must have a cloister or enclosure or something which outsiders absolutely are forbidden to enter except with the Superior or someone else in charge. They must protect themselves against noise and inquisitiveness and against everything. I agree that it is of the very greatest importance for them to be extremely careful of the influence this country can have on them, even with the best of intentions. They have to stay apart, and above all be very faithful to their life of meditation.

What is important is that they learn, however, to distinguish between what is simply a difference between their culture and ours, and what is a deeper spiritual matter. On merely cultural differences they may perhaps find less danger in meeting us halfway, though this is also questionable. But God forbid that they adopt any of the prevailing philosophy of life. Do please make sure that these thoughts get through to them. If there is anyone concerned there that I could or should write to, please urge them to consult me if they have any questions at all or if they need anything.

I am really very anxious to see them sometime if it is at all possible. It would be wonderful if they could ever come down here, or if three of them could, the rimpoches for instance. I do hope we can look forward to a time in the future when they would make a visit here to study our monasticism such as it is . . .

Please give my very kind regards to the Reverend Monks from Tibet and assure them of my deep respect and fellowship and my readiness to serve them in anything I possibly can. And may we share in a common desire for truth and enlightenment, and may this be blessed with success. Such is my prayer for them and I hope theirs for me.

On May 29, 1962, Merton wrote to Mother Mary Luke Tobin, Superior of the Loretto Sisters: "A quick note to you with this little letter I wrote to the vow class. I shall be there in spirit on Thursday . . . [Ascension Day] is a beautiful feast." He asked for her prayers: "Having a hard time with the work. The higher Su-

periors have decided I must write no more on peace . . . Other publishing affairs
are in tangle too, so I can use the help of the Holy Spirit even more than usual."

76. *To Nuns, Sisters of Loretto (making final vows), May 29, 1962.*

The day has come for you to give yourselves completely to Christ
Our Lord. You will never appreciate, in this life, what it means to surrender yourself totally to Him. This must, from now on, be part of the
mystery of faith in which you live. You will not *know* that you belong to
Him: you must *believe* it. And this will require more faith than you have
had up to this time. But He will give you the faith to believe it.

In the beginning, perhaps, this faith will not be too difficult. Later
on, under trial, it may become hard at times. A faith that is not tested is
not worth much. Your faith must grow always, without ceasing. This is
why trial is necessary.

The faith of a first communicant is not enough for a postulant in
religion. The faith of a postulant is not enough for a novice. The faith of
a novice is not enough for a professed, and the faith of a newly professed
is not enough for one who has been years in religion.

Sometimes we think that the purity of our faith is all in the past and
that what we have to do is "recover" the fervor of our first communion,
or of our days in the novitiate. On the contrary, we must go forward, not
back. And going forward may at times be grim, because later on, when
we go forward, we realize that we are getting to the end. However, at
that time whatever was valuable in the beginning will be brought back
to us in a new form by the Holy Spirit. It is not for us to be anxious about
arranging our lives, even our spiritual lives.

If we belong to Christ, we must also believe that He belongs to us.
And that is much more important. That is why we do not have to run
our lives, for He is our life. We must not imagine that we can dictate to
Him. Our gift of ourselves to Him is a surrender in joy, so that we
henceforth allow Him to have His way with us.

Wherever you may go from here, remember me and pray for me. I
will also remember you and keep you in my Masses and prayers. For
since our Lord has made us neighbors and friends on earth, I presume
He wants us to be neighbors and friends in heaven also. But first we must
accomplish our assigned tasks on this earth, whatever they may be. Let
us keep praying for one another that we may do this well, and with
confidence and joy, without anxiety, trusting in Him to whom we belong.

77. *To W.F. (Wilbur H. Ferry), Santa Barbara, June 4, 1962 (HGL, pp.*
211–12).

78. *To R.L. (Robert Lax), New York, June 4, 1962 (RJ, p. 175).*

79. *To C.H. (Catherine de Hueck Doherty), Ontario, June 4, 1962 (HGL,*
pp. 18–19).

80. To R.L. (Ray Livingston), Minneapolis, early June 1962 (reply to Livingston letter of May 2, 1962) (see this volume, p. 244–45).

81. To W.M. (William Robert Miller), Baltimore, early June 1962 (see this volume, p. 249).

82. To J.W. (John C. H. Wu), Newark, June 7, 1962 (HGL, pp. 621–22).

83. To J.H. (John Harris), England, June 8, 1962 (HGL, pp. 397–99).

84. To F.E. (Father J. Whitney Evans), Duluth, June 13, 1962.
The idea is a fine one and I think your draft is very promising [a pamphlet on nuclear war which Fr. Evans had prepared for his high school seniors]. By all means go on with it, a lot of good will be done by it. I have already mentioned it, or will mention it, to Justus G. Lawler, editor of Herder and Herder . . . Why not send him a copy to give him an idea of it? He will surely be very interested.

I think it could be somewhat expanded, to include perhaps some more material that has recently appeared, especially some of the work by Gordon Zahn on the way the German Catholics went along with Hitler in a manifestly unjust war, and the problem involved by this.

Most important, however, is I think inclusion of material by Leo Szilard, who helped Einstein get the first bomb project started, and who later protested against the use of the bomb at Hiroshima. He has evolved a plan, published in the *Bulletin of the Atomic Scientists*, April 1962, which comes as close as anything I have seen to fitting in with Catholic moral teaching and with the pronouncements of the Popes. It still permits the use of tactical nuclear weapons, but in a clearly and strictly defensive manner. I think Szilard's proposals are very sound and practical and he has implemented them in a way that might conceivably get somewhere. In a word, I think that his proposals are about the most effective yet made and may even stand a chance to prevent a nuclear war if people get behind him . . .

One more comment on your manuscript. I think the beginning (about putting their picture there) is arresting, but I think it puts too much stress on the idea of personal survival. The issue is not personal survival but moral truth, though of course the morality depends entirely on the destructive havoc wreaked by nuclear war. I think we ought to make clear it is a question of crime. Why not start out instead with the execution of the Nuremberg war criminals, and then suggest that those who start an all-out nuclear war might well be in the same position, and those who encourage and support them would be equally responsible? Anyway, God bless your zeal and your project. Can I have a few more copies? I would greatly appreciate some.

85. To W.W. (Will Watkins), San Francisco, c. June 15, 1962 (answer to Watkins letter of June 9, 1962).

Your gift of the Eatherly-Anders book arrived today and I am most happy to have it. It is something I had heard about and was anxious to obtain. So you have sent it, and I deeply appreciate your kindness. I will read it with the deepest interest and concern. Eatherly is a rare symbol in the history of war making, and a very significant one. We are a country of strange ambiguities, and there is good in them after all, I think. But unfortunately the less ambiguous and the less conscience-stricken are the ones who are the best armed and the most convinced.

I had heard about *Everyman* [CNVA boat that sailed into the atomic testing area in the Pacific]. I even got a letter from Hal Stallings, and I am following the case with interest. It is indeed a beautiful little boat, but I wonder if it would have been able to make it down there to the test area if there were any storms.

Thank you again for your kindness. We have to be true to our conscience in everything, and true to humanity, for man is the image of God. This image cannot be defaced or destroyed. It must not. To defend it is to defend that which is most dear to God Himself.

86. To D.D. (Dorothy Day), New York, June 16, 1962 (HGL, pp. 145–46).

87. To C.K. (Carl Kline), Wisconsin, c. June 1962.

I want to thank you warmly for your appreciative letter. It means a lot to receive such reactions because it shows that for all the confusion and self-contradictions in our society, conscience is not asleep . . .

The secularization of religion is of course one of the great tragedies of our time, but religion is secularized because everything else is too. Whether we can survive this illness is the great question. I mean as a society. For as individuals we have to have the courage and the effrontery to cling to spiritual meanings and direct our lives by them in spite of everyone.

I think I have about said all I will be able to say in print on the subject of war. I have a book finished, on the subject, which is not likely to be printed right now. But since you have expressed interest I am sending you a mimeograph of the text, which contains a few mistakes but is on the whole intelligible.

88. To G.M. (probably Gwen Myers), Watertown, c. June 1962.

Thank you for writing to me. I feel very close indeed to the Friends and I always have, so you must not feel embarrassed about the difference in our religious affiliations. Besides, you have read many books that are very much in line with the kind of contemplative life we have here. Dom Chapman is especially good. Caussade is of course a master.

Naturally the idea of a "Church" supposes that we all have an ingrained need for one another and that we all aspire by a kind of basic instinct of grace to a community in which the Spirit of Christ will speak to us and guide us. However, there are groups and groups, and community life is now more and now less transparent a medium for the action of the Holy Spirit. You must not be surprised or sad if in your prayer group your own aspirations are not understood, nor is it possible or easy to find understanding when you travel a rather lonely way.

We can always say that the way of the contemplative should not be unusual or lonely, and that for him to think of it as unusual is certainly dangerous. But the facts are there and so is the experience.

It remains for you to trust God, not to make you infallible but to protect you from serious error and to make good the smaller mistakes. And thus with confidence in His guidance, even though you may not always interpret it correctly, you can advance peacefully. I am sure He will guide you safely in everything if you take care to keep your heart quiet and pure, as best you can, and listen to His voice in simplicity, trying to avoid the more obvious illusions, and keeping as close as possible to the solid bedrock of faith. With that, He will do all the rest. And He will put books into your hands that will tell you what your friends cannot.

89. *To J.W.S. (John Whitman Sears), June 23, 1962 (see this volume, pp. 303–4).*

90. *To B.N. (D. Brendan Nagle), Malibu, c. late June or early July 1962.*
You are quite right of course, I do not claim to have kept up with all the latest technical terms in the Cold War and the arms race, this would not be fully possible where I am. Also, as I too am rather pressed for time, I cannot give this subject the fully leisurely development that a real answer to your letter would demand. However, I hope that I can clarify my position regarding the main points you raise.

Merkelbach may have a probable opinion when he says that an offensive war may be just, but it is certainly not incorrect to say that the more common statement of Catholic tradition on this point, as represented in Pius XII's numerous statements and especially his Christmas messages, is that the just war is a defensive war. It is certainly not "the common doctrine of the Fathers" that an offensive war is a just war. St. Augustine, who is the father of the just war theory as far as I can see, evolved his doctrine in the light of the barbarian attacks on the Roman Empire and was at pains to show that the previously common doctrine of Christians, who avoided participation in any war, usually was not a *prohibition* of all military activity on the part of Christians. Historically the Crusades present as much of a problem as a proof that a just war is also aggressive. However, as you say, this is secondary, a matter of speculation. Let's get down to business.

We can agree that your "minimum deterrent posture," which implies the willingness and readiness to wipe out enemy cities on a large scale if he attacks us, is immoral by Christian standards. It is a way of holding millions of civilians as hostages and destroying them if the need arises. Also I would add that this policy would not seem practical in any way, as our cities would also be destroyed to a great extent in such a war.

First counterforce strike. I will agree that this can be acceptable *in theory* in the light of the teaching of the moral theologians, and that a Catholic could hold this, but I would lay down certain very stringent conditions (and I would not hold this opinion myself in any case). Here are the conditions I would lay down:

a) I would say that first counterforce strike could be permissible in theory if there were reasonable certainty that fallout or other side effects would not do serious damage to neutrals and friends, or even to our own future generations.

b) I would say that for a counterforce first strike to be permissible at all there would have to be *real imminent certainty* that the enemy himself was planning such a first strike on our own installations or on our cities.

To make a first strike, even counterforce, simply because we felt the enemy was menacing us politically, or even because the enemy was about to effect a political takeover of an allied country like Austria, would not seem to me to fit the conditions for a just war according to Christian ethics. I would not think the counterforce first strike idea would be legitimate under any circumstances except in the extreme case when it was *the only possible way to prevent our own annihilation*, by nuclear, chemical, or bacteriological weapons, let us say. Or at least by nuclear weapons.

In this case I think one could legitimately appeal to the *ratio defensionis necessariae*. However, even then I think this is not a sound or practical policy and that as free men in a Christian society we ought to be able to come up with better ways of solving our problems . . .

Father, let's face it: there are all kinds of clichés and accusations flying around on this subject, and I have seen it stated, with what seems to me a high degree of probability, that the kind of thinking that claims to be "nuclear realism" is basically paranoid. I only mention this to show that psychiatric clichés come rather cheap and one can use them without much effort of thought. I prefer the diagnosis that sees traces of paranoia in the "hard" position, because this statement has been made by people of sound judgment and high professional standing—who have of course been attacked by others of high standing (though not in the same field!). Besides, the people I have met who are most apt to be breathing fire and smoke on this war question have seemed to me to be not quite balanced mentally, certainly they have profound emotional problems. However, this may be due to a chance sampling of specimens who have come my way . . .

Father, one does not have to be a pacifist to state with full assurance, as Leo Szilard and others have stated, that the continuance of such an arms race means full-scale nuclear war within ten years. And even the most sober analysts who favor the reasonable practicality of nuclear war —Kahn, etc.—assure us that there is almost no chance at all of the democratic society we now know surviving even a victorious all-out nuclear war. At best it might be "rebuilt" after a long period. I just cannot see that such a war is "realistic" . . .

The question, as I see it, is not one merely of political practicality. Nor is it (still less indeed) a matter of bodily survival. I would not give a hoot, personally, if this whole monastery and everybody in it were blown sky-high this afternoon. I hope that my brothers and I are ready for heaven, or at least for a relatively short purgatory!! By God's grace, not by our merits. I also am sure that God's mercy would take care of millions of innocent or confused people who might perish in a nuclear war. Survival is a purely secondary question.

We are Christians, and we are going to be judged by Christ, according to the standard of His Law.

We have just witnessed the execution of Adolf Eichmann. In Nazi Germany, you may or may not remember, honest people, including perhaps many Catholics, more or less seriously accepted the view that the purity of the German race, the power of the German nation, was gravely menaced by "international Jewry." The policy of genocide (which has since been explicitly condemned by the Church, though no such explicit condemnation is needed, since the natural law condemns it) was accepted, or at least put through without significant protest, even from Catholics (there were of course exceptions). It seems that Catholics just looked the other way, if they did not actively approve and cooperate (the commandant of Auschwitz was a baptized Catholic, but I don't know if he continued to practice his religion).

The Eichmann trial has shown that these people were "sane" and "normal." That they did their job like any other job. It was mostly a matter of paperwork, at the top level of course. But they knew very well what they were doing. They simply went by the fact that everyone in their society accepted this as "normal" and "right" and they shrugged off responsibility by saying it was their "duty" and that the needs of the state demanded this unusual procedure.

You and I can see Eichmann in a different perspective and we can agree that this was a horrible crime.

My main point is this: we are Catholic priests. Catholic means universal. We have a duty not only to our people—and your people, you say, are almost 75% employed in defense industries—but also to the entire human race. We have got to have universal perspectives. We have got to enter into the hearts and minds of "the others." This is demanded by the exigencies of the "whole Christ."

In this present world crisis, our duty is not merely to salve the consciences of our parishioners and enable them to go ahead in peace of heart with a job that may involve them in collective responsibility for

what, in spite of Merkelbach, may well turn out to be a collective crime.
I know this sounds mad, utterly extreme. Well, Father, we still have to
face the possibility. We are going to be judged by the way we have reacted
to this great moral and spiritual challenge of our time.

In all seriousness, in all humility, with all deference, and with no
personal reference intended, I must in conscience say that there is danger
of us Catholics, myself and all the rest, tending to think in some such
way as the Eichmanns did in Germany. Not of course that we will, by
God's grace, be so blind. But that kind of blindness is not beyond us,
even though in a lesser degree. How? By being so utterly and totally
convinced of the gravity of our danger that we forget the principle that
the end does not justify the means . . .

Anyway, Father, this is my opinion. In all charity, let us at least
continue to ask Our Lord to guide us through these difficult straits, and
trust Him. I keep you and your people in my prayers. Pray for me too.

91. *To S.E.M. (Sister Elaine Michael), Allegany, July 4, 1962* (SC, p.
145).

92. *To H.M. (Henry Miller), Paris, July 9, 1962* (CT, pp. 274–75).

93. *To E.A.S. (Evora Arca de Sardinia), Miami, August 2, 1962 (see this
volume, pp. 80–81).*

94. *To E.S. (Elbert R. Sisson), Maryland, August 2, 1962* (RJ, p. 323).

95. *To H.M. (Henry Miller), Pacific Palisades, August 7, 1962* (CT, pp.
275–78).

96. *To J.M. (Joost A. M. Meerloo), New York, August 1962.*
I have been meaning to write to you about the offprint you sent a
long time ago, and your letter with it. "Responsibility" is a very fine essay.
I find that you pack a great deal into every sentence. That is why it was
not too hard to "edit" the section of your book that I took over for the
anthology. Your statements all tend to stand on their own feet, as aphor-
isms almost. I find the present essay very rich, and of course profited by
it. I do hope you will keep me on your list for anything like that.

The book [*Breakthrough to Peace*] ought to be out by now, and for
all I know it may be. Generally things take a fair amount of time to
penetrate the walls and the community and finally come through to me.
I hope the book will do some good, but I find it hard to be optimistic
about the present situation. I must confess, however, that things look
better in a way than they did this time last year: at least in the sense that
there has been a reaction and that a significant element of the population
has thrown off its passivity. On the other hand, I cannot be totally happy
about every aspect of the peace movement. It is in many respects a sick

movement, and some of the people involved glory in the sick side of it. They make a virtue out of being sick, as if in that way they could somehow be revenged for the frustrations they feel they owe to the society they live in. Their feeling may in part be justified, but then are they themselves *not* part of the society they resent? I think they are very much part of it, and bear a good share of its karma, not only that but they add plenty, for all of us to carry.

97. *To A.F. (Allan Forbes, Jr.), Philadelphia, August 1962.*

Your letter of a month ago has been waiting for a brief answer: I have wanted to set things straight, if possible, regarding the peace book.

Of course, I had no intention whatever of calling in question the value of Quaker and Mennonite peace activity. I really am not sure whether the side remark I may have made, mentioning the two groups, was properly interpreted: doubtless it [was] unclear. And in my own mind, I did not intend to lump you all indiscriminately together with all shades of "pacifists." But it is evident that the whole statement was misleading, so I will try to clarify what I really think now, as I owe you this.

1. You are perfectly right to interpret my praise of Dorothy Day as praise also of the Quaker peace witness, and the genuine spiritual non-violent witness for peace. There should be no question about this. It seems to me that the long-standing Quaker position on peace is one of the most reliable and stabilizing forces we have at the moment, and I think it is of very great spiritual importance. I think it also has political importance.

2. You note that I am making a distinction between "spiritual" and "political" action. The two should not really be separate, but in fact there is a distinction all right. What may have great value spiritually may have little value politically. I certainly think that the rather simplified unilateralism that has been more or less accepted as a basic position by the peace movements is of doubtful political value. This is where my Romanism comes in, I am afraid. I think that if there is going to be political action it ought to have a chance of really working in the current situation. I think there is just no practicality at all, in the concrete situation, in a purely unilateralist position.

3. In terms of politics, I think that the issue is to get down to some real sincere and practical negotiation in regard to disarmament. And this means first of all a more general willingness on the part of responsible parties, especially in this country, to believe that negotiation can and will work. If they think that "negotiation" means "unilateral disarmament by the U.S.," this gives them the scapegoat they need to resist and to avoid all negotiation. It enables them to be irrational with what they think is a good conscience. Rather than twit them with their inability to see unilateralism I would prefer to make them see their own solemn responsibility to take negotiation seriously on a less drastic level, at least to make a beginning of serious negotiation and not to make proposals and withdraw

them as soon as they seem to offer a practical possibility of acceptance. In other words, negotiation must be honest and not just a question of "deals" and "blackmail" and "propaganda value." I think that for a while there was a serious possibility that the Soviets would have negotiated fairly honestly if we had shown a little confidence in them and a little trust. Maybe that time is now past. Maybe I am all wrong in having even the slightest hope for conventional and traditional political action. But it is the only action that can really prevent a holocaust. For the rest, the spiritual witness is in another dimension.

I see the spiritual witness which you and the other Friends so gloriously present, and I mean this, is most important as an expression of conscience, as a reminder of spiritual positions and obligations. It may by some miracle start a chain reaction in the moral order, and this we can always hope. But I do not think it will effect large-scale political consequences. Perhaps I am wrong in this. But in any event I do not intend this opinion to be interpreted as "disapproval," still less as a fundamental lack of sympathy. That is certainly not the case by any means. If anyone is worried about this point you can explain how I stand.

The situation does not seem to get any better, does it? This testing is a serious matter, and the renewal of Soviet testing on August 6th is a grave symbolic gesture. Let us trust in God and purify our hearts as best we can. This is a solemn moment and now above all we must be in a position to hear His voice and neglect no slightest indication of His will. It is most important that all who believe in His Name may open their hearts to His merciful light, because the fate of the world depends on this. And all must prepare themselves for any eventuality. The events of the next five years may fulfill all the worst expectations: or on the other hand there may be a merciful reprieve. Who can tell? We must be ready.

98. *To the Hon. Shinzo Hamai, Mayor of Hiroshima, Japan, August 9, 1962 (HGL, pp. 380–81).*

99. *To M.V.D. (Mark Van Doren), Connecticut, August 9, 1962 (RJ, p. 45).*

100. *To R.McC. (Robert J. McCracken), Iowa, August 1962.*
Thank you for your letter about the article on nuclear war, and for the questions it contains. I think that you have oversimplified my position a little. I do not declare that *all* atomic war is by its very nature sinful. I think it might be possible to construct an argument in defense of a very limited use of atomic weapons in a clearly defensive situation which would not be immoral. But I do think that in the present crisis we are going clearly in the direction of an unjust, immoral, and massive use of nuclear weapons, as well as chemical and bacteriological weapons also.

It seems to me that the extreme positions are to be avoided, because they aggravate the problem. I would say that the Church wants Catholics to follow Christian prudence. This means that just means of defense should certainly be maintained. But they must really satisfy the demands of justice, and that excludes, it seems to me, the massive use of nuclear weapons indiscriminately on cities or even on missile installations near cities, especially in a first-strike aggressive war.

It seems to me that the *duty* of the Catholic, whatever may be his choice of a defense system that fits in with just standards, is to *work for peace* in a reasonable and prudent way, by the use of the normal political means. I would say this meant giving close attention to the danger involved in the unlimited arms race, it would mean not voting for belligerent politicians, it would mean supporting those who favor a moderate, reasonable, and peaceful approach to international problems. It would mean favoring and supporting positive and peaceful measures in helping out undeveloped countries—such methods as the Peace Corps, for instance. In a word, I think it is a pitiful mistake for Christians to get rattled and to deceive themselves with a kind of crusading spirit that thinks our problems can be solved by nuclear war.

You have no obligation to join a group which you consider eccentric. You ought certainly to write your congressman and urge him to pursue peaceful politics rather than rash and aggressive policies. In order to do this intelligibly you have the obligation to form your conscience by intelligent reading and even some study of the question. Reputable Catholic magazines like *America*, the *Commonweal*, and others give different shades of opinion on the war question, whereas some of the more popular Catholic papers tend to be a little off-center. This is my opinion.

Should you refuse to serve your country? If you are absolutely convinced that the means taken to defend the country, or to advance its interests, are really unjust, then the question of refusing service would arise. I do not maintain that a Catholic must by the very fact be a pacifist. I would hold that in certain circumstances a pacifist stand by a Catholic would be legitimate. It is for you to form your conscience regarding the rightness and justice of our present policies. My opinion is that these policies tend to be dangerous morally insofar as they tend to an *unlimited* arms race, to a wasteful and artificial economy which may ruin the country all by itself, and ultimately to a disastrous massive nuclear war which would involve the destruction of what we are trying to defend.

My advice to you is: read the Christmas messages of the Popes for every year since 1948, and learn the principles they have laid down: judge current events in the light of those principles, and you will judge as a Catholic.

Trust in God and in His Holy Spirit. Have courage to follow your conscience. Seek the truth with deep humble sincerity. Love your country and your fellow man. You will be blessed by God and will see the right course if you earnestly seek to do those things.

101. To J.F. (James H. Forest), New York, August 27, 1962 (HG, p. 270).

102. To L.S. (Lou Silberman), Nashville, September 19, 1962.

Thanks for your letter and for the interesting offprints. I am glad to see our concerns are so nearly alike: how can we afford to ignore at a time like this the "scandal of prophecy"? The only hope we have is in scandals. All that is secure is a deception. I think that things are getting much more dangerous than they have ever been, and everybody seems to think this. At such a time we are forced to a kind of faith we had never imagined . . .

I have come across a manuscript of meditations by a Father Delp, S.J., who was executed under Hitler. Most of it was written in prison, and in reading it one gets the impression that only people like this knew what they are talking about. I am asked to write a preface to this, and I wonder what one can say, except that this is truth and what is not like this is untrue.

103. To L.D. (Leslie Dewart), Toronto, September 1962 (see this volume, pp. 281–83).

104. To D.S. (Dan Shay), Detroit, September 1962.

Your letter was very welcome. I think the idea is a good one, and I think you are very right to investigate reasonable ways of preparing yourself for the pilgrimage. This is quite important. With the help of grace I will try to think up a few ideas to contribute to your effort.

1. I would begin right away to think about people you ought to meet in Europe. First of all, the priests and intellectuals you may conceivably run into here and there will actually mean more, in many respects, than when you will meet in Rome: there you may meet practically nothing, or on the other hand it is possible you may get to see someone important. God alone knows. But in France you should try to get to men like Fr. Régamey and Fr. Hervé Chaigne, O.F.M. I don't know the latter, but the former can be reached through *La Vie Spirituelle*, 29 Boulevard de Latour Maubourg, Paris. I don't know if he knows English. Do you know French? You ought to read some of his stuff. Both these have written on non-violence. Recently a piece on Gandhian non-violence by Chaigne was in *Cross Currents*. They could tell you at *Cross Currents* how to contact him, no doubt. Later I can give you info about more non-violent activists in France. Fr. Régamey's book on non-violence has not been translated. He has a good book on poverty and another on the Cross, not directly about war but good spiritual material.

2. Of the Popes you should read and master all the important passages in the Christmas messages since 1948. Easter messages too, sometimes. It is in these Christmas messages above all that the statements about the immorality of total war come out clear.

3. The most important thing is to study carefully your purpose and your objective. Especially when making a statement of your intentions and desires to the Council itself. I wonder if this can have much value

at the moment. Isn't it too late? I mean for anything official. You don't want to just send something in that will get put on the shelf or get a rubber-stamp answer from somebody if it is answered at all. About this aspect of the matter I can't be of much help as I don't know anything about the court of Rome and I want to keep out of anything concerning it. But don't just go getting yourself a big cosmic runaround.

4. The more I think about it, the more I believe it is theologically as well as tactically inadequate to try to get the Council to condemn the bomb in some form or other. The bomb does not need to be condemned, since it is already in many ways condemned by its very nature, and in any case, even if the Bishops would go out on a limb and formally condemn it (which they wouldn't) it would not have that much effect. People who don't want to pay attention to the Church today never do, including Catholics, and including Bishops.

I am not in favor of the kind of pressure that strives to get Rome to approve this and condemn that. In the long run it tends to be glorified infantilism and it prolongs the infantile type of theological thought we are trying to get rid of. I think there would be more meaning in a less theological and more political approach, a concrete peace proposition of some sort, or a peace initiative that could be backed by the Church somehow.

The thing to realize is this: we are members of Christ, and we have a voice, whether as priests or as laity. If we as members of Christ protest against total war, then it is already in some sense a work of the Church. The protest in any case has already been clearly made by the Popes and I think the best thing for you to do is to reiterate in very clear terms what the Popes have already declared: that total war is a sin and that the psychology that strives to settle international differences by total war is murderous and criminal. The mentality that thinks *only* in terms of total victory, by any available means, is an expression of moral apostasy from Christ. The use of the Christian ethical doctrine that self-defense can be justified is not a right use, when it is taken to justify total war, that seeks total annihilation of the opponent's cities and economy as a means of beating him down. This is Catholic doctrine, and what is needed is a strong Catholic peace initiative based on this doctrine. I would concentrate, if I were you, on steps that will lead to the formation of such an international movement.

Write Dorothy Day and ask her about the Goss-Mayrs, who are coming to this country in the winter, I believe. They are the best people to know in this regard. You can quote anything I have said in this letter. I am with you in prayer and in the love of Christ's truth. May God bless you always . . .

Editor's note: In the typing of the Cold War Letters, the next two were mistakenly reversed. The carbon copies from which the letters were typed clearly label the letter to C.T., London, as 105 and the letter to E.E., Linz, as 106. I have put them in the proper order—the order Merton intended.

105. To C.T. (Charles Thompson), London, September 27, 1962 (HGL, pp. 574–75).

106. To E.E. (Elsa Englander), Linz, September 30, 1962.

I hope you are patient with my defects as a correspondent. I was glad to get your letter, sorry you did not meet Gordon Zahn. I understand how you feel about his book. That is the impression it will create upon most German readers. But perhaps the book was not really addressed to German readers. Naturally, when an author undertakes to make such an analysis, he must expect to be read and judged by those whom he analyzes. But nevertheless, speaking of his thought, it seems to me that he had in mind the American public of 1962 and not the Germans of 1945, or even of 1962. You are all very far from the days he describes, you have gone far beyond that, you have meditated in a long and anguished silence, and with open discussion and frank self-examination, upon the events of twenty years ago. There is no question that this is primarily an affair of the German nation, and once they have examined themselves and come to their conclusion, we cannot lightly revise their decision and come to some other conclusion. I do not think that Zahn intended to do that in any respect. But I do think he was treating the German question in an *abstract scientific* form with a view to the concrete present needs of America. Without this perspective, I do not think his book can be rightly understood.

There can be no question that what the German Catholics did under Hitler was humanly understandable and in view of the fact that in such a crisis there are hundreds of extenuating circumstances, hundreds of varied reasons for people not coming to an abstractly perfect conclusion, it is actually what almost anyone would have done in the same situation. Hence it cannot be said in any way that Zahn is singling out the German Catholics for special censure. On the contrary, I think his real point is his preoccupation with the sobering thought that this is the way we all act, and we are not likely, even now, to rise above this standard. In particular, there is every indication that the American Catholic not only *will* make much the same kind of compromise, but is in fact already doing so . . .

With this and the race troubles in the South one can see the beginnings and perhaps more than the beginnings of a Nazi mentality in the United States. There is in fact a Nazi party here, of little consequence at the moment because it is obviously part of a lunatic fringe. But much more serious is the presence of a very powerful and influential alliance of business and military men, backing certain politicians and leaders of anti-Communist movements, who are not content with opposing Communism as it really is, but who consider everyone who disagrees with them a Communist, a traitor, and a spy . . .

I have just finished writing a preface to the English translation of Fr. Delp's meditations in prison. I found them most powerful and deeply moving. I think this is one of the great spiritual books of the age, and here was certainly someone who opposed Hitler frankly and vocally, without hesitation or compromise. It is a noble and great document of German Catholicism in World War II. I do not have a great deal of biographical material on Fr. Delp. It would be good to write a biographical note. Can you send me anything?

Thank you for the very interesting material about the convent in Jerusalem and the beautiful, touching little book on the Jewish children. These too are evidence of the warm Christian love and faith of the German Catholics. I may add that we are looking with great hope to the German and Dutch Bishops in the Council. Germany may have been through some terrible times, but there is no question that German Catholicism is perhaps the most advanced and most living force in the Church today, together perhaps with the Catholicism of some of the African Bishops, who knows?

It is wonderful to be united in Christ, and to live at such a time, terrible though it is. Let us thank Him for having called us into His world and His Church in a day when the struggle is crucial, and pray Him to enlighten us and give us courage to open ourselves entirely to the Spirit given us by the Victorious Savior.

107. To D.S. (Dallas Smythe), Urbana, October 22, 1962.

I do want to thank you for sending me your very incisive conference on *Religion and the Mass Media*. I have read and reread it, and agree all down the line. It is very clear, and is right on the target. I think you will probably be interested in the review I wrote of the new J. F. Powers book ["Morte d'Urban: Two Celebrations," published in *Worship*, November 1962], which treats some of the same ideas indirectly.

Did your text come out in book form? I hope no cuts were made. I do not know much about Straus Hupe, but I have heard of him and know where to place him. I must say the mentality of Christians in this country is very disturbing. Except for a few minority groups like the FOR [Fellowship of Reconciliation], regarded as crazy by the others. Disturbing from a religious point of view above all, because it seems that there has been a real surrender, as your conference makes clear, to the values of what has always traditionally been called "the world," in the bad sense in which this term appears in the New Testament. What else is consumership but a systematization of one of the most essential elements in "worldliness." What has happened is, as you say, a complete secularization of religion in which the minister of God runs about frantically getting himself accepted as a member of the affluent society. The chief concern of Christians here seems to be to make sure they will never under any circumstances get excommunicated from the society of people who read *Time* and *Life* . . .

On the other hand, I have been extremely heartened by the opening speech of John XXIII at the Vatican Council. I doubt if the resonances would be apparent to those who do not listen closely to this kind of thing, but there are really deep and insistent notes of change and renewal. I am sure that if he gets any cooperation at all, the Council will certainly do good and even great things. Not everyone has been feeling that way, in the Church. There has been a lot of pessimism on the theory that the Curia would be able to do what they wanted with the Pope. Not so, I think. Pope John seems to know what he wants and to be determined to go after it. Also his talk the day after the opening, to diplomats in the Sistine, was powerful and significant: a great blow for peace. Trouble is that statements like that appear on page two and are forgotten the next morning.

In October it became clear that Soviet missile sites had been erected in Cuba. On October 22, 1962, President John F. Kennedy ordered a blockade of Cuba. On October 29, Nikita Khrushchev agreed to withdraw the missiles and to dismantle the missile sites in return for an American promise not to invade Cuba and to dismantle U.S. missile sites in Turkey.

108. To E.G. (Etta Gullick), Oxford, October 29, 1962 (HGL, pp. 355–56).

109. To E.S. (Evora Arca de Sardinia), Miami, October 29, 1962 (see this volume, p. 82).

110. To G.D. (George Dunne), Washington, October 30, 1962.
It was kind of you to send me a copy of the speech you gave (since bombs did not fall) last Thursday evening. I should be interested to hear how it was received. For my part I think you did an exceptionally good job, and I do not see how anyone can complain of your clear arguments on Christian grounds. At best they might heckle you most unreasonably on what they deem to be grounds of political urgency or expediency.

It does not seem to me, in the first place, that the Cuba crisis invalidated your thesis that the Communist push is political and not military. On the contrary, the fact that Khrushchev yielded when pressed shows that his first and main way of handling international problems is not military. The missiles are for him means of precipitating political action of one sort or another. He may of course get it in the neck, now, for being weak. But he may on the other hand reap a certain amount of benefit for his action "for peace," thus eating his cake and having it. I don't know, and it is not wise to make statements from behind such a wall as mine, when they may already have been contradicted by the event.

It is my opinion that the great danger is, as you say, on the political and economic front. Especially in Latin America, Africa, and Asia. Latin America is the one place where we might have (perhaps even might still) do something. But I am also much concerned about the economy of our own country: not that I know much about it. But one doesn't have to know the first thing about economics to know that this present war economy spells ruin. I am easily persuaded that Khrushchev is just waiting for us to collapse. He does not need missiles except to stimulate our frenzy to the point of self-destruction. But of course it is a risky game, because there are more and more who want to destroy him and Russia along with themselves. But I am speaking primarily of the economic collapse of a totally wasteful and destructive system. This statement does not apply to the system in its essence, but in its actual dementia.

May your work with the Peace Corps volunteers have great success. It is maddening to think that the work of the Corps is stripped down to a bare symbolic gesture, in comparison with the enormous war effort which is both symbolic and dreadfully real. It must be very frustrating to take part in something so largely symbolic, the symbolic character of which is less and less interesting to the ones who are pushing for the great power play.

111. To E.G. (Rabbi Everett Gendler), Princeton, October 1962.

My first reaction to the Peace Hostage Exchange [see letters to Stephen James in this volume] was to try to think of some way in which I could possibly get involved in it. But I am afraid it is out of the question for me. The main value of the pledge is its symbolic quality. Like everything else in this business about peace, it is a beginning of a way to communicate ideas. Where all the ideas are ready-made for everybody and disseminated by mass media, it is an illusion for individuals or small dissenting groups to imagine that they have some way of making themselves heard if they just join in the general cacophony by writing letters to *Time*. There have to be other ways of making oneself heard. The various devices of the peace movement, the non-violence movement, etc., are steps in this direction. I think this peace hostage pledge is certainly one of the best.

At the same time I am impressed with the fact that all these things are little more than symbols. Thank God they are at least symbols, and valid ones. But where are we going to turn for some really effective political action? As soon as one gets involved in the machinery of politics one gets involved in its demonic futilities and in the great current that sweeps everything toward no one knows what.

Every slightest effort at opening up new areas of thought, every attempt to perceive new aspects of truth, or just a little truth, is of inestimable value in preparing the way for the light we cannot yet see.

2. Postscript to the Cold War Letters

*[An ecological ethic calls for] restraint and wisdom in
the way we treat the earth we live on and the other
members of the ecological community with which we live.*
TO BARBARA HUBBARD

To Rachel Carson

A typed letter to Rachel Carson, author of Silent Spring, *dated January 12, 1963,
has at the top of the letter, in Merton's handwriting: "Appendix to Cold War
Letters." Above is an "N.B.," also handwritten. Two letters to Barbara Hubbard,
written several years later, touch on the same theme as the Carson letter.*

January 12, 1963

Anne Ford very kindly sent me your latest book, *Silent Spring*, which
I am reading carefully and with great concern. I want to tell you first of
all that I compliment you on the fine, exact, and persuasive book you
have written, and secondly that it is perhaps much more timely even than
you or I realize. Though you are treating of just one aspect, and a rather
detailed aspect, of our technological civilization, you are, perhaps without
altogether realizing, contributing a most valuable and essential piece of
evidence for the diagnosis of the ills of our civilization.

The awful irresponsibility with which we scorn the smallest values
is part of the same portentous irresponsibility with which we dare to use
our titanic power in a way that threatens not only civilization but life
itself. The same mental processing—I almost said mental illness—seems
to be at work in both cases, and your book makes it clear to me that there
is a *consistent pattern* running through everything that we do, through
every aspect of our culture, our thought, our economy, our whole way
of life. What this pattern is I cannot say clearly, but I believe it is now
the most vitally important thing for all of us, however we may be concerned with our society, to try to arrive at a clear, cogent statement of
our ills, so that we may begin to correct them. Otherwise, our efforts
will be directed to purely superficial symptoms only, and perhaps not
even at things related directly to the illness. On the contrary, it seems

that our remedies are instinctively those which aggravate the sickness: *the remedies are expressions of the sickness itself.*

I would almost dare to say that the sickness is perhaps a very real and very dreadful hatred of life as such, of course subconscious, buried under our pitiful and superficial optimism about ourselves and our affluent society. But I think that the very thought processes of materialistic affluence (and here the same things are found in all the different economic systems that seek affluence for its own sake) are ultimately self-defeating. They contain so many built-in frustrations that they inevitably lead us to despair in the midst of "plenty" and "happiness" and the awful fruit of this despair is indiscriminate, irresponsible destructiveness, hatred of life, carried on in the name of life itself. In order to "survive" we instinctively destroy that on which our survival depends.

Another thought that has struck me with powerful impact on reading your book: together with my friends Erich Fromm and D. T. Suzuki, I have been absorbed in the ideas of the mythical and poetic expression of the doctrine of the "fall" of man and original sin. The pattern in the Genesis account is very instructive. It seems to indicate that the meaning of original sin, whatever may be one's dogmatic convictions about it, is that man has built into himself a tendency to destroy and negate himself when everything is at its best, and that it is just when things are paradisiacal that he uses this power. The whole world itself, to religious thinkers, has always appeared as a transparent manifestation of the love of God, as a "paradise" of His wisdom, manifested in all His creatures, down to the tiniest, and in the most wonderful interrelationship between them.

Man's vocation was to be in this cosmic creation, so to speak, as the eye in the body. What I say now is a religious, not a scientific statement. That is to say, man is at once a part of nature and he transcends it. In maintaining this delicate balance, he must make use of nature wisely, and understand his position, ultimately relating both himself and visible nature to the invisible—in my terms, to the Creator, in any case, to the source and exemplar of all being and all life.

But man has lost his "sight" and is blundering around aimlessly in the midst of the wonderful works of God. It is in thinking that he sees, in gaining power and technical know-how, that he has lost his wisdom and his cosmic perspective. I see this clearly, too, in books like those of Laurens van der Post about the South African Bushmen. I am sure you must have read some of them.

Technics and wisdom are not by any means opposed. On the contrary, the duty of our age, the "vocation" of modern man is to unite them in a supreme humility which will result in a totally self-forgetful creativity and service. Can we do this? Certainly we are not going in the right direction. But a book like yours is a most salutary and important warning. I desperately hope that everyone who has a chance to help form public opinion on these vital practical matters may read your book. I hope also that lawmakers will be able to see the connection between what you say and the vastly more important problem of nuclear war: the relationship is so terribly close. It is exactly the same kind of "logic." We don't like the looks of a Japanese beetle. We let ourselves be convinced by a salesman that the beetle is a dire threat. It then becomes obvious that the thing to do is exterminate the beetle by any means whatever even if it means the extermination of many other beings which have not harmed us and which even bring joy into our lives: worse still, we will exterminate the beetle even if it means danger to our children and to our very selves. To make this seem "reasonable" we go to some lengths to produce arguments that our steps are really "harmless." I am afraid I do not relish the safety of the atomic age, but I hope I can use it to attain to a salutary detachment from life and from temporal things so that I can dedicate myself entirely and freely to truth and to my fellow man. A dangerous situation after all has certain spiritual advantages. Let us hope that we may be guided effectively in the right directions.

I want to conclude by sending you my very best wishes and every expression of personal esteem. I love your books, and I love the nature that is all around me here. And I regret my own follies with DDT, which I have now totally renounced.

P.S.: Sometime I would like to write to you about some of our problems here. Cedar trees dying out unaccountably, an awful plague of bagworms, etc., etc.

To Barbara Hubbard

The following letters to Barbara Hubbard, director of the Center of American Living in New York City, seem similar in tone to the letter to Rachel Carson.

December 23, 1967

Thanks for your letter. In the midst of the welter of Christmas I'll try to get a few thoughts on paper before I forget everything.

1. There can be no question whatever that mankind now stands at one of the crucial thresholds of his existence. In some sense it is the most crucial, since his entire future is to a great extent in his own hands. In the sense that he can determine that future, but not in the sense that he knows entirely what he is doing since he cannot foresee all the results of his decision. And also it will do him no good to hang back or try to avoid the decision, because even not deciding is a decision and will have its own (I think unfortunate) results.

2. Man now knows enough to determine his own future without knowing quite what all the implications are going to be. That is of course characteristic of human acts and human freedom. What is new is that now man can decide not just for himself and his immediate entourage as

individuals, but he can decide for the whole race. He can commit the future to a certain quality of life—or no life at all.

3. It seems to me that we must not be too naive about this situation. The fact that it is excitingly new should not blind us to the other fact that man is still acting in the same wrong ways that he should have learned to avoid. In other words, we have to face the new without forgetting crucially important lessons from the past. Our decision must be a life-affirming and loving one: but a life-affirming decision is not likely to emerge from a thought system that is largely programmed by unconscious death drives, destructiveness, greed, etc. And yet it still can, if we take account of a few vital and by no means new imperatives: to refrain from the wanton taking of life, to avoid selfish greed and the exploitation of others for our own ends, to tell the truth (and that goes for governments and corporations as well as for individuals), to respect the personal integrity of others even when they belong to groups that are alien to us, etc., etc.

4. We must face the challenge of the future realizing that we are still problems to ourselves. Where the religious dimension enters in is not just in pious clichés but in a radical self-criticism and openness and a profound ability to *trust* not only in our chances of a winning gamble, but in an inner dynamism of life itself, a basic creativity, a power of life to win over entropy and death. But once again, we have to pay attention to the fact that we may formulate this in words, and our unconscious death-drive may be contradicting us in destructive undertones we don't hear.

In other words, we have all got to learn to be wide open, and not get closed up in little tight systems and cliques, little coteries of gnostic experts . . . Your work in bringing people from different fields together is symptomatic. It shows the realization of one of our greatest needs: a real expansion of communication to its worldwide limits. I wish you success.

February 16, 1968

Let me get these few thoughts on paper before I forget them. First, thanks for your letter. Yes, I did enjoy Center Letter #3 and would appreciate having another six copies, if possible. May I? I also had not noticed that "Year One of the Noosphere" also happened to be the year of the Sputnik. You are right in noting the significance of this.

About our "birth into space": one reason why I am perhaps a bit backward about joining spontaneously and articulately in the celebration of a space age mystique is that I am not properly informed. Perhaps you can help me there. I do get the sense of immense technical skill and virtuosity and the opening of fabulous new horizons. But since my knowledge is largely based on magazines that I leaf through in the tedium of a doctor's office, I also get an impression of commercialism, hubris, and cliché, which frankly turns me off. I realize that this is a by-product which really has nothing to do with the seriousness of scientific exploration. There is another dimly sensed aspect of space flights as a sort of cosmic and ritual shamanic dance by which I could conceivably be turned back on . . .

All I am saying is that I am really not ready to speak on this subject.

Here is another aspect of the situation. The future depends very much on what we are thinking and doing *now*. Let me suggest a perhaps new and offbeat approach to what we are thinking now, ethically. I detect two broad kinds of ethical consciousness developing (over and above the sclerotic fixation on norms that are given by the past): (1) a *millennial* consciousness, (2) an *ecological* consciousness. The millennial consciousness is like this: all that has happened up to now has been at best provisional and preparatory, at worst a complete mess. The real thing is about to happen: the new creation, the millennium, the coming of the Kingdom, the withering away of the State, etc. But if you want to enter into the Kingdom there are certain things you have to do. They consist partly in acts which destroy and repudiate the past (metanoia, conversion, revolution, etc.) and partly in acts which open you up to the future. If you do these things, the big event will happen. This consciousness is found in Marxism, in Black Power, in Cargo Cults, in Church aggiornamento, in Third World revolutionary movements, but also doubtless in esoteric movements within the establishment, management, science, etc., which are all beyond my simple ken. The ecological consciousness says: look out! In preparing this great event you run the risk of forgetting something. We are not alone in this thing. We belong to a community of living beings and we owe our fellow members in this community the respect and honor due to them. If we are to enter into a new era, well and good, but let's bring the rest of the living along with us.

In other words, we must not try to prepare the millennium by immolating our living earth, by careless and stupid exploitation for short-term commercial, military, or technological ends which will be paid for by irreparable loss in living species and natural resources. This ecological consciousness can be summed up in the words of Albert Schweitzer: to wit, "life is sacred . . . that of plants and animals [as well as that of our] fellow man." And the conservationist Aldo Leopold spoke of a basic "ecological conscience," the source of an ethic that can be stated in the following expansion of the Golden Rule: "A thing is right when it tends to preserve the integrity, stability, and beauty of the biotic community. It is wrong when it tends otherwise."

The scientific exploration of space and of other planets—I say scientific, not military—can be seen in itself as neutral, neither millennial nor ecological. Since it reaches *outside* the natural ecological environment of our earth and becomes independent of it to a great extent, it tends to function in a different climate of thought. Nevertheless, as some scientists have reminded us, the ecological implications of interplanetary flight could be enormous.

My suggestion is this. The space age can be dominated by millennial thinking or by ecological thinking. If the millennial predominates, it may lead to ecological irresponsibility. If it does, then in terms of Leopold's "ecological ethic," it would be "wrong." That wrong can be prevented by a deepening of the ecological sense and by a corresponding restraint and wisdom in the way we treat the earth we live on and the other members of the ecological community with which we live.

The ecological consciousness is not predominant, to put it mildly, in business, in the armed services, in government, in urban and suburban life, in the academy. It tends to receive some notice from humanist philosophers, artists, psychoanalysts, poets, conservationists, hippies, etc. I regret to say that it is something about which the Church apparently couldn't care less, at least today. But in the past people like St. Francis of Assisi have stood for it in a primitive sort of way.

Well, not to draw this out too long: it seems to me that the important thing is to avoid a shallow millenarianism as we enter the space age, and retain a solid ecological consciousness. Then we will be all right. I suggest creating and distributing a new button with the following message: "Put Flower Power into Space."

3. The Bay of Pigs Invasion

*We become real in proportion as we accept the real
possibilities that are presented to us and choose from
them freely and realistically for ourselves.*

TO L. DICKSON

*Merton became involved in the Bay of Pigs invasion of Cuba (April 1961) through
the spiritual direction he gave to Evora Arca de Sardinia, who had fled Cuba at
the time of the Castro revolution.*

To Evora Arca de Sardinia

*Born in Manzanillo in southeastern Cuba, Evora Arca de Sardinia, after her
preliminary education in Cuba, attended high school at the School of the Holy
Child in Suffern, New York, and Knox College in Cooperstown, New York. In
1950 she returned to Cuba, where she lived with her parents and where she met
her husband, Eugenio, with whom she had five sons. She was actively involved
in works of social justice and relief of the poor. She was instrumental in organizing
the Boy Scouts and ran a club for shoeshine boys who roamed the city barefoot
and in rags.*

*After the Cuban revolution which brought Fidel Castro to power in 1959,
she fled with her family to the United States, where she gave help to émigrés from
Cuba seeking refuge in the United States. Her husband was one of the leaders
of the 1,200 anti-Castro forces (trained by the American CIA) who invaded Cuba
on April 17, 1961, at the Bay of Pigs near Havana. The invasion proved a disaster
for the invading forces, most of whom were taken prisoner. Castro demanded
ransom for their return. In a state of sadness and desolation, Evora wrote to
Merton telling him that her husband had been captured. She speaks of her concern
for the refugees, her deep desire to do the will of God, and her uncertainty about
whether or not the ransom money ought to be paid to Castro. Merton's first letter
was written to Evora and her friend Marta Elena, whose fiancé, Manuel Artime,
was a leader of the invading forces.*

*Merton writes with a deep sense of compassion to this woman of deep and
simple faith. In a moving way he shows his concern for the pain and the darkness*

she was experiencing. His role is that of the spiritual director, giving strength, consolation, encouragement. Warning her against those who would turn to violence but also against those who would embrace a comfortable and wealthy Catholicism, he seeks to help her achieve personal inner freedom in the face of much hardship.

May 15, 1961

I write to you both as to friends, with deep compassion and concern in this moment of anguish. Your letter, Evora, came to me only today after a long delay. I have just read it. I would be failing in charity if I did not address you both a few words to assure you of my prayers and to tell you that my novices will be praying for Manuel Artime and for your husband. I remembered all your intentions at Mass this morning very particularly, before I had received your letter.

This is a bitterly sad and frustrating situation. I hope that the Holy Spirit, who gives strength to the martyrs, may bless and enlighten your two beloved ones and enable them to sustain the torments and even the death that may perhaps wait for them. Perhaps, indeed, they have already ended their sufferings. If so, they will have given themselves gloriously for the cause of freedom and for truth. But I shall pray that if possible their lives may be saved and that they may escape in order to work for a truly free and prosperous Cuba.

Have great courage and trust God. And pray that those who fight for freedom may learn the wisdom that is necessary to confront the enormous and cleverly integrated machine of Communist tyranny. The tragedy is that the democracies do not yet realize that goodwill and high ideals alone are no match for the sustained, worldwide, monolithic machine of Communism. The situation in Cuba is terribly complex, and though Castro is hated, we must remember the latent power of all the false hopes that have been roused by the intimate presence of Soviet power in the midst of the people. They really do dream of a new world: that is the poor, who should be the greatest concern of the Church. I am very much afraid that the curtain is rising on a long and tragic era for all of Latin America, due to the false hopes and illusions aroused in radicals by the Castro regime. Remember that these false hopes are fed by immense and profound resentments and by wishful thinking which cannot be silenced by the belated gestures of the United States. We have to face realities, because we are in real difficulty and God alone knows what may come of it all.

Hence we must purify our hearts and our faith, seeking the will of God not in a negative resignation only, but with every hope that He may show us some positive way of action that can counteract the forces that are inexorably advancing against the Church. No doubt His way will be to purify the Church by suffering and persecution . . .

I will not add more. We do not see the way that lies ahead of us. It seems dark, but God is the Master of all destinies and His will is love.

Let us then put aside everything else and trust ourselves completely to Him, giving ourselves to His love, and asking Him to enlighten us and guide us in the way of positive action if any such action is feasible. For the rest, we must have great patience and sustained fidelity to His will and to our ideals.

On July 26 Evora wrote of the depression in the Cuban community in Miami and her own sense of powerlessness. She feels as if forsaken by God, yet she has great trust in God.

September 9, 1961

I do not have time to give you a really full answer to your good letter, though I have waited in order to answer you adequately rather than just by a note. However, this much I can tell you. Naturally you will want to serve the cause of Cuba with all your strength, and yet there is no point in exhausting yourself in efforts that may be fruitless. It seems to me that in politics one has to take great care not to simply waste one's time and energy. Politics is the great realm of waste. What you can do to help individual persons is another matter. Especially refugees, or people trying to get out, and so on. But here too, be wise with the wisdom of the spirit, which is humble. Do not expect too many great things from yourself and realize that patient and humble work with few apparent results, but in the way of charity (not politics), can be very sanctifying and helpful to the Church and to your compatriots. Also it is important to devote yourself to social activities that help preserve the unity and the morale of your Cuban group. But the most important thing remains prayer and faith . . .

1961—Christmas Greetings

All blessings and joy at Christmas. May God give you strength, patience, light and love . . . The interests of Cuba should be the aim of all who love her. Each group and faction claims to be right. This will lead only to tragedy . . . God will bless your faith. If you see a chance to get your husband released it might be good, but do not be rash or irrational. All blessings to you and the children.

On January 27, 1962, Evora wrote of the divisions and the spirit of revenge that existed among the Cuban people who now lived in exile from their home.

[Cold War Letter 27]   January 31, 1962

This time I want to try to answer you immediately. I think you are quite right, and that the ideas that have come to you are true. You should accept them in peace and in humility and ask for the patience and perseverance to cooperate with the truth that has been shown to you. It is a long and weary business, and very difficult because it means being in conflict with good people who mean well but who are radically wrong in their view of things.

It seems to me that the darkness that has troubled you, and the same darkness which many good people and souls of prayer suffer these days, comes from one very serious source. Without wanting to be in conflict with the truth and with the will of God, we are actually going against God's will and His teaching. We are actually refusing Him what He asks of us as Christians, while at the same time proclaiming to heaven and earth that we are the best of Christians. We are, however, without knowing it, adhering to a Christianity that is scarcely Christian. It is infected with worldly values, and it is corrupted by love of wealth and power. In fact, the Christianity which we have subtly substituted for the will of God and for true Christian tradition is really the Christianity of the rich, the powerful, the selfish. It is a Christianity of individualism, of greed, of cruelty, of injustice, which hides behind specious maxims and encourages a kind of spiritual quietism. It is a Christianity of formulas, which are to be accepted blindly and repeated without understanding, a Christianity of passive conformity, in which under the name of obedience we are often brought into subjection to the most worldly influences and powers . . .

Many Catholics make the mistake of thinking that the problems of our time are very clear-cut, that there is no difficulty in seeing the truth, and that since the just cause is very evident, we need only to apply force in order to achieve justice. But precisely this illusion that everything is "clear" is what is blinding us all. It is a serious temptation, and it is a subtle form of pride and worldly love of power and revenge. Only if we are humble and contrite of heart and admit that there is much wrong in our so-called zeal will we merit from God the light to understand our problems . . .

The great error of the aggressive Catholics who want to preserve their power and social status at all costs is that they believe this can be done by force, and thus they prepare the way to lose everything they want to save. On the contrary, the force that preserves the Church is love and patience and suffering and courage to overcome cruelty and violence. So many Catholics think this is "defeatism." They dismiss it without even thinking about it. That is natural, they have never really been taught these things. It has been totally overlooked. This oversight is now having terrible consequences . . .

Read carefully the wonderful statements of the Popes, especially all the Christmas messages of Pius XII and John XXIII. Have you read *Mater et Magistra*? These have wonderful and inexhaustible teachings for our meditation, and above all they need to be put into practice . . .

February 27, 1962

If I answer you now it has to be a very quick answer. You cannot help suffering the way you do, and feeling restless. You have to gradually give up the hope of the kind of support you used to know in the past and depend on God alone in spiritual poverty and naked faith. It is hard and bitter, but it is necessary, for this is God's will for you. In the depths of your soul you will have peace but on the surface you will have restlessness and conflict. Continue peacefully to give to others as to Christ Himself, realizing that He will reward you in His own good time . . .

In the following letter Merton refers to Cobre in Cuba. Some twenty-two years earlier, at Easter time in 1940, he had visited Cuba and made a pilgrimage to the Church of Our Lady of Cobre. He prayed that her intercession might bring him to the priesthood and promised that, if he became a priest, his first Mass would be in her honor. This visit inspired one of his best poems, "Song for Our Lady of Cobre." See Collected Poems, *pp. 29–30.*

May 24, 1962

On Saturday, the 26th, I shall celebrate my 13th anniversary of ordination and shall offer Mass in honor of La Caridad del Cobre, to whom I think I owe the grace of the priesthood. I shall include in the Mass all the needs of Cuba as well as your own and the needs of all you love. This goes for Marta Elena and friends also.

I would not say exactly that it was completely wrong to pay ransom for the prisoners in Cuba, although in so doing one helps an unjust cause. The Christians, after all, ransomed captives of the Moslems in the Middle Ages. It is of course better not to help Castro. But I am afraid of the element of hate and fanaticism that is creeping into this whole question.

Unfortunately, I do not think that violence is going to solve any problems, but it will only create more problems. The world is at present in a very serious condition, and prospects are not good. It is because men are completely taken up with hate and fanaticism and violence and cannot see the truth. It does not matter how much they may think themselves justified: everybody is wrong, no matter how right he may appear to be. Everybody is wrong when he lives by hate and violence . . . Even with the best motives the use of force tends to bring about enormous evils and to multiply still more violence and blindness . . .

[Cold War Letter 93]   August 2, 1962

I deeply feel with you all the emotions that have shaken you, on meeting the prisoners returning from the Isle of Pines. I want to try to help you weather the storm, but God alone can really do that. God and the Church.

One thing I have always felt increases the trouble and the sorrow which rack you is the fact that living and working among the Cuban émigrés in Miami, and surrounded by the noise of hate and propaganda, you are naturally under a great stress and in a sense you are "forced" against your will to take an aggressive and belligerent attitude which your conscience, in its depth, tells you is wrong. You react rightly against the pressure of hate, and you strive to "be a better Christian" and take more and more sacrifice upon yourself. In this you are following the right instinct, but because of your position you are not able to follow it far enough, or in the right direction. I could wish you were able to get away from Miami for a while and restore your perspective, and calm down, and get some peace of heart that would enable the Holy Spirit to strengthen and teach you in silence.

The noise that surrounds you at Miami is necessarily misleading and in very great part it is false. The picture of the U.S. and Cuba that underlies all this pressure and hate is exaggerated and distorted. We have got to base our ideas and our action on a greater and more stable element of truth and justice. The evil that is taking place in Cuba is partly the fault of bad Cubans, but it is also partly the fault of the United States. When did the U.S. ever make any fuss about Batista? This aggravated situation is not at all simply due to Castro and Russia, though they have their part.

Whether you should raise money to ransom your husband, when he wants to stay on the Isle of Pines. Evora, it is a complex question.

1. He wants to stay with his fellow prisoners and suffer with them. This in a sense is a greater supernatural good for him. He will do more for Cuba there, *he is closer to the truth there*, than he could be in Miami. If you buy his way out, you may perhaps be diminishing his merit and his power to help Cuba spiritually.

2. On the other hand, his situation may also be spiritually dangerous, and it may constitute a temptation. If you think there is danger for him, spiritually, or if you believe that in some way it is a great evil for him to stay in prison, in every sense of the word, then you should ransom him.

3. The principle to follow is charity. Your clear-sighted charity must seek what is his real good, his highest good, such as he himself would want it, in his heart . . . If he is willing to stay, honestly, I would not raise such a tremendous sum to ransom him.

4. Remember that by paying a hundred thousand to Castro you are working against what your group believes to be the true political interests of Cuba. I am in no position to judge in this matter . . .

August 17, 1962

I am sorry I have been busy and have not been able to write. This is just a note to say that I think the decision expressed in your letter is reasonable and right. In any case, you can always change your mind if the situation changes. I would then say do *not* pay the ransom at least yet, as long as there is chance of them all getting out together. It would be better if they came together, without ransom.

The complications of your married life make the situation very difficult to you, but do not worry, you are objectively right in not giving the Communists a large sum of money to ransom your husband, when he is doing well where he is. If you hear that things are very bad, that he is in serious danger of death perhaps, you might reconsider.

September 19, 1962

As this tense situation gets worse and worse, we must all realize that no strain or effort of ours is going to change the essence of the problem. We cannot make anything better by our anguish or our worry. The dimension of faith is the only one that can be of any service here . . .

Frankly, I believe that most of your troubles come from the conflict of grace with your own nature and with the obscure awareness you have that all is not well with the political cause you have embraced, or with Christianity as a whole, as it is manifested in the comfortable and wealthy Catholicism of the U.S. The situation is full of ambiguities and contradictions, and right and wrong is inextricably mixed up on both sides. The evil of Communism grows in Cuba, but the evil of moral injustice is not absent on the American side. There is no question that there *is* some truth in the accusation of U.S. imperialism: in the sense that the big money is what determines all the decisions, and people like you have to pay with your happiness, with your health, and even with your lives. This is a bitter injustice, and you obscurely realize this: you cannot help doing so.

Do what you reasonably can in the political sphere, but you cannot do much. You are bound to see your best efforts frustrated and brought to nothing. Do not place undue hope in impossibilities. Do what you can, be detached from the results, do all for the love of God, trusting in Him to bring fruit from your efforts. It will be fruit you cannot see, probably.

As for your husband, you have made the right decision, but that does not mean it cannot be changed if there appears to be a good chance of saving him: but I think it would be foolish, especially now, to pay an enormous ransom to the enemies of your country.

[Cold War Letter 109]   October 29, 1962

This is a troubled time, in which you are going to have to collect your forces and muster up even more spiritual discipline. I know how you feel, but you have no right to get so discouraged. There is a sort of self indulgence in it, and you cannot afford that at the present time. None of us can . . .

Certainly it is hard to see your world broken up around you. No man can take that without suffering and self-questioning. But God has sent these trials to deepen your faith, not to destroy it. If you feel that it is hard to believe, this is because God is no longer presenting to you the image and idea of Him you once had. He is different from what you think He is and what you want Him to be. If he does not do things the way we want Him to, and we cease to believe in Him, then that means we only want to believe in a God made in our own image. That is why we have to have our faith purified and conform to His inscrutable will. So courage, and keep in the fight.

Like all of us, you have got your faith identified with a certain way of life. But we have to keep our faith even if our way of life is changed or destroyed . . .

January 1, 1963

. . . Your telegram was very welcome and it enabled me to share something of the experience of so many Cuban families. I hope it was a really happy Christmas for them all, and especially for you. I hope the men got back in good enough shape to enjoy the reunion with their families. I am sure it must have been a heartbreaking experience in many ways. So much suffering, such confusion, in many ways, such waste.

All this is characteristic of our time. We live in an age of revolutionary turmoil, and there is no getting away from the confusion and suffering that are involved. The ones to blame are not just Castro and Khrushchev and people like that. We must take a far wider view: this is just one part of a huge historical and social cataclysm and the root of it all is the technological revolution with its myriad consequences.

Nevertheless, one must still hope that peace and justice and order will be restored to every part of the world, and that Cuba will find its way again to freedom and to the development it so badly needs and desires. How tragic it is that everywhere men fall victims to the tyranny of absurd ideologies and empty slogans, which have such awful far-reaching consequences.

I can certainly wish you all the graces and joys of the season and I am sure God will pour down special blessings upon the family because of the sacrifices and sufferings so generously undergone by your husband. You owe him a great debt for all he has suffered for you and for Cuba, and your love will now be, in his life, a blessed force for healing and renewal. How wonderful it is that the Christian family should be a source of such deep and unending blessings . . .

February 22, 1963

. . . As to the political situation, if you expect any good to come out of it you will be disappointed. I recommend that you be detached from the political aims and hopes of the Cuban exiles, and do not place any hope in American action . . . You must not be too involved in the immediate political hopes and plans which will probably only add to the frustration you all feel. Be detached and go forward in faith, and use prayer as the great weapon for the liberation of your country . . .

April 17, 1963

It was good to hear from you, both before and after Easter, with the copy of the letter from your friend in Cuba who is now, thank God, in liberty. All your news is therefore not bad, by any means. Though you have trials and sorrows, I still think you have more to be thankful for than to lament about, though the state of Cuba is really tragic.

Where I think the real problem lies is in the peculiar situation of the Cuban émigrés. It is difficult for me to talk about this, since it is so terribly complex a problem and so many things are involved in it. But I think this is the source of most of your sufferings and confusions, and it strikes at the depth of your spiritual life. It cannot help being extremely painful, and no easy answer exists. You will suffer, you will be hurt, and you may on occasion do things that are wrong and that will block grace in your soul. This is because in a situation dominated by hate and passion, no matter how just the cause may be, it is almost impossible to keep a real Christian balance. It seems to me that inevitably the tensions and frustrations of such a situation end in obscuring the perspective. I wish you all had a long-range view that would cover the whole of Latin America: because this is a problem of all the "Americas" together, actually. And the tragedy is that it is broken up into fragments, and everyone sees the part that is most crucial to him.

July 25, 1963

I have not forgotten your letter of June 6th, but summer is a very busy season. I have had a great deal of mail and retreatants to take care of, with new postulants, and with some writing work of my own. Hence I have neglected you, though I remember you in prayer.

There is no question that God is sanctifying your heart by strong medicine . . . The Cuban question is so tormented and complex, there is so much suffering that could have been avoided, but it seems that the devil himself is trying to drive everybody to hate more and to commit greater acts of injustice. Behind it all is the basic confusion of the materialistic U.S., which does not really grasp and understand issues like that of Cuba. If there had been better understanding, all would have been simpler. Yet I personally do not reduce the whole thing to one "simple" answer: helping the exiles to get back and to destroy Castro. It is more complicated than that. I assure you that if the exiles took over Cuba tomorrow, then the whole thing would start over again, there would be other exiles planning bloody revenge, and the new ones in power would savagely execute their former persecutors. This is no solution to anything. Yet you are correct in sensing that the ambiguities and confusions of democracy are very dangerous and self-defeating. You simply cannot put your trust in American arms, but you cannot trust in any arms. You have to rise very far above this whole issue, you have to try to see it as Christ Himself sees it: and what one of us can say that this is easy? But Christ is not in politics: and yet the Church should have enough political sense and experience to guide the faithful morally in ways that will lead effectively to justice. This is very difficult in individual cases. Your words that we must pray to God and hope for the victory to be given us over and above everything else, are quite correct. And furthermore, we must seek only His victory. This is most important. When we insist that our victory is His victory just because it pleases us or is profitable to us, we are mistaken. Yet the sufferings of all those who have been killed and tortured for His love must not be in vain: but it is not our part to punish the ones who did these things. We must leave that to God.

September 5, 1964

I am sorry your letter has gone so long without an answer, especially when you feel so lost and abandoned. I would have liked to help you a little if I could. But really your life is not a *fracaso* [failure] at all: you feel that it is emotionally and this is a great suffering, but there is no failure for those who are loved and sought by Christ. He loves you, even though you may feel that you have lost your religious energy and that your faith does not have its old drive. To feel oneself a great and vital Christian is a luxury that we have to do without today when God is so hidden and so unknown in His world . . . Perhaps He wills to be hidden even in our lives. We must be content to be united with Jesus in His passion and in darkness, for it is thus that we cooperate with Him in helping others. There are many others whom you can love and help. Perhaps you feel that even in this you are poor and helpless. But do what you can and you will find that even a little means much. God loves you, so trust Him. I know that the sufferings of your broken marriage are very difficult, and God knows this too. Have courage, He will help you, though perhaps not in a way that you will easily see.

Christmas 1966

Peace and joy in the New Year. God bless you—fear not. Blessings.

4. The Peace Hostage Program

*Your plan is a very effective symbolic statement of what
the ordinary man feels about the absurdity and insanity
of the international situation.*

TO STEPHEN D. JAMES

Stephen D. James, concerned about the problem of how to prevent nuclear war, rented a post office box in Grand Central Station in New York City. He invited correspondence from anyone who had some idea for preserving peace. His own thought was the exchange, on a large scale, of peace hostages with the Soviet Union (for instance, President Kennedy's brother for Premier Khrushchev's children). He received a large volume of responses to his appeal, among which was Thomas Merton's.

November 30, 1962

Your letter was no surprise to me and I am already familiar with the Peace Hostage Foundation [see Cold War Letter 111]. I have already been asked, unofficially, about it and have gone on record more or less as being in complete sympathy with the idea. I want to repeat that statement now with a few embellishments.

First of all, however, let me say that my own position here is one that puts me in difficulties. As a member of the Order I have to be careful not to involve the Order itself in my statements, as I cannot claim to speak for it officially. Then also I have been asked to go easy in controversial statements, but I generally do not go "easy" enough. I don't think one can abstain at a time like this. Finally, and most difficult of all, it is not feasible or licit for me, as long as I am a member of the Order, to make an independent decision to move from the monastery even for a good cause. And it seems to me this is an admirable cause, and even one that involves a distinctly Christian and monastic witness. In my own private opinion a monk should be absolutely the first to do a thing like this, and we should have beaten you to the gun in even suggesting and organizing it. Alas, that is only my opinion, and it is not likely to be shared by everyone.

I do not like to come out then with an unqualified commitment to your plan when I obviously cannot commit myself to fulfill its primary obligation. What would really be the value of a rousing cheer on my part to encourage somebody else to go to Russia and sit "under the bomb"? All I can say is that I wish I might possibly be able to do what seems to me such an obviously good and reasonable thing. But if I even bring it up, my Superiors will think I am nuts. They have been conditioned to this impression long since, as I am always coming up with such "idealistic" notions, and by now their reflex is conditioned beyond the point of hope. However, I do hope you will keep in touch, and if there is any significant possibility of the plan going into effect, and if there is some strong argument in favor of my being part of it, I mean an argument that would register with people who shrink from the extraordinary, i.e. if someone like Robert Kennedy got in on it, so that it was manifestly so respectable as to be almost square . . . You see what I mean. I might be able to put up an argument that would be listened to.

But setting that aside, I would, if it were up to me, want to be the very first to go to Russia. Not being married, I would want to offer myself for one of the most dangerous and unpleasant "posts" there, for instance to work in some population center near one of the missile bases in Siberia. How easy it is to say all this when you won't get sent. But at least that would be what I would want, or hope I would want.

Apart from that, I can say in general that I think your plan is a very effective symbolic statement of what the ordinary man feels about the absurdity and insanity of the international situation. We have got to be able to make our thought register, and writing to congressmen is not going to be enough. Nor will the papers make themselves our mouthpiece if we have only words to offer. There have to be deeds that make sense more than words can. This plan is of course not the universal, complete solution, but it is a step in the right direction and any such step is of inestimable value.

So far as I am concerned, within these limitations, you have my wholehearted support, and I am sorry it is not more than moral support . . .

February 12, 1963

Forgive me for not answering your two letters sooner. I feel guilty in alleging that I am "too busy" when I know how busy you are. But, also, at the same time it is not clear what help I can give.

Certainly you can quote me anytime as being wholeheartedly in favor of your plan, which seems to me to be a bold and original effort to meet the inhuman situation with some kind of human response: with a gesture that focuses attention on the fact that what is at stake is *man* and not just a lot of pompous abstractions. In this I am completely with you, and I would do anything I could to join you. But, unfortunately, my position here is such that this is not permitted. Hence I hesitate to make loud statements when the only statement that is required is some form of action.

5. The Second Vatican Council: Schema XIII

What matters is for the Bishops and the Council to bear witness clearly and without any confusion to the Church's belief in the power of love to save and transform not only individuals but society.

MERTON'S OPEN LETTER TO THE
AMERICAN HIERARCHY

This letter was published in the September 1965 issue of Worldview, *as the Bishops were preparing to return to Rome for the final session of the Council.*

You are about to return to Rome for the most decisive session of the Second Vatican Council. Schema XIII—"On the Church in the Modern World"—is, from a pastoral viewpoint, of such unique importance that one may believe the whole work of the Council stands or falls with it. You who have listened with patience to so many opinions will surely bear charitably with this expression of deep concern, written not in order to defend a merely partisan view, but to insure that the great work done by the previous sessions is not damaged by a failure to meet one of the most crucial problems of our time.

The task of the Council remains that of proclaiming the Gospel of love and hope to modern man in a language that he will understand, without any alteration or distortion of the essential Gospel perspectives. The message of love and of salvation is not bound to any particular time or culture, and its true perspectives look above history and beyond it. Hence, in order to convince the world that Christianity is not necessarily identified only with a medieval or baroque Christendom, we do not need to assert that it is fully identified with technological society in its present confusion. The Christian is called, as always, to a decision for Christ, not to a decision for this or that kind of society. He is called to obey the Gospel of love, for all men, and not simply to devote himself to the interests of a nation, a party, a class, or a culture. The message of the Church to the modern world therefore remains, as it has always been, an eschatological message.

Not only should we resist the temptation to ignore or evade this aspect of the Council's task, but we should frankly admit its special relevance in a time when man has in his hands incalculable power for destruction and can, indeed, if he so chooses, even destroy himself along with his civilization. While admitting that there is no sense in getting hysterical about this danger, and while retaining a hope that man will never go so far as to madly abuse his awful power, we must nevertheless soberly take into account the fact that he *has* this power. He has it permanently, and remains perfectly capable of abusing it. We are aware, too, that in spite of a universal desire for peace and in spite of the Church's reiterated and anguished appeals for peace, governments continue to devote by far the greater portion of their budgets to armaments and preparations for war, and indeed continue to show a marked preference for settling international disputes by violence, or the threat of violence, rather than by more peaceful and reasonable means. In a word, if we consider this as an expression of a basic moral attitude, we are compelled to admit that with all its humane possibilities, the modern world remains committed to force and indeed can be said to "believe in" the primacy of power and of violence. The modern world is one which still believes in war, from guerrilla warfare to total and even nuclear war, while cold war and deterrence by terroristic threat of violence seemingly remain with us as permanent features of our civilization.

Whereas a few years ago it was common for our statesmen to protest that they never expected nuclear weapons would actually be used, or perhaps they proposed the use of tactical nuclear weapons only, more recently we find strategists and publicists, speaking with a certain note of authority, advocating the calculated use of nuclear weapons even on a large scale (v.g., "city-trading") as part of a rationale (if not a mystique!) of escalation. Such proposals may exercise a nefarious fascination on those theologians who are willing to equate "controlled use" of nuclear weapons with an uncontrolled use that is in fact brutally and cynically *calculated*, and which includes in its calculations the deliberate and terroristic destruction of defenseless and innocent non-combatants *precisely because they are defenseless and non-combatant*. This is what "city-trading" would involve.

In the article on modern warfare, which you will, we hope, be discussing, you will understandably not wish to deny to nations a right which the Church has traditionally admitted—namely, to defend themselves by just means against an unjust attack. On the other hand, remember that you, the American Hierarchy, will be sitting in the Council as citizens of a nation which is waging an undeclared war and which may, at that time, be even more fully engaged in warfare than it is now. It is not beyond the bounds of possibility that you might be identified, in the Council, as members of a nation which would willingly carry its escalation of warfare to the point of once again involving the entire world in a global conflict. Let us hope that this will not happen, but it can possibly happen, and the world even now looks at our government with great trepidation, fearing that we may already have gone so far along the road to global war that it may not be possible to turn back.

It does not require much imagination to see that if, in these circumstances, the Council elects to give official approval to certain modern weapons and, by implication, to total war, the effect will be a scandal of such proportions that it will neutralize the great pastoral good that has been so far accomplished.

Certainly the theoretical issue of the morality of this or that modern weapon is something that admits of technical debate. But even assuming that the Council could exactly define the limits within which such weapons might properly be used, we would have to recognize that in practice there are few, if any, governments on this earth today that would ever confine themselves to moral limits defined by the Church. But on the other hand every militarist and political opportunist would gladly and noisily avail himself of the Church's declaration, in order to justify his own unprincipled use of force. Meanwhile the average man, unused to fine theological distinctions, would interpret the declaration simply as an unqualified approval of war in all its forms, and without limitation.

The common man, the poor man, the man who has no hope but in God, everywhere looks to the Church as a last hope of protection against the unprincipled machinations of militarists and power politicians. Would it not be a dreadful thing if the Council were to say something, even by implication, to destroy the hope of the defenseless and thrust them further into despair?

It seems that in the discussion of this issue there is a serious danger of losing the Christian perspective which should be ours. If the question of modern war resolves itself into a split between two radical positions, which we might call "militarist" and "pacifist," this loss of perspective will inevitably occur.

A "pacifist" position would be one which, at least by implication, would condemn all use of force in principle as evil, by stating that since even moderate use of force is liable to lead directly to unrestrained and terroristic use of force in total war, which the Church has repeatedly deplored, then all use of force should be condemned. While some of us may find considerable merit in this position, it is perhaps questionable that the Bishops would ever adopt it in the present circumstances. And when our own country is thought, by so many, to be "attacked" (by reason of the fact that our political ideal is threatened in Vietnam and elsewhere), one would not expect the American Bishops to be enthusiastic about it. One might simply remark that this is a good instance of the way in which no nation ever goes to war without having what appear to be solid reasons for thinking that it is resisting an unjust aggression. When Hitler went to Poland in 1939, he was allegedly "defending" the German nation. A little hindsight would enable one to call the Japanese attack on Pearl Harbor, analogously, a "preemptive first strike" on the Pacific Fleet, which would, according to some of our own nuclear moralists, be perfectly licit.

Rather than expecting a formal, technical assessment of the precise morality of this or that weapon, the world rightly looks to the Council for the strongest and most unequivocal appeal for the renunciation of force in favor of reasoned negotiation and other peaceful means of settlement. Above all, the Church cannot evade her duty to speak out in defense of the innocent and uninvolved non-combatants who, in ever greater numbers, necessarily become the victims of massive and terroristic use of force in the modern war. The indiscriminate slaughter of *all*, combatant or non-combatant, must be condemned.

Obviously any position which would in practice result in blessing the use of force and explicitly *extending* the Church's approval to new weapons of far greater destructive power which our Popes have already repeatedly deplored, would seem to deserve the name of "militarist." It would certainly neutralize any appeal for peace to the point of making it seem little more than a trifling form of words, repeated out of routine and without conviction. Much more could perhaps be said about this position, but in the interests of brevity one need not go into arguments which are by now familiar. It is surely reasonable to applaud the prudence of those who, at the time of the Third Session, thought that the Council ought to say *more* against the use of force than modern Popes have said, and *not less*.

But one may ask if the real issue can be reduced to a choice between these two positions, which we called "militarist" and "pacifist."

Let us return to our principle: the task of the Council is to affirm the Church's eschatological message of love and salvation in terms which are most relevant to the modern world. In this instance, then, the problem is that of stating *the Church's view of modern war in the light of the eschatological message of salvation.*

The New Testament writers never make fine distinctions between one or other of the policies used by worldly powers. Admittedly, it later became necessary for theologians to do so. But perhaps we should consider that one of the more important aspects of renewal in theology consists in a restoration of more authentic and essential perspectives. Whatever one may think about the morality of modern war, it is hardly likely that the world will interpret an official blessing of nuclear weapons, however tactical, as an affirmation of Christian love. The preaching of Our Lord opened with these words: "The time is accomplished and the Kingdom of Heaven is at hand: repent and believe the Gospel" (Mark 1:15). This summary of the whole message of salvation includes, in the one word "repent," the summons to total obedience to God which is in turn summed up in the New Commandment of Love. Whatever the Council says on war must be said in such terms that the primacy of love is stated with a clarity that cannot be doubted or misconstrued. Any attempt to introduce fine moral distinctions that would savor of evasion and pharisaism must be regarded, in this context above all, as a most serious temptation and a grave danger for the Church in the modern world. Any impression of equivocation in this matter which is a source of anguish and horror to so many men would tend to give irreparable scandal.

But ambiguity cannot be absent from any statement on modern war that is dictated by an implicit practical belief in power. It is of course quite natural that Bishops should share in the public opinion of the society to which they belong. But the Church is in the world as a Body that is not able to agree with all that the world believes. The Church is implacably opposed to principles of thought which imply an enslavement to the powers in the world that are completely hostile to Christ and to His love. One of those principles is the practical belief in the efficacy of power and force to accomplish ends which love and faith "cannot achieve." Characteristic of that "realism," which St. Paul called the wisdom of the flesh and of the world, is its conviction that the love which Christ preached is illusory and inefficacious in the conduct of everyday affairs, at least in public life.

We are not unfamiliar with a Christianity which in effect compromises with this ruthless spirit. The compromise is quite simple, and consists in this: as to our interior motives, yes, we admit the primacy of love. But in the conduct of political life we agree with the world: what counts is naked *power!* Hence, one concludes upon a use of force that is guided by motives of "love." The exigencies of a modern power struggle do, of course, demand one's entire attention, and hence, having started with an initially pure intention of "love," one gets lost in the brutal realities of an escalating conflict. A love which was at best abstract to begin with soon vanishes altogether. When the dust and smoke clear, one devoutly hopes one will be able to return to himself and make an act of contrition for any excess that may have occurred . . . Or one hopes that there will still be someone left to be sorry!

It hardly seems sufficient for the Council, speaking as the Church in the modern world, to make a practical option in favor of power over love, and then hastily add that even though power is in effect more efficacious, one must try to prefer love at least *in abstracto.*

What matters is for the Bishops and the Council to bear witness clearly and without any confusion to the Church's belief in the power of love to save and transform not only individuals but society. Do we or do we not believe that love has this power? If we believe it, what point is there in splitting hairs about the superior morality of killing a thousand defenseless non-combatants rather than a million?

In the November issue of Worldview, *Thomas Molnar, in a letter to the editor, wrote a caustic criticism of Merton's "open letter." He declared that, while seeming to advocate a non-political position based on Christian love, Merton is in fact inviting the Bishops to choose a particular political position, "in this instance" (as he puts it) "to repudiate Washington in favor of Hanoi." The editors of* Worldview *invited Merton to reply.*

November 1965

Mr. Molnar, having summarily reduced me to the lay state as a punishment for pride [he addressed the monk as "Mr. Merton"], proceeds to a massive distortion of my open letter on Schema XIII, and ends by calling me a Communist. Actually, what I was trying to say was nothing more—and nothing less—than Pope Paul VI said at the U.N. I have no doubt that Mr. Molnar also considers Pope Paul a Communist, since he implies that Pope John was one. I must confess that I feel some movements of pride at finding myself condemned in the company of two great Popes.

To begin with, there was nothing whatever in my open letter that could be interpreted as being in favor of Communism, regarding the Vietcong as freedom fighters, and so on. This is all gratuitously assumed by Mr. Molnar, who is addicted to the usual stereotyped right-wing line of thought: "Anyone who does not see things exactly as I do must be a Red." Therefore I take this opportunity to declare that I have no desire whatever to find myself living under the rigid and coercive rule of any totalitarian dictatorship, whether of the right or of the left. In my opinion they boil down to pretty much the same thing, and those who insist that we must choose between one or the other are in fact much closer to their mirror images on the opposite side than they are to the rest of us who look for other solutions.

If Mr. Molnar had not been so swept away by accusations of treason, he could have cogently stated a difficulty which I see as well as he does. It is this: If the Church utters a sweeping condemnation of modern weapons, this will bind the consciences of Catholic statesmen and soldiers, but Communists will ignore the condemnation. In fact they may even take advantage of it in order to use those same weapons against more scrupulous opponents. This, in Mr. Molnar's view, is tantamount to making a political decision in favor of Communism. Hence he argues that the Church should not commit herself to any moral decision that would have unfortunate political consequences for the West. Rather she should make moral decisions which can be used in favor of "our side." This amounts, in effect, to a subordination of faith to *raison d'état*. That is why, though I see the objection, I do not come to the same conclusions. I believe, on the contrary, that the Church must put faith before politics. She has the obligation clearly to define revealed truth in matters of morality, even of public morality in international affairs. She has the obligation to do this in a prudent and reasonable way (which incidentally I think the Council is doing) and Catholics are obligated to form their consciences accordingly, trusting in God to prevent any untoward consequences which they may fear in the immediate future. By this obedience and trust they will save their souls and serve the cause of God, which is not always clearly manifest to us in all its details. The Old Testament and the New are full of warnings that those who trust in human weapons and alliances, rather than in God, will be destroyed in punishment for their unbelief. I do not utter this as a veiled threat against the Pentagon, but only as a plain statement of fact.

As a Christian, a monk, and a priest, it is my obligation to state such truths, and to do so forcefully when necessary.

It is my opinion (and here I do not speak of matters of faith) that a rigid, aggressive, and opportunistic use of force will in the present circumstances be not only futile, but harmful to the cause of the West. There are certainly arguments that can be advanced in favor of taking a strong stand in Vietnam, but as far as I can see it is doing no good whatever, and will only help the cause of Communism in Asia. I am certainly not one of those who believe that "Communism will win." On the contrary, I do not think either Communism or capitalism will win. I think that even if they do not knock each other out they will evolve, along with the rest of the world, perhaps very painfully and violently indeed, into something neither I nor Mr. Molnar have yet imagined. Whether it will be "good" or "bad" I have no idea. That is a matter for prayer.

6. On War and Peace

The way to silence error is by truth, not by violence.
MERTON TO JAMES MORRISSEY

To the Editor of Liberation

December 30, 1961

The San Francisco-to-Moscow Peace Walk was probably the most significant single measure of moral protest that has been made against war for several years. Its significance is perhaps evident in the seemingly strange disproportion between the effort that went into it and the results achieved. It hardly stirred a ripple in the mass media either of the United States or of Russia. As Karl Meyer remarks in his very pointed and moving statement, printed in your issue of last November, they did not "touch" the Soviet Union, though they "flicked in and out." They did not "touch" the Soviet Union because they did not even "touch" America. They touched nothing. Yet they walked for nearly a year.

The moral degeneration of mass society calls for these seemingly useless actions that "touch nothing" and make no impression on the mass media. Actions which, on the contrary, through innumerable direct human contacts, brief exchanges of ideas or of looks, attempt to share some kind of human understanding. Whereas the mass media seem able to corrupt the best things they "touch," this kind of primitive and almost helpless contact by fraternal "presence," by "passing through," can do nothing whatever but good. The good will not be apparent and that is perhaps the best and most necessary thing about it.

So we are reminded of the necessity for complete "purity" in our non-violent action: complete detachment from results. We must act only because the act itself is true, and expresses the truth. We must not even demand that the truth be immediately recognized. Still less must we expect to be congratulated. On the contrary, it may well mean a cracked skull. This purity of action is the fundamental guarantee of its truth. It is the only thing that gives the non-violent demonstrator power against the mass media with all their money and all their influence.

As for results: the truth needs only to be manifested. It can take care of itself.

To Herbert Burke

Professor Burke was at this time a member of the English faculty of St. John's University at Collegeville, Minnesota.

December 11, 1962

I got a letter from Jim Douglass this morning. It was a good one, too. I think I will send "Peace in the PCE" [Post-Christian Era] to Bishop [John J.] Wright. I think, too, that the new Lapp book, *Kill and Overkill*, is a very important one to clarify the issues, and to bring home the fact that this is not a war with bows and arrows, or even with blockbusters anymore, but that the whole concept of war has been stood on its own head, which it has always wanted to do anyway. And that if we persist in thinking it is a matter of easy syllogisms based on familiar premises, we will end up in the worst tragedy and justify the worst crimes. I am more and more convinced that the issue is one that involves a necessary cataclysm, overturning some of the most familiar axioms of our thought. If we cannot give up these apparent first principles (which are rooted in Constantine and Augustine), we are lost. Of course others have given them up long ago, and are operating without any principles at all. It sounds like Zen. I wish it were, because Zen is sane. But not the Pentagon.

You are probably better off at St. John's than you would be in some other Catholic colleges: as far as I know the Fathers there are broadminded and understanding. I think in English one can actually say a great deal and more effectively than in some other courses. We have forgotten, perhaps, that our "arts" course is really a pre-philosophy course and rightly concerned with matters that can be better said poetically than philosophically: and that until one has passed through this first stage of wisdom, philosophy will never be a wisdom at all. You have, therefore, a right and a mission to say the things you want to say. And as for the question of courage, there again I think we have probably more than we think. Or we can have. For it is not a matter of doing spectacular things but a matter of very clear-sighted ordinariness and sense. People are so awfully confused that one can actually say a great deal without frightening them if one says it in a way that does not interfere with some of their more absurd patterns (which, of course, may have to be shaken out of line sooner or later, but which may not concern the real issue at all). It is still largely a matter of reminding average people that they still do want freedom and truth, and that they have not yet given up completely, though they want to.

To John and Barbara Beecher

January 9, 1963

As you gather, I have more or less been told to stop writing about nuclear war. But with *Breakthrough to Peace* (which I am sure J. [Laughlin] must have sent you) I think I managed to get a considerable amount said before the expected ban. As a matter of fact, the introduction to that volume, which summarizes my attitude in a general way, got printed all over the *Los Angeles Times*, so I didn't get so hermetically sealed after all, did I? In this matter of war and every other form of injustice, we must, of course, keep articulate and vocal in whatever way we can. I am a firm believer in the power of the offbeat essay, printed or mimeographed in a strange place and handled by interested people. The material that goes from hand to hand is much read, at least by the people who are responsible enough to appreciate information and unconventional opinion.

One thing that one can always protest about is the treatment of the Indian. I think of the recent violation of the very old treaty with the Senecas, who have been driven off their "inviolable" land, now ready to be flooded by a big dam. So it goes on. If we have no concern for rights and freedoms in the concrete, how can we expect the world to respond to the perfunctory mouthing of ideals?

To Madame Camille Drevet

Madame Camille Drevet, who lived in Paris, was a member of the group, founded by Louis Massignon, known as Les Amis de Gandhi (Friends of Gandhi).

January 17, 1963

Do you know the Goss-Mayrs in Vienna? They are interested in this book and are trying to get permission to publish parts of it in German in their magazine *Der Christ in der Welt*. They are also actively using material of mine in Rome, trying to interest theologians in it, and they are also using work of Father Régamey.

I am very interested now in pushing forward the study of the more positive aspects of the question of peace—i.e., the theological bases of non-violence and of a social action based on redemptive love. Father Régamey's writing strikes me as the best thing so far in this line. Please let me know of anything new either by him or by P. Chaigne.

The introduction to *Breakthrough to Peace*, in which you are interested, has had some rather good fortune in this country. It was printed in its entirety in a prominent place in one of the largest newspapers in the country, the *Los Angeles Times*. Los Angeles is in the center of the area most consecrated to the production of nuclear weapons and missiles.

The reception of the article was quite good, although the people in California are extremely reactionary.

Basically the conditions continue to be very serious everywhere, because the real trouble is never touched. The real disease is spiritual, a sickness of thought and of the will. It is very deep-seated, and little or nothing is being done by the Catholics in this country to get to the real root of the trouble. Unfortunately, the U.S. and Russia continue to be in a position where bad thinking or perversion of the will can have disastrous consequences for the entire world. There are still serious evidences of possibility of an American fascism growing up.

It is of the greatest importance that we pray and take every spiritual means to dispose our hearts for union with the will of God and for action based on truth and love. We will certainly meet no end of obstacles and failures. It is useless to think too much of results. We have only strength and integrity enough to concentrate on the truth and sincerity of our action itself. This is the essential. God Himself must do all the rest, and indeed without His continued assistance, without unusual graces, we cannot even maintain the strength necessary for our ordinary task. Today even the ordinary is apt to demand heroism.

December 27, 1964

I must thank you for your new book, *Par les routes humaines*, which reached me some time ago. I have not yet finished reading it, but it is really a most absorbing and fascinating book, full of all kinds of good things. You have had a rich and fruitful experience and have indeed traveled the ways of men and found Christ in them. I compliment you on the book, which is very fine and I am delighted to have it. I will continue to enjoy it and profit by it at leisure.

Thanks, also, for the bulletins of the A. de G. [Amis de Gandhi]. I was especially impressed in the October issue by the wonderful hymns from India, which I am discussing with the novices here. They are most moving. Incidentally, I was happy that Pope Paul made such an open and clear plea for world peace at Bombay. I hope he will be heard. The Hibakusha, from Hiroshima, were here on their pilgrimage last summer: or rather a half dozen of them were, and I had a very good afternoon with them. I am still in contact with one of them, a poet and calligrapher. The way of human friendship and personal contact is the one basic way of peace.

My selections from Gandhi are not yet printed in this country, but I hope the book will be out early next summer. Perhaps it may appear in France before it does here. We are also working on an edition for Brazil, and this will be very important. A non-violent movement (led to a great extent by the Goss-Mayrs) is being started in Brazil and it may have crucial importance in the future of the country which can hardly be anything else than revolutionary. Indeed, the whole future of South America seems to invite revolution, and this is not properly understood in the

United States, because too many people here are in fact involved with the forces that are keeping South America in tutelage. Yet I think the future of Latin America is great.

It is a pity that the discussions in the Council on nuclear warfare were so inconclusive. Archbishop Roberts had a fine intervention on conscientious objection, which, however, he presented only in writing.

July 1, 1965

This is a time of very serious decision for all of us in this country, and I for one am beginning to see many things I had not taken into account before. One has to reevaluate the whole concept of political witness here at this time. Merely to make a moral judgment, to decide for justice, and non-violence, and to make the decision known in some way, this is good, but it is also a kind of moral luxury, and at times it seems to be perfectly meaningless. There is certainly the question of sustained nonviolent action, which has been very meaningful in the civil rights field, because here everyone pays attention and the issue is clear. Strangely enough, in the area of peace, non-violence is regarded quite differently in this country. It is treated differently by the press in the first place. Then there is the conviction that anyone who opposes the war in Vietnam, or war as such, is simply a traitor. There is a great deal of dangerously naive and irrational thinking, or rather not thinking but just prejudice and emotion. I think the most dangerous thing in the world is the stupidity and moral blindness of the American leaders today. They are blindly and absurdly convinced of their moral rightness, and they think that anything they do is in some way perfectly justified merely because they feel that they have good intentions. They will maintain against the whole world, and against all intelligent and objective criticism, that they alone understand what they are doing. The basis of this super-stition is twofold: first the inane confidence that a superior technology and more elaborate cybernetics are a sign of moral infallibility and superior wisdom. And second there is the ancient American myth of rejuvenation, justification, and a totally new start. By definition this is the land not only of "liberty" but also of primeval innocence and indeed complete impec-cability. The evidence, unfortunately, is all to the contrary, and one cannot evade the guilt which the evidence produces. Nevertheless, the greater the guilt, the more frenzied and complacent are the arguments that the U.S. cannot possibly be culpable in anything and that in the long run all is to be blamed on the enemy . . .

To what extent is political action really meaningful here? I do not know. One must certainly try to act and make some sense out of the situation. On the other hand there are implications that are too deep for comfort. As a monk I am especially limited. It is true that I can make certain judgments and express certain opinions. I have lately concentrated on the question of the Church and the Council. The tragedy in this country is that the majority of Bishops *believe in the bomb.* I do not mean that they are willing to have the bomb proclaimed a just weapon of defense by the Council, which they are: but this is rooted in a basic assumption that force is really effective and reasonable and is in fact the only truly effective way of resolving international conflicts. This assumption is *unquestioned* by them. Such being the case, they naturally look at the use of total violence in a prejudiced and basically unchristian light. I have been trying to get some of them to question this basic assumption. Naturally one does not get very far. Polite letters acknowledge one's remarks, and it is said that attention will be given to them. I did get a good letter from the Papal Secretariat of State saying Pope Paul was glad of a letter I had written to him, and I know he is taking things very seriously. His trip to this country might conceivably be a great turning point. That is my prayer.

I must stop now, but I am glad to have your good news, especially about the books . . . I am delighted with the little book on Abbé Manchanin.

To Larry Murphy

November 21, 1963

Thanks for your long letter of October 22. Thanks, too, for the *Monthly Review* and for writing to *Minority of One* on my behalf. I haven't heard anything from them. It does not make much difference, I mean, whether or not they publish it, but I appreciate your kindness.

[W. H.] Ferry [at the Santa Barbara Center for the Study of Democratic Institutions] keeps sending me very good things, as I suppose he does also to you, and he is a remarkable, very alive and wise person. He does not have much hope for a really secure peace or reasonable settlement of the problems of our time, and I must say I see very little reason to disagree with him. Looking soberly at the facts, it seems to me that an optimism that is not based on an almost irrational hope of miracle cannot be accepted: and as for an almost irrational hope of miracle, I do not include that in my present equipment for interpreting reality. I, of course, accept miracles as a rational possibility, but my idea of God is not such that I imagine He would be working miracles to make all the causes fail to achieve their effects. And the amount of causality that is now in action . . . Almost everything is being done to produce war, and almost nothing to avoid it: except, of course, a little talk here and there, and the ridiculous sophism of deterrence.

I do not blame you for moving to NZ, though I do not think it solves any problems, it only puts them off for a few years. But even that is quite worthwhile, for you never know what a few years can mean. I have very often seriously thought of being in a country that would not have and could not have the bomb. At times it almost looks like a moral obligation. Unfortunately, for me the complications are beyond measure and I think the best thing is simply to sit here "under the bomb," with Fort Knox thirty miles away as the crow flies and Oak Ridge, Tenn., not a great deal further (perhaps two hundred miles).

As to the point you raise on humanism: there is, as far as I know, no set, airtight compartment into which one can place humanism by itself. There are different kinds of humanism, whether religious or agnostic (the positivist nineteenth-century type) or atheistic. Atheistic humanism, a very definite entity, is also totalistic and collective because it envisages the fulfillment of man's possibilities only on a collective scale: "man has to make himself" by getting into line with the forces that drive society wherever it may be going and turning them in a direction that will be friendly to man. The Cold War is a struggle between two kinds of humanism which I regard as more or less gross and ineffective: the liberal kind and the totalist kind. Neither is, to me, an effective and realistic humanism at all. I hasten to add that conventional religiosity is not offering anything much better. Your statements about the existence of God I heartily agree with, because the God you depict in them would be a monstrosity and a contradiction. However, I also admit this is the God that a lot of people believe in, and his status may well be for all practical purposes official in a lot of quarters. Perhaps the crisis of our time is among other things a symptom of our total lack of a genuine, valid humanism—as well as of a really living religious sense. I personally see no way at all for a genuine and valid ethical sense to exist without a religious basis (at least one that is implied or hidden). I find this, actually, in most of my friends who claim to be atheistic and who also have a genuine ethical concern. That is why I don't waste time quarreling with such people about the ordinary notions of religion. It is a perfect waste of time.

I was happy that Linus Pauling got the Nobel [Peace] Prize, it is another of the small signs which seem hopeful but are perhaps not really so. But still, for his sake, I am glad. But as you say, quite rightly, nothing more than lip service is being paid to peace. The arms race continues and will certainly continue, because of the complete and total incapacity of society at large to face the risk of a peace that would in fact be ruinous to the rich and to the powerful on both sides. Peace cannot be afforded and therefore no one really wants it. Man's greed will lead us, I am afraid, into a frightful mess. I can only offer the diminished optimism that the underprivileged (i.e., those who do not have the privilege of an economy and a power that can make bombs) will take over the remains of our society and construct something a little more rational.

August 28, 1966

I have your interesting letter and notes on war and on your hope for humanizing modern methods of war. It is certainly true that if violent conflict is unavoidable it should, nevertheless, be conducted with as much restraint as possible. This is nothing but the old classical doctrine of the

Just War, and maybe there have been instances in history when it applied. Perhaps there might be some hope of someone taking an interest in this theoretically.

However, it seems to me that you are dealing with the symptom and not the disease. The real source of the trouble is in man's mind, both individual and collective. The roots of war are to be sought in error, perversity, pathology. As long as these remain the chief causes of war (along, of course, with the economic and sociological factors that aggravate them) then the conduct of war will be as irrational and as brutal as the war itself. The problem is enormous: it means nothing less than an entire revolutionizing of man's thought, *everywhere*. We have at our disposal media of communication that might help us to do this, but the chances of our using them in this way are problematical. Again, because we program our error and pathology into the media themselves. It is a demonic, vicious circle, my friend. We are in grave trouble, and without the help of God we can do nothing. Fortunately He is not dead as some claim. So let us hope.

To Dr. Albert Belden

November 29, 1963

Thank you for your very kind letter of October 19th. I am sorry to have delayed in answering, but I have been ill and have had some difficulty getting my correspondence up to date.

I want to say that I am in perfect agreement with your Pax Christi Plan and of course you can count on my signature and my cooperation. I certainly believe that it is the duty of all Christians to do whatever they possibly can to work toward the abolition of war, which is no longer to be regarded as a reasonable and efficacious way of settling international disputes. I set aside the controversial point whether it ever has been fully reasonable in fact: this is made irrelevant by the presence of nuclear, bacteriological, and chemical weaponry. War today is certainly unreasonable and unchristian, especially total war. Consequently, I repeat, I believe it is the duty of every Christian to work actively for the abolition of war. Obviously there can be a wide area of discussion about the most effective means for doing this. About the end in view there can be no really serious discussion, it seems to me.

With special reference to one point in your pamphlet; the question whether the Catholic always and without distinction acts in obedience to ecclesiastical authorities: in this matter of war, where the Popes have called into question the morality of *laymen* to discern the practical morality of certain political measures (about which the clergy may not be fully informed), I think one might hesitate a little to say that the hierarchy would take upon itself rightly to say the last word in deciding whether a war was or was not immoral in a given case. I don't know about that.

There would obviously be much room for argument on this point, but in any case if the individual felt he had sufficient information for believing that a war *in fact* was going to be total and therefore immoral, he would be bound to abstain from participation, even though theoretically it might still be established that he had a duty to defend his country. There would in reality be no conflict here, because he would within the terms of this case have reason to believe that the defense would be utterly inefficacious and that therefore the idea of a "just war" would not apply. I repeat, many of my fellow Catholics might disagree on this point, which has yet to be satisfactorily discussed and decided upon.

I do know Archbishop Roberts and he is a friend of mine. I know you can count on him fully. I also know Norman Cousins and he too is a friend of mine.

However, I must say that because of my peculiar situation in a monastery I do not have the same contacts and liberties for action that others have, and I would not be able to give you the same kind of active help that a secular priest might. Also, there are at times certain limitations put on my writing and I am at the moment not able to say as much as I would like to say on this subject in print.

The great thing is indeed an international agreement on a code of law and on measures for the control of armaments and their reduction, and for the liquidating of problems and tensions by effective negotiation.

You can certainly count on my support and I certainly will naturally be praying for the success of this enterprise. It is most important that all Christians, of whatever denomination, cooperate in this urgently necessary effort for peace.

May 9, 1964

Perhaps the most influential and important Catholic theologian who is interested in this, and very much interested, is Father Bernard Häring, C.SS.R., whom you can reach at Via Merulana 31, Rome. He can do more for you than anyone, perhaps, though he is more in the field of theological definition than of practical organization . . .

As I may or may not have mentioned, I am not in a position to be writing articles specifically about war. I have to be content to get in my digs obliquely, in reference to other topics, and also I am rather hampered as far as supporting causes is concerned, because it often takes a lot of time for anything of mine to be cleared and printed. I just am not living at the tempo required for active and effective help in practical affairs, and I am too out of touch with what goes on.

Nor am I particularly in touch with Rome. I suppose they have heard of me there and my existence is not unknown to the Pope, but that is about all. In the past I have found that when I tried to get something done by writing to Rome about it the effect was usually not what I wanted and it ended by being more of a nuisance than a help. I can be of more value to you if I keep my fingers out of that huge machinery.

Humanly speaking I have come to be a bit discouraged by the institutional aspects of all this. The machinery does not and will not move. Occasionally a statement emerges. That is all. However, perhaps one of the most hopeful signs is the organization by a strictly nonreligious group of an important conference on *Pacem in Terris.* I urge you to get in touch with Mr. W. H. Ferry, of the Fund for the Public, Box 4068, Santa Barbara, California, about this. This is almost the only concrete and definite thing that is being done, and on a world scale, in spite of official coldness on all sides, including the Catholic side. Here is something that might fit your plan. Do please get in touch with him, he is a good friend of mine and I will mention you when I next write . . .

To Mrs. Hermene Evans

A resident of Chicago, Mrs. Hermene Evans wrote requesting Merton's support of the Peace Study Union.

February 27, 1964

Your letter of Ash Wednesday was quite late in reaching me and hence I did not have time to reply in such a way that you could give the reply to Marjorie Swann. I think the best thing is to write to you and you can pass the letter on to whoever seems best to you.

Certainly I want to give my support to the World Peace Study Mission. I particularly want to give any support I can to the pilgrimage of the Hibakusha. I have asked Father Abbot if we could invite them here, when they are in America. I think I could arrange for them to give talks at various places in the Louisville area, and I know a lot of Protestant seminaries would be interested. Also one of the Catholic colleges would be interested, and we would like to have the Hibakusha out at the monastery. I think this could be an interesting and rewarding part of their trip. What do you think? Could you pass this idea on to Barbara Reynolds?

As regards the various peace movements, I have a rather hard time keeping up with what is going on and reading the necessary literature. Thus my ideas tend to be rather confused. But this particular project is taking good shape in my mind now and I have it well identified. I will be glad to do what I can within the limits of my position. Meanwhile I hope that you will keep me posted . . .

The grace of God is our only support and the more we rely on Him in faith, the better off we will be. But this means a great deal of humble and receptive dialogue with those who do not share our faith.

To Olaf Anderson

Mr. Anderson was a member of the Presbytery of Louisville, Kentucky.

April 18, 1964

It was good to get your letter. I rather suspected that you were implicated in the arrangements for receiving the *Hibakusha* in Louisville, and I was thinking of writing to you directly if I heard nothing more from the people running it. Now I am glad to know that they, or at least some of them, will be able to come out on the 16th. We cannot invite them for lunch if they are a mixed group, but certainly men and women together can be received in the afternoon, though the women would not be able to enter the enclosure. We will think of some way to spend a pleasant and profitable afternoon, perhaps up at the cottage for part of the time. I even toy with the thought of getting a hibachi and letting one of them make some tea, Japanese style, but that may prove too complicated. But I *look forward with joy to having them here*, and hope they will have a pleasant and restful afternoon. The Catholic member of the pilgrimage is not apparently in this group. I would like to see him too, but he will be in Cleveland or somewhere I believe.

It is good to hear from you again. I am enclosing a mimeograph that might be of interest. I have just been doing some work on Gandhi, and it is certain that he was one of the few who have really taken any steps in the right direction. We have to learn the lesson of *satyagraha* if we are to preserve a meaningful human society on this earth. I am totally convinced of this. It is of absolutely primary importance.

May 12, 1964

Thanks for your letter and for the details about your visit with the Hibakusha group next Saturday. This is to change a few minor details at this end and to clarify everything as much as possible.

Do not rush over your lunch in Bardstown and I will be ready for you at 12:45, *at the hermitage.* Jack Ford knows very well how to get here, and it is a matter of turning off on the side road just before you reach the monastery, in fact just before the reservoir in front of the waterworks. The gate will be unlocked. There is room to park cars in front of the barn, and then it is easy to find the hermitage walking up the path through the woods. Jack Ford will have no trouble finding it, but even if for some reason he could not come, you could find it.

We can then have time to get acquainted and to talk a bit up at the hermitage. About 2:15 it turns out there is a Solemn High Mass. I had completely forgotten this, as I had not checked the Ordo. This Saturday is the Vigil of Pentecost and the only day in the year when Mass is at this time. I have no doubt most of them would like to see this from the balcony at the back of the Church.

After the Mass, we could get together in the gatehouse and the men who would like to see the monastery could then be taken on a tour. The rest of the afternoon could then be free for conversation and you could then go back to Louisville according to your schedule. While the men are going on the tour the ladies and those who do not wish to go would remain in the gatehouse and some of us would be there to converse with them . . .

To Theodore Roszak

Mr. Roszak was the editor of Peace News, *London.*

August 22, 1964

I am happy about the new job, and congratulate you on it. I got your notice about it some time ago and was going to send something, but then forgot. Thank heaven you are persevering in your requests. This time I am sending a basket of stuff.

The poem "Baroque Gravure" appeared in *Commonweal* here, but that does not interfere with you people. "Paper Cranes" [a poem Merton wrote when the Japanese Hibakusha people visited him] is unpublished.

The "Tribute to Gandhi" is coming out in a book and perhaps also in the magazine *Ramparts*, which is unknown in England. Then, finally, the bit on the race question is written for a French magazine, and could bear very light editing for you . . .

You are right that in the matter of peace the English Catholic is much more enlightened than the American, but I am very much afraid that the English (and Irish!!) hierarchy are terribly conservative, with the exception of Archbishop [Thomas] Roberts, who is a great man, and who might do something for you. He is with the Jesuits at Mount Street.

In any case, whether any of this is useful or not, I hope I can earn myself a subscription. Some time ago those who had given me one failed to renew it. I got a dolorous message, asking was I mad! I was not able to reply that my benefactors had defaulted. I am not in a position to ask for money for subscriptions here. But the magazines get through if the subscription is given me: this is already a largesse . . .

September 10, 1964

Yes, I will review Gordon [Zahn]'s book [*In Solitary Witness: The Life and Death of Franz Jägerstätter*] when it comes, but it may be a very fast job. I will do my best, depending on what kind of situation I may be in at the time. However, I plan to send you another article in a day or two, also a review. Meanwhile, I will give some thought to the race article. I have material here to read on it, and will get the whole thing to you as soon as I can. I will quite probably make a few changes.

November 20, 1964

Thanks for your letters, etc., and for the copies of *Peace News*. I certainly understand your difficulties about editing the long article I sent and have no objections to the fact that it came back. I am glad you were able to use a little of it anyway.

Here is the review of Gordon Zahn's book, which I reviewed in proof. I hope it will be satisfactory. I thought the book was really first-rate. I hope it will be read and understood especially by those who need to read and understand it, and not only by those of us who already agree with it anyway.

I have especially liked Tom McGrath's things in *PN* and also the article by John Wilkinson in the last issue, which is very much to the point. I have also been reading [Jacques] Ellul.

January 15, 1965

Yes, I would be interested in Simone Weil's book [by Jacques Cabaud], provided that you give me lots of time. I could get the review to you perhaps later in the spring. Perfectly all right about the delay on the Zahn review. I really liked his book. I have not seen it reviewed here much, but then I do not get around. Has the publisher sent *Peace News* my new book, *Seeds of Destruction*? If not, I will shoot a copy along to you. I don't know what is coming off about English publication of this, but if you were interested in having it reviewed soon, that would be fine with me. It is going fairly well so far.

Your project for the book sounds like a good one, and I am a great fan of Huizinga. I would like to help you, but let me tell you quite frankly that letters from me to these foundations just don't work. I do not have the knack. I never know what to say, and when I do get articulate it turns out to be in some wrong way and they are miffed. I just don't have that grip on the cool double-talk of these mandarins. So I tell you quite honestly that a letter from me would be futile, and your best interests lie in not having me write. No one for whom I have ever written one of these letters has ever got anything. Though I must admit they are doing fine without the grants, and are probably better off, like my friend Lax, who has been living on Greek islands for several years now *without* that Guggenheim he thought he needed to get there for a year. He will probably stay there for keeps . . .

A. J. Muste and a whole bunch of good people were down here for a retreat and discussion in November. I think of you often. Please let me have a few extra copies of the issue in which my review appears. Many thanks, and good luck in the New Year. I hope you get that grant. Would it mean leaving *Peace News*?

June 24, 1967

Your note reached me yesterday with the open letter of the ex-Trappist. Maybe my last letter crossed with yours and in any case it had little bearing on your problem: about which I will clearly say this:

Objectively the present war situation is one in which there is such evident injustice that your subjective scruples about the purity of your own motives seem to me to be negligible. Are you going to participate in the burning of little children in a way that is questionable even on its own political terms (i.e., will it save anyone from Communism?). Certainly our motives can be very mixed up and if we try to get to the bottom of all their implications we can work till doomsday and never finally clear everything up. Before God we have to do our best to be true and then rely on our act as objectively and simply as we can and make a decision neither for nor against participation in what we know the war to be.

The open letter of the ex-Trappist is quite true! I have seen the same thing over and over again myself. I don't know what you intend to do about it, but I am returning it to you and if you want to use my comment with it, that's all right. As I say, I find it to be a very accurate reflection of the suffering, the disillusionment, the near-despair, and the final disgust of so many who have been completely unable to cope with the monastic institution. Even those of us who seem to have "coped" must recognize that our exploit is not entirely admirable and some of us have not carried it out entirely without injury to ourselves and perhaps to others as well. At the same time, I would like to say quite definitely that I have long ago ceased to be any kind of spokesman for institutional monasticism in its present state. I ceased to be this ten years ago, and my last word on the subject was *The Silent Life*, which was, in fact, a simple formulation of the monastic ideal as incarnate in four traditional institutional Western forms. I would like to make it quite clear that I do not think that the ideal has been realized or is being realized unequivocally today. In fact the whole situation at present is one of hazard and speculation. I do not know to what extent the current monastic experiments are proving helpful, because I am not able to get sufficient information about them. It is of course impossible for me to explain in detail my own position in regard to the Trappists: my notes on the solitary experiment should have suggested that I was "separate but equal" and definitely not a member of the establishment. Far from it: I am not even fully integrated. In no sense do I claim to be representative of anything that is going on among the Trappists, except that in my case this solution has been found by all at once expedient and respectable. As to the past: I did not come here in order that others might follow me, and I do not intend to leave here to justify the fact that others have left. I have my own business to mind, and in minding it I am perhaps more in communion with the struggles and ambiguities of others than they themselves realize.

To Père Hervé Chaigne, O.F.M.

Fr. Chaigne was the editor of Frères du Monde *at Bordeaux, France.*

December 28, 1964

I am finally getting around to thanking you for the issues of *Frères du Monde* and especially for your excellent translation of the Freedom Songs [see *HGL*]. I was very pleased with them, and with the whole magazine.

In November a group of peace workers, including A. J. Muste, who is the dean of American pacifists, and some from *The Catholic Worker* and Jim Forest of the movement, came here for a retreat and discussion which was very successful and full of good lights. There was much discussion of a book which I had at the time just read, Jacques Ellul's great work on technology [*La Technique* (1954), published in English as *The Technological Society* (1964)]. Do you know Ellul? You must, I am sure. I admire his work and find it entirely convincing and indeed it has the stamp of prophecy which so much Christian writing on that subject seems to lack. I am very anxious to read his book on propaganda.

I am sorry to have left you so long without answers to important questions, but I hope the above brings a little light. Best wishes to you for the New Year. Let us be united in prayer and faith.

April 21, 1965

I would be delighted to have Ellul's book on propaganda. That would be ample payment [for the article Merton had sent]. I know Ellul is a pessimist (I suppose that fits in with a certain Calvinism about the modern world) and he has been much discussed. His book [*The Technological Society*] was not liked in America (naturally) but for that very reason I think there is a definite importance in his rather dark views. They are not to be neglected, for he sees an aspect of technology that others cannot or will not recognize: it does, in spite of its good elements, become the focus of grave spiritual sicknesses, and since they are so evident, it is well to pay attention. To begin with, the folly of the United States in Vietnam—certainly criminal—comes from the blind obsession with mechanical efficiency to the exclusion of all else: the determination to make the war machine work, whether the results are useful or not. The course of the war in Vietnam from the American point of view is entirely dictated by the demands of the machine, and this may lead to World War III.

I hope my Gandhi book [*Gandhi on Non-Violence*] will soon be out in this country and it is also rapidly being translated in Brazil, where there is at the moment a most hopeful non-violent movement developing. You might get an interesting article from Jean and Hildegard Goss-Mayr about this. South America might possibly see the growth of a real Christian and non-violent revolution that would be of momentous importance . . .

You mention two other books of Ellul: I can tell by the titles that they are negative, but perhaps they might have some interesting intuitions nevertheless. If you care to send them along, I would be delighted to have them . . . Do you see *Peace News*? I had an article on the pacifism of Simone Weil there ["The Answer of Minerva: Pacifism and Resistance in Simone Weil"].

June 27, 1965

There is good news about the Freedom Songs (which you translated). A good modern composer (young) [Alexander Peloquin] is setting them to music for a concert of chorus and orchestra and a young Negro singer will be soloist. I hope it will have a good effect. [See Robert Lawrence Williams correspondence in *HGL*.]

In this country the question of civil rights is somewhat in the background and that of war is once again the most prominent problem. The stupidity of [President] Johnson and his advisers is meeting considerable opposition, and the peace movement is getting more active. But unfortunately the peace movement here seems to act only sporadically. It becomes articulate at a moment of crisis and then subsides when the crisis seems to be resolved. Which means that it is not fully serious as a movement, and in effect when something like the Cuba crisis occurs, the peace movement fails. The only reason why it is active now is that the claims of the government are so obviously preposterous. If there were, by chance, something like the bombing of Pearl Harbor in the last war, the peace movement in this country would collapse.

The military strategy of this country depends more and more on its technology and on the computers. It is more and more a war of machines. For instance, the enormous number of marines sent into Santo Domingo (far too many to be rational) was dictated by a computer. This also applies to the decisions in North Vietnam. A merely human protest is not regarded as having any meaning. It is not "scientific."

The fact that the Pope plans to come to the U.N. is due, I think, in large part to protests and letters he has been receiving from this country, as well as from Europe. We depend very, very much on all of you . . .

October 5, 1965

The Gandhi book has appeared here, and I am sending you a copy. I also enclose a piece on Schema XIII [preliminary document from the Second Vatican Council, "On the Church and the Modern World"—see pages 88–92 for Merton's letter to the Bishops], which was unfortunately delayed here and came out rather late to do any good. If it interests you, you can use it, and if you want it in the book, that is all right too. I was very happy about Pope Paul's speech at the U.N. and I hope people in this country will finally get the idea that the Pope is not blessing our adventures in Asia. As a matter of fact the Vietnam War continues to be

very unpopular, and the unpopularity of it does have a restraining effect
on the President, but on the other hand he is pressured by the Pentagon
and the Pentagon is stronger than public opinion, unfortunately. Also I
don't think Johnson is a genius in foreign affairs.

What about the French elections? Is Mitterrand a good man? Sounds
hopeful to me. I am sorry that the Gandhi book came out just at the
moment when India is enthusiastically waging war in Kashmir. Gandhi
was right about the non-violence of India being the non-violence of the
weak. It is a shameful war.

To Dr. Benjamin McLane Spock

*Dr. Spock wrote to Merton asking him to participate in a rally for peace sponsored
by SANE which was to take place in June 1965.*

June 2, 1965

The question of my being one of the sponsors of the SANE rally next
week is one that would require clearance with my Superior and he is
away. Also, I think that possibly he would not be cooperative, in spite of
the fact that it is a good and urgent cause.

The involvement in public events of this nature creates a conflict
with the monastic vocation in which I find myself. Hence it is necessary
for me to express my opposition to the Vietnam War in other ways than
this, though there can be no question of my solid agreement with your
purposes. I hope the rally will be an immense success and that it will
help bring home to policy makers the fact that the whole country does
not agree, or passively submit to, massive escalations of the violence in
Asia.

To Miss Jeanne Beaumont

December 24, 1965

Thanks for the book, first of all. I had heard about it, and I am sure
I will profit by reading it. I know the clergy do not and really cannot give
women the right kind of understanding for the simple reason that their
seminary formation makes this impossible. Most clerics and religious have
a completely unrealistic and fanciful idea of women.

About the point you bring up, on war, peace, and conscientious
objection. The simplest thing is to follow the guidance of the Church. I
am not doing anything rash or new in recommending that you and your
sons read *Pacem in Terris*, the Council's Constitution, "On the Church
in the World," especially the section on international relations and peace,
and of course speeches like Pope Paul's at the U.N.

There are certain things which are simply forbidden to the Christian conscience. They are mortally sinful and even criminal. Total and terroristic war with indiscriminate destruction of combatants and non-combatants, for instance in an entire city, is a war crime. The soldiers who willingly participate in carrying out such an action are responsible before God. Now, the danger to the Christian conscience in modern war is that one may get into the war for very good and seemingly moral reasons, and then the situation may build up to the point where one must participate in criminal actions. This is the case in Vietnam for instance, especially if the war escalates even more. Thus far the bombing of North Vietnam is, to say the least, morally dubious, and certainly the enormous amount of civilian casualties in South Vietnam is hard to justify. How can one participate in such a war and not be partly responsible for such things? And what good will this ever do the cause of freedom? However, these are isolated political judgments. It is best to stick to matters of principle.

It seems to me that the best thing for a concerned Christian to do is to offer his services to society in some constructive and non-violent manner that can be offered in substitution for military service. I don't know what these would be. Does the Peace Corps give exemption from the draft? If so, then if I were of draft age I would feel myself morally obligated to join something like the Peace Corps. As a matter of fact, in the last war I was classified as a non-combatant objector and I would have tried to get into the Medical Corps, except that I was myself rejected in the medical examination. However, I think that this classification is very nice in theory only, while in fact I believe that those who are drafted as non-combatants actually are given the business by the sergeants when they get in uniform and have a very bad time. Also they end up killing anyway.

The Council says explicitly that it is good that there be legal provision made for those who object to modern war and that these should consider themselves obliged to serve their society in some peaceful capacity. This being the case, no one should regard a Catholic objector as an oddity anymore. You are right, of course, that crazy and irresponsible protests on the part of pacifists do more harm than good and I have been in some arguments with them recently on this score. They are antagonizing good, honest people who really want to find out what the score is.

You might also read Gordon Zahn's book *In Silent [Solitary] Witness*, on the Austrian Catholic objector [Franz Jägerstätter] executed under Hitler. The boys might enjoy it also. I don't say you ought to give them a forceful indoctrination, but they should have an opportunity to learn the other side of the question. The problem of social pressures is, of course, always going to be difficult, and it will perhaps be much worse in the future.

To James Morrissey

Editor and staff writer for the Louisville Courier-Journal.

November 21, 1965

My good friend Dr. [Daniel] Walsh has told me about the story you are writing. I am glad you are going about it so conscientiously. I really appreciate the care you are taking, and I wish I were a subject really worthy of such attention. Anyway, thanks.

Dr. Walsh is one of my oldest friends and he can be trusted to say what corresponds to my own thought in most matters. There is, however, one sensitive point of concern that I would like to make sure of. It concerns the current demonstrations for peace. Since (confidentially) I am engaged in a difference of opinion with Catholics in the peace movement close to the card-burners, I would not want to say anything or be quoted in a way that would go too far one way or the other. Hence I have thought it best to write a considered statement of my views on the contemporary war situation. I mean the protest about the Vietnam War. I would appreciate it if you would confine yourself to this statement in quoting me on this subject. You can either use the whole statement or, probably better, use it by working it into your story in pieces here and there. I leave you to judge.

It should be clear to everyone that I do not consider myself a competent judge in commenting on current events, simply because I am not informed. Therefore, for this very reason, I do not attempt to take an active part in any political movement or any movement of any kind. And, although I did write a book recently about civil rights and world peace (*Seeds of Destruction*), I was more concerned with general principles than with specific events.

Also, one other point: about my present position at Gethsemani. Since people often think I have left, and irresponsible rumors to this effect have circulated for the last twenty years, it would be well to say that I am still here, have never left, have no reason to leave, and am firmly committed to the monastic life until my death. (This you can quote if you want.) Also, I am living as a member of the Gethsemani community, but have been granted permission to live a more retired and silent life, less involved even in community activities. My time is given entirely to prayer, work, meditation, study, and philosophy. I will naturally continue to write, but hope to avoid writing about current crises insofar as I can possibly do so. This information is for your use as you see fit. I would appreciate your not going into further details about my life here (I am in fact a hermit in the woods, but that is off the record, please) since this is not a matter of public concern to anyone.

You may make use of anything in this letter except the points I have formally asked you to keep confidential. I wish you luck with the story and again thank you for your consideration. I regret that the rules of this

Order do not permit me to encounter you personally and answer directly. However, if you have any further doubts I would be glad to settle them by mail if I can. I would add that recently some very good pictures were taken here by Art Fillmore of St. Louis and I think Fr. Abbot would be willing to let them be used. They are of the Abbey, etc.

A STATEMENT [ENCLOSURE]

If a pacifist is one who believes that all war is always wrong and always has been wrong, then I am not a pacifist. Nevertheless I believe that war is an avoidable tragedy, and I believe that the problem of solving international conflict without massive violence has become the number one problem of our time. As President Kennedy said, "If we do not end war, war is going to end us." Therefore the entire human race has a most serious obligation to face this problem and to do something about it. But every time we prefer to solve a conflict by force we are sidestepping this great obligation and putting it off. How long can we go on doing purely this?

The human race today is like an alcoholic who knows that drink will destroy him and yet always has "good reasons" why he must continue drinking. Such is man in his fatal addiction to war. He is not really capable of seeing a constructive alternative to war.

If the task of building a peaceful world is the most important task of our time, it is also the most difficult. It will, in fact, require far more discipline, more sacrifice, more planning, more thought, more cooperation, and more courage than war ever demands.

The task of ending war is in fact the greatest challenge to human heroism and intelligence. Can we meet this challenge? Sometimes the prospect seems almost hopeless, for man is more addicted to violence now than he ever has been before, and we are today spending more for war alone than we spent for everything, war included, thirty years ago.

I do not advocate the burning of draft cards. It is not my opinion that the draft law is so unjust that it calls for civil disobedience. But nevertheless I believe that we must admit patriotic dissent and argument at a time like this. Such dissent must be responsible. It must give a sane account of itself to the nation, and it must help reasonable and concerned minds to accept alternatives to war without surrendering the genuine interests of our own national community. Such dissent implies a belief in openness of mind and in the possibility of mature exchange of ideas.

When protest becomes desperate and extreme, then perhaps one reason for this is that the ones protesting may have given up hope of a fair hearing, and therefore seek to shock or to horrify. On the other hand, perhaps the public is too eager to be shocked and horrified and too easily refuses a fair hearing.

This is a serious problem for all of us today. We are Americans and we have a duty to live up to our heritage of open-mindedness. We must always be tolerant and fair and never persecute others for their opinions. The way to silence error is by truth, not by violence.

To the Nobel Institute

This institute at Oslo, Norway, awards the annual Nobel Prize for Peace; the Swedish Academy at Stockholm awards the other Nobel Prizes for Literature, Medicine, etc.

June 27, 1966

I am sending you this letter and the accompanying statement ["Nhat Hanh Is My Brother: A Statement by Thomas Merton"] in order to support the proposals of those who have asked that the Vietnamese Buddhist monk Thich Nhat Hanh be considered for the Nobel Peace Prize.

It was a pleasure and privilege to meet Nhat Hanh here at our monastery and to spend almost two days in conversation with him. Speaking as a Catholic priest who has had some experience in dealing with spiritual men, I wish to say that I was profoundly impressed with the great and special qualities of spirit and character which the Venerable Nhat Hanh seemed to me to manifest. He struck everyone he met here as a true messenger of peace and of spiritual values.

The visit of Thich Nhat Hanh to the United States, to plead for peace in the awful war that is uselessly ravaging his country, has been one of the few really constructive and hopeful measures taken in this direction since the speech of Pope Paul VI at the United Nations. It has had the same kind of impact though on a much smaller scale. It is the same kind of appeal. But since Thich Nhat Hanh is a Buddhist intellectual, his appeal to university circles in this country has been especially effective and important.

What is most important, however, is, it seems to me, that Thich Nhat Hanh made this journey and delivered his message of peace at the risk of his own life. As the accompanying statement shows, there is considerable fear that he may be imprisoned and even killed as a result of his efforts for peace. Therefore it seems to me that he is eminently worthy, on the highest moral grounds, of consideration for the Peace Prize on account of the heroic character of his witness for peace.

I therefore heartily endorse the proposal that Thich Nhat Hanh be considered for the Nobel Peace Prize of 1966.

To Joan Baez and Ira Sandperl

On December 8, 1966, Joan Baez, songwriter, folksinger, and peace activist, and a friend, Ira Sandperl, visited Gethsemani and spent some time with Merton at his hermitage. Wilbur H. ("Ping") Ferry had arranged the visit. Joan Baez tells about it in Paul Wilkes, Merton by Those Who Knew Him Best, *Harper & Row, 1984, pp. 41–45.*

December 14, 1966

I don't know if this will get there ahead of the card and note I sent yesterday. It may. I thought I would send along a couple of more or less singable poems I dug up. Not that I think that these particular ones are of any use. But I will keep attentive to such rhythms and songs as present themselves and we'll see, maybe a song will come out one day.

Once again, it was good to have you here, good to have someone to talk to about things that matter.

I can send you a couple of fairly bulky mimeographed sets of notes of courses given here on things like Syrian monasticism, if you are interested. May find something that would be of use to you there. I cannot find a copy of a thing I did on non-violence ["Blessed Are the Meek"] for the FOR people in Vienna, but it is supposed to come out as a pamphlet if the Catholic Peace Fellowship gang ever do anything about it—or get their hands on money.

The record [her Christmas record "Noel"] is lovely. I especially like the first side. Many thanks for it. It is great to have around. It fills my place with a good sound. There are scores of birds all around now and the other night a flying squirrel got in somehow and woke me up running around all over everything.

God bless you always. Peace, joy, love, grace, light: all the best things of Christmas to you. Keep in touch—always remembering the mail is heavily censored. And come again when you can.

February 14, 1967

Thanks for your note from Tokyo. I hope the trip was very good in every way. After you had gone I thought of some people in Hiroshima I could have recommended. You probably saw plenty of people anyway. I hope Joan's concerts were a success.

I was going to write Joan back there at one point when I heard about the Al Capp business [Li'l Abner cartoon ridiculing Joan Baez]. Totally sickening. I hope that is all ancient history by now. Joan is big enough to take anything a twisted bird like that can give out, anyway. His cartoons tell all that one needs to know about him these days.

Nothing particularly new here. I keep working on the usual things. I wish I had talked more about things you and Joan are more interested in when you were here—meditation, etc. But I find I talk less and less about all that. The great thing is the desire and the blind insistent humble pushing to get through whatever it is: and yet be nothing and still push anyway. And be dragged through also.

In any event it is terribly important for us all to be in contact with those of like mind, and I am always here for discussion about anything, within the limits which the administration will tolerate. I'd say if you are coming East again late spring or early summer, keep Kentucky in mind. Or write anyway. I am hoping to see Ping Ferry in April.

All my very best to you and Joan. I am always very close to you both. It's good to know you are there. Still haven't written anything on Dylan, and perhaps won't after all. I lack perspective. I may send on some of the pieces on Faulkner I have been doing, but the typist has murdered them.

To James Schulte

A senior at St. Louis University who was thinking of applying for conscientious objector status.

April 10, 1967

One has to distinguish pacifism in the strict sense—a belief that all war is evil—from the belief that a particular war is unjust and cannot be accepted in conscience. The problem of the Vietnam War is not only that it is a war, but that it is also an unjust war in the opinion of anyone who knows what is really going on there. Hence one can oppose it and indeed should oppose it without being necessarily a pacifist. This is what a lot of people do not seem to realize. On the other hand, a completely pacifist position is also quite reasonable in our time, when any war is likely to escalate to a nuclear war and even conventional wars are hardly likely to be waged by purely legitimate means.

To the Editor of The Record

The Record is the Catholic diocesan newspaper of Louisville, Kentucky.

March 10, 1968

It seems that there has been some controversy about me in *The Record*. I do not want to waste your space by adding unnecessarily to this controversy. But it might be a good thing if I brought the following to the attention of your readers.

The other day in Hue, Vietnam, a monastery of Vietnamese Primitive Benedictines was destroyed, some of the monks were killed, some have "disappeared," one is in Laos. This is a community with which I had been in close contact. Their loss is something I feel deeply. But the monastery was not destroyed by Communists. It was blasted by American bombs. Now, I am not blaming anyone for this. Obviously this was not "intended." But the point is that this happens over and over again. It is not just an isolated incident, it is characteristic of the entire war: what does it all add up to? Simply to the fact that we are "saving the Vietnamese from Communism" by destroying them. It is getting more and more clear to more and more people that there is something radically wrong with this war. It has become, for very many, a most serious problem of conscience. No amount of bluster or derision can alter the fact. For that reason I am also opposed to a war which involves a needless waste of American and Vietnamese lives, which is not likely to attain any useful purpose, which is definitely not helping America or democracy in any way whatever, and which is, in fact, a scandal to this entire world.

To Mary Lanahan

June 24, 1968

It is not always possible for me to answer letters but chance or Providence has arranged that yours gets answered. All I can do is say as simply as possible what I think the problem is.

Pope John and the Vatican Council have both clearly stated that nationalistic wars are no longer reasonable means of achieving political ends (at least legitimate ones). They just don't *work*. In other words, what people don't seem to realize is that in Vietnam it's either commit genocide or permit the Vietnamese to work out a solution that does not fit the plans of people in Washington. In terms of the traditional Catholic just war theory (which is also insufficient, but let that pass) when a war produces only massive slaughter out of proportion to any good that can conceivably come of it, it is unjust and immoral.

Obviously we have a right to try to prevent the spread of a political ideology which we deem harmful to us. But as a matter of fact, anyone who knows what is really happening in Asia knows that we are not stopping Communism at all by our conduct of the war. Quite the contrary. We are driving the Asians to Communism by our stupidity.

I am not a "pure" pacifist. I can certainly see that the use of force may be necessary to maintain a certain international order. I do not say that evil must be passively accepted. It must be resisted. But I believe that with the advent of the atomic bomb war has taken on a new shape which makes it at the same time stupid and pointless. The power is so *great* that it is good for only one thing—massive extermination on a scale so big that it is no longer worthwhile. The threat of such extermination is really not such a viable means of achieving real ends. With all our bombs we can't change things in Cuba, and with all our force we can't curb the Vietnamese. The only thing left is to wipe them out. I don't know if that is what will be deliberately done, but bit by bit we are getting there, so to speak, without looking.

As to the Berrigan brothers, they are friends of mine. I don't agree with their methods of action, but I can understand the desperation which prompts them. They believe they have to witness *in jail* to the injustice of the war. That is their business. It is certainly not a necessary teaching of the Church.

I know, for a fact, that Pope Paul is deeply distressed by the war and has done everything he can to persuade the U.S. to make a *real* move toward a compromise agreement. Johnson persists in wanting nothing short of total victory. The price to be paid is not within the range of Catholic morals. On the other hand, he can certainly continue the war in some *just* way in order to reach a solution. I don't think that is what he is doing. That, of course, is only my opinion. You don't have to approve of the Berrigans, but I do suggest that the war is something deplorable to a Catholic and neither of the two main presidential candidates seems to have anything to offer but more of the same. That is why I am for [Eugene] McCarthy—and agree, also, with what seemed to me to be Robert Kennedy's peace stand.

We certainly don't have to be pacifists in the strict sense, but as Americans and Catholics we ought to see that with all our influence in the world we could do more by strong but peaceful means than by sheer force, which is *not* getting us anywhere and is just wasting lives. I am afraid our leaders just don't have the sense or the imagination to look for new and creative solutions. I think Johnson is a disaster. And Humphrey and Nixon are no better.

To Rupert A. Lutz, O.F.M.

Merton's correspondent is a Franciscan priest serving as a chaplain in the U.S. Army.

July 31, 1968

I don't want to get into a long controversy, but I just want to answer your letter as a Christian and a fellow priest, admitting the big differences in our view of things.

First of all, I don't like to use the term "hawk" and I don't like to call names. I think perhaps the term was used by the interviewer rather than by me. What I said about nationalism has been said before me by Popes Pius XII, John XXIII, and Paul VI. There is a difference between nationalism and patriotism. Nationalism puts the private interests of one's country before the common good of man. Unfortunately it is my belief that the Vietnam War is not at all for the good of our country and is really doing more to help Communism than to hinder it. However, I suppose that is where you and I differ.

Certainly I can understand that as a chaplain you are bound to be for the war and to accept the government's view of the war at its face value. That does not make you an ogre, I agree. And you see the problems of the men in the service: for you they are the most important thing. Okay. But as a priest I think you ought to be aware of the growing moral corruption of your country as a result of this war. Take a look at Saigon: the place is a whorehouse, a black market, a mess. Is that what we are fighting for? Asians are asking themselves if we are trying to turn the whole of Asia into something like that. Look at the people who have become millionaires at home as a result of this war. We are not fighting for money? It's obvious that we are. Our professed aims are of course not quite that.

Father, as I said, I don't want to argue. But I think we can both agree that this war is tragic for our country and that it ought to be brought to an end. But of course one can't just drop everything and leave. What bugs me is the apparent unwillingness to really try to reach an agreement that would at least, hopefully, get somewhere. Johnson loudly proclaims a bombing pause and then steps up the bombing. The proportion of civilians killed in this war is astronomical, far higher than the military and far higher than in any other war.

We may not agree on what the problems are or on how to solve them but let us at least agree that there are terrific problems and that they cannot be solved by more and more killing. It should be evident by now that this doesn't work.

Anyway, I keep you and your men in my prayers. The situation here at home is ugly, very ugly. Because of the war. Let's hope we can solve our problems and get down to fulfilling some of the great capacities our country has. We could be far different from the sort of image we are now presenting in Vietnam.

III.

Merton's Life and Works

*I am pretty sure by now that I am not meant to follow
any beaten track.*
TO NAOMI BURTON STONE

[*Since this section covers a variety of subjects, the terms of the title should be
taken in a very general way. "Life" may include events of his life, or reflections
on life, whether within or outside the monastery. "Works" is used to designate
both his writings and the things he did in his lifetime. Some of the subtitles I use
will attempt to clarify these different categories. Since Merton's individual letters
often touch upon a variety of issues, none of the categories will be entirely
satisfactory. However, they should offer some guide to the reader regarding the
substance of particular letters.*]

1. To Naomi Burton Stone

*[Between us] there is just the right balance of being the
same and being different.*
TO NAOMI BURTON STONE

Naomi Burton Stone came to America from England in 1939 as a literary agent.
In 1951 she married Melville E. (Ned) Stone. She early recognized Thomas Merton's talents as a writer, though she was unsuccessful in getting his early novels
published. When she learned he had entered a monastery, she felt that a promising
literary career had come to an end. Little did she realize that it was just beginning
and that she would represent him in bringing to publication some of the finest
works of spiritual writing in this century. His initial success was of course his
best-selling The Seven Storey Mountain, which Naomi had sent to Robert Giroux
late in 1946.

Naomi was more than a literary agent to Thomas Merton; they became close
friends. Not only was she sister and sometimes "mother" to him, but Merton
valued her counsel, even the occasional "scoldings" she found it necessary to give
him.

What follows is a brief selection of letters and parts of letters that Merton
wrote to her. There is a mounting interest as Merton moves from a purely professional relationship, having to do with his books, to much more personal revelations
of his own identity, his fears, his needs and concerns. In their exchange two
strong personalities meet; at times sparks fly when they don't agree, but the sparks
helped to deepen their friendship—a friendship that meant much to Merton.
Naomi Burton Stone and Dom James Fox were perhaps the two persons who
contributed most to his growth as a monk, a writer, and a human being.

To get the full benefit of this correspondence, it would be necessary to read
both sides of it and in its entirety, but still the selections given here (brief compared
to the size of the total correspondence) shed a good deal of light on Thomas
Merton and his struggle to achieve personal freedom and maturity.

January 2, 1947

Naturally I was delighted to get Bob [Giroux]'s wire [accepting the
manuscript of SSM. See SJ, pp. 20–21] and your letter. I will write to

Bob when I hear from him. Meanwhile please assure him that I give him a free hand with the editing. There is one idea that I would like to keep or get in somewhere else: the one about the identity of disinterested charity and true freedom, because that is important. I guess it is evident enough that the whole book is more or less about that, but I'd like if possible to keep the part that says it explicitly. Also I'd like to keep as much as I can of the references to Duns Scotus because even Catholics don't know him, and they should.

About the contract, Father Abbot says you can send it out here in the ordinary way. He will know what to do about it. Address it to me. I suppose it will be a contract with the monastery because I can't make any contracts.

February 18, 1947

Incidentally I think *The Seven Storey Mountain* would be better not described as a novel, since it was by no means written as one. The others [his pre-monastic manuscripts] were novels, but this I felt bound to keep as close to literal truth as I could because I felt that some of the impact of the book depended on it. So it is a straight autobiography, and I feel, don't you, that the publicity should make that clear when it gets around to that. I hope all this does not communicate my own mental fog to you, on whom I depend for clarification and clear vision!

Easter (March 30) 1947

I am working on a book about our Order [*The Waters of Siloe*] which I think Harcourt, Brace might conceivably take. There are interesting things about our history, and some unpublished stuff about the first Trappists in America, and anyway a book about what the life is all about, by someone on the inside of a monastery, ought to have some appeal. What do you think? I am writing it anyway, as it is in connection with our hundredth anniversary next year.

The Abbot General of the Order [Dom Dominique Nogues] is here now and he told me to go on publishing under the name Thomas Merton, so that is the name I use for all business purposes, contracts, etc. The General likes the idea of the work I am doing.

May 13, 1947

Since I last wrote to you the censor came through with a complete capitulation on everything [in *The Seven Storey Mountain*] that mattered and wrote me a very nice letter into the bargain. So in matters of style I am left to my own devices and can follow the inspiration I happen to get. Incidentally I put the thing up to the Abbot General of the Order —who is a wonderful person—and he told me to go ahead and write as I pleased and to use all the slang I wanted: but he would not force anything upon a censor.

The upshot of the whole thing is that all I need to cut is what is really useless anyway, and I am now working on the ms. and cutting far more than the censor suggested—because it is tedious. I have rewritten a few pages. The whole thing has not yet come back to me from the censor but the rest will be along soon. Meanwhile I would be glad to get Bob's suggestions and editing and clean the whole thing up.

August 1, 1947

I thought I had better drop you a line to try and find out how things are coming at Harcourt, Brace. I still haven't heard a word from Bob about the final changes he wants made—or any changes he wants made, for that matter. It occurs to me that he might possibly have written, and the letter was mislaid around here. If so, it is getting to be time to straighten things out, don't you think? His original intention was to publish the thing in the fall, but it is getting to be too late for that.

As I told you before, I rewrote quite a lot of it, especially the whole last section, and cut all the parts that seemed to slow things down. I have the copy I worked over sitting here now. What do you think I should do—send this one in to Bob also, and let him look it over? On the other hand, that would leave me minus everything and perhaps things would still not progress any further . . .

March 8, 1948

[James] Laughlin [publisher of *New Directions*] sent this check here by mistake. He is in Europe and I guess didn't get my reminder about sending everything through you. I'll remind him again, though.

I am nearly finished with a book, *Waters of Siloe*, about the Trappist Order and life which I will shoot along to you. I have promised it already to Bob Giroux. It ought not to be delayed too much because the centenary of the monastery will be celebrated next year and the book ought to coincide with that. If Bob does not want it, then I would like to take it back and send it independently to Bruce and Co. in Milwaukee, with whom we always deal personally, because Father Abbot makes special arrangements with Bruce, who is a friend of his.

Does that suit you? I hope Bob will take it anyway. But if he doesn't I know these other people will: only, personally, I would rather see it go to Harcourt because it would reach a wider field.

Also, Laughlin is interested in another project that is under way, a book of more or less random thoughts about the contemplative life called *The Soil and Seeds of Contemplation*. That will be ready, I suppose, about midsummer. The St. John of the Cross project has stalled somehow.

July 9, 1948

Copies of *The Seven Storey Mountain* got here and they look fine. I am not sore at the book in any special way—although I am grieved at having written a book as corny as *Exile Ends in Glory*, which Bruce may have sent you by now. Some parts of it make me writhe. I apologize. Don't disown me, please.

November 8, 1948

This just to thank you for the wonderful job you and Bob have done on *The Seven Storey Mountain*. It certainly seems to be going quite well. I am getting so much fan mail that it makes me nervous. Everybody around here seems fairly pleased at the idea—that is, everyone who knows about it or whose knowledge of it makes any difference.

April 28, 1949

The carbons of the *Mountain* were given to Boston College Library, which is in the care of one Rev. Terence Connolly, S.J., Librarian. Father Abbot here does not object to anyone using unpublished parts, at least on principle. Evelyn Waugh [who edited the British edition of *SSM* under the title *Elected Silence*] tells me that he thought it possible that he might consider some of the parts that were cut by Harcourt as suitable for insertion in the second English edition. I think it would be unwise just to publish unused sections of the book indiscriminately. This man [who had contacted Naomi] can write an article if he likes. But I leave it finally to your better judgment. Do whatever you think would be best for the book. The magazine he speaks of has no standing.

January 14, 1950

I am typing the *Journal*, which, provisionally, I am calling *The Whale and the Ivy*. It looks as though this might well turn out to be the next one for publication, as I have more than enough for a book. I will send you a good part of it between now and Easter. Besides that, Mme. Sauvageot (the French photographer) has come through with a batch of admirable pictures. Quite enough for a book too. What should I do: send the pictures right away to Bob, or wait until I have got up a text to go with them? This latter will take time, as I will have to read up on the material. I do not intend to write much in this book, let the pictures do most of the talking. Mme. Sauvageot needs to be paid, if she has not been already, for the pictures used in *Waters*. Will you check with Bob on these points?

February 13, 1950

You wanted me to send all articles through you. Here is one I promised *Commonweal* for Lent ["Self-Denial and the Christian," March 31, 1950]. Edward Skillin is the editor. I suppose they are in a rush.

I am just writing to Bob to catch him before he leaves for Rome.

Holy Thursday 1950

I am glad your reaction was a little better than I thought it might be. I was afraid that although the *Journal* seemed lively to me it would seem dull to people outside. And this is the least lively part. I haven't seen the penciled remarks but I am sure they will all be very helpful. Really, you offend my secret pride not by criticizing me but by saying you are sorry to criticize . . . don't you know how *modest* we monks are supposed to be? We love criticism. To give us the impression that you think we might wince a little—why, it makes us positively blue with indignation. Everything you say about religious language is very reasonable and right. I am awfully glad to have somebody say it because it is extremely important that I should avoid the kind of faults you mention and it is also almost impossible for me to avoid them. It is part of my "mission" to be completely straight and unsentimental about everything I believe in: but also not to be too light about it. Yet of course one can be rather light, after a while, about superficial things in our life: and people would be, as the saying goes, "scandalized." I have to watch it and I am glad to have your eye on the book.

Privately my feeling is that the *Journal* does belong with the *Mountain* and that Harcourt can best handle it: but I promised it to Jay [Laughlin]. If he fully understands that the decision is in your hands and if he is content to abide by that it is all right by me. If he will let the book go, why not let him have the collection of articles, which will soon enough be big enough for a book. And on top of that I might try to write him a lively little formless notebook with all sorts of amusing things, more scattered than this, less autobiographical—I could play around with all sorts of things for a few years and then give him the bits and pieces and on the whole it would be more his kind of a book. But I think if he lets this go he should get something too in its place and the articles are solid enough. In a collection of articles he could also include "Poetry and the Contemplative Life" [*Commonweal*, July 4, 1947], which was already in *Figures* [*for an Apocalypse*], and I would rewrite the conclusion. Then too maybe he would like the picture book of those cloisters and honestly it will be a swell collection of pictures. There—three consolation prizes.

And so, in the fullness of happiness of this day: Naomi, look, you have a divine mission, no less, which is to keep me in order as a writer and tell me when I am getting completely stupid and cheap and all the rest. And it is easy for me to get that way, as I write in such a hurry when I get the slightest chance to sit in front of a typewriter. Those chances are getting rare. Father Abbot is trying to keep the way clear for me to have time for the two big jobs I am supposed to do—writing and teaching. They dovetail together well, as long as other stuff doesn't land in the middle and disrupt everything. But there are always things cropping up. I need a full-time secretary, I guess. Pray for me to get a lot of sense and to be guided by the Holy Ghost and not my own mad impulses.

Holy Week 1950

Thinking about the *Journal* again, whatever anyone may think about publication, I can't get rid of the feeling that I ought to forge ahead this summer and at least get the thing ready, sending out bits to various magazines. And I am really beginning to be a little more definite in thinking that it ought to come out in book form fairly soon in the lineup—shall we say after *St. Ailred*? That would mean in 1951 or early 1952. I do not think we ought to let too many medieval saints get in between this and *The Seven Storey Mountain*. This has more life in it than anything I have done besides the *Mountain* and may well turn out to have the most appeal after that one.

March 28, 1950

I suppose by now you have seen the book [*What Are These Wounds?*, the life of a Trappistine, St. Lutgarde, published by Bruce]. What a cover! Please inform me as soon as it receives the golden raspberry award from all the critics.

April 29, 1950

Well, the settlement is very easy, Naomi. There just isn't any problem anymore. Father Abbot read over part of the *Journal* ms. and got to talking with some prominent Catholics somewhere. The latter were all up in the air with surprise and dismay at the thought of a cloistered monk writing and publishing a *Journal* in his own lifetime. Of course you can't write a *Journal* when you are dead. But they convinced Father Abbot that the *Journal* simply should not be published. At least not while I am still walking around on the face of this earth. Such a thing had never been heard of before. And that is quite true: it hasn't. Maybe it isn't such a wonderful book either, I don't know. Anyway, Father Abbot is quite definite about not wanting it to go into print because he feels that it would get him and the monastery into a lot of nasty criticism from people who just wouldn't understand.

September 16, 1950

Please excuse the mess this letter is going to be. I am not writing about anything important. The chief reason why I am writing is that in this hospital [St. Joseph's Infirmary, Louisville, Kentucky] where they have 2 or 3 hundred rooms named after saints, they put me in a room named after St. *Naomi*. You will be glad to hear it is a very swanky room, one of the best in the place. For that I am somewhat ashamed, since I was supposed to be poor—and am getting it for nothing too!

May 10, 1951

Several weeks have gone by without my saying a word to you about my happiness to hear that you were married and to send you my very best wishes and my prayers and my blessing. It was not necessary to be in a rush about it. You know I always keep you in my prayers anyway and that I always ask Our Lord to make you very happy.

The reason why I held things up was that I wanted to send you a tangible sort of a wedding present. I knew you would be pleased to hear that Father Abbot had reconsidered his decision about the *Journal* and that he would allow the publication of special selections from it [under the title *The Sign of Jonas*]. I have tentatively made some selections and am sending this copy to you for Bob. The book will begin more or less where it started out last time. Bob has the old beginning. Very much will have to be cut out of that, and this will have to be cut also.

The principle we must work on is this: Father Abbot is strongly opposed to anything that might make narrow-minded people look askance (whatever that is) at the monastery. The book should be principally a collection of personal meditations—with just enough color and background to give the thing a lot more life than *Seeds of Contemplation*. But realism about the side of the monastery that would appear to be too human is to be cut out altogether. I think, too, that we might cut practically everything that is directly personal about myself as a writer. The business about ordination to the priesthood cannot very well be depersonalized. In any case, that is the heart of the book. I believe that the present selection is a good enough basis to build on—or to cut down on. Would you go over it, and have Bob do so, and both let us know what you want to go ahead with. After that it will have to be combed by the censors of the Order with Father Abbot's own very special limitations on the script in view. After everybody has taken a crack at it, we can begin to think of publication. It might do for next summer??

In September 1952, Robert Giroux was told by Abbot James Fox, who was returning from France, of the decision of the Abbot General, Dom Gabriel Sortais, that The Sign of Jonas *could not be published. In the eyes of a European censor—Dom Albert, prior of the Abbey of Caldey—the book was "inappropriate" and would ruin Merton's reputation in Europe. Robert Giroux was dismayed. Having been cleared by the American censors, the book had already been set up for publication and had been accepted by several book clubs. Giroux got in touch with Jacques Maritain at Princeton, asking him to write the Abbot General in French. Maritain lauded the book as a deeply inspiring spiritual work. This letter to the Abbot General was surely crucial to his final decision releasing the book for publication. At the same time Naomi Stone had contacted Tom Burns, the British publisher, who got help from Fr. Bruno Scott James in persuading Dom Albert to withdraw his objections. By November 3, 1952, Merton was able to inform Giroux that the book could be published without further changes.*

October 10, 1952

Many thanks for your very kind letter, written at home, and also for the other mail from the office. The fact that *Jonas* got into trouble is no particular surprise or worry to me. I am sorry for Bob's sake. It is certainly true that we all rushed ahead too much. I have written to the Abbot General to see if things cannot be patched up, since the work has gone so far that to stop now would make the public raise a lot of eyebrows about the Order and what is going on inside it—or what they might think was going on inside it. The only thing about the censorship that nettles me a little is that, after I have put myself on paper as simply and straight-forwardly as I could, the all-round conclusion in the Order seems to be as follows: "When a person is as bad a monk as that he ought to keep quiet about it." I do not disagree with the conclusion. In fact I see more clearly than ever the wisdom it contains. But . . . oh well, I do not even feel that writing the book was a waste of time. A lot of it was prayer. I am by now used to the fact that what seems to me to be prayer seems to many holy men to be folly.

March 3, 1956

I was so glad to get your long letter and to hear that things are working out all right. Of course they will have to go slowly. Don't be impatient about anything in yourself. After all, if we just try to correct one tendency by going in the opposite direction, we end up swinging back and forth on a pendulum. You have to accept even what you want to reject before you can reject it effectively. You run the risk of making yourself too restless now when you need to realize how true it is that you have "arrived." I don't say you never had the grace of God before but you certainly have it now: and Christ lives in you. Let Him do that. He accepts you as you are, so you have to do the same yourself, or run the risk of trying to be more exacting than He, which is not precisely wise . . .

Shall I add to the immense list of books you ought to read? The February issue [of *La Vie Spirituelle*] has an excellent article by Régamey on psychoanalysis. Not just saying that analysis is okay for pious folk, but much more, doing a lot of good analytical thinking on Catholic lines. Also if you don't know Gustave Thibon, get to know him real quick. He is excellent. Régamey has other good books—*Poverty* is one, *The Cross and the Christian* is good. Louis Bouyer's *Paschal Mystery* is good. You might like Hilda Graef's book on Edith Stein—but oh well, there we go again. Everyone probably forgets that all you do is read books. I don't know how you can possibly stand it. I read actually very little now. Just walk around and think.

It was so good to have you here, and of course I don't mind at all having a sister who is sensible. Not all are. But as a matter of fact that was what I was thinking about sitting up there at Gannon's [the residence for lay visitors]: that I had always secretly regretted not having a sister and now all of a sudden one shows up. There is just the right balance of being the same and being different. I certainly trust your opinions and your observations, since they are the first things I have heard that made sense in a long time.

As a matter of fact, I can't imagine why I don't enjoy my job more. I know I can do it, etc., yet I refuse to enjoy it. Not as explicitly as that: I want to and I even try to. But something inside me has been hit so

hard that I just go bitter every time. However, it does not worry me.
The first thing that I feel about it is that I have to go through positively
everything that the others go through here, so that I will know what I
am talking about when I try to help them. Secondly, as I am now beginning
to realize, my own neurosis is so old and so well entrenched that it is a
wonder I have not felt it long before. Actually it is a good thing that I
am feeling it at last. My sensitivity to it seems to have coincided with my
ordination to the priesthood. Before, I had no idea that I wasn't going
along perfectly. (I should have had an idea of course, there were ample
indications!)

The bitterness in me comes from the fact that I have at last opened
up the area in which it is impossible not to notice that in all this solitude
business and in my other outbursts of idealism I have been reliving all
the brat experiences of my childhood, magnified and adorned. Secondly,
the bitterness comes from realizing that now there is definitely *no hope*
of my ideals being realized, that they are more or less fictitious and illusory
and that perhaps I don't even want them myself—that indeed I may not
even know what I really want, except that I am rather sure I don't want
the big pot of spiritual adolescence which is called the monastery of
Gethsemani. I mean that I find it distasteful and frustrating—although,
of course, I "want" it in the sense that I mean to keep my vows. Thirdly,
the bitterness centers on my writing. My ambivalence about writing is
not as great as I have made it seem. I really have little ambivalence about
writing as such, provided I can just write. That I really enjoy and I profit
by it and it comes easy, etc. But of course writing against the obstacles
we have here is another matter. Then again, I know that my writing has
been a safety valve for the neurosis, too. Being without the safety valve
is a strain at times, but perhaps it is a good thing. I shudder to think how
many pages I have written beating people over the head for not being
spiritual and which I now realize to have been just egotistical junk. In
fact I am awfully aware of the shallowness and superficiality of most of
the writing I did between 1945 and 1950—and some of what I have written
since then, too.

Yes, dammit, your heart *should* ache for me. Don't repent of that.
Somebody ought to ache along with my ache, even if it's selfish. But don't
go and ache too much, because if you do it will be another subjective
and unattached ache that will be wasted. And that is the next reason for
my bitterness—the awful feeling that all this suffering (I don't claim it is
tremendous) is really relatively useless. Well, if I learn from it, that is
something.

Honestly I don't think the vow [not to accept the office of abbot] was
that smug. As an abbot I would have nothing to offer the Order. I would
be a liability, not an asset. Of course, you might say that I ought to trust
in God and let things take their course. I have seen so many things go
disastrously wrong that way (of course Divine Providence keeps them
from going *too* wrong) but they go wrong enough for it to be terribly

painful and frustrating for all concerned. And in the end, these mistakes are terribly costly in the lives of good people: so many men twisted up beyond repair and suffering uselessly. Of course it is not all completely useless, and naturally in God's designs much is salvaged that we do not know of and there is no reason why a bunch of spiritual wrecks should not be of tremendous value to the Church, because precisely it is the weak and helpless who are most used by God as His instruments.

Well, I plow through things and seem to come out all the time anyway. I am really very happy that in all this wrestling with myself, I am really getting rid of an awful lot of Merton, but the void that replaces him is a bit disconcerting: except that I know God is there. One thing is sure: I do not particularly want the survival of the person and even the writer I have been. Although I do have enough sense to realize that this is what I shall always probably be. But my true self is not one that has to be thought about and propped up with rationalizations. He only has to be lived, and he is lived, in Christ, under the surface of the unquiet sea in which the other one is busy drowning.

P.S. Please don't stop "bothering" me and don't apologize for it. For heaven's sake I need it. And so do you, I guess.

April 4, 1956

I hear you had lunch with [Robert] Lax. I have been meaning to write to him and still do. Has he suddenly left for France again, or is he still around?

I was in to see the man about those Rorschach tests we took as an experiment, and lo, I discover from my own that I really love everybody and am socially adapted and that all I am really looking for is a chance to help people. I say to him: "But I want to live a solitary life." And he says to me firmly: "Clinically you are social." "No," I gasp, "I am truly a hermit." He replies, inflexibly: "The Rorschach test says you are *social*." Dom James will be ten years younger when he hears it. But I still hope I can get enough solitude occasionally to continue breathing. But nevertheless this type declared, and I believe it, that there is a whole lot of potential creative and productive stuff in me going to waste because I spend most of my time rejecting everybody and telling myself that they are rejecting me. So, maybe I'll be seeing him again . . .

Easter was wonderful and today is wonderful, all the way into town the pear trees and cherry trees and redbuds were in bloom and the farms looked clean and fresh instead of being the usual mudholes, and everything was sublime, even the hogs . . .

April 27, 1956

What they are always saying about confirmation is that you must not expect to feel anything special. After all, they told me that when I was confirmed in the C of E at Oakham. And I didn't feel anything either.

Nor did I, as it happens, get confirmed at that time, as every one supposed.

In May 1939, about six months after my baptism, I remember Fr. Moore grabbed me and said I should be confirmed by Bishop Donohue —which I was. The thing that most occupied me was the choice of a new middle name. That is where I came up with James. (Do you remember, I used to be definitely Thomas James Merton.) (Everything spelled out in all letters.) I don't think it makes any sense to say whether I felt anything or not. We made a procession outside of Corpus Christi, about ten feet along the sidewalk, out one door and in the other, and all the heathens in Teachers College stood at the windows and looked at our Popish pranks, and what I felt was embarrassment or resentment. Yet it was a big day.

About receiving the Holy Ghost: of all the things about which we talk glibly (Catholics talk glibly about everything Catholic) the one I hate most to talk glibly about is the mystery of the Holy Ghost given to our souls—the one I hate next most to talk glibly about is the mystery of Our Lady, the Bride of the Holy Spirit. It comes to the same thing. The Holy Spirit is He Who is most intimate to us, closest to us, "sweet Guest of our souls," and the One we know least about because we see Him least in perspective. We know more of the Father, and of course more of the Son, than we know of the Holy Ghost. Nothing, practically, is revealed about the Person of the Holy Ghost, beyond His procession and mission: I mean nothing about His "identity" if I may so speak. He Himself is His own revelation. He is the Revealer of the Father and the Son and in revealing Them, reveals Himself.

He is the "Spirit of Truth Who cometh from the Father" and all that is most real and most true in us, is of Him. "Devotion to the Holy Spirit" is a thing that can become most false and misleading, insofar as we make the Holy Ghost another, bigger, more mysterious object of devotion than the saints: He is a sainted, canonized Spirit, the chief of the Saints, according to this human approach. He has His Feast—Pentecost, Feast of St. Spirit—as March 19 is Feast of St. Joseph. No, that is crazy. Pentecost is the celebration of the Mystery of His visible Mission—and to love the Holy Ghost is to love all that He has done: His Church, in which He makes Christ live: His life in ourselves which we can never see or measure or look at.

In confirmation, we get the strength and the perspective, first of all, to get along with a Spirit Who is our Spirit, as intimate to us as our own selves and more so, and yet the Spirit of God and infinitely beyond our clear knowing. In confirmation we get the strength to keep up with the pace He sets, which is the pace of the wind blowing where it listeth and you don't know where it is going. The thing we have to avoid above all is being untrue to this Spirit by saying He has said something when He hasn't, and saying He has not said something when He has. And first of all, we must not saddle Him with all our own foolishness, and blame Him for our own wacky visions. At the same time, however, we must be able, in a quiet, confident way, to do the seemingly crazy things He asks of us—the craziest of which is, perhaps, to be ordinary.

About you—certainly the Holy Spirit given to you in confirmation will come to straighten out whatever needs to be straightened out with Ned and with everything else. If you ask Him, and believe, and be quiet and let Him work it out in His own way, that is enough. But above all, give yourself the silence, once in a while, to listen to Him. He says most when He says nothing.

May 2, 1956

First of all, here are a couple of poems . . . Matthew Scott is sending the long one to Graham Greene [called "The Sting of Conscience," with the subtitle "Letter to Graham Greene"]. I hope Greene will be appropriately edified at the effect of [his novel] *The Quiet American* on a Trappist monk. Come to think of it, it is not the kind of book that is usually read in the monastery. Somehow I reacted—responded, what have you—strongly to the basic moral point. It touched off something very deep in me, that whole business that is boiling around down there. Resistance against the beautiful moral façade which gets built up in front of our very iniquity—including perhaps my own. Our wonderful capacity to eat our cake and have it, especially when it is cake righteously taken away from someone else who is starving to death. Our ability to ruin others in order to feel clean ourselves. Oh my.

Perhaps you would not suggest that this poem be published just now, or in the book. Someone might understand it, or connect it with Greene's book, and I'd get sent to Alcatraz for un-American activities. But it seems to me it should be published anyway, just for that reason . . .

Yes, Bob [Giroux] can show "The Neurotic Personality" [article] to [Dr. Gregory] Zilboorg.

P.S. The thing I can most think of, after *The Quiet American*, is that the Holy Spirit is the Spirit of truth but not necessarily the Spirit of big catchwords and bright slogans. And that is why we need His protection against the noise all around us everywhere.

The poem—which Merton later admitted was a projection of his own troubles onto his mother, America, the monastery, and the Church—has eight stanzas. Here is the first stanza:

> You have written, Greene, in your last book
> The reasons why I so hate milk.
> You have diagnosed the war in my own gut
> Against the innocence, yes, against the dead mother
> Who became, some twenty years ago,
> My famous refuge.

The poem was not published till 1987 in the spring issue of the Merton Seasonal, *with a fine accompanying article by Patrick F. O'Connell.*

May 17, 1956

Honestly, you may be surprised to learn that your letter of May 13 surprised me. I don't mean that I imagine I ought never to be scolded, or that I thought you were going to go up into ecstasy over the Graham Greene poem. After all, I said I didn't intend to publish it right now— or ever, if you don't want me to. And I remember vaguely you never liked him.

What surprised me was that you said I had been hurting you by the letters I wrote. That is one I just can't figure out, except of course I know I said a lot of things about not liking living so much with other people, etc., etc. But haven't you caught on to the fact that that is mostly a line and that when I say it I am automatically filling up paper (which I admit is a very bad habit). What on earth is there in any of that stuff to hurt you or anybody else? Do you mean to say you take it seriously? Do you take it seriously when everybody thinks rainy days are horrible or nice days are wonderful? Who cares what kind of a day it is? Who cares about solitude? I like it, and if I can have it, all right, and if they ever put me where I get a lot of it, swell. As for living with people, I do find it uncomfortable, and it is not something I can make myself entirely happy about by pressing a button. But I was only rattling the bars of my crib because I thought you liked it. Since you finally tell me that you don't, I'll gladly stop.

The key sentence of your letter appears to me to be this one: "Every time I tell you that I think what you are doing is wrong, this is the way you reply—if you reply."

Okay, so you think the Greene poem is a *reply*. God help us. Do you really think you are my mother? It was sent you purely as a matter of business, and contains no veiled or open message either to you or to someone else except Greene—and God and I suppose my mother, God rest her soul. It is, by the way, not intended to be read to the Senators in Congress either, or published on handbills and distributed in the subways.

"What I am doing is wrong." Well, what am I doing? I am being novice master. I am not writing much of anything except five million conferences. I am trying to get a little time each day to read a book and think and catch my breath. Oh yes, the dreams. Well, I am *not* typing out dreams and distributing them all over the Middle West either. That obviously could not go on and it is all washed up since several weeks. I would never have time. What else am I doing? I am not griping as much as you think, and I am certainly griping less than I have at any time in the past twelve years. Only during that time I didn't express my gripes much to anyone, certainly not to my agent. The Greene poem contains aggressive thoughts? Well, yes. That is, by the way, one of the reasons why it is a good poem. It contains a lot of things that are in me, rather than a lot of things that are not in me.

Analysis? Yes, I can use some. With the full approval of everyone concerned, including several people who know and who say that I am neurotic enough to stand treatment, I shall be going in to the man in Louisville for a while. Maybe he'll make things nicer for you, as well as for everybody else around me. Believe me, groups of people did not "suddenly" start to become a problem just when I stopped writing, and as a matter of fact I have been griping a lot less since I have stopped writing—because I don't have to try to write and listen to machines all over the place at the same time. It is a big relief.

Believe me, I am doing nicely without the *eremos* and shall consider the subject of solitude as closed.

Of course I don't know all the context of Greene's present situation and I might be making a mistake about him, but in any case I have always found his books more interesting than those of most people who claim to be writing about the way people behave. I am sorry you are allergic to him. We don't have to discuss him either, if you are.

I think fundamentally you are sorry that I am not the person you want me to be. I am fully prepared to admit you want me to be better than I am, and even that you are able to see things that I cannot see about what I ought to be. But you ought to be warned of the fact that I react strongly—and unconsciously—against any thought of being made anybody's ideal. Maybe that is something I have to learn to take with equanimity, even though I see them making a mistake. I don't know. But for the time being I can't stand it . . .

So what's the conclusion: I am childish, I am selfish, I love to gripe. I want to complain and have someone to complain to, and for a while you were elected. I am sorry. It won't happen again, and at the same time I will make a serious effort to grow up. But please be patient. I am neurotic, you know: and I am not just using that as a convenient cover. Because it isn't a convenient cover, it makes things quite difficult in the sense that there is no quick immediate solution that can be effected by some one thing that I clearly know about—even assuming that I know about it.

This, for the moment, will have to serve as a reply to yours of the 13th. If you think it is inadequate and unsatisfactory, please let me suggest that communication is not as easy for me as you think: I mean real communication on a really personal level. You don't know yet that for me communication is not communication but a narcissistic gesture of some sort at which I happen to be quite clever. Do you think that I have ever in my life communicated with another person? Sacramentally I hope, but not in writing.

Maybe that sounds horrible, or maybe I am exaggerating because of an ideal of communication that I know will never be attained on earth— or something. But I am trying to tell the truth. That is one of the real problems for me here. It is true I seem to contact people (like novices, etc.) better than others do. But I know that in fact I am not that much in communication with them, in fact very, very little. I wish I could be, and I suppose it is really quite simple, but what do you do about the wall, twenty feet thick, that is in between?

Thanks for your letter anyway. It ought to establish definitely in my dim mind that complaints are not an effective way of getting over the wall to another person. (Especially when they are unconsciously intended as a device for reinforcing the wall.) God bless you.

June 4, 1956

One of the reasons why I write such bad letters is that I write a lot in a hurry without previously taking a moment to think what I am about to say. I haven't thought about this one either, not directly. So perhaps the best thing I could do would be to make it a little shorter and try to think a little while the paper is in the machine.

First of all, something concrete. Yes, I like the type for the prayer. I think it turned out very nicely and I hope you will let me have a few. We have Lydian [typo] here and do some cards in it (they are printing some of my bright sayings) but I hadn't liked it as much as I did on seeing this one. What is the typeface you used for your initial letter? I think Jay had it on the cover of *Thirty Poems*. Incidentally, too, I am very happy about the Cummington people and trying to think of any number of things we could have them do, but I can't think of anything. Maybe some booklet for the monastery someday. Maybe.

Now about me. (At once I get discouraged at such a beginning. You wouldn't think it, but to some extent I freeze up, even though I seem so glib when I talk about myself.) There is something I am groping for, anyway. I hope I can get to it in the next fifteen minutes. Without too much beating around the bush.

First, in a way it seems silly that I should write about myself to you. But I don't think it is. You are my good friend and one I can talk to, and I can't talk to most of those here as I can to you. It is still unconventional. Okay. But I am pretty sure by now that I am not meant to follow any beaten track. Let us assume, anyway, that it makes sense for me to occasionally tell you what is going on. I won't say cry on your shoulder, because actually I don't cry on people's shoulders, I just pretend to because I think they like it. Hence the trouble that comes from the misunderstandings created by my ambivalence. In fact, I am probably too proud to cry on anybody's shoulder, and yet at the same time I need to.

Second, I am really beginning to discover that the solitude I need is a solitude in which I talk less about myself, while staying where I am. That seems to make a little sense, doesn't it? There is such a thing as just clamming up, finally. It will at least save me from experimenting and saying things I don't mean.

Third: in point of fact, let it be known and recorded that I am, I confess, far happier now than I have been at any time since I came here.

In the last six months, for the first time, I have consistently felt that I belonged here for days on end. I have been consistently unbothered by the things that used to drive me nuts. I have found a way to fit into the place by being detached from places, in effect. I honestly am ceasing to care much *where* I am or what I am doing.

Fourth, yes, I project my troubles onto everybody else—in the Greene poem, I projected them on (1) my mother, (2) America, (3) the monastery, (4) the Church. An interesting lineup, of which I am conscious, and I think it makes a good poem. What the poem says is not that I really have anything fundamental against 1, 2, 3, or least of all 4, but that I am definitely conscious of being in hidden rebellion against all of them. (I am a fallen man, and I guess there are a few others around.) I am certainly boiling with hostilities and resistances, which are the expression of my pride as they are also of my weakness. And I am also definitely conscious of the fact that for ten years in the monastery when I was following the straight ascetic-mystic line, I was getting nowhere except into a few pretenses with which I did not quite kid myself, but did, apparently, kid a lot of other people. At the present time, by the grace of God, I am starting over again and the going is much rougher, much more colorful, and much more honest, less publishable, more fruitful, I believe. And also I do not doubt, have never doubted for an instant, that I am very much loved by God, and in fact in some way favored by Him, why He alone knows. I am always more and more aware of the fact that I am united to Him, even though, paradoxically, I become more and more aware of the fact that I am sinful enough to be plenty separated from Him. Again, I am in some things rather sure of His will, in a diffuse sort of a way (in others I am in black perplexity about the whole business). But the thing that I am surest of is that I am somehow on the right track, and the path that He wants for me is the one I am walking on, and I have no need to seek another. But by the path I am walking on I mean the concrete one I am walking on, not just the institutional Cistercian path—I mean *my* path. Which oddly enough seems to be Cistercian too. And it is going into the desert but not the desert that anyone expects. It is not going anywhere that anyone expects, including myself. And that is where I want to go; and where, by God's grace, I will go.

Meanwhile, I think I had better admit that I really have no more axes to grind and nothing to chop. Woodshed or no woodshed, my solitude is pretty much of an accomplished fact. As for the novices, sure I love them (but again, through my own fault, when I get subconsciously lazy, it sometimes becomes inordinately difficult to give them another bloody conference). (The adjective is purely rhetorical.)

As for you, you want me in the worst way to be a saint, and that of course gets me upset, because I am not, and it is precisely difficult for me to accept the fact that anyone expects anything of me. That is when I go into one of my tantrums, and is one of the natural roots of my love for solitude—a weak root, and a diseased one.

Actually, what I usually look for unconsciously is a big smoke screen of double-talk, behind which I can go the way I know I am supposed to go, without comment.

This being the case, all I need to do is get rid of the smoke screen and go my way without observing myself or thinking anyone else is too interested (because in fact they can't see it anyway).

And it occurs to me to wonder how all this may affect *you*. But I think you will be glad if I just say, or try to say, what I mean. This time I am not just saying it because I think you will like it, but if you like it I am glad, and I know your prayers for me will do me good, and your advice will too, and I also know that God has put you there on the way I am traveling, as He has put me on the way you are traveling and we are going to get there fine: that is the way we help one another into heaven. It is the Christian vocation.

P.S. Is Zilboorg['s number] 33 [on] 70th [Street]? That is where I wrote him.

On July 22, 1956, Merton in company with Fr. John Eudes Bamberger, flew to St. John's Abbey at Collegeville, Minnesota, for a conference at which the well-known psychoanalyst Gregory Zilboorg was to speak. For Merton his meetings with Zilboorg, especially the one on July 29, were an unexpectedly shattering experience: Zilboorg defined him as neurotic in his need to have his own way, and pathological in his demand for solitude.

July 30, 1956

Zilboorg has been terrific. I am infinitely grateful for the possibility of contact with him. His lectures were terrific (and there is to be another week of them) and the whole thing has been for me like a retreat—not so much a question of picking up a lot of magic technical devices as of getting a real orientation for the human needs of sick people, a sense of how to handle them (*not* manipulate them) and help them to get well. This week Fr. Abbot is here too. And six other Trappists from all over the place.

As for my own personal problems—clearly Zilboorg is the first one who has really shown conclusively that he knows exactly what is cooking. And something is, though not so serious, but serious enough to mess up my work and my vocation if it should get worse. He has told me, more directly and more forcefully than I ever thought possible, the exact home truths that need to be told, and I need not insist that the desire for absolute solitude has finally been disposed of completely and forever as pathological. Moderate isolation and silence, sure. Okay. I will never give anyone any trouble about vocation or stability again, as long as I am in my right mind. He has a solution or a possibility, about which he intends to speak to Rev. Father.

Finally, Zilboorg is absolutely against publishing "The Neurotic Personality" [the article Merton had written was sent to Zilboorg before the conference]. He says it is sheer trash and can do nothing but harm and I shouldn't even try to revise it. I should put it on the shelf and get busy really learning something about the subject, and that will take time. I thoroughly agree with him about the article.

August 3, 1956

Everything is going very well indeed, and I am very glad I was able to get up here. It was a wonderful session and I have got a great deal out of it. Zilboorg is going to keep in touch with me and will give me whatever advice he can.

December 29, 1956

[At the monastery] I am getting so used to the new dry-up campaign that I find there is really very little to say in a letter. Everything goes fine, and on top of it all for a Christmas surprise who should show up but Zilboorg. I walked in the Chapter room the other morning, on the Feast of the Holy Innocents, and there he sat, mustache and everything. All the monks fell over. He gave us a couple of talks, I had some good conversations with him from which it transpires that, though I am indeed crazy as a loon, I don't really need analysis. He now has me all primed and happy with slogans like "Pipe down," "Get lost," etc. Nothing I like better.

Everything is quiet and peaceful in the novitiate. All the novices gorged with candy and Christmas mail. Just sent them all out to the woods, so that I could get the mail out of the way—total of three letters I am writing. Virtue. One to you, one to Lax, one to Sister Thérèse [Lentfoehr]. Also wrote one to my aunt in New Zealand.

Not only do I write nothing, but I lose all desire to write anything. At least for a while. Zilboorg keeps assuming that I will want to write "afterwards."

My French translator, Marie Tadié, sent this in her Christmas card: it is "from an old Irish story."

> I said to the man who stood at the gate of the year: "Give me a light, that I may tread safely into the unknown." And he replied: "Go out into the darkness and put your hand into the hand of God. That will be to you better than light and safer than a known way."

I think that about sums up everything. Most of the time we only think we have problems. Because we want to have problems. Because to have problems is our way of being important somehow. It is not that we have to learn to be unimportant because we are already that. But not to refuse the privilege of being unimportant. Which is what we always do.

And now to return immediately to my important and business self —a nonexistent personage, kept in being by my own unaided efforts—I like the proofs of the poetry book [The Strange Islands]. I like very much the progress of the Gerhardt Marcks special edition of *The Tower of Babel*.

April 25, 1960

Thanks for the big picture of Stams. It was duly posted on the board for all to admire at Easter. I must say your adventures in Austria were not *edifying*. ("Kiss me, Kate" indeed!) Perhaps your spiritual musings will be a warning to the young and flighty. In our menology (catalogue of saints of the Order) there is a story of a boy who went about begging and playing the fiddle, entered Stams, became a big wheel of some sort, like subprior (no, it was cantor), and he hung up his violin somewhere prominently to remind him of his ascent from the depths. See any violins around when you were there?

(I got myself a new typewriter with some specially chosen funny accents, mostly for French, but after I got all through my plotting and planning I came out with no question mark.)

My own spiritual musings are about as usual, only worse. Never had such troubles with censors, so complicated, so unreasonable, so long-drawn-out. I stand surrounded by the massacred books they have rejected, and both the General and I are dizzy. Dom James has given up trying to keep up with us. Mainly they have finally sat on a project of my collaborating with the Zen man, [Dr.] Suzuki. Even when I offered to invite other equally edifying collaborators—Fromm, Tillich, etc. Why not Khrushchev? (There I go again!)

Every time I open my poor trap the least bit about the solitary life the censors set up an anvil chorus that can be heard from here to Brooklyn. After all, I am not agitating about *anything*, just saying things which people in a contemplative order theoretically ought to appreciate. Not Trappists.

We have a new setup of studies for novices, which looks good on paper but will probably come out a little differently in practice. I am at present trying to find my way out of the bushes. I suppose it will just mean a few more classes, and I hope I can get them a little more time to study, because all in all there is very little of that. I can never give them any intelligent assignments.

We are busy ripping out the floors of the dormitory wing, to replace them with concrete and so make at least part of this place fireproof. The other day I had my novices practice sliding down ropes from our third-floor window. We all did fine until we landed on the roof of the cloister, from which there is a further fifteen feet down which nobody apparently has thought of. We decided not to try jumping it unless there was a real fire.

January 7, 1964

The main thing I have on my mind, and I have written about it to J. [Laughlin] and spoken to Fr. Abbot about it, is having you and J. be my literary executors. Of course there are a lot of ins and outs, and the main thing is that you are my publishers, or about to be, but that is an advantage. You are the two people who really understand what it is all about anyway, and no one here does. Also Fr. Abbot agrees that up to a point it would be a very good thing to have this matter in the hands of someone outside the Order. Provided that it were guaranteed that the monastery would get the royalties and other monies due to it, and also that someone in the monastery would have a chance to veto the publication of any passage of a book that might bring serious discredit on the monastery or someone in it. Fr. Abbot made a point of this and this only. Wonder why? Does he think I have written a secret biography of him or something, or a novel about the place? (That last is certainly something I have often been tempted to do.) But since in fact there is nothing of this nature, that ought to leave everything else clear, even of ordinary Order censorship, once I am dead. The problem about Order censorship is precisely that it goes far beyond what is just and legitimate even in the strictest ecclesiastical censorship, because it concentrates not on "faith and morals" but on a strange vague category called "opportunity"—that is to say, whether it is "opportune" for this book to be published. Anything whatever under the sun, with or without reasons given, can cause the book to be stopped under this rubric. The head American censor agrees with me perfectly on this and has now come to a tacit agreement letting me publish magazine articles without censorship (which is perfectly normal outside our fence in any case). I am not trying to put anything over on my Superiors here.

Of course the main problem is that both you and J. are my age. But we could bring into it, as J. suggests, some young lawyer who might be interested. We can discuss it. I just wanted to put the thing before you and see what you thought. If I kick off, or get shot by the local patriots after my latest book, there will be a certain amount of unpublished material, quite a lot, much of which is already stored away at Bellarmine College. It will be made clear that they have no rights, only the "physicality" of the manuscripts. Is that word real? It is the one J. used.

I guess *Seeds of Destruction* is officially out by now. If you happen upon any review that looks interesting, please send it along.

March 3, 1964

Well, the unthinkable has happened. It usually does. A letter from the new Abbot General [Dom Ignace Gillet] came in concerning the articles on peace in *Seeds of Destruction*. [These articles were part of a manuscript Merton wrote in 1962 called *Peace in a Post-Christian Era*.] I was sure, since these had been cleared before by the previous Abbot General, with difficulties, but yet cleared and published, that I had the right to go ahead with them. However, the new Abbot General dug out all the correspondence, had a meeting with the definitors, and said that these articles are not to be "republished" in book form and implicitly in any other form.

He has, however, approved the Letters, which I was afraid he might possibly object to. This is probably to compensate for the prohibition of the other articles. But Dom James, in writing to him about the contents of the book, apparently did not make clear that the "Black Revolution" is there too, and since this has been published in France with Dom Ignace's approval, there can be no doubt that this will easily be cleared up.

Hence though formal approval for the whole book is still to be obtained, I am sure it will come soon, but we have to take out the articles on war. I am sick about this, not because of the lack of publication, but because I really thought that I was in the clear with them and did not anticipate them digging up all the old arguments. But they did. I am sorry most of all because it had to happen with this book when we had so much trouble with Bob before.

Naomi, frankly I must say that this whole thing leaves me a bit dizzy. And sick. I can't say exactly that it constitutes a temptation against my "vocation," but it certainly raises some pretty profound questions indeed. I know, one must just take it on the chin and shut up, etc., etc. But with all the attention that has been drawn to the obedience of an Eichmann and now even the question of Pius XII [the reference is to Hochhuth's play *The Deputy*], the props given by the conventional arguments don't offer much support. One is faced with the very harrowing idea that in obeying one is really doing *wrong* and offending God. I know of course that my conscience tells me that this is by no means certain and that the only thing is to trust Him and hope for the best. But it certainly wrings all the last drops of alacrity out of one's obedience and one's zest for the religious life. It is a bit weird to foresee that one may have to end his life in something that may have turned out to be the most monumental mistake. Again, I am not saying this with absolute seriousness. There is enough irony left in the whole thing, and in me, to see it also as a good enough joke. And I hope I can have the grace to be somewhat less than bitter about it. I do hope you are taking this in the right way and not too seriously, because I am not thinking drastic and deadly thoughts (much), but I do want to say something to someone and you happen to be in the position of listening at the moment. Sorry. One thing is that this probably knocks out the journal stuff that I thought would make a book. But I can prune the verboten peace stuff out of that. We'll see. Will you break this thing gently to Bob [Giroux]? I will write him when I am in a more placid mood.

March 13, 1964

I have worked out the reason for the misunderstanding with the new General [Dom Ignace Gillet]. I had asked the old one [Dom Gabriel Sortais] for permission to publish the book on peace [*Peace in a Post-*

Christian Era], and in order to sell him the idea I had said that it was *based on* the three articles which he had permitted me to publish, though there were additions and so on, since they were expanded into a full-length book. He refused this, and the present man seems to have taken this as a denial of permission to reprint the articles even in their original form.

Naturally I am feeling much more philosophical about it after the first day. When I wrote you the cut was open and full of salt. Thanks for your good letter and advice. I suppose there is not much point reflecting on it and making statements. I know exactly what the thing is. I am always grumbling about solitude and this is one of the forms it takes in my own life: a progressive alienation from people with whom normally I ought to live in perfect understanding and agreement. Having to get along without too much support in an area where no one is either very sympathetic or very interested in my ideas. Above all it means having to figure things out in a somewhat lonely and insecure way, and this brings out the fact that I have always been more dependent than I realized. But at the same time that being "dependent" is just totally useless and even dishonest in this kind of situation. The net result is having to face things alone before God and hope for the best, and to go on with this even though other people may not quite like it or understand it. I don't want to upset anyone else, and I don't think I am really doing so. But there is only one answer—that is, to get my own Cross on my shoulder and carry it, whether others think I am making sense or being heroic, etc., etc., or not. Of course the worst element in it is that I am getting in so many ways disillusioned with the Order and the Church even (that is the thing that upsets people). But I have no intention of making any kind of fuss about it, or starting a row. I will have to live with this as everybody else has had to live with it since the beginning. The modernist crisis is long since over and I am not a modernist in any case. This is a different era. And I am afraid it is a much more dour and serious era too.

Thanks for everything. Happy Easter.

August 9, 1965

Thanks for your letter of the 4th. There is of course a lot more of the journal material scattered about. I will try to send you a batch of what we have, but it is in no way to be regarded as final. Before we get busy on the publication version, I will get more typed up, and we can cut out the numbers, etc. "Truth and Violence" will be little more than one section of the whole thing. As a tentative title for the book I have thought of *A Temperature of My Own*, if not the other idea I had long ago, *Conjectures of a Guilty Bystander*. Maybe *Temperature* fits it better . . .

At the end of this month I am out of my novice job and permanently in the hermitage. I am of course very glad, and also I see that it will not be any big joke either. The more I get into it, the more I see that the business of being solitary admits of absolutely no nonsense at all, and when I see how totally full of nonsense I am, I can see that I could wreck myself at it. Yet I really think God asks me to take this risk, and I want to do this. So please pray hard, really. I am an awful fool, and I know it, but if I can just be obedient and cooperative for once in my life, this can be a very good thing for me, incomparable, in fact. Do please keep me in your prayers. I am almost getting a humble and chastened attitude toward the whole thing. Wouldn't it be amazing if after all this I really went at it in a spirit of humility and faith, instead of just making noises and demanding it all as a right?

August 10, 1965

Here are the roughest rough copies of two other sections of the Journal. "Night Spirit" and "Dawn Air" are to be in *Blackfriars*. "Barth's Dream" was in the *Sewanee Review*. The only other copies that are decent I am keeping here to work on, as I don't want to lose them, and this is only to give you some idea what is cooking. You can keep all those sections together there, but they are not intended in any way to be definitive. I will also enclose with these a copy of "Truth and Violence," which is perhaps more complete. I don't know. I can't remember exactly what you have.

August 17, 1965

This is just to thank you very, very much for your really understanding letter. In a thing like this, which is so strange in its way, it is good to have you really catch on immediately. And it is better still to have your support and your prayers. I am grateful for all these things. And I am really very hopeful for the future, even though my system is acting up furiously at times. That is the way it has to be, and I am glad it is so.

One thing that is very clear to me: this going into solitude is really what I must do. I know, if one can ever be said to know, that this comes from God and that I must obey Him. Of course, what my mad stomach tells me is that He has lured me out there to destroy me. But of course I don't "believe" such a thing. And in the long run what is happening is the kind of acceptance where one says: "Look, if you want to destroy me, that's fine, because I would rather be destroyed by you and to please you than to have everything else in the world and not be pleasing to you." And the funny thing about this is that I absolutely mean it, and I can't think of anything else in the world that makes sense or calls for two seconds of interest, compared with this. Of course I would like to go out and be a hermit in grand style, but I realize that I will probably be a pretty silly one, but I don't care, I'll make the best of it I can, with God's grace, and if it is absurd, well, classify it as existentialism and forget it. But I think, in my stubborn head, that it is the real fulfillment of my monastic vocation. Also, however, I am aware that since there is much lacking in me, the lack is going to make itself felt. That is where I am going to rely on people's prayers to tide me over, because the list of things I lack would take up more paper than the pile of junk I sent you and which, it does not surprise me to hear, was so packed that it all came apart. I think I know who does the packing out there, and I suppose he must be fed up with all the stuff he has to pack up for me and for everyone else, and perhaps does not think too hard about what happens to mail in transit.

Meanwhile, I am really confident that, as you say, if I just plunge in everything will really be fine, and it actually has been so far with the quiet semi-hermit routine I have had all year. What happens now is just that it is taking on the shape of an "event" and I suppose even a drama, though I don't consciously get dramatic about things. This time perhaps, without meaning to, I am. So let's hope I calm down by next week. Saturday is the day I officially "begin." Actually all this stuff about beginnings and the BIG DAY is most of the trouble. It is too artificial, but that is the way we operate.

I am certainly thinking of all the people you mention and will keep them all in my prayers, all the more so as it is a good thing to think about other people's troubles rather than one's own. I had a good rest in the hospital but everything started acting up again when I got home, what with the cleaning out, the moving, etc. However, it is not all psychosomatic, because the bug that began it all this spring was for real.

Meanwhile I propose to keep happy by working on the *Guilty Bystander* or whatever we want to call it. I like the title with *Guilty* in it, the way I feel now (feel guilty for having it so good). And will keep after other writing, peacefully and quietly. Incidentally, my friend John Wu is doing a terrific book on Zen, though he is having a time writing it so it connects with the reader. But the material is most interesting. I mentioned it to New Directions, but I think you should know about it too. It might be more for Doubleday than for ND.

God bless you, and I do appreciate everything so much, and though I am such a damn defensive being, I do love you very much, as you know. God bless you in everything.

August 25, 1965

About the hermitage: the five days I have been here all the time have been simply perfect, and everything seems to indicate that it will go on that way, but of course the original joy of it will doubtless wear off but for one thing I have no doubts: this is exactly right for me. It is all that I ever hoped for and more. For once I have got something that I can bite into and really work at without wasting time looking for something else. And that is really quite extraordinary, I think. I still see that it is going to be hard, but at least it is going to make sense. No one minds doing something difficult if he has sufficient reasons for tackling it. I can see without difficulty that if I really want to live the kind of life I came here for, then this is the sort of situation I must do it in. They have been the best days since I came here to Gethsemani twenty-five years ago, without any shadow of doubt. This is what I am here for, and thank God I have found it, because it was very likely that I might never have done so. Think of that: living all your life right next to what is just what you came for, and never getting into it. I hope that I have the sense and the faith and all the rest it takes to get into this and make of it what is there to be made of it. Still sounds incoherent. But I am very happy and thank you and everyone for all the prayers. Keep them up, and I pray for you too, and God bless you always.

August 31, 1965

I enclose a long article on existentialism which I did for *The Critic* ["The Other Side of Despair: Notes on Christian Existentialism"]. (Do you know this magazine? It might be interesting.) The bit for *Motive*, a magazine you don't know, I imagine, mostly Protestant, published in Nashville, might possibly go with the "Behavior of Titans" stuff. J. wanted a new title for that and I have what I think is a fairly passable one: *Raids on the Unspeakable*. It is an improvement, I think, on a phrase from Eliot's *Four Quartets*, "raids on the inarticulate." It sounds a little more sinister, and therefore good for a title. What do you think?

Before putting me away in my state of rest Fr. Abbot gave me a rush job to do for the monastery, a postulants' guide, you know, one of those things where the monks blushingly tell everyone how wonderful monks are. After that I want to get down to typing out more journal material for you. I would like to have the whole book in your hands by late fall. But I can't promise to be too exact about that. I will do my best.

Am settling down fine, actually I have stopped thinking about whether I am a hermit or what, and am simply living, with plenty to do, lots of reading, work, long meditations, and really this life makes an enormous amount of sense for me. It really does, and is doing me a lot of good in all sorts of ways. I am much less frustrated, spend less time mentally arguing against the ideas of the Abbot, stomach is much better, am utterly simplifying all meals I take up here, cooking practically nothing except soft-boiled eggs, and everything is working out fine, only problem I have had really was that I got into a difference of opinion with a nest full of hornets and was quite badly bitten. Believe me, those things are fierce. But fortunately it seems that I am not allergic to hornet bites so I didn't swell up as some people do. They were painful, however.

Thank God they finally got around to letting me live this kind of life. I can see now how much I have been needing it, and also I can with difficulty see how I lasted so long in the community setup without going into orbit around Mars. I see how much support I have had all along from grace, when I thought I was navigating on my own. Here one realizes that very keenly. It is the best thing about living alone.

October 26, 1965

Tomorrow I hope to send off the manuscript of *Barth's Dream and Other Conjectures*. (This strikes me as a better title, but you may not agree.)

I am just finishing proofreading the ms., which has a lot of typing errors in it, and I don't guarantee to have caught them all. In particular, though, I think it needs cutting. If you feel that there is too much pessimism and too many lamentations about the technological society, please feel free to cut where you see fit, because I am bothered by this myself. I think you will probably be most annoyed by the same bits that leave me wondering. I turn out to be a very querulous character. One can get by with this in community, because one can spread the querulousness out nice and thin over a wide area. In solitude it gets a bit concentrated, and I am now quite earnest about getting rid of it.

October 30, 1965

Thanks for the letter. It is perfectly all right about the title. I recognize that you are the best judge on that and I agree that the title is really better [*Conjectures of a Guilty Bystander*]. As to the list of books, here is a more complete one. But I don't think they should all be printed anywhere in any list you put in a book. I think we should customarily leave out the really bad ones, *Exile Ends in Glory*, *What Are These Wounds?*, etc. I usually leave out *The Last of the Fathers* too, as being not much more than a pamphlet.

Thirty Poems	New Directions	1944	Verse
A Man in the Divided Sea	" "	1946	Verse
Figures for an Apocalypse	" "	1948	Verse
Exile Ends in Glory	Bruce and Co.	1948	Biography
The Seven Storey Mountain	Harcourt, Brace	1948	Autobiography
Seeds of Contemplation	New Directions	1949	Religion
The Waters of Siloe	Harcourt, Brace	1949	History
The Tears of the Blind Lions	New Directions	1949	Verse
What Are These Wounds?	Bruce	1950	Biography
The Ascent to Truth	Harcourt, Brace	1951	Theology
The Sign of Jonas	" "	1953	Journal
Bread in the Wilderness	New Directions	1953	Theology
The Last of the Fathers	Harcourt, Brace	1954	Theology
No Man Is an Island	" "	1955	Religion
The Living Bread	Farrar, Straus	1956	Theology
The Strange Islands	New Directions	1957	Verse
The Silent Life	Farrar, Straus	1957	Religion
Thoughts in Solitude	" "	1958	Religion
The Secular Journal	" "	1959	Journal

Selected Poems	New Directions	1959	Verse
Spiritual Direction and Meditation	Liturgical Press	1960	Religion
The Wisdom of the Desert	New Directions	1960	Religion
Disputed Questions	Farrar, Straus	1960	Essays
The Behavior of Titans	New Directions	1961	Poems, Essays
New Seeds of Contemplation	" "	1961	Religion
The New Man	Farrar, Straus	1961	Religion
The Thomas Merton Reader	Harcourt, Brace	1962	Anthology
Life and Holiness	Herder and Herder	1963	Religion
Emblems of a Season of Fury	New Directions	1963	Verse
Seeds of Destruction	Farrar, Straus & Giroux	1964	Essays
The Way of Chuang Tzu	New Directions	1965	Verse
Seasons of Celebration	Farrar, Straus & Giroux	1965	Religion
Raids on the Unspeakable	New Directions	1966	Prose Poems, Essays
Mystics and Zen Masters	Farrar, Straus & Giroux	196?	Essays
Conjectures of a Guilty Bystander	Doubleday	196?	Essays, Notes

TRANSLATIONS: *Clement of Alexandria, Selections from the Protreptikos, The Solitary Life, A Letter of Guigo the Carthusian.*
TRANSLATIONS OF VERSE BY: Raïssa Maritain, Jorge Carrera Andrade, Nicanor Parra, Fernando Pessoa, Ernesto Cardenal, Pablo Antonio Cuadra, Cesar Vallejo, etc. Published in New Directions anthologies.
EDITOR: *Breakthrough to Peace*, New Directions, 1963; *Gandhi on Non-Violence*, New Directions, 1965.

February 4, 1966

Let me assure you that I am in much better shape than I would be if I were in the community. They have flu there and the overheated place gets you sweated up, so that when you get out into the open you are immediately chilled. I have not yet had a cold this winter though we have had one of the longest cold spells I can remember. As to the food, since I get one good cooked meal daily at the monastery I really think there is nothing to worry about. Breakfast is simple, toast and coffee, surely I see no harm in that. I don't make a steady diet of sardines but after all there are Fridays. I can boil an egg or two whenever I like. There is absolutely nothing whatever to worry about. I am in good shape and very satisfied with everything . . .

July 15, 1967

I have always thought it would be a good idea to do *Seven Storey Mtn* and *Sign of Jonas* together like in a Modern Library Giant. Maybe that is a silly notion. Or even *Secular Journal* too: thus all the autobiographical stuff in one fat book. I am not attached to this idea, but think it might be done.

September 26, 1967

John Slate, my friend who was going to take care of the legal end of the literary estate, has died. However, today I talked on the phone to a man at his office, Barry Garfinkel, who wants to carry on with it and sounds interested and efficient. I am willing and glad to have him do this, though at first I had thought it might be better to transfer the whole thing into the hands of a Louisville lawyer.

The way it was explained to me: under Kentucky law, executors for a will have to be in Kentucky itself. But the lawyer suggests setting up a trust and you and J. would then be the trustees. I have authorized him to get in touch with you both. Or at least to catch J., who might be easier to see than you. With my friends dying right and left (Ad Reinhardt died a few weeks ago) I would really like to get this all tied up shipshape, finally.

The next book I hope to deliver will be, unless you strongly object, the *Journal of My Escape*. I have got the ms. from Ed [Rice] and gone over it making a few more changes, and it is now being typed. I do think it reads well, just as well as it ever did (at least to me), and I think this is a reasonable time to try it out again. I hope you agree.

October 19, 1967

I am answering your letter right away because . . . if you can possibly come in November, I wish you would. Several things have come up, and if you can possibly make it then, I'd be most grateful . . .

First of all, in strict confidence (though it is now generally known not only in the monastery but all over Kentucky!), Fr. Abbot is planning to retire . . .

Then, on Jay's urgent advice, I have dropped the idea of going on with Barry Garfinkel and got a Kentucky lawyer who is well on the way to having things sewed up pretty soon. Dom James may want to discuss this around about mid-November, and it would be immensely helpful to have you there when, by exception, I make a new will (which is probably what will be required). The plan is to set up a Trust with you and J. and a Kentucky resident (Tommie O'Callaghan) as trustees, and to have the Abbey formally agree to this. Then we will be in the clear and everyone will presumably know where everyone stands and be happy with it. And the next Abbot won't have to worry about it.

January 19, 1968

The new Abbot is Fr. Flavian—one of the other hermits and hence obviously all in favor of hermits. That is fine, because other candidates were not! He is the best of the lot, and the one I voted for, the one most people seem to like, the one most in favor of a serious monastic life, not wildly experimental but for real development. I think he still needs to develop, he is young and inexperienced, but has possibilities.

No more for now. I must warm up some soup, haven't had anything to eat for a couple of days practically. Just tea and fruit juice.

February 27, 1968

This is about the Cargo idea. First of all, the tape is on its way back to you. I checked it and it is perfectly okay.

Cargo movements properly so called originated in New Guinea and Melanesia around the end of the 19th century and developed there especially after World War II. But analogous movements have been cropping up everywhere in formerly colonial countries, and starting from Cargo as such I tend to find analogies all over the place, not only in "Black Power" but even to some extent in Catholic renewal as practiced by some types.

A Cargo movement is a messianic or apocalyptic cult movement which confronts a crisis of cultural change by certain magic and religious ways of acting out what seems to be the situation and trying to get with it, controlling the course of change in one's own favor (group) or in the line of some interpretation of how things ought to be. In some sense Marxism is a kind of Cargo Cult. But strictly speaking, Cargo Cults are means by which primitive and underprivileged people believe they can obtain manufactured goods by an appeal to supernatural powers (ancestors, spirits, etc.) and by following a certain constant type of pattern which involves: (a) complete rejection and destruction of the old culture with its goods and values; (b) adoption of a new attitude and hope of immediate Cargo, as a result of and reward for the rejection of the old. This always centers around some prophetic personage who brings the word, tells what is to be done, and organizes the movement.

Though all this may seem naive and absurd to Western "civilized" people, I, in common with some of the anthropologists, try to spell out a deeper meaning. Cargo is relevant to everyone in a way. It is a way in which primitive people not only attempt by magic to obtain the goods they feel to be unjustly denied them, but also and more importantly a way of spelling out their conception of the injustice, their sense that basic human relationships are being ignored, and their hope of restoring the right order of things. If they want Cargo it is not only because they need material things but because Cargo will establish them as equal to the white man and give them an identity as respectable as his. But if they believe in Cargo, it is because they believe in their own fundamental human worth and believe it can be shown in this way.

All the essays in *Prophets and Primitives* point somehow in this direction: "Sacred City" = the primitive order. "War and Vision" = another primitive way of understanding life. "Shoshoneans" = the relationship disturbed, Indians as inferiors. "Cross Fighters" = an attempt at violent resistance (with apocalyptic and Cargo-like doctrinal background). There will be a piece on the Indian Ghost Dance v. important Cargo-like movement in Western U.S. Then Cargo itself.

A generalized sort of approach like this is feasible for an amateur such as I am. It permits me to reflect on these things and bring out insights here and there. My type of approach.

If, on the other hand, I attempt a whole book on Cargo I am more or less committed to deal with some of the very tricky professional and technical problems that are arising all over the place. The field of Cargo Cults [is] one of the most active spots in anthropology today and I just am not up with all the material: that is a full-time job. But a reflective essay or two may not be out of place for someone like me, along with other essays like the ones I have. I have got good reactions from an anthropologist on the "Sacred City," for instance.

Also, really, if I were to do the type of book you want (okay, amateur!) I would then have to visit the scene and meet some of the people, which is impossible. Since I can neither deal with the technical questions as a pro nor go to Melanesia as a cultured and hep amateur, I think I'd better keep my sails trimmed the way they are.

I hope I can get this stuff on paper sometime in the next two months. I can (I mean now "Cargo" and "Ghost Dance"). I may have something of a book ready for delivery in the late summer, though I have no desire whatever to rush it, to sign a contract, or to tie myself down. *Vow of Conversation* will be along in, say, two months . . .

Many thanks for the CARE package, which got in yesterday. I love Riceroni, had it before, and the Lipton Dinners look superb . . .

March 3, 1968

More I think of the other, *Vow of Conversation*, the more I see it will have to be held up, because it gives too many details about the hermitage and so on. Problem is that people come here and can find their way to it. And more and more people come. I've been chasing them out. Lately, too, one mystical (?) lady appeared on the scene. Quite a sane-seeming girl but with a whole new lowdown on the Apocalypse and a whole new program for *me*, if you please. It looks as if she is going to be a problem, but she has not, thank God, come up here yet. Only to the gatehouse. If I need a refuge, can I escape to Maine and stay with you and Ned?

May 4, 1968

Well, here it is the evening of Derby Day and I do not even know who won. (Just feel funny, not superior. After all, in Kentucky!!—everyone in Louisville having big Derby Day parties, at which I confess I am glad not to be) . . .

By the way, my old aunt [Agnes (Aunt Kit) Merton] (the one who visited here four years or so ago and who is in *Conjectures*) was lost in the Wahine disaster (big shipwreck in New Zealand). I was awfully sorry about it. Survivors said she was terribly courageous walking about and telling everyone to cheer up. She was among the many who were lost between the ship and the nearby shore, even though they had life belts. Heavy waves, etc. It must have been very wretched for them all. (Life rafts capsized and all the rest.) Do pray for her. She was a very dear person and about the last one in the family really close to me. I'm sure she is in heaven anyway, but I pray for her. Dom James has finally moved into his hermitage, all finished, with all kinds of modern improvements. It is the awe of the land.

June 27, 1968

The reshuffled ms. is on the way to the NY office with a new title: *My Argument with the Gestapo*. Could be subtitled "A Macaronic Journal" 1941. I have rearranged the chapters and now I think the sequence is as it originally was intended to be, more or less.

Take a look at the Contents and see if it would not be fun just to title the chapters like that. I think it has a curious effect.

I have cut a little, drastically in a couple of places, and am willing to consider more cuts and making the macaronic language more intelligible to "the average reader" in spots. Open to suggestions. But am very attached to the speech on literature to the storm troops just as it is, length and all.

And even open to a little judicious additional writing to fill out on some of the people, if that would help. Note that my guardian has been a bit disguised because his wife [Iris Bennett], a prize neurotic, wanted to sue me for what was said in the *7 Storey Mtn.* I might disguise them both a little more.

August 19, 1968

Monks Pond has turned into a nice little magazine, I think, but having accumulated material for four issues, I'm quitting. The business of losing poems, failing to answer letters, hunting all night for mss., and getting buried under piles of material in 100 degree heat—this is finally turning me off. But I expected it.

Be sure you have your four copies, your set, which will one day be not only historic but fabulously valuable.

2. Merton's Schools

OAKHAM

I have many glowing memories of Oakham.
TO CHRISTOPHER DIXON

To C. (Christopher) J. Dixon

Merton attended Oakham School in England from 1929 to 1932 and during his stay he became editor of the school paper, The Oakhamian. In 1954 Dixon, who was then editor of the paper, wrote to Merton, who replied on November 9, 1954. In the spring of 1991 this letter was forwarded to the Abbey by Danny Rondo, who found the letter tucked into a book he had purchased at a secondhand bookstore. Noticing that Merton's letterhead read: "Our Lady of Gethsemani, Trappist, Kentucky," he thoughtfully mailed it to the monastery, expressing the hope that it would be "useful" for their archives.

November 9, 1954

Your letter was a very pleasant surprise. I assure you that I am glad to hear from my old school, and to hear that things are going along well. Above all I am glad to hear so many familiar names. Thank you.

I have often thought of Oakham in the years that have gone by since I was there. How long it seems! I even remember dreaming about the place once, during the war. I dreamt there was an air raid and—oddly enough—I sought refuge in Wharflands. So doubtless my subconscious feelings about Wharflands are still very good. I remember two of my closest friends were in Wharflands—C. A. P. Winser and J. R. Dickens. J. L. Barber, of course, I remember too. And his brother "Carnera." I take it Barber is now a Master there.

And then Mr. Moore, and Mr. Duesbury! How well I remember them both. Especially the cavernous tones in which Mr. Duesbury used to recite the "Road to Mandalay" during the supper we had at the end of each term (or was it each year?). Give them both my affectionate regards. Mr. Moore will be surprised and, no doubt, edified to hear that one of the things I most regret about my stay at Oakham was my lack of zeal in the study of Greek. I really wish I had used my opportunities. I could use some Greek now. I would like to read the Greek Fathers in the originals—the best I can do is find my way through the New Testament.

I am glad to hear that Hodge Wing has been tidied up a bit, and that you have so many new buildings. And you play hockey now! Glad to hear about the victorious seasons. Do you still play the same teams? Worksop, K.E.S., Boomsgrove, Bedford Modern, Trent? (I don't think I have typed those names, or thought of them, since I was editor of *The Oakhamian*.)

Really, I have many glowing memories of Oakham and the O.O.'s [Old Oakhamians]. The last person I have heard from was "Tom" Sargant, who, at the time, was living in Devonshire. I have never been in contact with any of my contemporaries there, although I tried to reach some of them. Is the old Head, Mr. Doherty [Headmaster 1929–1934], still at Lancing [College]?

Above all, I remember the countryside around Oakham most vividly. I can still see Burley fishponds, and Egleton, and Lax Hill. I remember the village of Brooke. Do you still run cross-country through that valley, and over Brooke hill, down by the rifle range? [These places are all mentioned by Merton in *SSM*.]

With all these thoughts in mind, I am glad to be able to tell someone at Oakham that I really bear the school a deep affection, with sentiments of gratitude that will not die. I know that what I wrote about the school in my book was perhaps not flattering. But I am sure readers will have seen that I was not trying to describe the school objectively, but rather the state of my own mind there. I never regret having gone to Oakham. On the contrary, I am very glad that I was sent there rather than to some larger school, for Oakham had something of simplicity and sincerity about it that one might look for in vain elsewhere. The school, the masters, and the boys were quite genuine. I hope they still are, and do not doubt that everything is as it was in that respect.

So I close with the hope that Oakham will reach its zenith not only in sports but in the deeper things as well. A school is a place in which one prepares to lead a productive and happy life. Therefore it must be a place in which one comes to know something of the ultimate spiritual values that men have to live by. I have never believed in professional piety, or sanctimoniousness. The sanctimonious generally manage to make spiritual things unattractive. But I hope that Oakham will always be able to teach her sons that they have souls, and that there is no more important

task in life than for a man to safeguard the integrity of his deepest self—
to know himself and to know God and, in a word, to "save his soul."

This is my prayer for you, Dixon, and for all who are now teaching
or studying at Oakham. It is above all my prayer for all my friends and
contemporaries who doubtless remember me as anything but a man of
prayer. God bless you. Needless to say, I send my best regards to all
those who remember me.

COLUMBIA

*There is a kind of sanity and magnanimity about Colum-
bia that has a profound importance in the world of today.*
TO GRAYSON KIRK

To Alfred B. Hailparn

*In 1936, Merton was named editor-in-chief of the Columbia yearbook, The Co-
lumbian, to be published in May 1937. During the summer he wrote to the
managing editor, Alfred B. Hailparn, whose father was a liquor distributor in
Yonkers; Merton's well-known fondness for beer makes its appearance in the
second of these two letters. They are among the earliest Merton letters yet discovered; he did not graduate from the college until June 1937.*

Douglaston, L.I., N.Y.
June 18 [1936]

Many thanks for the letter. I had been trying to think up some way
of getting in touch but didn't have your address & couldn't get hold of
[Peggy] Noonan [secretary in the King's Crown office at Columbia] to get
it.

First & most important: tell Anne Donohue to go to hell. It is too
late now, as we have signed with White [as photographer]. I'm sorry you
didn't get a free picture or something.

We signed Garamond Press as printers again and I'd like to know
where the hell they are with that stationery: if, for instance, they sent it
to Columbia or what?

I was up on the campus yesterday. I took White's man along & got
a number of swell shots around the place. Just wait until you see them!
Furthermore I am going to make another trip up there with him, & get
a lot more: I want plenty of pictures of campus in the book, & there are
lots of swell old cuts too.

Thanks for taking the trouble to write out the names of the people.
I shall get to work on the motley crew with an encouraging letter in July
or August. Meanwhile as soon as stationery & stuff arrive I'll try to rally

[Robert] Veitch & [Frederick] Mackenthun around the banner for some concentrated selling.

I am working 8 hours a day up at Radio City these days, so I have not had much time to scout around myself. However—the time will come.

As to engravers—they can wait. I have my eye on a bunch called Hammersmith Kutmeyer now signed for Yale & M.I.T.—they are nice people.

Much later. Meanwhile, take it easy.

Douglaston, L.I., N.Y.
August 20 [1936]

Fred Mackenthun & Bob Veitch came down to see me on the job today, & we had a little talk about advertising. They will probably write to you for some blanks, although we are more earnest in getting prospects lined up than hopeful of getting any signatures on the dotted line as yet.

At any rate we got together & talked things over, and we are each going to work independently on a bunch of prospects that appear good to us individually, taking care not to overlap on each other's preserves. This is all more or less independent & informal but it is a step in the right direction. I thought you would like to hear about how things are progressing so as to know what is what up until the time comes when you can join in.

By the way, I was wondering if you might not have some likely connections through your father's business—do you think there are any possibilities through such channels? Far from being a question of advertising out of charity it would show certain advantages—college men drink a lot of beer!

Well, let's hear from you, Al. Meanwhile so long and good luck.

To President Grayson Kirk, Columbia University

June 16, 1961

Yesterday evening I received from the Father Abbot of our monastery the University Medal for Excellence which was awarded to me *in absentia* at the recent Commencement Exercises. The time has come for me to break the silence which has hitherto been my only contribution to the rather complex arrangements which have permitted me, by your kindness and by the indulgence of my Alma Mater, to receive this honor without being personally present at the Commencement. And so I want to say now, very warmly and sincerely, that I am deeply touched by this gesture.

As a monk of sorts, I suppose I have reached the point where, through confusion as well as through virtue, the honors of the world no longer have the kind of impact I would have expected in the days when I longed for them without receiving any. But this does not mean that my heart does not respond to the human meaning of this award. On the contrary,

I can and must say that my response is to acknowledge very heartily the love which I have never ceased to have for Columbia and which has grown with the years. And by Columbia I mean, of course, not the plant but the people. Hence, to be recognized by men whom I respect as the movers of a great and forward-looking body of learners and teachers is to me not at all insignificant. On the contrary it has about the only kind of significance that counts for one who is concerned with the future of his country and of humanity: it gives a sense of solidarity and approval in the attainment of aims which are, in their deepest essence, spiritual.

As a Christian thinker and as a priest, I know it is my duty not only to pay homage to the God of truth but to serve Him in His world, by helping to build the ever changing but ever living organism whose real destiny is to manifest His truth in action. Though human society is almost always far from this ideal, and perhaps very far from it in our own day, we must remember that the important thing is the striving and not the realization. We are only responsible for what we are able to accomplish.

I have said elsewhere, and I repeat it here, that there is a kind of sanity and magnanimity about Columbia that has a profound importance in the world of today. Receiving a medal from the University makes me feel somehow part of this, and encourages me to hope once again that a little of it brushed off on me while I was there, and that I can communicate something of it to a coming generation.

The work that is being done at Columbia in the humanities, in Oriental studies too, continues to interest me. I am presently engaged in studies that work toward a broad integration of Oriental and Occidental philosophy and spirituality (not, I hope, purely eclectic). I feel it is necessary for Christians to recognize the profound meaning of the natural wisdoms that have remained alive in the Orient, and that this recognition can help us to appreciate forgotten elements in our own spiritual tradition. I am very interested in keeping in touch with those who might be working along these lines at Columbia.

I might also throw out a kind of suggestion, since I am on the subject: among your Oriental and perhaps African students there might conceivably be some who would have an interest in seeing our monastery here and perhaps discussing matters of this kind. I am at present engaged, in a small way, in what one might call retreat-seminars of this type, occasionally. Last year a couple of faculty members of Union Theological Seminary were down and I hope more will return. I leave this to simmer in your thoughts.

Needless to say, President Kirk, if you yourself happen to come to this part of the country you should consider yourself cordially invited to our monastery. I would ask permission to speak with you and thus have the pleasure of meeting you. Just drop us a line if you are coming down this way. There are no complications, we have a roomy guesthouse and always a lot of visitors on retreat.

Once again, I am deeply grateful to the University and yourself not only for the generous award but also for the added favor of allowing me to receive it through the gracious intervention of my dear friend and teacher Mark Van Doren. I hope you will convey these sentiments of mine to all the others who have a part in giving me this happiness, among whom I have no doubt Dr. [Jacques] Barzun is to be numbered.

To Arthur Hays Sulzberger

Mr. Sulzberger (1891–1968), chairman of the board of The New York Times, *wrote to Merton that Grayson Kirk had shared the preceding letter with him. He said: "It moved me very much . . . I take exception to only one thing you have to say. You 'feel it is necessary for Christians to recognize the profound meaning of the natural wisdoms that have remained alive . . .' As a Jew I should like to share in that. I can sense no conflict." Sulzberger also asked Merton for his thoughts on the situation with respect to Nationalist and mainland Chinese.*

July 26, 1961

Your very good letter of the 6th has reached me. I am of course delighted that Grayson Kirk saw fit to share my letter with you. I am sure there is much that can come of an exchange of ideas. He speaks of perhaps coming down sometime, or of some of the Columbia Faculty coming down for some conversations. If you should feel inclined to join such a group you would certainly be very welcome. Nor is there any need that one come as part of a group as the doors of the guesthouse are always open. The only problem is that my own contacts with guests are limited and my schedule requires that I give top priority to the novices, whose spiritual director I am.

I have just spent a couple of days with a very lively young rabbi [Zalman Schachter] who is in the Hasidic tradition. We have discussed all aspects of spirituality, the Bible, and natural wisdom, ranging from Rabbi Nachman to Zen and the Christian mystics. From this concrete example you see that there is no disagreement in my mind with your statement that it is necessary for Christians and Jews together to share these same interests.

You mention the problem of the political recognition of Red China. As I do not know the terms of the treaty made with Chiang Kai-shek, or too much of the historical details of what has taken place since then, it would be very rash for me to say anything too specific about what should be our policy at the moment, from a purely pragmatic viewpoint. But Red China is getting to be more and more of a fact. Moral obligations are certainly realities in their own order, but facts too have to be taken as they are. Whatever we are to do in the political sphere, it is certain that we have to "recognize" Red China as a reality of huge import. I think that we have tended to confuse loyalty to our Nationalist Chinese friends with a sort of tendency to treat Red China as something quite provisional.

As if it would be bad form to admit interiorly that they are here to stay. And Mao Tse-tung is one of the greatest minds in Communism, one of the more formidable powers in that formidable movement. So the "recognition" which I suggest is in the order of knowledge. The *Times* can certainly, in every way, take cognizance of the realities that are there and see them objectively, and *study* them.

Americans, as a whole, are in a state of appalling ignorance with regard to the world they live in. Most of them have not even the vaguest notion of Marxism. Their reaction to Communism is emotional, irrational, because not based on knowledge. This is the most dangerous possible situation, because when irrational and easily scared people also have at their disposal immensely powerful destructive weapons, awful consequences can result from a mere movement of shadows, a mere stirring up in the imagination. And in actual fact the threat is greater than we imagine. Yet at the same time knowledge is the beginning of strength and of effective resistance, as well as of creative solutions. And we are, I believe, obligated before God not merely to defend what we have but to advance toward the creation of a society that transcends what we have and what they have. We have the obligation to build, and not with wishes. Truth is the solid foundation of freedom, and truth only.

As I stop for a moment to reflect on this uncalled-for sermon, I see that it may imply things by no means intended. As I do not often see the *Times* (or any other paper), I cannot say exactly to what extent our papers are giving accurate and objective information on China today, and how deep the probing goes. But we really need to probe. I do get the Paris weekly digest of *Le Monde*, in which there has been some excellent material not only on China but on many other countries. I am sure the *Times* is doing much the same thing. And if I make a suggestion, it is with the awareness that it has probably already been done long ago.

But since we need to know Communism: how about a series on Marx in the Sunday *Times Magazine*. Say six articles on various crucially important aspects of Marx. Marx and history, Marx and business, the Marxian dialectic, and one article, for which I might rashly offer my own inadequate services, *Marx and religion*. From what I know of this last question, this is extremely complex and also interesting. Because the religious alienation which Marx fought has been more perfectly actualized, I believe, in the society from which he thought it would automatically vanish. Now here is, I think, the point where we need to use Marx. We need to know Marx in order to turn him against the present-day pontiffs of Marxism.

Permit me one more paragraph to enlarge on this. It is the pseudo-philosophical aspect of Marxism—I almost said the pseudo-religious doctrine—that gives it its greatest power of appeal in a world of disoriented people looking for a coherent set of beliefs that will seem to fit the modern world. It is because America has no coherent philosophy to offer to the nations of Africa, or at least none that is easily recognizable

as such, that we tend to get nowhere among them. This also goes for
Latin America. We underestimate the intellectual appetites *and capacities*
of these people, who, because they are economically underdeveloped,
we imagine to be inferior in most other realms besides. This is a fatal
error. It is lack of respect for the Latin American mind and its culture
that has helped, among so many other things, to ruin us in those countries . . .

I have gone beyond the proper length of a letter and by now you
must be ready to turn to something more important. But in any case I
am sure I have convinced you of a deep and friendly interest and involvement in the problems of the *Times*, which is a great paper, and one
for which some of my closest friends have worked and probably still work.
I think, for example, of Foster Hailey, from whom I have not heard in
about ten years now. If by chance he is around I hope someone can
convey to him my good wishes.

To Mark Van Doren

The Van Doren letters may be found in The Road to Joy, *edited by Dr. Robert*
Daggy. The following letter was not available when that book was published.

August 30, 1957

Your letter was wonderful. The idea of the autobiography is a fine
one, and I am sure it will be a fascinating book. I cannot wait to read it.
I hope you will put me on the list for a copy, if you have a spare one.

I would be a hypocrite if I tried to pretend I was not very happy to
be in it. Of course you can quote and say anything you like. I do not see
how I could possibly say no to any such request, coming from you. And
I would hardly be tempted to do so.

You have really seen a lot of events and people. And I am sure that
looking back you have thought that really the last thirty-odd years around
Columbia and New York, and wherever else you have been, have been
filled with life and very productive—not only in you but all around you
as well. I cannot say I know precisely what sort of "movements" have
been moving in America. I am hardly placed for announcements as to
where everything is tending. But I feel sure that things have been moving
with you and around you, and in the right direction—there are other
movements in the other direction.

I can only say that I am sure the book will teach me much, and leave
me more indebted to you than ever, for it is not always possible to see
a whole section of a century through the eyes of someone like you. You
are one of the few people around to whom God has given wisdom.

The best news of all is that you hope to come through here on the
way to Illinois. I am so glad we will have a chance to talk again and this
time I hope I can arrange to show you a little more of the monastery. Of

course everything will be all right. I have Father Abbot's permission. The 28th will be on a Saturday. If you get here before eight in the morning you can hear the conventual Mass sung, and from nine o'clock on I will be able to be with you and Dorothy.

Did I ever send you the notes on Genesis I promised you last year? I think I did not. So I am sending them out today. They are only a skeleton, of course. I have no intention of making anything more of them. I am going on with Exodus and not even trying to hold on to the notes this time—it is better to prepare sitting under a tree with a pencil, rather than pounding a typewriter.

My novitiate is getting along nicely. There is a Nicaraguan poet [Ernesto Cardenal] in it, a quiet and pleasant fellow who was once at Columbia for a while, about ten years ago I should imagine. He did not take your courses, but sat in on one occasionally, he says. We are getting others from Latin America, and I am beginning to hope we may make a foundation down there. Nicaragua would be ready to roll out all sorts of carpets for us, and a man down there who grows ipecac in the jungle (a Scotchman who has become very rich) tells of a big island in the Lake of Nicaragua—an island with two volcanoes and hence very fertile, which used to be sacred to the Indians and might just as well become sacred to Trappists. Here it is not jungle, and one could farm at the 3,000 level growing more temperate crops as well as coffee . . . Father Abbot, however, spurns Nicaragua. All right—then there is Venezuela, Colombia . . .

I am enclosing a picture of the St. Benedict statue we have here in the novitiate. It is not bad, and we have another like it of St. Bernard.

ST. BONAVENTURE UNIVERSITY

St. Bonaventure's represents one of the happiest periods
in my life. It was a transition stage.
TO ANTHONY L. BANNON

To Anthony L. Bannon

On February 7, 1966, Anthony Bannon, editorial staff writer for the Magnificat, *the weekly journal of the Roman Catholic diocese of Buffalo, wrote Merton informing him that the paper planned to publish several feature articles on St. Bonaventure University. He invited Merton to put in writing some recollections of his brief teaching career at St. Bonaventure. Bannon wrote: "An important strain of thought and reference that runs through the University is a remembrance for some and a legend for others of you and your brief stay there."*

February 12, 1966

First of all if you want material about me, there was an article in the Louisville *Courier-Journal* recently. If I can dig up a copy I will send it, but I know Fr. Irenaeus has several and could lend you one.

I will briefly say a few words about St. Bona's, of which I have the most pleasant memories. It was really a providential step along the road of my vocation. As you know, I first thought of being a Friar, but that did not work out because Fr. Edmund, down in the provincial's office in N.Y. (he was the provincial's secretary at that time), thought I was still too new a convert and was not yet ready. I had had a rather wild life, certainly wilder than most of the holy postulants who were entering that year at Paterson. However, I decided that I wanted to at least live with the Friars, in the atmosphere of a Franciscan college. St. Bonaventure was really ideal. I felt that I was in contact with the authentic simplicity, cordiality, and charity of St. Francis. These Friars were good, warm friends. I felt they accepted me and I certainly liked them. I also liked the Sisters of the Immaculate Conception, also Franciscans, who worked in the kitchen and worried about my eating, and packed up box lunches for me when I went off to spend the day alone in the woods. The box lunches they gave me seemed to indicate that they thought I was not one man but a squad.

It was when I was teaching English at Bona's that I first began to write poetry that was halfway respectable, and I wrote quite a lot. Living there in that quiet atmosphere, under the same roof with the Blessed Sacrament, I was able to cut out drinking and smoking and with my head clear I was discovering a lot of new things about life: namely, that it could be pretty good if you gave it half a chance.

I remember especially among the Friars Fr. Richard Leo, O.F.M., who was teaching English along with me, Fr. Cornelius, who was my boss, and of course Fr. Tom Plassman, who was the President and a great good friend. Of course there was Fr. Philotheus, the expert on Occam, who gave me some tutoring in the philosophy of St. Bonaventure along with one of the seminarians, now Msgr. Richard Fitzgerald, of Erie. Fr. Philotheus was the one to whom I went for advice about entering the contemplative life. There were other Friars I knew well, like Fr. Joseph Vann, whom I had met at Columbia, but who was at Siena when I was at Bona's. Fr. Juvenal I remember, and of course all those too numerous to mention whom I used to meet and talk with on campus. Of course last but not least was my old friend Fr. Irenaeus, who remains my link with Bona's, as we occasionally correspond about books and other such things. He still lends me books, I have one of them here now.

Naturally there were lots of lay professors and other eminent lay figures such as Griff on the campus, whom I will never forget. The lay profs used to eat together and razz each other a lot: Ray Roth, Dick Engel (who was head of the ROTC at that time), Sunny Behm (is that how it was spelled?), and others who lived off campus like Jim Hayes. It was a great bunch and I enjoyed every minute of my time at St. Bona's. If I tried to recall all the students there would be no end, and I still remember a lot of the names.

To sum it all up, St. Bonaventure's represents one of the happiest periods in my life. It was a transition stage. God had something else planned for me, but it was a necessary stage. I will be forever grateful for the hospitality of the Friars, and will always feel that I am still in some secret way a son of St. Francis. There is no saint in the Church whom I admire more than St. Francis.

3. *Reading, Writing, Reviewing*

*Thoreau . . . expresses the real spirit of American per-
sonalism and freedom, the ability to be a non-conformist
and to "listen to a different drummer."*

TO HARRY J. CARGAS

To M. R. Chandler

M. R. Chandler of the San Francisco Examiner *invited Merton to respond to a
questionnaire about book reading being sent out to the paper's readers.*

July 19, 1963

I hope these answers are satisfactory. I read a lot in Latin, French,
and Spanish, besides English, and I always have at least three books going
at the same time. I tried to keep it simple and understandable, and hope
I have not failed.

One question you have not asked: about authors whom one might
consider too little known and too little read. One of these in my opinion
would be the late Ananda K. Coomaraswamy, whose field was Oriental
art, but who actually had a great deal to say about the meeting of Eastern
and Western culture. This is a topic of vital importance today. One rarely
sees this great man in paperbacks, though almost everyone manages to
get there at some time or other.

Reading, to my mind, means reading *books*. I don't think magazines
alone meet the requirements, because even with a heavy magazine you
can get in the habit of skipping around (of course you can do this in a
book too). But normally with a book you have to get down to business
and keep on reading continuously, so that if it is a book with any substance
at all you are forced to think. The real joy of reading is not in the reading
itself but in the thinking which it stimulates and which may go beyond
what is said in the book.

Traditionally, for a monk, reading is inseparable from *meditation*. I
would be interested in seeing the column in which you make use of this
material.

The following are the questions, with Merton's answers:

1. *Name the last three books you have read.*
   The Platform Scripture of Hui Neng, translated by Wing Tsit Chen
   The Proslogion by St. Anselm of Canterbury
   A Different Drummer by William Melvin Kelley
2. *Name the books you are reading now.*
   Homo Ludens: A Study of the Play Element in Culture by John Huizinga
   Ratio Verae Theologiae (The Real Meaning of Theology) by Erasmus
   The Historian and Character by David Knowles
3. *Books you intend to read.*
   Apology to the Iroquois by Edmund Wilson
   The Silent Rebellion: Anglican Religious Communities, 1845–1900 by A. M. Allchin
   Cur Deus Homo by St. Anselm of Canterbury
4. *Books that have influenced you.*
   Poetic Works of William Blake
   Plays of Aeschylus and Sophocles
   Summa Theologica of St. Thomas Aquinas
   Sermons of Meister Eckhart
   De Doctrina Christiana, *Confessions*, and *Sermons on Psalms* of St. Augustine
   Rule of St. Benedict
   The Bhagavad-Gita
   The Imitation of Christ, etc.
5. *Why have these books been an influence on you?*
   These books and others like them have helped me to discover the real meaning of my life, and have made it possible for me to get out of the confusion and meaninglessness of an existence completely immersed in the needs and passivities fostered by a culture in which sales are everything.
6. *Name a book everyone should read.*
   Besides the Bible (taken for granted and not included above) and such classics as *The Imitation of Christ*, I would select a *contemporary book* which I consider to be of vital importance and which I think everyone should read at this time: *The Fire Next Time* by James Baldwin.
7. *Why this book?*
   This is the most forceful statement about a crisis that is of immediate importance to every American, and indirectly affects the whole world today. It is something that people have to know about. The Negro has been trying to make himself heard: in this book he succeeds.

To Lorraine

April 17, 1964

You ask how a Catholic writer can have "the greatest possible influence on his public." A seemingly innocent question, but to a writer, and to one in my position, it is more complex than it appears.

What do you mean "his public"? The writer's "public" is a very mysterious entity and it is certainly different from the Publisher's Public and the Reviewer's Public. There is a public that reads the blurb on the jacket and then, if it reads the book at all, sees it only in the light of the blurb—or the review which copied the blurb. If that is the public one is to "influence" then what matters is to have good blurbs and lots of advertising and bang-up reviews, and if possible a pretty good and original image of the writer himself.

This, of course, is a waste of time and an indignity, and is not worthy of consideration in a serious man's mind.

The writer who has "influence" on the people who really need to read him must have something important to say, and something that is important *now* or perhaps tomorrow, later than now. And he must want to say it to the men of his time, perhaps even to others later. But it must be a bit desperate if it is going to get out at all. And if it is desperate, it will be opposed. Hence no writer who has anything important to say can avoid being opposed and criticized. Thus the writer who wants to—let us say reach, or help rather than influence people—must suffer for the truth of his witness and for love of the people he is reaching. Otherwise his communion with them is shallow and without life. The real writer lives in deep communion with his readers, because they share in common sufferings and desires and needs that are *urgent*.

Of course the writer has to be articulate and he has to write well. He has to take his craft seriously. As for the Catholic writer, he has got to do something better than to put the catechism in a new form that will appear to be "catchy." He may have to say some things that shock his fellow Catholics. I don't claim that he says *nothing but* these things that shock, but sometimes he may have to.

To Mr. Lunsford

December 12, 1964

It was very kind of you to think of sending me the little book of Terrence Gray. It is most valuable and full of very accurate insights. I appreciate very much having such a book at my side and I have been reading it often and thoughtfully in the hermitage, where I am fortunately able to spend quite a lot of time, day and night. It is a good book to keep one spiritually alert. I have no hesitation in saying that the "Buddhist" view of reality and of life is one which I find extremely practical and acceptable, and indeed, I think it is one of the very great contributions to the universal spiritual heritage of man. It is by no means foreign or hostile to the spirit of Christianity, provided that the Christian outlook does not become bogged down in a slough of pseudo-objective formalities, as I am afraid it sometimes tends to do. But I am very grateful for this book, and will be looking for a way to get some of the others. Perhaps the simplest thing would be for me to write to Mr. Gray and propose an exchange of some of my books for his.

This fall I had the pleasure of meeting another student of Buddhism, Marco Pallis [see *The Hidden Ground of Love*], who has written a couple of excellent books on Tibetan Buddhism, from firsthand contacts.

May 26, 1965

You will certainly enjoy the Nishida book [Kitaro Nishida, *A Study of Good*]. My review is not yet published, as things move very slowly with our quarterly. When it does eventually appear I will be glad to send you an offprint, if you remind me. That will probably be toward the end of the year or early next year. [It actually appeared in *Collectanea Cisterciensia* in 1967 and in *Zen and the Birds of Appetite* in 1968.]

Has Dr. Suzuki said anything about coming to this country again this year? I suppose it must be getting harder and harder for him to travel. You mention the possibility of coming down here yourself. There is no question of my being here, I am never anywhere else. But my visits are very limited and I have only one or two more allowed me for this year. One of these is precisely at the end of October, a friend from Vienna [Hildegard Goss-Mayr] who is active in trying to get something said in the [Vatican] Council for peace and against the bomb. It is very important that I see her, so I will not be able to fit in another visit at that time. I am sorry.

I am hoping that New Directions will soon bring out a book I have done on Gandhi [*Gandhi on Non-Violence*], and I will gladly send you a copy when I get it. Again, you may have to remind me of this, say about July.

As I am reviewing books on Buddhism for the magazine of the Order, if you run across anything important I would be glad to have it drawn to my attention so that I can get a review copy.

To Mr. L. Dickson

Mr. Dickson managed a bookstore at the University of Delaware in Newark.

September 12, 1965

In replying to your letter of August 25th, I will be glad to say something about the importance of *reading* in college since I know, from my own personal experience as an undergraduate and then a graduate student at Columbia, that reading and personal contacts in college can be absolutely decisive in a person's life.

It seems to me that a man or a woman goes to college not just to get a degree and a good job, but first of all to find himself and establish his true identity. You cannot go through life as a mask or as a well-functioning biological machine. Man is a being whose reality cannot be left entirely to forces outside himself, nature, society, events. We become real in proportion as we accept the real possibilities that are presented to us, and *choose from them freely and realistically* for ourselves. This act of choice implies a capacity to judge, therefore to think. It implies some kind of personal philosophy and a personal faith.

The reason why judgment and decisions are so important today is that a person, especially in college, is suddenly presented with such an overwhelming amount of material—ideologies, philosophies and pseudo-philosophies, religions and religious fads, movements in art, literature, politics, and new developments in science and technology—that he *has* to make a choice somewhere. If he fails to choose, he is lost in a confusion of contradictory notions that end up by meaning absolutely nothing. In which case he can either go crazy, or else become an insufferable square with a few mechanically pronounced dogmas instead of genuine thought.

Therefore, if a man is going to make authentic judgments and do some thinking for himself, he is going to have to renounce the passivity of a subject that merely sits and "takes in" what is told him, whether in class, or in front of the TV, or in the other mass media. This means serious and independent reading, and it also means articulate discussion.

If this letter will encourage students to read more widely, more critically, more eagerly, and if it helps someone to find books that will revolutionize his life, then I am glad to have written it. I might mention, though, that the quality of the books one reads and of the thoughts one "buys" certainly does make a difference. The mere fact that an idea is new and exciting does not necessarily make it true. Truth is important and the whole purpose of thinking is to be able to tell the difference between what is true and what only looks good.

I don't care whether or not the readers of this letter buy *my* books. But I might mention a few authors who have helped me a lot. Among moderns: Maritain, Gilson, Karl Barth, Camus, Pieper, Pasternak, Fromm, Eliot, Jaspers, Gandhi, Guardini, Suzuki. Among writers of the past: Plato, Lao Tzu, Confucius, Plotinus, St. Augustine, St. Thomas, St. Anselm, St. John of the Cross, Dante, Shakespeare, Cervantes, Pascal, Blake, Kierkegaard, and of course above all the Bible.

To Harry J. Cargas

Formerly of the Queen's Work, *Harry J. Cargas was editing a series of articles for a book for Herder and Herder. He invited Merton to contribute an article on St. John of the Cross. The two letters Merton wrote him touch on other subjects: the just war, pacifism, solitude, and Thoreau.*

October 13, 1965

I have been pondering on your letter of September 30 and of course if you are so anxious to have me in the series that you will do most of the work, that changes matters for me, doesn't it? I will certainly change my attitude to the point of doing a book for you if you get me the material and I have only to pick the best essays and write an introduction.

The hesitation that remains: does it have to be St. John of the Cross? I like him fine and all that, of course, but I hate to get simply identified with his kind of spiritual outlook as if I had no other interests but the contemplative life precisely as it is seen by him. How about somebody else?

The question then arises: must it be a Catholic? Is someone like Eliot excluded? Does it have to be a writer? Or are painters and sculptors included? Here are a few people I might perhaps prefer to John of the Cross in this instance: St. Anselm, Origen, Pascal, Soloviev, Bultmann, Bonhoeffer, Dostoievsky, Auden, Pasternak, Wm. Blake, Flannery O'Connor.

Boiling those down to the three best (for me to handle, I mean) let's say St. Anselm, Origen, and Soloviev—with Flannery O'Connor. In case you don't want a non-Catholic.

Whatever you have to say about peace, Pope Paul's speech at the U.N. certainly cleared things up a bit. I would say in parentheses that you should probably be a little critical of the term pacifist, which implies a religious or ethical code based on the idea or article of faith that all war is by essence evil always and everywhere. The present position of most Catholics is that war has ceased to be a reasonable and just method of solving conflicts (I mean most modern Catholics who see that it is evil at all). It is important not to be identified merely with a sort of fringe group mentality, though I have all the respect in the world for the bona fide pacifists. But they don't cut any ice, just precisely because they are a fringe group and one can dismiss it as an article of faith which they believe and no one else does. The position of the Pope and of the Council (I hope—I haven't seen what has been said) is that war can no longer be tolerated as the normal form of last resort in international conflicts, and this by reason of universally accepted moral norms. Much stronger . . .

February 14, 1966

Okay, a word about Thoreau since you ask.

The only references to him in my writing are few and I think really only one in *The Sign of Jonas*. And I do not know exactly where. I don't think I have any unpublished references to him either. I do remember once saying to Mark Van Doren in a letter (unpublished, I think. I don't believe it is in the letter section of *Seeds of Destruction*) that Thoreau and Emily Dickinson made me glad of being an American.

At Columbia I had Joseph Wood Krutch as one of my English professors, as well as Mark Van Doren. Both Thoreau men, but I did not have them in any class where Thoreau was treated. I liked Krutch and we got along very well (he gave me all A's and in fact an A+ on some of the work I did for him). Hence it is not so much that I was indoctrinated with Thoreau's ideas as that I have always agreed with his outlook and with those who see things the same way. In fact I did not seriously read him until I came to the monastery, and the one book of his that I have really read is *Walden*. I am living a Walden-like sort of life now, as a matter of fact. Some of my students have acquired a great liking for him here in the monastery. In fact, however, I have been attacked by a rather stuffy old professor in Rome (a Camaldolese, whom Dom Leclercq calls an arrant conservative) because he says my love of solitude is too much like Thoreau's. Hence my love for Thoreau is something that conservatives have against me.

One of the things I like best about Thoreau is not usually remarked on. It is the fact that he is something of a bridge builder between East and West. Gandhi liked his essay "Civil Disobedience," and Thoreau had a liking for Oriental philosophy. So do I. I have a book on that coming out this year [*Mystics and Zen Masters*], I hope. Thoreau, to my mind, expresses the real spirit of American personalism and freedom, the ability to be a non-conformist and to "listen to a different drummer." I remember now I have a line or two on him in my book *Conjectures of a Guilty Bystander*, which is a notebook, parts of which have appeared in *Harper's* and elsewhere, and which is slated to appear in the fall. Actually, though, I only quote something Emerson said of him.

That's about it. I wish I could have given you more. It is not that I have immersed myself in Thoreau, it is just that we are birds of a feather, I suppose.

To David H. Scott

Mr. Scott was the religious book editor for the McGraw-Hill Book Company.

January 25, 1965

It was a great pleasure to receive Pope John's *Spiritual Journal* in proof. I had heard of the book and was very anxious to read it. It did not deceive my expectations. It is a record of deep piety and unquestionable sanctity, full of delightful and unexpected details about the inner life of a great and holy and utterly simple man. But I think the importance of the book lies partly in the fact that it is the expression of a very traditional and in some ways almost hackneyed spirituality. It is utterly *ordinary* in its content: there is nothing in the piety of Pope John that would surprise or disconcert the ordinary and average "faithful." This might at first sight seem strange to those who particularly appreciate the breath of renewal and change which began to sweep the Church when Angelo Roncalli became Pope John XXIII. But in fact it shows, to the Catholic mind, that the Johannine renewal was not a revolutionary break with the past but a charismatic fulfillment of the living and timeless demands of the Gospel.

To N. Chatterji

A Rabindranath Tagore scholar who was living in London.

October 29, 1965

Thanks for your kind letter in which you ask for my personal reaction to Rabindranath Tagore. I am sure that in asking for this, you were prepared to get only a partial and perhaps not very profound answer, since I am by no means a student of Tagore: I have an educated Westerner's acquaintance with him, nothing more. I will give you my thoughts for what they are worth, and if you feel that they are of any use to you, please feel free to quote them as you please.

Tagore is the kind of writer whom my Father and Mother admired and whom I therefore grew up to respect. But also, as often happens in such cases, I respected him more than I read him. I might say that I neglected his whole generation, apart from dutifully reading a few plays of Shaw and Ibsen. Thus I am afraid that I have never seriously read his poems. It is not that they repel me, they never aroused any special interest, and it is possible that as I grow older I might one day turn to them. So far I have not. I have indeed a little book of his translations of Kabir which I like very much indeed.

I have read his prose here and there, I know of him through Romain Rolland's letters on India, I admire his ideas. I honestly think that though he is dated in some ways, there is a genuine and lasting value in his "wisdom." It is more than just something that goes along with the white beard. I really think that he said a great number of sensible things, that he had very sound judgment, I respect his insight, which at times seems to merit the name "prophetic." In a word, I think he knew what he was talking about. He was not simply fabricating pompous clichés, though one might be tempted to think so from the tone, at times . . . I think he makes unbiased and nuanced judgments about East and West, and I agree with his insistence on the need for a unity between them that preserves essential differences. Thus, though I have never participated in a Tagore cult, I can say that I have a healthy respect for his thought and for his person, and he remains in my mind as a great man of the early twentieth century. But I think I have been more influenced and impressed by two other Indian writers of his time. The first—not really a writer—is of course Gandhi. The other, perhaps less well known, is I think the Indian to whom I owe most, and that means a great deal. It is Ananda Coomaraswamy. It is in him that I find the most valid synthesis of Eastern and Western thought. I think he is much neglected, and I certainly think he went very much deeper than Tagore and had a greater mind.

Why was Tagore popular with my parents' generation? Because so many of them were open to the East without knowing precisely what they were open to. They wanted some Eastern figure with whom they could, to some extent, identify themselves, and Tagore made a definite enough impression to fill this role admirably for the West. Hence his popularity, and hence the readiness of the Europe of the turn of the century and World War I to listen to him with reverence as a spokesman of Asia. Naturally it was too big a responsibility for any one man, but he did not altogether fail to meet it, at least in a rough-and-ready sort of way. Do you think I am wrong? Today, of course, we see the whole situation in perspective, perhaps a better perspective, and he seems a bit of a cultural entrepreneur. In all fairness I think him a great man.

I hope these few lines are of some use to you, and I will be interested to hear how your work progresses, perhaps even to see the book when it is published. I realize that you cannot give copies to everyone, but I would appreciate hearing when the book is out, and I can get it from a library.

To Marie Cantlon

Ms. Cantlon was an editor at Harper & Row, New York.

May 5, 1968

It took some time for Mary Daly's book [*The Church and the Second Sex*] to reach me. However, I am reading it now with great interest. I wish I had time to write a review of it for some publication, but unfortunately I have too many other things to do. Here's a statement, which, of course, you may quote if you wish.

Mary Daly has given us a hard-hitting, highly original, and even revolutionary little book unmasking the latent anti-feminism of so much Catholic thinking and practice. The real impact of the book is not just in the area of crass and obvious discrimination, but in its "exorcism of the mystique of the eternal woman." She has brought out with relentless and sometimes infuriating clarity how this supposed idealization of woman in fact masks a mutilation of human persons—both men and women. She writes with such passion that some readers might think she was advocating conflict and competition between the sexes: actually, she is talking about the more difficult and important work of achieving authentic partnership on a personal level. I am grateful to her for many new insights.

To Hugh Garvey

Publisher and editor at Templegate, Springfield, Illinois.

September 3, 1967

Yes, I like the Rosemary Haughton book [The Transformation of Man]. I think it will really help. You are right that I am swamped by such requests, and each time I respond to one I am likely to get more. But one acquires a certain independence in these matters. If I like a book and have time to say so, I'll say so.

Historians of theology will quite possibly look back on our age as the "Age of Rosemarys" (at least in English-language theology). Or perhaps the "Age of the Mothers of the Church." Some of the more interesting theological insights today are coming from women and mothers. Evidently there is an aspect of theology which is not revealed to you until you have a baby, or several, and tried to bring them up. This is an admirable book, an existential theology of love and encounter, a fundamental statement and witness to the salvation event in daily life and in areas where, to an exclusively clerical theology, it was not previously visible.

To Jack T. Ericson

Jack T. Ericson, curator of the special collections at the University of Syracuse Library, wrote to Merton asking for some of his writings, especially unpublished works, that could be placed in the collection of distinguished American writers. There are presently four large boxes of Merton materials at the university's library.

March 23, 1968

I quite understand your problem. Several years ago I came up against it and realized that in my case a fully tidy and professional solution was already impossible. Several collections had already sprung up spontaneously—and doubtless irresponsibly. I had left manuscripts at St. Bonaventure when I came to this monastery thirty years ago. I had also given many manuscripts to a friend [Sister Thérèse Lentfoehr] who was intent (and is still) on bequeathing them to Georgetown [actually they went to Columbia]. Manuscripts had found their way into other collections. Bellarmine College came on the scene quite late. When I pointed out that other collections existed, they said at Bellarmine that this was a fact they were prepared to live with—always hoping for a merger with one or other of them later. In all these collections there is a mixture of manuscript and printed and other material—drawings, photographs, etc.

For my own part I have become accustomed to this plurality: it has one advantage at least for me: material is in different places and will not all be destroyed if an accident happens to one of them. Copies can easily be shared.

Your letter is the first one I have seen that takes a very definite stand and represents what seems to be now a universal policy. I would like to know more about this. Would you spare a moment to spell it out clearly for me? Could you send any brochures or other information? Is it customary for an author to establish *one* collection only and put *everything* in it? I can see this would be most convenient for scholars. Yet with the grants and travel money available today I don't think I for one would mind going around to two or three different places. It would make a nice change.

However, one thing I cannot do: I cannot give Syracuse a complete and exclusive collection of manuscript material. This is out of the question. If you feel it is not ethical to give manuscript material to another collection—or for your collection to accept it—then return the mss. I have sent and I will put them in one of the existing collections. But if you feel you can keep them, you are certainly welcome to do so. I presume there is no problem about mimeographed and printed materials. But perhaps these do not concern you? I can, at any rate, gladly continue to send you any material that you are prepared to accept and what would be useful for you.

Meanwhile, interested as I am in this question of collections, I would very much appreciate complete information on what is now accepted as the most professional policy. None of the curators so far has made any kind of problem about it. Any references to pertinent articles, etc., would also be most welcome . . .

April 13, 1968

Many thanks for your letter of the 9th. The solution suits me very well, though it is not in every respect perfectly tidy—and cannot be. I suppose that if anyone ever decides to work on my mss. and other materials he will have to get a special grant to chase them all over kingdom come. Actually, though, since I tend to have a lot of mimeographed material and offprints, tear sheets, etc., which will probably never come out in a book, a collection such as yours can be helpful to students even when it is not "the" collection. I shall certainly keep you in mind for material of this kind above all. And if I send you anything unique, a manuscript or something, if the Bellarmine or some other collection needs it they can contact you for a Xerox. I will inform them, and of course they will be glad to do the same for you. In this way I think that the various collections will supplement each other instead of competing—or appearing to do so.

I am mailing two more envelopes, and will continue to send things from time to time, including old materials as they turn up. I would say that I probably have a very unusual amount of material printed in strange out-of-the-way places and in publications to which few if any libraries in this country subscribe. So I will keep you in mind with all of these. And with future issues of *Monks Pond*.

A couple of items are enclosed.

To John Allen Eastman

Merton mentions frequently in his letters that people continually sent him man-uscripts and asked for advice about publishers. Some he answered; some he did not. Eastman, a poet, had sent Merton a collection of his poems and asked for the usual advice and help. Merton did not respond and Eastman wrote a second letter asking that his poems be returned, with or without a critique. This letter is included here as an example of Merton's responses to such requests.

September 13, 1967

Most sorry. If you knew. I get buried under manuscripts every day of my life, they are lying all over the place, they are blocking the view, they are falling in my food.

It happened that the other day yours fell out of a pile when I was looking for some drawings, so I knew just where it was when your letter came.

Really I like the poems very much. The one called "Poet," with the interpretation attached, is very sensitive and rich. One that moves me most is most curious dream of dead child.

New Directions very stuffy about taking on anyone new now. I wouldn't send it to them. Have these been to the mags? Lots of new magazines would be friendly to them . . .

Sorry again. I'm not really that much in touch with publishing, etc. For some reason people imagine I know everybody. I am better ac-quainted with, say, the possum who came up and sniffed at me during my meditation at 3:45 a.m. today. He does not publish books as far as I know. Very gentle delicate dumb possum.

4. Religious Life

*We should avoid forms of spirituality and piety that make
us too aware of ourselves and of our precious interior
lives and inner experiences . . . The great thing is to be
free in the forgetfulness of self.*
TO A RELIGIOUS

To Sister Anita (Ann) Wasserman, O.C.D.

*Ann Wasserman, daughter of Edmund and Margaret Wasserman, entered
the Carmelite Convent of Cleveland in 1952. Several years earlier her
brother, Edmund, had entered the Abbey of Gethsemani, where he became a close friend of Thomas Merton. His religious name was Brother
John of the Cross, and Merton refers to him as "Cap" and "Cappy"
(nicknames which resulted from his father's remark the day he was born:
"The captain has arrived!"). When the Wassermans visited their son at
Gethsemani, Merton was always included; in fact, they "adopted" him
into their family. Ann, whose religious name became Anita, had written
to Merton once before entering Carmel. The rest of the letters were written
after her entrance.*

*This set of letters is of special import, as it is one of the few ongoing
series of letters dating from the earlier period in Merton's monastic life.
The spirituality expressed, especially in the earliest letters, provides an
insight into Merton's earlier views on the spiritual life. They tend to show
a more devotional spirituality (somewhat comparable to what one finds
in* The Sign of Jonas) *than do his letters from the 1960s, where a more
contemplative view of spirituality predominates.*

May 3, 1952

Many thanks for your letter. I was glad you wrote. The element of
attraction is not the most important thing in a vocation. You do not need
to reflect on that too much. The attraction is there. I am glad you think
it is more an attraction to God than to Carmel. You ask if the apparent
monotony of the Carmelite life (which now does not seem as exciting as
it seemed at first) affects your vocation. If the attraction to a life with
Jesus remains, even gets stronger, while the sensible attraction to the

Carmelite life diminishes, and if at the same time you feel a kind of obscure conviction that you can really find Jesus in Carmel, then I would say this was a very good sign and that you had a real Carmelite vocation . . .

Look at it objectively in the light of faith and with common sense. Do you really think that you will find Jesus in Carmel? Then go. What you are looking for is Jesus, and He is hidden. You are not just looking for an interesting life with Him: you are looking for Him. To find Him is to be hidden, even from oneself. To live thus is sometimes very monotonous: but under the monotony is deep peace and pure joy which we are sometimes hardly able to understand, but which is worth any sacrifice: it is the joy of pleasing God alone and of living in such a way that our left hand doesn't know what our right hand is doing. However, before you make any decision for final action, I would visit those three Carmels at least and speak to the Mother Prioresses. Do not feel that you have to wait until you find an ideal Carmel. There is nothing ideal on this earth. When I came to Gethsemani I knew it was only going to be partly what I "wanted," but I found God here anyway.

Would you like me to show your letters to Father John of the Cross? He would be happy. I send you his love with my own prayers and blessing. I'll have to answer the question about prayer later.

November 21, 1952

If Cleveland is as cold and gray today as Kentucky is, I will take that to be a good sign, because it is good to begin the religious life without sensible consolation and to continue without it. Not that consolation is useless: but since Jesus knows when we need it, we can safely let him decide when we ought to have it.

I don't know whether it was a sensible consolation for me to offer Holy Mass for you this morning, but my heart was certainly full of joy and gratitude, and I asked Jesus with all my heart to make you one of His saints. And if you are faithful to Him He certainly will. I know you will be faithful, because I think you will be able to understand what is the true way to sanctity. It is simply a way in which we lose all esteem for ourselves and find out more and more that we are nothing and that we are worth nothing, and that Jesus is everything. Souls who fail to find Him in religion are those who never learn to appreciate their own nonentity. That is something very hard to appreciate. It is impossible to feel good about being what we are. But we must take our eyes off ourselves and realize that all our joy comes from Jesus and from Him alone. Then we no longer strain our eyes trying to find some reason for rejoicing in ourselves. There is none . . .

Forgetfulness of His love is the one thing that saddens Him. You have come to Carmel only to seek His love and to let Him love you. You belong to Him alone, and that should be enough to keep you happy always, no matter what may come. Pray for me, Ann. I owe Jesus so much, and I thank Him most of all for having made me even more of a nonentity than anybody else, so that I can love Him more— I am nothingness twice over.

February 25, 1953

I swear your name is spelled with one "n." [She had spelled it "Annita," as she wanted to keep "Ann" in her name.] It is a Spanish name, and in Spanish Ann is Ana and Little Ann is Anita. But that is not what I wanted to write about . . .

You seem to be fitting in to the life of Carmel just as you ought. I think you are made for Carmel, and Carmel is made for you.

It takes a little time before you get a really balanced and well proportioned view of the life. At the beginning, the adjustment calls upon so much inner stress that, whether you know it or not, you do not quite see things in perspective. That is why some of the details you mention seem so large and yet, as you yourself realize, they are probably not the "important things that will lead me to Him."

All these isolated observances are means to an end, and you will soon get used to using them: in fact I am sure you are already using them as they should be used. It remains for you to see them, not as isolated means but as parts of a whole.

The "important thing that will lead you to Him" is the life itself, Carmel as a whole, or rather Jesus Himself, living in you and living in that little community which He has chosen and formed to be all His own . . . One of the things that pleases Him most is to see a soul who lives the religious life trusting far more in His mercy than in her own merits or virtues. In practice, that will mean falling short of the highest perfection in almost all that we do, but making up for it by finding consolation in being loved by Him and in realizing that His love for us is in a certain sense all the greater in proportion to our weakness and involuntary imperfection. We do not want to be imperfect. On the contrary, we desire perfection. But we see quite clearly that our own powers can never raise us to perfection. We are content to try, to make the poor efforts that are within our reach, and not be saddened by the poverty of the results. For after all, one thing is necessary: to please Him. If we want to please Him, we succeed. That is very easy, and it is everything. But it demands great faith, because we seldom see any evidence that we are pleasing Him, especially if we are not very pleasing to ourselves . . .

You know, in your letter, there was a great difference between the questions about meditation, etc. and the little paragraph about your walk with Jesus. The latter was the real thing, and it was so simple and so completely you. It is really quite easy and spontaneous for you to be with Him when you don't have to think about it too hard and when you don't have to observe yourself "doing something."

In examination of conscience, we should never think about faults that do not constitute any problem for us. Our conscience will tell us when they really constitute a problem. If there is no problem, then general dispositions of sorrow for sin and of love for God are enough to occupy us at that time . . .

In meditation, the less conscious you are of performing some special "exercise" the better off you will be. If a book helps you to keep relaxed and free and un-self-conscious, then it is a good thing. However, don't just read all the time. The purpose of meditation is to get us in contact with Jesus. It is like making a phone call. When you have got the person you want to talk to, you don't hang up immediately and then ring up all over again. Sometimes the line is busy, however. Then you ring again. Only make sure that the line is not busy at your end when He is trying to reach you . . .

I keep you in my Mass and in my prayers. Happy solitude!

May 21, 1953

. . . Ann, I think your soul is just as it should be. Do not try too hard to see anything special in yourself or in your actions. You must be very simple and value all the little ordinary things of Carmelite life for no other reason than that they are pleasing to Jesus. Soon the life will seem just as ordinary as every other life. Probably does so already. And that will strike you as struggle. You will feel as if there were something lacking. Nothing is lacking, if you have the faith to see that there is one big difference—the only difference: you are leading an ordinary life that is *entirely consecrated* to God. It is not yours, but His . . . What is valuable is what is real, here and now. The present reality is the reflection of an eternal reality, and through the present we enter into eternity. That does not mean that everything becomes shadowy. The saints more than anyone else appreciate the reality and value of everyday life and of created things around them . . .

We have to see not only the nothingness of things and not only their value but their nothingness and their value both at the same time. In that way we avoid a temptation of contemplatives who despise ordinary things not so much because they are nothing in the sight of God but because they are boring to ourselves. Boredom and detachment are two different things. This may seem strange: but sometimes, when prayer is dry, it is good and praiseworthy to look at some real created thing and *feel* and *appreciate* its reality—a flower, a tree, the woods (for you, the garden!) or even a person. (But there you had better be careful.) Just let the reality of what is real sink in to you, and you find your soul spontaneously begging to pray again, for through real things we can reach Him Who is infinitely real .. .

November 6, 1953

Since I have been adopted by the family, your letters rate as family mail and the last one was held up until All Saints. I don't know if they are going to do this regularly. Anyway, I was happy to have it and to hear from you.

Cappy is just beginning his retreat for solemn profession today. The weather is beautiful and yesterday he went by triumphantly waving the key to the enclosure gate so I suppose he is out in the depths of the forest, God bless him. I am glad he is so happy. You must use the good qualities you share with him—reserve and good sense and a good kind of independence and fidelity to God's will for *you* which may be quite different from His will for everybody else in the universe. And he really loves God with a lot of deep spontaneity. He is a real person, and an unspoiled person. I have watched him go through the rough spots of early religious life in which he could quite easily have become slightly warped and artificial, but he didn't. I know you won't either. The first rule of all life is to be yourself, because that is the only way we can be real. We have to take ourselves quite simply as we are . . .

And now for your letter . . . As for Scripture, I do not say you should strictly read it every day. But I do think you should try as best as you can to get a taste for it. That, I admit, is not easy. It means reading something about it—and you may find the books on St. Paul a little heavy. I have not yet found a practical introduction to Scripture that really clicks with the scholastics here . . . I still think you are right to stay out in the garden alone when you can. You ought to see our hermitage—it is called St. Ann's, by the way!—it looks out over a rather ragged sort of landscape: blue distant hills, lots and lots of sky, and then closer at hand a yellow bluff with a lot of cedars climbing all over it. It is in an out of the way corner that no one ever goes to, but even there you can hear machines in the distance . . .

. . . With the list of books you send, your reading seems to me to be orthodox but a little thin. I hardly know what to suggest to put more vitamins into your diet of books. That will help your prayer more than anything, though. Stick to things like St. Theresa and St. John of the Cross—and the Bible. St. Thomas' "My Way of Life" is very good too.

As for your prayer: we have to face the fact that man is naturally a little lazy and doesn't *like* to pray a lot of the time. We bring useless trouble upon ourselves if we imagine that we must always be sweetly and passively attracted to prayer, and that if we are not something is wrong. No: we are more often than not cold and dull. But we have to revive our prayer with real acts of *faith*. Faith is the virtue which really puts us in contact with God: the true God, the living God . . . He is always there, even when He is not felt. Finally, we owe Him our sincere efforts and He does not owe us any results or any satisfaction in return, and so we should be perfectly happy to make a lot of efforts without any apparent result . . .

Really, though, I think you are going along very well. I do not think you should worry about yourself. I think you should always remember that sooner or later you will reach a stage where you no longer think about yourself much at all, and this will solve most of your problems. Such a condition is a gift of God. We dispose ourselves to receive the gift by refusing to take ourselves very seriously but taking Him extremely seriously and living, as I have said, with lots of faith.

We have been praying for your new convent—be sure to let us know the news . . .

May 8, 1954

I was happy to hear that your profession is to be on Ascension day. You are giving yourself to Jesus practically on the fifth anniversary of my ordination. You are just one day later. And I know of no more beautiful feast than the Ascension. It teaches us to live in heaven. Our desires must be where our true rest is found . . .

Jesus leaves us on this earth long enough to learn that although this life seems drab, it is already heaven. And being in heaven does not mean escaping from our own poor limitations and littleness: it means learning to find heaven with our own littleness. Jesus emptied Himself in order to teach us this. We do not have to be great but simply to be ourselves —the selves whom He loved. And so, when you make your vows, do not think that you cease to be Ann. The closer we come to God, the more we begin to be the person we have always been. You would be very mistaken to try to put yourself entirely out of the picture. The "old man" we put off is not our real self, only the false self we have created for ourselves in our efforts to improve on God's work. But Ann is God's child, and His creation, and He would not want you to try to be someone other than He has made you to be. Do not feel frustrated, then, if you cannot be someone other than yourself.

Cappy and I are both reading the new book about St. Therese, by Hans von Balthasar. It is a good book on the whole, although I do not agree with one or two statements and I suppose it will be received with mixed emotions in Carmel. But on the whole it is one of the best books about Therese. The introduction and the chapter called "Truth" are fine, and there is a wonderful chapter on the family life. All through it I could not help thinking of you and Cappy and "our" family. You have so much to thank God for in having given you such a good family and surrounded you with the warmth and affection which make God almost visible. It is beautiful to see souls echo one another as you and Cappy do. Your love for Cappy makes it easy for you to see and love Jesus: and it is He Who has already secretly loved you hidden in your brothers and sisters and Father and Mother. He still surrounds you, though in a more hidden way, in your Carmel. It takes far more faith to see Him in your sisters, but He is there. But above all He is in your own heart . . .

To Edward Wasserman

October 16, 1954

This is to thank you and Peg for your letters at Assumption and to let you know that everything is going along fine. Cap got through the tobacco harvest and its attendant acrobatics and we crammed the barn full of two grades of burley. The hot weather kept up even until the other day but it finally rained and got cool on the Feast of St. Theresa when I said Mass for all the Carmelites I could think of, including especially Ann. And of course one of the Carmels of Rio de Janeiro, with whom I am very thick. They keep sending me the great big hosts they bake down there, and I am glad to get them. We are big buddies . . .

It seemed like a good idea, to me, that Robert is staying home. Peg is very right in saying there is nothing to compare with a good Catholic family. That is true. And your family there is such a good, happy atmosphere, that I do not see what Robert could gain in boarding school. I think he would only lose, really, at his age. I have been in enough boarding schools to be skeptical about them. College is time enough to go away— if he intends to go to college . . .

How is Carol [Ann's sister]?

I often think of you all and beg God to bless you—"my" family. I haven't talked much to Cap about what he would want for ordination . . . If I find out anything more specific I'll let you know. It seems to me to be foolish to pay two hundred dollars or so for a chalice when we have so many now and when Cap himself would hardly ever get to use it.

To Sister Anita

February 8, 1955

Before Lent comes, I want to write you at least a few words to let you know that I am still praying for you to be a saint. Our way of silence and poverty is the surest and happiest way although not always the easiest. The companionship and example of others is a help. Yet in our contemplative life we are always in some sense solitaries. Jesus makes sure that we enter into an interior solitude in which He alone can guide us.

Cappy is doing very well. This week I am singing the High Mass and he is my subdeacon. It is assuring to me that I often see the other members of "our" family in him when I see him from an unexpected angle in the sanctuary—sometimes I see a glimpse of mother, sometimes of Carol, those two especially. I wonder why? But anyway it makes me think of the mystery of the priesthood that makes *all* the family present in the one who becomes a priest. You will all be in the sanctuary and at the altar with him . . .

Also I am excited about Carol's wedding taking place at Cappy's first

Mass. That is wonderful! We will probably all be so uplifted that we will not be able to walk on the ground at all . . .

I hope you can read my handwriting. I am writing out at St. Ann's [the temporary hermitage the Abbot was letting Merton use] today where it is quiet. May you enjoy a holy and silent Lent with Jesus in the desert and be very close to his heart at Easter. Pray for me—I have a very special intention. So will you all remember it, please!

June 10, 1955

I will try to give you a little news of the ordination although I believe you will be hearing about it from the rest of "our family" in great detail.

Everything was wonderful. I think I enjoyed it and derived as much inspiration from it as from my own ordination six years ago. In fact, I think I got more sensible consolation from Cappy's ordination than from my own. I was so happy to be at his side in his first Masses. He did very well, made no mistakes, and one could feel how close to God he was. I especially enjoyed the little talks he gave, one before his first Mass, and the other at the nuptial blessing.

The first talk came as a surprise to me. He knelt a few minutes at the foot of the altar, before blessing the new vestments, then stood up and turned around and spoke to all who were there. They practically filled the tribune, upstairs in the back of the Church. He said that the Mass was for them, and that no priest is ordained for himself alone. He was ordained for them all—for us all (since you are included)—all our hopes and problems would be placed before God by him. Then he said there is only one priest, Jesus, who entered the holy of holies covered with His own Precious Blood. And he said that now he too would enter heaven and present the divine Victim, for them, to the Father. It was very simple and yet made a great impression.

Carol's wedding was very beautiful, too. I thought it was a fine idea that they had it here, yet I did not think it would work out so well. I hope Carol and Stan will be very happy. They looked it that day.

I know that you were present at everything in the spiritual silence of your retreat, and I often thought of you. Jesus will give you special graces in compensation for the sacrifice of your bodily presence there . . .

I had a lot of fun with the family, except that I must admit the first day I went out there I got rather a workout. After that I waited until the tide had gone down a little. Monday there were only the six of us and it was much nicer . . .

Apart from this there is not much news here. For my own part I badly need your prayers. I am hoping against hope that something can be done in the matter of solitude . . . Anyway, the Holy Spirit seems to be indicating that the time has come to open the question one way or another. I need prayers, then. One of the things I will probably be doing is that I will stop writing either for a while or altogether. But that is not what I mean by solitude, as writing is not too much a distraction to me. Writing books has always been more or less like weaving baskets. But if I can dispense with that too, so much the better. But Father Abbot is trying to work out some way in which I can have real solitude, so that is why I ask prayers. It requires more than the good will of the local superior!

April 30, 1957

I was very glad to hear about your profession coming up on May 27th. How time flies. It seems like only a week or two ago that you were down in the gatehouse wondering whether or not you should enter Carmel. And now you are on the eve of your solemn profession.

There is no doubt about your vocation. God has been very good to you, and He has proved over and over again that His love wants you for Himself in Carmel. I know you too are sure of this now, and that you will never be surprised if the weakness of nature sometimes goes into confusion on this point. That is quite natural, and is no sign of a lessening of His love, or of yours . . .

You are offering your life in sacrifice to God. It is a true and very pleasing sacrifice. It will be all the more pleasing if it is more positive than negative . . . We too easily tend to focus our eyes on our sinfulness and nothingness and then we forget that we have risen with Christ, that we have a wonderful new life to live in His Holy Spirit, that we have been overwhelmed with His gifts. It is true that we do not appreciate them enough: but the best way to appreciate them more is to look at them, and look at God's love, instead of constantly looking at our own failures. If we wish to please God truly by our religious life, we must see that it is really a *life* and not just a living death . . .

Realize, then, that you are loved. And open your heart to that love, and even if the world collapses around you, do not let anything turn you aside from loving and praising God. We have been saved and Redeemed by the Precious Blood of Jesus, and there is no room for sadness or doubt in our lives, no room for preoccupation with our faults and miseries. We must not only trust, but we must go forward and make our lives fruitful with the offering of our own love: our giving of ourselves in a positive creation, a living of a new life in a new world, in a new dimension. It means rising above the pettiness and triviality and prejudice and half truths that tend to narrow everything down in this world, even in a genuine life of faith! To arise above these things does not mean to despise those in whom they exist: after all, they will be found even in our own selves. The secret of rising above these things is to realize that Christ's victory over sin and death and error is so complete and so perfect that even where there may be falsity and triviality He also can be present and act as He wills, provided that there is no bad will.

I don't know if this sermon is any use in your own life, but I am putting it down on paper for you because I know that for almost all religious this is one of the truths that needs to be stressed above all. We have become too negative, too supine, too passive. We make a virtue out of discouragement and we think that to eat our hearts out with secret resentment and frustration is to go through a "passive purification." Well, it does mean that, but only if we go *through* it. We must not get stuck in it and stay there permanently . . .

. . . And when we have reached solemn profession, we have reached the stage when we can no longer expect everything to be done *for* us by the community: we must stand on our own feet and support the community by our own work, and example, and prayer and by the power of the Spirit living in us. It is a great responsibility, when we realize it, but one from which we need never shrink, for since God has willed it for us, He gives us all the grace we need and much more. Your greatest strength will always be your littleness and the humility which will make you trust in Jesus. And don't ever lose either your common sense or your sense of humor. And since abstract truths are not always too much help, you can always see all these things embodied in a concrete person in your Foundress, St. Theresa. I hope you will love Jesus as she did, with as much drive and joy and self-forgetfulness and naturalness and good balance. That will always be my prayer for you, Ann . . .

July 18, 1958

Yesterday, on our heterodox feast of Our Lady of Carmel, I had the pleasure of offering Mass for the Cleveland Carmels . . .

Cappy has been a little under the weather but don't worry about him. I don't know if he is getting an ulcer or not but I hope not. He is going through a kind of crisis of growth and there is nothing anybody can do about it. Except encourage him and stand by him. He is struggling to adjust his potential bigness to the narrow limitations of a life like ours where people are so tied up in trivialities, necessarily. Only God and Our Lady can help him. Pray for him—and for me. I think it is good and wonderful for people to go through the trials that will make them more pleasing to God and deliver them from mediocrity (and since he is the kind of person for whom mediocrity is impossible, trial is unavoidable). He will have to struggle . . .

Yes, I was crazy about my little niece, Anita. I caused a beginning of confusion in her life by the fact that she also has an Uncle Louie in Rob. Two uncle Louies at such an early age is already quite a problem . . .

April 9, 1959

Thank you for your letter—and all the letters I have not answered, because I have been very remiss, I am afraid. I nearly did not get around to this one today, I have been having an absorbing and wonderful time translating things from the Desert Fathers. They are wonderful. I hope someday to send you the results in a little book. That is real spirituality —so simple and down to earth and far removed from the cerebral and gabby "spirituality" that flourishes among us these days. Acts, resolutions, and all the rest.

Thank you also for the beautiful palm. You are like the Desert Fathers yourself: they used to weave baskets out of palm leaves, and you have woven me a cross, so I accept it with love from the desert of Carmel . . .

Cappy is doing well in the Guest House. I heard from "home" that they regarded it as a kind of demotion. I would not say that exactly. But it is true Cap has been passing through a kind of rough phase, and things have not been easy for him. He is very independent and sometimes people are not quite ready to make allowances for character. But everyone who comes in contact with him is helped by him and he really *helps* them, does not just give them a line and let them go. He is very generous with his time and with his attention and he really gives himself to the people who need him. It is wonderful and unusual. Few people have such a gift for doing this as he has . . .

As for me, I am happy with the novices and with the woods and with the desert through which our Lord leads me. It becomes vaster and vaster and embraces the whole world and many souls and though I am alone in it I have everybody in it with me . . .

November 19, 1959

Many thanks for your good letter. Now is the time when I really need your prayers because at this moment everything is being decided in Rome. In fact, Father Abbot himself flew over there on Monday, not telling anyone why he was going. I think it must have certainly been partly concerned with my petition. There are other matters as well. In fact he was *summoned* over and maybe they are asking him a few questions too . . . It is quite a situation. The head of the Congregation, to whom I applied, and whom I met once before, has just been made a Cardinal [Cardinal Larraona] so I hope things will come out well and that I will soon be heading for—Mexico . . .

Cap is interested of course but whether or not he would ever go down there is another matter. Maybe when I get squared away I can start a hermitage for a dozen people and he would be one of them, I think.

He has done very well in the Guest House and there were even some articles in the Louisville paper about the retreats here, with mention of Cappy. I have not seen them.

It is not surprising that you get distracted in prayer if you have a distracting job. It takes a little time to learn to do a new job with sufficient detachment to be undisturbed, relatively, at prayer. So the first thing is patience, and prayer of petition for the grace to be more recollected. Then be careful about throwing yourself into the job: take it calmly, trustfully, and don't be too afraid of mistakes or too desirous of success. Just let the job get peacefully integrated into your life. In prayer, emphasize the strong virtues, like faith, and hope and love which give prayer real substance. If you just hope to let your imagination and affections do it for you, you will be pushed all around the lot. So begin by really believing in the presence of God, don't take it for granted. And renew the element of realization in your faith. A little polishing on that won't hurt . . .

February 29, 1960

Last chance to answer your good letter—probably you haven't heard from Cap either. You know his job by now—vocation secretary. Runs in the family, doesn't it? Right now he is a little under the weather with a kind of flu and a fever, but isn't feeling too bad, just has to lie low. It is hard to keep him in bed though. I know how he feels. I can stand it for about a day then I have to be moving around a little, at least to walk up and down saying the office. No, I am not in bed or sick . . .

I am glad you liked the little Christmas book. I am sending a mimeographed thing on no less a subject than the primitive Carmelite vocation. Meaning the Fathers of Carmel, not you sisters. I sent it to the Friars at Holy Hill (the Provincial, Father Albert, to be exact), to find out if I had said anything revolutionary. I probably have. I would be glad of your reaction—any reaction . . .

I love Lent, not that I fast wildly, or go to heroic extremes. But I love Lent anyway. It is a season when nature is more quiet: the fields and hills are our own selves, all waiting to be born again. And the spring sun and rains preparing the way. So let us be united in Alleluias . . .

January 1, 1962

I shared your emotions at the death of Sister Florence [who had entered Carmel with Ann]. It must have been a real blow to lose someone so close to you. So far all those who have died here in my twenty years in the monastery have been ones who were years my senior or else were in the brothers and I hardly ever saw them. Only one or two have been anywhere near close to me. But I suppose that will change now that I am becoming one of the seniors. However, the death of a Carmelite is never purely a matter of sorrow. It is right that we "miss" those we have loved in the convent, but also more right that we should rejoice in their joy. And of course I am sure that her sacrifice will be very fruitful where it is most needed. In any case I do not omit to pray for her.

Here is the hot news: Cappy has been named master of the Brother Novices. Just this morning in the big lottery of jobs which we have every New Year's Day. I think he will do very well. I am still with the choir novices. It will mean that I will have to change confessors. Cap was my confessor and the Novice Masters can't hear confessions even in the community as they are too busy. I don't know who I will get. Cap was about the only person around here that I could really talk to spontaneously about all troubles and headaches, so I will miss that opportunity. It will be a form of solitude. We have to learn to get along with only God for our confidant, I guess. Cappy never gave much advice anyway, but he listened, and that was important.

Let us keep praying for one another in the New Year. The Lord alone knows what it will bring . . .

Say hello to the folks for me, I will drop them a line if and when I can . . .

To Edward Wasserman

August 7, 1962

I have been a pretty bad correspondent this last year or so, having been occupied with a million things. But I do at least want to drop you a line and say I am very sorry to hear how things have turned out with your sickness. All I can say is that I hope you are not having too hard a time of it, and that the graces God will give you all along will be fully accessible . . .

I had looked forward to seeing you all again this year, but I suppose the trip is out of the question: you must take it easy and rest. I hope the blood transfusions have been a help. It is consoling to think I was able to give a pint the other day with the bunch when the Red Cross came. One realizes the value when a friend needs blood: otherwise you just give it in a vague sort of way thinking more of general and abstract "people" who might need it.

There is nothing much new down here. Cap is doing fine as novice master. Things are quiet as far as postulants go. He received one recently and one has just arrived for the choir, but there is not much prospect of large numbers, and I am satisfied with that . . .

To Margaret Wasserman

September 4, 1962

It took a little time for the news of Ed's death to get to me as I am in the hospital for a check-up. But I am praying for him at Mass these days and will offer Mass for him when I get a chance. I am happy that he received the grace to die so well—that is a wonderful thing and we can all be happy for him and with him. After all it is the eternal values that really count, and it is the mercy of God above all that is the crown of a good life. So be consoled, and the Lord will also guide and provide for you in your loneliness. He has given you a wonderful family and I pray there may be fruitful and happy years in store for you yet. Anyway I send my blessings and sympathy to all, and will pray for the repose of Ed's soul.

In 1963 "Cappy" left Gethsemani.

To Sister Anita

September 1963

Thanks for your letter. It reached me in the hospital in Louisville, where I have a cervical disk, but they did not operate and I am going home to try to take care of it in the infirmary at the monastery. Pray that it may work out all right.

I will say the Mass for Cappy—hope everything gets settled all right for him. I think he really would be better off in a monastery but he really has to work it out himself.

Sorry for the scrawl. My blessings and best wishes in XT.

September 23, 1964

Thanks for your good letter. I am sure everything is right with Cappy. He does not write to me and I have heard absolutely nothing direct from him for months, but indirectly I heard recently from someone who visited him and who said he was doing well. It seems that he is facing his problems realistically and doing well in his studies. I am not too worried about him. I think he is grappling with the thing in his own way and that is the best we can expect. If he had stayed here he would be climbing up the walls by this time. I wish there were some way to figure these things out. I know the family was very grieved that he left, but merely trying to keep himself here by willpower would not have worked out . . .

I do miss the visits that used to come along annually. Do tell Peg [Margaret] that if she is ever down this way I would love to have a chat with her. I would love to see the whole gang but know that is hardly possible. I think of them all often, however, and keep you all in my prayers . . .

I have been pretty busy all summer. Do pray for us please, we are having an important meeting of abbots and novice masters here the first week in October. A lot of important things will be discussed, or should I say kicked around? I still have hopes the Order will see the light and begin to permit a little more of the eremitical type of life. This is very important because there are unquestionably genuine solitary vocations around and the way we are set up now only frustrates them. This is a serious matter. So I do recommend it to your good prayers and to those of the sisters. But I have no hopes of immediate action. One thing is sure, I am really aware that solitude is most important in my own life and I know that this is not just a subjective opinion. Maybe it will eventually work out, and as a matter of fact over the years I do have more and more solitude. Since I got my bad back, I now get up and say vigils and make meditation privately in the novitiate chapel which is an immense boon for me. It is something to be grateful for. And I do get to the hermitage almost every day at least for part of the afternoon, so I am not kicking. This is all wonderful. But I could use more, if God wills.

Have to go now. Bless you always, keep me in mind as you pray and let me have any news.

To Sister Vera [also a member of the Cleveland Carmel]

March 21, 1965

. . . The contemplative Orders, while understanding the need for discipline and austerity, and not sacrificing their truly contemplative ideal, need a greater flexibility and maturity. This would allow, for instance, on the one hand a venture into dialogue with others. The important thing is to make sure that the contemplatives keep themselves free from routine active work and odd jobs that oppress and overwhelm the freedom they need to be alone with God. I mean schools and what not. It is imperative that contemplatives do not get roped in to these organized "works." Anything that threatens their freedom and disengagement from routine obligations in the active life must be fought and fought hard. There must be no confusion about this. Once the bishops get you signed up for this or that little job, you are in the rat race. And may God help us if we get ourselves imprisoned in a system of relationships that involve constant talking, contacts on a superficial level, etc.

On the other hand, I think the great problem is getting ourselves free from silly routines with our own cloistered life: the gestures and activities that used to be very much to the point, but have now become formalities which are carried out more or less as ends in themselves, without anyone really knowing why. At the same time, we must remember that a lot of these things may still have a meaning which American girls are likely not to have understood, but could be capable of understanding.

In all things we need patience, tact, prudence, willingness to wait. With us, sweeping reforms are not a matter of immediate and urgent necessity. We can take our time, though many will not be willing to do this. But at least, let us try to see clearly where we are going . . .

To Sister Anita

May 3, 1965

. . . I did not have Vietnam on the brain, though I do now. You probably don't know much about it but the situation is very serious and the people who are making it serious, deliberately, are our own government. They are engaging in a new game called "escalation" which is a cynical political power play that is extremely dangerous and will in any case cost the lives of thousands of innocent Asians who are in a bind between us and the reds. No thought is being given to these wretched people who only want to get both us and the reds off their backs and try to settle their own affairs without interference. A Vietnamese Buddhist is now (in Brooklyn) on a fast unto death, that is to say he declares he will not eat again unless the firing stops and they agree to enter negotiations. Do pray for him and for this whole mess to be straightened out. Of course there are many conflicting opinions, but it is basically a dirty and unjust deal and the hands of the U.S. are not lily white, though I admit the reds are not angels either. I think of the poor innocent people caught in between who have no desire to be involved with either of us, and are being used by power politicians . . .

August 1, 1966

Thanks for your letter of Trinity Sunday. I have been slow in answering letters this summer because since my back operation, and with other things like bursitis, I have trouble typing and so do not type more than I can help. It stands to reason that I can't write most letters in my own handwriting. That would be asking too much of my friends.

. . . It is no joke that being a hermit makes you much more vulnerable to all sorts of things and one needs very special grace. So pray hard for me, too. Things are fine again and I love the hermit life tremendously. But as I say you can really fall on your head if you don't watch out. I can well understand how Cappy, having batted around rather rootlessly for several years now, feels discouraged and at loose ends, maybe rather hopeless about everything. I will certainly keep him in my prayers. Do what you can to encourage him.

December 10, 1967

Thanks for your letter. I am so sorry I didn't answer the one you mentioned. Probably I *did* take your word when you said I didn't need to! Anyhow, the problem as you stated it was just one of those normal things and not a matter of crisis, so I did not feel that you needed me to call out the fire engines.

. . . We all have to be realistic about the fact that we need human love and often do not realize how that need creeps into other things we do. And our bodies are not always perfectly docile to the spirit. But the struggle is healthy and good and it all gives us opportunities to make up our minds on deeper and deeper levels, and really commit ourselves to our vocation. In my case I think I was taken by surprise by the fact that after an operation that really reached into the center of my nervous system, the spine, I was in a state of helplessness for a couple of days and it almost threw me. When someone came along with an enormous amount of tender and devoted care, it made an impression. We were both set up for it, without knowing it, and before we could really give it a thought, we were in love. Where I made the mistake was of course in continuing to see her after I got out of the hospital. Time has taken care of it. She moved away from Louisville, and I have more or less stopped communicating with her. I hope she isn't mad at me for that . . .

A fine thing happened this week. Fifteen cloistered superiors (including two Carmelites) were here for a meeting, a kind of retreat and conference on renewal problems. I was in charge of it and we had a very fruitful time. They were all very good indeed and I got the feeling that there are really solid hopes for our communities getting somewhere, and that all the hopes are not to be placed merely in the more far out experimental projects that are going on. I think we can have a first rate contemplative life within the structures we know, but that serious changes need to be made. The whole business is on tape and you can get it from Sister Elaine Michael, the Cloister, Allegany, New York [published as *The Springs of Contemplation* by Farrar, Straus and Giroux, 1992].

Sister Ann continues to live as a professed nun at the Carmelite monastery in Cleveland.

To a Woman Religious Superior

October 1, 1960

It is certainly a fundamental truth that all religious not only work to save their own souls and the souls of others, but in so doing they manifest something hidden in the mystery of God, some aspect of the inexhaustible truth of His mercy to men. Each time we come in contact with a religious community that is truly faithful to its mission, we are struck not only by the joy of its members and by the calm, fruitful, and productive atmosphere, but over and above this we are somehow aware of a divine reality manifested in their midst, seen only through the eyes of faith.

We know that our heavenly Father has a very special concern for the poor and the abandoned, who are the apple of His eye. We know that He pays very special attention to the needs of those whom the world ought to care for, but whom the world tends to reject. Recently I had occasion to talk to a writer from India who said he was shocked by the way the old people in American society tended to be set aside and tacitly forgotten. I wished he could have visited your community in order to correct this impression.

And yet it is sadly true that in this country which worships youth to the point of obsession, old age is not understood. There is a kind of foolish legend about old people, a legend in which the old are rendered acceptable because they retain some vestiges of youth, but only for that reason and no other. (The foolish platitudes which praise the old for being "like kids" rather than for the dignity of their age.) It is certainly very fine for old people to be full of the vigor and verve of youth, but they should not have to cling to that *alone* as a way of being acceptable to the rest of the world. On the contrary, their age itself has a wonderful quality which makes them worthy of special respect and love. This is what the Little Sisters of the Poor are able to recognize and live for. What they see in the old people is not some vestige of natural "pep" but the light and the joy and the mystery of Christ, which gives them a far greater and more wonderful energy, in spite of the feebleness of their limbs. You have been able to see in the sick poor not just "specimens" of aging humanity but temples of God, persons of unutterable dignity who have traveled to the threshold of eternity and are waiting to be called into the joy of their Lord. These are in many respects the most interesting and exciting people on earth: for they are sitting right in front of a door that may open to them any moment. There is nothing else for them to be interested in. This is a truly marvelous condition. Would that the rest of us could live like that. But those who have the cult of youth and success and pleasure are prone to turn their eyes away from the beautiful mystery. They do not want to think of another world. The mystery which you serve is the mystery of charity and the mystery of heaven, and God loves you because you love His little ones.

To a Religious

December 30, 1964

It must be about a month since you wrote your letter. It got here and got buried in the pile, so that I did not get to it until today. There is really not a great deal I can do for you except to say be patient, pay attention to obedience and to grace, trust God, pray that you may fulfill all His desires in your regard, and then let Him act. He often does surprising things.

Religious life is, I am afraid, so organized and so systematized today that there is a great deal of frustration and development is often slowed down or even blocked to some extent. I think that we should all be praying for a genuine renewal and opening up of new perspectives. Certainly in most Orders the Superiors are beginning to work on it. There are very few religious who can say that they are exactly in a perfect spot for living a life of real interior prayer. Yet if one desires sincerely to love God, that desire will never be completely frustrated. It would indeed be blasphemy to think it could be.

Hence, your task is to seek, with purity of intention, to give yourself as completely as possible to God, even in a contemplative way if possible, pray for it, be patient, be open with your Superiors and guides, and hope for the best. I do not promise you an easy path, but in such circumstances the Lord will certainly send some help.

Meanwhile we should avoid forms of spirituality and piety that make us too aware of ourselves and of our precious interior lives and inner experiences. This all gets us confused and brings on more trouble. The great thing is to be free in the forgetfulness of self, but that does not mean that we have to plunge madly into action and never be conscious of anything but jobs to be done. Quite the contrary. There are enough

people in the rat race outside convents without making convent life itself
a rat race too.

To German Seminarians

March 11, 1965

Forgive me for not answering your letter sooner. I will try briefly to
indicate something that you can follow up in your ideas of philosophy and
contemplation. The contemplation I speak of in *New Seeds* is more than
philosophical. However, philosophy, when it is not purely abstract and
cerebral, and when it is truly philosophy, tends to a level of metaphysical
wisdom, a unified vision or even intuition and experience of being: not
being in the abstract, but the ground of our own being. This is of course
analogous to the contemplative intuition and certainly a good disposition
of the mind for it. In fact, Christian philosophy being impregnated with
the life of faith does in practice open up the way to theological contemplation, the understanding and wisdom given by the Holy Spirit. Philosophical contemplation reaches to being and to God as the author of being,
and theological or mystical contemplation is an intuition of love recognizing our union by grace and gift with the indwelling Holy Spirit "in
whom we cry Abba Father." Properly speaking, Christian contemplation
is Trinitarian, and sees the connection of our own inner life with the inner
life of the Three Divine Persons since we are united to the Father, in
the Son, by the Holy Spirit.

To a Woman Religious

June 30, 1965

Yes, it is certainly true that our solitude is for others. As Heidegger
would say, we are free *from* the world in order to be *for* the world. And
it is precisely our freedom from the mechanisms and processes of the
world that can enable us to bring love, understanding, and peace to
persons who are in the world. If we fail to do this, there is instant punishment: we become implicated in the trivial processes and mechanisms
of our own life and the monastery becomes a little "sacred" world in which
everything is permitted once it fits in with the machinery, and everything
gradually becomes meaningless and inauthentic. Then we end up as phar-
isees, and spend our time formulating arguments to prove why our empty
existence is really "the best" and much superior to any other.

It seems to me that the most difficult problem today is that of authenticity in our monastic solitude. A solitude that is really for God and
for the world, and not simply a selfish evasion. I see more and more that
the merely negative answer is fruitless and deadly. At the same time there
is an ill-considered desire to find oneself acceptable to and accepted by

the "world" in its own confused sense, and then one ceases to be of any use, and the witness to Christ is silenced. It is a problem for every one of us. And I am sure that it is formulated in very different ways everywhere, though it is basically the same. We are not as far advanced in trying to solve it here as you are there. The monumental problem of poverty, for example, is one we have hardly touched in this country, though there are sporadic experiments. I think, however, that the "small community" is not a fully satisfactory answer and I think that for us the problem is far more complex than we realize. It means a new understanding of technological society. We are still trying to solve the poverty question in a thirteenth-century context. I admit that I do not have much to offer in this field.

To a Carmelite Nun

January 20, 1967

I am glad you wrote to me about that prayer problem. It was necessary that you should. I regret very much that now, as always, there are people running around and busying themselves with things they do not understand and doing great harm to people who are living the contemplative life. I think it would be well for you all to realize in Carmel that you cannot believe everything you hear from priests about your kind of life and what you are doing or ought to do. It is most unfortunate that men who have no experience whatever of our problems and our way of life presume on scant information to advise us to turn everything upside down. They rob people of the peace which God has given them and provide nothing instead but something of their own agitation and disorientation. They can assuage their own needs in their active lives, but when they create this kind of a stir in convents they can so upset people that they can do real harm.

From what you wrote of your life of prayer, it seems to me that it is just about what one would expect it to be. St. Theresa wanted to have convents in which precisely that kind of prayer would be easily and spontaneously developed. For heaven's sake, that is what Carmel is *for*. And now this man, without even inquiring into the details or asking you any real questions, just on the basis of a few guesses of his own, tries to sweep that all aside. I am sure he must have done the same with others. I hope that you will all know enough to realize that instead of helping you in your vocation he is simply hindering it, at least in this respect.

My suggestion is that you go back and read the passage from the commentary on the Our Father in St. Theresa's *Way of Perfection* where she speaks of "Thy Kingdom come" and also the part in the "Living Flame" of St. John of the Cross, Stanza III, see especially Vol. 3 of the Peers translation, beginning at the top of p. 74 and going on from there.

I am quite sure that if you take care to purify your intention and your faith, and seek humbly to love God alone in peace and silence in your manner of prayer, and open your heart to Him without attempting to see Him clearly or even to feel anything, and simply wait upon Him in silent humble love, repeating as you do some phrase of Scripture and drawing light from it, He will do the rest and will work with His grace in your heart without you even knowing it. But you will grow in union with Him without understanding how. The basis must be real faith in Christ and total trust in Him and the desire to obey His call to love Him in simplicity and purity of heart. Just take care not to indulge in self-complacency or merely to seek refuge from the trials of life in a little inner sanctuary of your own. In other words, don't make it a mere evasion from reality. But if you have real faith, you will be in contact with the highest reality and that is surely no evasion. Drat those retreat masters anyway. They are a pest.

To a Woman Religious

March 27, 1968

I can't go into your questions as I would like to. In large contemplative and monastic communities such as ours, yes, the majority seem to thrive on a sort of cloistered activity, but not bustling activity or external activity: the vocation of service and self-forgetfulness, combined with a very simple kind of union with God in faith and devotedness. This is really not an "active" life in the sense of one that "goes out" into the world of activity.

As for continual prayer: certainly this was always the monastic ideal. Or at least one tradition in the monastic way: that of continual actual awareness of God. Yes, *but*. The problem about it comes when people who don't know what it really means try to concentrate all the time on some concept or object of feeling, etc. St. John of the Cross makes quite clear that this is an error, and can have very bad results. But if you teach people to seek continual conscious awareness of God this is what most of them will try to do. What is really meant of course is continual openness to God, attentiveness, listening, disposability, etc. In the terms of Zen, it is not awareness *of* but simple awareness. So that if one deliberately cultivates a distinct consciousness *of* anything, any object, one tends to frustrate one's objectives—or God's objectives. If one just thinks of it in terms of loving God all the time in whatever way is most spontaneous and simple, then perhaps the error can be avoided.

To Sister Maria Blanca Olim

October 16, 1967

I am really dreadfully ashamed of having left your letter for seven months without an answer. I suppose the reason is that the questions would have called for extended treatment, and I wanted to put them aside until there was "time." But I have been so taken up with other things that I have not answered you. And now I suppose it is too late to answer in detail.

In my opinion it would be a mistake if Benedictines took too active a view of the monastic life today. The motto PAX still says volumes about the Benedictine life. Not that it has to be "contemplative" in the Platonic sense: but our cloisters do have to be places of silence, peace, prayer, humility, and love. The thirst for God has not dried up in the heart of modern man: it is only that some of the familiar ways of talking about God may have lost their meaning to him. There is still a great need to find an absolute and ultimate meaning in life, and there are many young people who are *not* content with the busy and dynamic conception of life. There is great desire for freedom, simplicity, spontaneity, true poverty, authenticity in everything, and the total absence of formality and pretense. Hence the old aristocratic approach to the monastic life will tend to appear unsympathetic and unappealing. But whatever we may do about the details of observance, I am sure that the basic thing will always remain the need for deep prayer in the heart, and the deepest and most authentic response to the word of God. We must certainly bring renewal to our liturgical worship, but we must also preserve a place for silence and for contemplative prayer. However, it must be admitted that entirely new ways of explaining contemplative experiences must be found. However, when we see the Beatles (you've heard of them in England?) going to an Indian Yogi to learn meditation, it can certainly not be said that all desire for the contemplative life is extinct in modern youth!!!

To Sister Margaret Mary

November 16, 1967

Maybe I am a bad one to give ideas about what a retreat for a community ought to be like, because for my own part I prefer a whole lot of silence and free time to think and read—and not a lot of conferences. From what I have observed I would say the following:

1. Flexibility is needed. Religious should be able to choose to make a solitary, personal retreat somewhere if they find the systematic planned retreat oppressive.

2. The routine of three and four lectures a day is no longer really effective. If it is felt that there should be quite a few organized activities, I would say then let there be two conferences at the most, and one seminar or discussion period, and perhaps something of another nature such as a Bible vigil.

3. It would seem that retreat should be a time when there is less pressure, less organized activity, and more time simply to get oneself back in one's right mind.

4. I would, however, suggest that even for those who find silence and solitude oppressive: there is a certain value in just disciplining oneself to be "empty" and to spend a certain time *doing nothing*. Those who can try an hour a day of this will soon find that instead of going nuts they may profit by it more than they expected. Walking in the garden is permitted in such "empty" periods, but no talking, no reading, no formal prayer, just plain "nothing."

5. The talks—which remain of course necessary—should be completely basic, and not lectures but really simple and direct utterance of the Word of God in all its purity and truth.

The kind of priest who could do a good job on this would be Father Barnabas Ahern, C.P.—but of course he is terribly busy. I am sure some of the Benedictines at Collegeville could provide. Doubtless you have had them before, up your way.

5. Vocation Crisis: 1959–1960

I have often manifested to my Superiors my sincere desire
for a more solitary, primitive existence in a monastic life
stripped down to the essentials and at the same time more
authentic.

TO ARCHBISHOP LARRAONA

When Merton came to Gethsemani in 1941, he made it clear that the Trappist monastery was his second choice. He would have preferred to go to the Carthusians, but at that time they had no foundation in America and the war prevented him from going to a European monastery. His desire for a more solitary vocation was a thorn in his side (and also in that of his Superiors) which tormented him periodically. This is the theme of The Sign of Jonas. The desire for a more solitary life became almost an obsession with him in 1959 and 1960. The following letters reveal the story of his struggle, as he sought a more solitary life in various places—Nicaragua, the Virgin Islands, Reno, Nevada, and Cuernavaca, Mexico. It was the last of these alternatives that especially appealed to him. Dom Gregorio Lemercier, prior of the newly formed (1950) Cuernavaca Benedictine monastery, did all he could to encourage Merton to come to Mexico and join his struggling monastery. In the summer of 1959 he visited Merton three times.

To Bishop Matthew A. Niedhammer, O.F.M.

Bishop Niedhammer headed the Apostolic Vicariate at Bluefields, Nicaragua. The priest Merton refers to is, of course, himself.

June 13, 1959

I am writing on behalf of a Trappist priest who has been nearly eighteen years in the monastery and who, in order to seek a more solitary and contemplative existence—something along the lines of Charles de Foucauld—has thought of the Corn Islands, which fall under your jurisdiction. This vocation seems genuine and has been approved by prudent directors and theologians. It is likely to be strongly opposed by Superiors.

This priest is seeking to settle on a thinly populated island, like Big Corn Island, away from the beaten track. He would take care of such

Catholics as are on the islands, and lead his life of prayer as best he could, benefiting by the solitude and primitive simplicity of the place. There is no idea of any kind of new foundation, only of a very informal, solitary priest's life. He would not be looking for a very extended apostolate, with projects for buildings, etc. But just the simple and necessary care of souls as an obvious concomitant to his presence there as a priest. He speaks Spanish, though I understand English is the language of the islands.

The purpose of this letter is, then, to ask if you would consider it practical for someone to live on the Corn Islands, on this basis, and if so, would you be willing to have the Father incardinated in your Vicariate? In the event of a favorable reply, we could go into further details and start the necessary steps with Rome. But I would beg you to keep the whole thing in strict confidence, and in replying, please see that the envelope is clearly marked *conscience matter*. It would also be of great help to us if you were able to reply without delay, at least to say yes or no.

Any information about the Corn Islands would be welcome. We are going on the information of a Nicaraguan novice who says that the islands are quite healthy and pleasant, and very quiet. Is there any airfield there yet? Is there any danger of a large tourist hotel being put up there?

July 27, 1959

Your friendly letter of June 29th was very welcome. I thank you for it, and have remembered to recommend in prayer your episcopate, in commemoration of the anniversary on that day.

I see we both agree that the Corn Island project is a good idea, in fact a very good one in many ways. And because of that, I believe Our Lord will not just let it drop into oblivion. However, there are obstacles, and great ones. Not that this should discourage anyone. On the contrary, it is perhaps a good sign. In any case, I brought up the matter of a permission to come down there myself. I asked for this permission, but my Father Abbot is absolutely opposed to the whole thing, in no uncertain way. All the more so since, as I might as well admit, I myself am the one who wants to try out this experiment in solitude. So he has refused me permission even to come and look at Corn Island, on a temporary leave of absence. You may find this surprising, but that is how things are in some houses of this Order.

It is not even possible for me to get away to New York.

The only permission I have been able to obtain is that of conversing with you if you should come down here in September on your way home. And so if it is at all possible, and if it is not too great an inconvenience, I hope that you will be able to stop by at Gethsemani on your way back to Nicaragua—or whenever else it may be convenient.

For my own part I firmly believe that this idea, or something like it, would be an important solution to spiritual problems of my own, and would also be a vital new development in the way of a monastic experiment (though it is not a matter of "making a foundation"). It seems to me that the rigid institutional structure of our big monasteries, while having certain advantages, soon reach the point of diminishing returns. There comes a point where real development ceases and the life enters into a kind of stagnation and futility except in certain cases where people called to be Superiors go on in a kind of *active* perfection. For the rest, the monastic community is like a convoy of ships in time of war, in which every vessel takes the speed of the slowest in the convoy. However, that is not the point. I do hope that someday it will be possible to make a really genuine new departure in a truly isolated and primitive place like Corn Island. I emphasize the word "primitive," because I think that is a very important note and one which has ceased to have any meaning in our overdeveloped monastic setup.

Without writing a treatise on the subject (I hope we can discuss it at length) I do want to say that I am, as far as in me lies, set on seeking a solution to this problem or at least on getting permission to reasonably examine the situation—for without this I cannot settle the question at all. I shall keep trying to get permission, and I hope that someday we will be able to take really practical steps to realize this idea. Meanwhile, I hope we will both continue to pray for it to work out. The Church must always be growing and sending out new, living shoots. Mere inert contentment with the status quo has never made saints: at least that is my perhaps presumptuous opinion. No doubt some will think it demented. I know you will agree, though. And with this conviction, and in union of prayer, I hopefully await a chance to discuss the matter further. Please give me your blessing, and receive the assurance of my prayers.

To Bishop Robert J. Dwyer of Reno, Nevada

June 6, 1959

I am surrounding this delicate matter with certain precautions because I would like to keep it in the strictest confidence. In point of fact, I am inquiring for myself. I would like to find out if there might be some possibility of my being incardinated in your diocese. I am not at present seeking to start a new type of foundation (though Frank Kacmarcik may have spoken to you of this). What I seek is first of all a benevolent bishop who might understand the desire of a priest to live as a quasi-hermit in a very isolated locality, while attending to the needs of a small number of souls in a nominal apostolate.

I know you have plenty of mountains, deserts, and Indian reservations in Nevada. It would certainly be possible to find an out-of-the-way spot, perhaps on an Indian reservation, which no other priest would be able to take care of normally. I would be delighted to be among Indians or Mexicans (I speak Spanish). But when I say "among" I still want to leave room for physical solitude. I could live in the same area, somewhat apart, and say Mass for them on Sundays and feasts and attend to their other ordinary needs (short of schooling, etc.). It is not my plan to give up the contemplative life but to continue it in other surroundings and circumstances, outside the institutional framework in which I now find myself subjected to and limited by many ironbound conventions.

This step results from earnest conversations held some time ago with Dom Gregorio Lemercier, O.S.B., Prior of the primitive Benedictine community in Cuernavaca, Mexico. He strongly encourages a move in this direction, as does also the theologian Dom Leclercq, who teaches at San Anselmo. My Superiors, however, are opposed. In fact I have not yet fully acquainted them with the plan. Dom Gregorio has invited me to come and live as a hermit near Cuernavaca, and is speaking to the bishop about that. I thought it might also be prudent to inquire about a possible place in the United States. A third possibility would be the Virgin Islands, about which I have not yet inquired.

It seems to me that the most honest and practical way to solve this long-standing problem is simply to get an exclaustration and be done with it. I know this will shock many, but I can't help it. Of course, that would be an added reason for keeping everything as secret as possible. I have good reason to believe that Rome would grant the indult, if the request is properly presented. Do you know, by the way, if one goes through the delegate or direct to the congregation?

If you approve of my project, and are willing to consider adopting me, will you please let me know soon in the enclosed, addressed envelope and *not* in one with a letterhead. If you think it is practical, I would be grateful if you would even enclose the document that would be needed in requesting an exclaustration. I might not have much liberty in corresponding in the future, especially after the project becomes known. If by any chance you could stop by here I might get permission to speak about it later, but it might be difficult after I have made everything known to my Superiors, which I plan to do in August.

What I have said above about the project is, I know, sketchy. I am open to all kinds of suggestions. The essence of the plan is for me to live a semi-eremitical priestly life much as Charles de Foucauld did in Africa. All I ask is sufficient isolation and liberty to lead the contemplative life, in combination with whatever restricted form of apostolate you would think worthwhile. I would prefer it to be among disinherited groups, like Indians: but always allowing for a few restricted contacts, perhaps with intellectuals and others. The great thing would be to avoid becoming the center of any kind of unwholesome publicity or attention.

Will you please give me your blessing and pray for this intention? I would be grateful if you would also ask the prayers of your Carmelites and of other such souls without telling them, of course, who is involved. Thank you. I hope to hear from you soon.

To Bishop James P. Davis of San Juan, Puerto Rico

June 9, 1959

Not having forgotten the pleasure of meeting you and speaking with you some years ago, I am addressing to you in this letter a request which concerns me very deeply. It is a matter of strictest confidence. I shall try to be as simple as possible, recognizing that you may feel some surprise.

I know that your large and important diocese contains the Virgin Islands. And that among those islands are two which have no priests. Islands on which there is a very small Catholic population. I know that you would be delighted to have a contemplative foundation somewhere in the diocese. Unfortunately, I am in no position to offer you that. However, recently, after discussing the matter with very solid spiritual guides, including the Benedictine theologian Dom Leclercq, who has taught at San Anselmo in Rome, I have decided at last to solve a very long-standing problem of a desire for the solitary life.

I have been invited by a Benedictine Superior to live as a hermit near his monastery in Mexico. This is tentatively being planned. However, I feel it would be a good idea to think of other places, especially since the location in Mexico is at a resort town, Cuernavaca. The Virgin Islands seem to me to be ideal. My plan would be to get a benevolent bishop—your excellency—to allow me to settle there in charge of a small mission so that I would be solitary and yet have a small pastoral charge to take care of the souls around about, who, in turn, would perhaps be willing to help me supply slight material needs of my own. This kind of plan is now working well in the case of several Benedictine solitaries in Europe and I am sure it would work very well in the Virgin Islands. I know you would prefer to have someone in Puerto Rico, but I think it would be wisest for me to go to the most isolated and least populous place.

It is my desire to live in a remote place, near poor people. I presume the population of the islands is mostly Negro. I speak Spanish, but suppose the language of the Virgin Islands is English. I have no pretensions to the austerity of a Charles de Foucauld, but the life I envision is somewhat the same as his, without a similar emphasis on the apostolate. Pastoral care of souls would remain something quite secondary, and contemplative solitude would be the primary concern. In order to carry out this plan it would be necessary to obtain an exclaustration. In spite of the disadvantages of this, I am willing and ready to do this. It is the simplest course to take, and it is what I intend. However, I have not yet consulted my Superiors on this point, they only know in a very general way of my desires, which they do not wish to favor. I have been strongly urged to take the matter to Rome.

I would therefore greatly appreciate it if your excellency would write me in a plain envelope, without letterhead, clearly marked *conscience matter*. Please let me know if you think we could work out something on the above lines. If you are strongly in favor, I would appreciate your sending the document necessary for me to obtain an exclaustration. I will then place the matter before my Superiors. Please pray that if this is the will of God, all concerned may give their full cooperation. And please give me your blessing and pray for me.

To Bishop Robert J. Dwyer

September 1, 1959

It has taken me a long time to acknowledge your very kind letter of July 4th. Actually I have been trying very hard to see some light in the problem I mentioned to you and have not yet reached a fully satisfactory solution. I have discussed the matter in a general way with Father Abbot, without bringing up the specific question of Nevada, because I felt that it was not close enough to being the real solution, unfortunately.

I do want to express my gratitude for your very kind letter and for the proposal you made. In effect, it would certainly provide solitude and time for prayer and isolation. But of course, as you understand, it is not merely a question of that. And there would be so many other factors involved that would make it, practically, a step down rather than a step up, that I do not feel there could be any question, before God, of my taking it. But I must admit that there was much that was attractive about the idea of being a poor priest in a parish lost in an exhausted mining area, "with no future." Thank you for offering to help me in this way. I think of the good people of Eureka and keep them in my prayers.

My situation here seems at times to be in an impasse because of the apparent impossibility of getting a permission to go and investigate reasonable possibilities for a more solitary and simple life. This is my great difficulty, and I would ask you to remember it in your prayers. Meanwhile I have modified my hopes and ideas by renouncing as impractical the thought of starting something among Indians. Whatever I do will have to have a clearly monastic stamp on it, one way or another, otherwise people just would not understand it. Though of course I have no idea of doing anything that people in general will know about.

To Archbishop Larraona

Archbishop Larraona headed the Sacred Congregation for Religious at the Vatican.

September 8, 1959

You will remember that in 1955, when I was looking for a contemplative life that would be more simple, more primitive, and more solitary than that of the Trappists, you advised me to wait a few years, at the same time indicating that, if the problem persisted, I should address myself once again to the Sacred Congregation. This is what I want to do now in a formal and decisive way by asking the Sacred Congregation to kindly grant me an indult of exclaustration for three years, in order to resolve the very serious problem of my vocation, while having a practical and concrete experience of the contemplative life under conditions entirely different from those which exist or can exist in the monastery of Gethsemani and in the Order of the Cistercians of the Strict Observance. Without this practical trial I am unable to resolve the problem of conscience which seriously threatens my spiritual life and my psychological health. My progress in the monastic life seems to depend on a solution.

I entered the monastery of Gethsemani in 1941. I made my solemn profession on March 19, 1947. I was ordained a priest on May 26, 1949. I have often manifested to my Superiors my sincere desire for a more solitary, primitive existence in a monastic life stripped down to the essentials and at the same time more authentic. In effect, the monastery of Gethsemani is a business center, where the monastic life is very busy and lacks the true life of contemplation. The changes in the Constitutions of the Order have not contributed a solution to my problem, which is a question of the solitary life. But my Superiors categorically refuse me permission to try out the solitary life with the Carthusians or the Camaldolese.

Since 1952 I have been writing to different Superiors: the Carthusians in Vermont, the Camaldolese of Frascati. All have invited me to their monasteries to talk about my problem or even to experience the life they live there. Permission to do so has been consistently refused by my Superiors. Finally I have asked permission of my Abbot to examine the conditions of a solitary life. That permission was also refused. But I guess from the Abbot's attitude that he realizes that they can't continue in this way. He knows that the problem has become an agonizing one for me, but just the same he does not want to take the responsibility of granting me permission to leave the monastery.

Therefore I am addressing myself directly to the Sacred Congregation, taking this responsibility on my own conscience, convinced that I owe it to God to resolve this problem.

My spiritual directors strongly advise me: (1) to leave this monastery, at least for a time; (2) to leave the United States, where I am the object of an unhealthy publicity and where my participation in a monastic façade constitutes for me a serious problem of conscience.

The Carthusian life is no longer a solution. My health, affected by the troubles and conflicts resulting from this problem, would prevent me keeping the Rule of the Carthusians. They advised me to look for a modified solitary life under definite conditions in one of the following situations:

1. His Excellency the Bishop of Cuernavaca in Mexico, who knows me well, has offered himself as the "sponsoring bishop" (*episcopus bene-*

volus). I would live a life that would be simple and quasi-solitary in the shadow of the Monastery of the Resurrection in his diocese, under the hospitable direction of the Prior of the monastery and as a guest of the monastery. This is the same Rev. Prior Gregorio Lemercier who is willing to present this letter and explain all the details of my case.

2. The Bishop of San Juan, Puerto Rico, is willing to receive me into his diocese, where I could live a very solitary and primitive life. He would put me in charge of a very small mission, where there are 50 Catholics and no priest.

In the first solution, there would be *de facto* monastic life. I would be truly part of a community, while not being *de jure* a member of this monastery. For this reason, it is the first solution that I prefer as being more in the spirit of my vocation. My canonical situation could be settled after three years. In the meantime, the test would take place and it is that which is necessary.

In the second solution poverty and true solitude, with the addition of a bit of missionary life, would be very concretely a very sanctifying solution.

Thus I present these two possibilities to you, Most Reverend Father, leaving to you the task of pointing out which would be the better choice and then to enable me to get the indult, so that I can make my way as soon as possible to one of these two dioceses. I have explained to you frankly and sincerely my desires and my situation—a situation which is truly serious after so long a time—and I appeal to your fatherly compassion. Therefore, I ask you formally to submit to the Sacred Congregation my petition for the indult.

I remain cordially and devotedly yours and ask that you give me your fatherly blessing.

To Ernesto Cardenal

This letter was not available in its entirety when Dr. Christine Bochen edited The Courage for Truth, *which contains the Cardenal letters.*

October 8, 1959

I have received very good news from Dom Gregorio in Rome. He has seen Father Larraona and it seems that the dispensation will be granted, but still the Superiors of the Order must be consulted and this may be quite an obstacle. But it seems as if in the long run the move will be completely successful. This is very fine and encouraging news, and is certainly the result of much prayer, including your own prayers, for which I thank you. Keep them up, they are more necessary than ever.

I have written Dom Gregorio a letter which was mailed in the usual way, open, and so I was not able to speak very freely. Father Abbot does not know all the details as yet, as far as I can tell, though I have told him in a general way that since I cannot obtain a leave of absence from him I am appealing to Rome. I do not know whether or not Rome has yet contacted Father Abbot. At the moment he has been in the Bardstown hospital with a hernia operation.

Since I can more easily write you a conscience matter letter, I think I will take this opportunity to send you some important remarks which you can convey to Dom Gregorio at the proper time.

First of all, about entering Mexico. I think it would be safer if I got a passport and a regular visa to enter as a permanent resident. This will take time. If there is some special difficulty I will simply enter, as you did, on a tourist card. I imagine that to obtain a visa I would have to have some kind of document or affidavit from Dom Gregorio. I hope he will know what to do, and will take steps to produce the necessary evidence that I will have a home and support in Mexico. This could be sent when it is definite that I am to come.

The plan I thought would be most convenient would be, when I get the indult, to leave here and go to Albuquerque, New Mexico, and take up the question of the visa with the Mexican consul there. While I am waiting for things to materialize I could then take a look at some of the Indian pueblos in that region, which would be very interesting. I could even perhaps spend a few days on one of the missions and make a kind of retreat in the desert.

If Dom Gregorio thinks best, I would simply come to Mexico as fast as possible on a tourist card and then get the visa later, as you have done.

From time to time I will send you packages of books—they will be *our* books and perhaps you could keep them for me. I think there is still one book of yours here, Max Jacob. I will enclose that in one of the packages.

One small trial is my health, at the moment. There have been some complications in my usual infirmities. I hope I do not have to spend any time in the hospital. I think it is just a providential event that will help me prepare for a new step. Often sickness has the function of slowing a man down when he is about to turn a corner. Please pray that it may be no more than this and that everything will go well. This is such a wonderful opportunity to reach out for a more simple and solitary life, and to put into practice the ideas that have come to me for so many years. It would be a shame to spoil it. I am very happy that things are turning out well, and I want to correspond perfectly with the opportunity. It is so important to try to realize in actual fact the simplicity of the monastic ideal, and to get away from all the artificiality which grows up in the monastic institution. Let us pray that we may find the ideal of a simple, non-institutional, contemplative life in the mountains, in true poverty and solitude. Meanwhile I hope there will be a little house available soon, when I get there.

P.S. How are you? I have not heard anything from you since Dom Gregorio brought your poems. I am wondering if a letter of yours had failed to reach me. If you answer this one, it had better be conscience matter. Let me know any other hints or suggestions you think would be useful. When traveling in Mexico perhaps I ought simply to dress as a layman. I will need prayers this two or three weeks as the struggle with Father Abbot may be quite definite—though there is nothing he can do now, at least as far as I am concerned. Keep well, may God bless you.

On November 19, 1959, Merton wrote to his friend Dom Jean Leclercq telling him of his request for exclaustration and suggesting that, if Leclercq happened to be in Rome, he might put in a good word for him with the Abbot General, Dom Gabriel Sortais. This letter may be found in The School of Charity, *edited by Brother Patrick Hart.*

To Father Jean Danielou

December 5, 1959

I have been hoping that by this time I would have written a letter from Mexico saying that everything had gone well and that I was established at Cuernavaca, ready to start a new life in solitude, collaborating with Dom Gregorio in his effort at a revival of more primitive and genuine monastic life. Unfortunately I am still here, and though I have been expecting some news from Rome, the situation is beginning to look a little dark and I am wondering what has happened.

Dom Gregorio said he had seen you but I do not know how much of the events you know. The petition for an exclaustration was presented in Rome at the end of September. Larraona said that he would almost certainly grant the indult even though there might be opposition (this of course in strict confidence). He felt that it was well founded. However, at the end of November my Abbot suddenly flew to Rome: to be more exact, it was the middle of November. He returned on the 24th. I knew, and later confirmed, the fact that he went because of my petition for an indult. But when I spoke to him about it he refused to give any information whatever, or even to say explicitly that he had seen Larraona. He said he had been forbidden to speak by the Abbot General. Even the American definitor in Rome had not been told anything about the affair and learned of it only from me. The impression the Abbot gave was that he was very satisfied with the "coup" he had evidently pulled in Rome, though I still continued to hope that Larraona would stand by me. Now I am beginning to wonder if perhaps Father Abbot and the General between them did not play a strong hand in Rome and defeat the whole project. Certainly they are very shrewd and efficient politicians, and besides Father Abbot has immense influence and prestige because of this rich and famous monastery.

The thing that most perplexes me at the moment is my inability to communicate with Dom Gregorio. I am completely in the dark and have no way of getting advice or help from anyone. My letters are very carefully controlled. Until recently, one of our former novices, Ernesto Cardenal, a Nicaraguan poet, who went to Cuernavaca, had permission to write me conscience-matter letters for direction in his own problems, and messages from Dom G. could come through in that way. Two days ago Father Abbot informed me that a conscience matter from Cardenal had arrived and would be *sent back* to Mexico without being given to me. He pretended to have no other reasons for this than that "it is too much work and Trappists are not supposed to give direction by mail." He completely ignores the bona fide fact that Cardenal has a very valid reason for consulting me about his own personal problems, which are serious, and which, as a poet, artist, etc., can be well handled by someone who understands those things. Of course he is also my contact with Dom G. The Abbot keeps up the pretense that he knows nothing of this and thinks only of "my interests."

One of the only ways I can think of, for getting around this difficulty, is to ask you to forward this letter to Dom Gregorio, and receive a reply written by him to you, which you can then incorporate in your reply to me. In this way I will get the advice of both of you. I believe Father Abbot will at least respect my liberty of corresponding with you, since the Father Immediate gave permission. But in the past he has *opened* conscience-matter letters and given them to me only after long delay. You see what kind of man he is. Extremely convinced of his own rightness in everything, *absolutely incapable* of understanding that there can be a more perfect form of contemplative life than this, unless perhaps the Carthusians. But utterly incapable of seeing anything outside the conventional cadres. He scorns and refuses to help emissaries from little, experimental new types of monasteries like the Cistercians of Erlach in Austria, and has the usual contempt for men like Dom Alexis Presse. In other words, he is utterly committed to the prosperous, established, bourgeois type of big monastery with all its comforts, façade, etc. At present we are becoming a very prosperous cheese factory, and our advertising is utterly sickening. I will send you some, to get an idea of the publicity, which affects the spirit of the whole monastery.

I have an acute problem as regards liberty of conscience. I would be much better off if I felt I was able to settle the question of vocation by a free and frank discussion with those concerned, especially Dom Gregorio. Instead, Father Abbot acts in practice as if it were a sin to consult anybody but him. He arrogates to himself sole rights to decide the question, in both forums, internal and external. This is a clear violation of the rights of conscience. Only recently, when Father Immediate gave permission for me to write to you, has Father Abbot even allowed me to consult anyone outside the monastery by sealed letter. It is because of this problem that most of all I sought the indult. Normally, it would have been logical and relatively simple just to get a leave of absence to go to Cuernavaca and work the thing out. On the contrary, rather than let me go to Cuernavaca, Father Abbot himself will go to immense trouble and expense to fight the project in Rome . . .

I hope Dom Gregorio will be able to do something to help the case in the Roman curia. If he thinks it is a good idea for me to write another letter to Larraona, then I hope he will let me know and say in what terms I should approach the question afresh. Perhaps it would be best if he himself wrote. I would appreciate any other advice, practical and spiritual, that either of you can give me.

The alternative, as I see it, presents itself as crucial. It is a question of choice between a bourgeois, inert, decadent façade of monasticism, and a genuine living attempt to renew the inner spirit of the monastic life. If I stay here, there is nothing I can do—except write books, and more and more these books will tend to become embittered, critical reflections of the state of affairs. I feel convinced that only in a more primitive monastic setting can I really develop and grow as God wants me to. In such circumstances I have no choice but to go on, no matter what, to make every effort to seek a more solitary and primitive life, in which of course God Himself would take good care of whatever apostolic element He would desire to have in it. Writing would not be excluded except for the first two or three years. Meanwhile I have enough written to bridge any gaps.

I am trying as hard as I can to accept the difficulties of the situation without bitterness. My Superiors cannot help having the self-righteous, deluded complacency of their class. But I have seen what harmful effects it has. I must strive to correspond with God's will in my own life, without showing bitterness or displaying a wrong kind of resistance. Not being a rebel, in other words. I would deeply appreciate the help of your prayers. Looking forward to a reply from you both—with all fraternal solidarity in Christ, and with firm hope for the future of monasticism.

On December 7, 1959, Merton received the decision of the Congregation of Religious: his petition for exclaustration was denied. The decree was signed by Valerio Cardinal Valeri and also by Archbishop Larraona, secretary of the Congregation.

To Dom Gregorio Lemercier

December 17, 1959

The Reverend Father Prior has allowed me to write this letter in the absence of Dom James, who returns tomorrow. Yesterday morning I received a decidedly negative answer from Rome. Nothing could be clearer, more precise, more final. It is a long letter signed both by Cardinal Valeri and Cardinal Larraona—yes, both of them. The most important part is the following: "Here is what we ask of you: as a true son of Mother Church, obedient to the example of your Master, for whom you have left all, who said in a Gethsemani other than your own: '*Non mea voluntas, sed tua fiat*' ["Not my will, but yours be done"], live in peace in the monastery which shelters you and where God has called you to seek Him and to find Him . . . *Vir obedience* [sic] *loquetur victorias* [The man of obedience is the one who speaks of victory]. Do not hesitate to enter into this narrow way . . . where one is committed to renounce more than one project even when it may seem good and where one rids oneself of illusion."

The reasons given: "unpleasant repercussions and scandal . . . in the Order and in the world." *Nemo judex in propria causa* [No one can be a judge in his own case]. "The reasons given by your Superiors seem valid to me."

Fr. [John] Eudes believes that Fr. Abbot has told them what the psychiatrist Zilboorg said on one occasion, in passing, that my desire for solitude was "pathological." Fr. Eudes was not at all in agreement with this judgment, and told me yesterday that Zilboorg was a fellow who quickly changed the opinions that he tossed out like that into the air. Indeed, later he seemed to think of me in an entirely different way. But Fr. Abbot has clung to this word and others Zilboorg had expressed—namely, that I might well leave the Church, go off and marry a woman, etc., etc. Obviously we are all human. But the Abbot will have a great deal of ammunition from these arguments. So that's it.

It appears to me that the letter of the Congregation is quite final. I don't know how they could have done otherwise. All that is left is for me to accept wholeheartedly. Which is what I am going to tell Cardinal Valeri.

Clearly it is hard to see an ideal so close to realization vanish before your very eyes, because of the remarks of some fellow [Zilboorg] who says fantastic things at times, while still being a great psychiatrist. But he was an intuitive type, an artist (he had been an actor), a talkative person, a teaser, very sociable—and now deceased, which complicates matters even more.

It seems to me that I ought to see another psychiatrist; this would be useful. I am going to try to see one in Louisville who can help clarify matters. But in the meantime, given the tone of finality in this letter from Rome, I must accept their decision. This is what I am doing.

As for me, before God I believe that the best thing to do is to renounce all direct and positive initiative to leave the Order. I must leave this in the hands of God and the Church. If you believe that something can be done, I authorize you to take whatever steps you can to discover the will of God and to make it known to me. But for my part, I must remain inactive; otherwise I am disobeying the Sacred Congregation. Only if Rome itself changes or opens some way for me, would I be able to do something by myself.

In writing to Cardinal Valeri, I am going to tell him also that I am not thinking of a solitude that would be purely egotistical, but of the possibility of a little eremitical foundation, with a ray of apostolic endeavor added to it. But I do not think that this is going to change his opinion. The fact is that the Abbot will have pictured me before the Congregation as an unstable and emotional type who is trying to avoid the regular life [i.e., life according to the Rule]. So I will always have this reputation in Rome. That will be the end of any idea of getting out of here, no matter what the reason.

Besides, I should tell you that when Dom James wanted to forbid me to correspond with Cardenal, and when I advanced my reasons, saying that I considered Cardenal as an intimate friend, at that moment I could see Dom James's expression. He was triumphant. To say that I had an intimate friend was quite simply to acknowledge a particular friendship. How happy he was. He was totally vindicated. I was a homosexual . . . You see how he makes his judgments. And because of the reasons given by this kind of superior, the Congregation has thrown out my application.

So I have made my "submission" or I shall do it. I will not ask Dom James for permission to be a hermit in the woods. I will doubtless continue as Father Master [of the novices]. He has no one else for the position. I promised him not to make any positive move toward getting out of the Order, at least while he is Abbot.

Have I anything still to hope for?

1. Under another Abbot, I would certainly ask permission to come and see Cuernavaca and even to make an experiment of six months, either at your place or Dom Damasus' [at Mount Saviour Monastery, Elmira, New York]. After reestablishing my reputation by consulting with your psychiatrist down there, I could begin again to ask for exclaustration, if the Church is not opposed. That is to say, I would be there only to *show* that the situation was different and favorable.

2. Under another Abbot, it might perhaps be possible to make a small and more solitary foundation, or to live in solitude within the Cistercian Order—something that would be more in conformity with the will of the Sacred Congregation . . .

I have told Father Abbot that I would ask for permission to live in the woods here, but this I am not going to do at the present time. What good would it do? It would not amount to much.

So long as Rome considers me a Don Juan in prison, there is nothing to hope for. It is very heartrending. It is an injustice which I accept; and since it is my own case, they refuse to acknowledge me as judge or lawyer.

By the way, I did not tell you that Fr. Abbot has told us nothing of what went on in Rome.

If you have something you want to communicate with me, you can write to Fr. John of the Cross before the end of the year. The privilege he has of telephoning his family expires at the end of the year. He will no longer be Retreat Master. Let us know what your telephone number is. Someone tried to call you the other day, without success. After that, there is always a friend whom Cardenal knows. I was told that Cardenal had written that all was arranged and the indult had been granted. I shall know more about it in a few days.

If I could, I would very much like to have you as director and continue to write to you. Dom James will not permit it. Do you think I could ask this permission of the Congregation? Have you any other ideas on the subject?

Fr. Abbot is usually away in September. He makes regular visitations in May and July. But this is not certain. I have no desire to make a lot of moves. I just want to tell you that one can pierce through the iron curtain.

As for me, I am just letting myself be. I accept, I consent. This is for me the will of God. I believe that God Himself will intervene either to arrange things exteriorly or to give me in my heart the solitude I seek. I am experiencing a great deal of peace, an emptiness, a truly wonderful silence, and an enormous amount of freedom. I am perfectly at peace, in union with the Christ of Gethsemani and very near our heavenly Father.

I thank you for your charity—very great indeed. God will reward you. I pray for you and I remain one with you and with all the monks at Cuernavaca. And with Ernesto. I regret very much that I cannot write him even a brief word. At least we shall meet in heaven. But I hope before that. With much charity, in the union of peace and poverty, in Christ who is poor.

To Dom James Fox

December 17, 1959

I want you to receive this news when you come home, and before I see you. The whole question of my vocation has been finally settled once for all by Rome. There is no question in my mind that this is God's will, and that I am to accept it without hesitation, and this I do. The Sacred Congregation feels, in view of the circumstances of my writing, etc., that I cannot leave Gethsemani and that I am to go on here as before.

The Lord has given me the grace to see this without difficulty and to accept it gladly and with deep peace of heart. I only took the steps I did in order to find out what the Congregation thought, and hence what was the will of God. I know of course that the Congregation was considerably influenced by you and Dom Gabriel and I know that human feelings must have entered in, but still I have sufficient faith in my Superiors and in the Church to see that this does not matter. It is a clear and comforting assurance of the will of God.

Here are the following resolutions, which can be stated as promises if you see fit to regard them as such.

1. I intend to take no further positive steps as long as I live, to leave the Order. I will make no move to do so, and will apply no pressure to

do so. At most, I will content myself with manifesting my thoughts to Superiors or those competent.

2. Since the present job of Novice Master implies a certain solitude and since I have been better off here than at any other time in the monastery, I make no offer to resign, leaving you to fire me if you see fit. It is my hope that I will be able to continue here as I am now, with due regard for opportunities to be alone in the woods, etc.

3. However, if it is your mind that I should cease to be Novice Master, then I would like to put in a request to try out living as a hermit in the woods. I will renew this request at any time when cessation of duties leaves me free to do so. But of course I remain completely subject to your decision and will not press the point in any way—e.g., by writing to the General.

4. I regret any inconvenience I may have caused you. According to the above, this will not be renewed. I will devote myself as best I can to forming the novices and making real monks out of them. I am sure that we can work together on some of the difficult problems of formation that arise with the new generation coming in (college, etc.).

I really love Gethsemani in spite of the reaction against certain aspects of the setup. I am grateful to God for the graces He has given me here and know that He has many more in store. The decisions made have left me very free and empty and I can say that they have enabled me to taste an utterly new kind of joy.

There is no need for me to write to Dom Gabriel about this. I am sure you can give him the gist of the above when you write to him. So this will be my Merry Christmas to you, Dear Rev. Father. Please give me your blessing and pray for your devoted son in Christ Jesus.

c. December 17, 1959

Concerning the rights of conscience:

The reason why I did not directly consult you about my application for an indult was that there was in fact no necessity to do so. I was fully aware of your views on the subject. I had every right to appeal to a higher Superior.

To demand that I appeal to the higher Superior through you is to demand, in effect, that I should *not* really appeal to him, or not do so in a way that would represent my own views, but yours.

To demand that I consult you about my interior motives is to demand that I come to you for direction whether I desire it or not, but this is contrary to the Canons. In point of fact, I had arrived at my decision in conscience as the result of consultation with other directors. But in the past, as I know from experience, you have shown a tendency to *overrule* the opinions of directors in order to substitute your own. This, in the internal forum, is nothing else but demanding that the subject regard you as his *only* director, when in point of fact he has no obligation to regard you as his director at all.

I had frequently consulted you on this matter before, including early this summer, and I was fully aware of your opinion. I took it seriously into consideration and did not neglect it at all. I was grateful for it. However I felt in conscience that this did not represent the way God wanted me to follow, as far as my own interior was concerned. I then decided to submit the matter to higher Superiors, which I had the right to do, and this was in no way disobedience.

To interpret my act as disobedience is, in effect, to deny me the right to go direct to higher Superiors.

I fully recognize your right to refuse permission for a leave of absence. In this you were following your conscience and within your rights. But I wonder about the way in which you have done everything possible to prevent me obtaining permission from anyone and in any way whatsoever. I do not deny you this right, but in point of fact it seems to me to represent an arbitrary and tyrannical spirit. Are you not so intent on your own views, in this matter, that you are willing to stifle the Holy Ghost in a soul? Can you say with certainty that you have not stifled Him in souls before, in the question of vocation particularly? Do you not have an inordinate tendency to interfere in the workings of conscience and to suppress by violence those desires and ideals which run counter to your policies?

Do you not tend to assume that your own policies represent the last word in the spiritual perfection of every one of your subjects, and that anyone who is drawn to another way is leaving the path of perfection, simply because he is not following your ideas?

In charity and justice I appeal to my right to settle affairs of conscience with directors, and that I be allowed to do so without violent interference. I appeal to the right, granted and assured by the Father Visitor, to consult directors outside the monastery by letter, without interference, so that this problem of mine can be settled. I am only asking for things which the Church wishes her subjects to have, not for anything unreasonable.

I have always striven to be perfectly obedient to legitimate commands in the external forum, but I beg the right to form my conscience according to the guidance of directors, in the internal forum, without demands that I follow your directions and no other. I hope you understand this rightly as a humble and filial petition.

To Valerio Cardinal Valeri

January 2, 1960

The fatherly wisdom with which your Eminence wrote to me on December 7 (No. 5390/59) indicated very clearly to me the will of God and of the Church. I hasten to express my obedience to this holy will for all the reasons your Eminence has suggested to me; and, thanks to your prayers, I am able to make this acceptance without difficulty and even with a great deal of peace—which was surely a grace from the heavenly Father to do what by myself I would be incapable of doing. I assure you, then, that I have abandoned my plans for an exclaustration that would enable me to live a solitary life: a life that could be dangerous for me and I willingly accept the duty of devoting myself to the tasks which obedience has entrusted to me here for the good of souls and for my own well-being. I am entirely at the disposition of Holy Church, whatever it may be. I do not belong to myself but to Christ and to souls.

If your Eminence believes that the question of possible scandal should suffice to advise against exclaustration, I accept this decision. I don't want to do any harm to souls. I love the Order of Cistercians and my brothers who seek God here. The fact that I am not a normal Cistercian (and certainly not a very good one) changes nothing in their love and esteem for me, which I by no means deserve. So I can say that here is my rightful place.

Will Your Eminence allow me to make two clarifications, in order to manifest and reveal my own conscience? These are two thoughts which come to my mind at times, though without troubling me too much.

The first is that I myself am quite convinced that I do not have a vocation to the hermit life, and, in asking for exclaustration, I was not exactly asking simply to be a hermit. What I wanted and what I was advised to do was to join Dom Gregorio Lemercier and his plans for a primitive Benedictine monasticism. I wanted to help him in forming a small group, more or less solitary, under his direction and with a limited apostolic outreach: that is to say, with the possibility of certain limited contacts with intellectuals in Mexico City who are somewhat communistic in outlook, but who would have accepted me with much goodwill as a person who would understand them. Certain ones among them were awaiting with lively anticipation my coming in Mexico and this small foundation. The fact that I did not come is a great disappointment to them, and even something of a scandal. I am not suggesting that this scandal could be compared to the other, clearly much more serious, which would have been caused among my confreres, though they would probably not be greatly surprised.

The second thought is more difficult to express and more personal too. Fr. Abbot has not said a word to me—which leads me to guess that his trip to Rome in November had something to do with my "case"—and I have no exact idea of the reasons he gave you to make you see that I should not leave the monastery. But my guess is that his strongest argument must have been based on a few words about me from the lips of the late Dr. Zilboorg, a famous psychiatrist well known in Rome. This good gentleman, who was my friend, told the Abbot on one occasion four or five years ago that the desires I had at the time could be dangerous for me and that I could even do some very foolish things. Doubtlessly he said this with good reason and I accepted it with prudence. But those who knew Dr. Zilboorg knew that he had a flair for the dramatic and was fond of theatrical tricks and exaggerations. I don't think that Fr. Abbot realized sufficiently this feature in his character—especially since Dr. Zilboorg had said on that same occasion some rather strong things about Fr. Abbot himself, which the Abbot didn't need to hear. For my part, I am not paying much attention to it, because I knew Dr. Zilboorg well.

Before presenting my petition to the Sacred Congregation, I have consulted with a psychiatrist [Fr. John Eudes Bamberger, now Abbot of the Abbey of the Genesee in New York] here at the monastery, who was aware of the whole situation, who knew Dr. Zilboorg and also Fr. Abbot. This psychiatrist, who is one of our priests, simply told me not to worry about what Dr. Zilboorg had said, that my petition was on solid ground, that the plan seemed to him to have nothing to do with any neurosis whatever, and that it was all right for me to do what I was doing. Above all, he and I were convinced that I had much to gain by placing myself under the direction of Dom Gregorio Lemercier. Far from seeking to avoid religious obedience, I wanted, on the contrary, to place myself under a spiritual father who seemed to me much stronger and more clear-sighted than my own Abbot. What I mean to say is that I believe that the monasticism of Dom Lemercier is more alive and more effective than what we are practicing here.

And, finally, realizing that I can still be a victim of illusions, I have just received permission for a series of consultations with the best psychiatrist in Louisville (Dr. James Wygal), who incidentally was once a student of Zilboorg, who is acquainted with the monasteries of this area, having worked a good deal with religious, including Cistercians here.

While accepting wholeheartedly and without reservation the decision of the Sacred Congregation and of Your Eminence, I wonder if—after these consultations have taken place and the psychiatrist assures me that there is no danger for me in making a change of this kind and that I might even have something to gain by it—I might not be able to submit to you his decision to see what Your Eminence thinks about it.

I am not thinking of renewing my request for exclaustration. But the thought still remains with me that there still exists the possibility of a transfer to the monastery at Cuernavaca, where I would be assured of a regular Superior and an excellent community, and so there would be no dangers such as my Superiors fear [when they think] of my petition for exclaustration.

Without doubt there still exists the big question of possible scandal. I don't want in any way to impose my own will. For my own peace of mind I need to know in some definitive way if this desire rises out of some psychological problem. But even if it is something perfectly normal, as I think it is, obedience still means the same [the obligation it has always been], and I am entirely in the hands of my Superiors.

I hope Your Eminence will pardon this letter of simple and candid thoughts from a son who is completely loyal and who seeks only the will of God, nothing else. The letter of Your Eminence by itself is quite sufficient to resolve all my doubts and to answer all my questions. None-theless, I wanted, with filial trust and simplicity, to share these two thoughts with you. I accept fully all that Your Eminence wants and I ask for Your paternal blessing.

To Father Jean Danielou

January 2, 1960

Thank you for your very fine and heartwarming letter of December 26th. I was glad to get it and it was indeed a consolation. It was good to hear from so many friends in Europe.

Meanwhile, however, I had received a letter from Rome, signed by both Cardinal Valeri and Cardinal Larraona—a long detailed and sympathetic letter, in which, however, it was said that they accepted fully the ideas of my Superiors and desired definitely that I remain here at Gethsemani, first by reason of the scandal and trouble it might cause for souls inside the Order and outside it, and then because of my own "spiritual good." Now, since before this Cardinal Larraona seemed to have decided that the question of scandal was not sufficiently weighty to prevent the granting of the exclaustration, it is evident that my Father Abbot's visit to Rome was the deciding factor and that he must have told them something strong. I believe that he told them (he has said nothing to me) some rather lurid and exaggerated statements that were made at one time about me by Gregory Zilboorg. Zilboorg, as you may know, was a wonderful person and a great psychiatrist, but also a man of the theater and a great talker. He was not above making highly exaggerated statements, and what he said of me among other things was that I was a megalomaniac (which is partly true—otherwise I would not be a writer) and then that if I once got away from the monastery and the control of Superiors I would probably seize the first opportunity to run away with a woman. Well, I know we are all frail, but after all a categorical statement like that is not meant to be taken absolutely literally. Certainly I feel that to have the case negatively decided because of an irresponsible remark of a fine talker is not quite just. But of course I fully accept the decision of the Cardinals and recognize that their will seems to be quite final. However, I have dared to write what I hope is a humble letter, expressing my further thoughts, along with my full acceptance. I do not think there is any hope of their revising their decision and I personally remain totally indifferent. I am perfectly content to stay here if it is God's will. I will do anything they say, I no longer have any preference one way or the other. I really feel perfectly free, and if I express these further thoughts it is not so much because I "want" to go to Mexico as because I still think it may be God's will for me to express these ideas and to clarify. That is all. As far as desires go, I really can say that I am indifferent as to where

I live and die, or what I do. There is no difficulty in my spending the rest of my life here.

As I said in the letter to the Cardinals, I intend to have some consultations with a psychiatrist in Louisville who is a good doctor and a pupil of Zilboorg's, very reliable. Whatever be the outcome, I would like to know if there is any foundation to those damaging statements, and what I ought to do about it. In any event, it ought to be useful to me and to my work.

Father Abbot is really obsessed with the idea that I should not be allowed out of the monastery for more than a day and not further than Louisville—he has many funny ideas about his men, and trusts no one in certain matters. Especially me, though I have never given any reason whatever, in the monastery, to rouse suspicion on this score. However, he would certainly never permit me to go to Florence in June, much as I would like to do so for many reasons. It seems to me that it is very necessary to take a political stand in these times and I have been, I regret to say, foolishly apolitical—even in the article on Pasternak (the second one) which I have just sent you. About this I will have to write to you more later. I just wanted you to have this copy of the letter to the Cardinals as soon as possible. I do not know if you have any other news. It does not seem to me that there is anything else to be done, and I must simply accept the situation as it is and serve God in it with all the fidelity I can. This year I have been reappointed as Novice Master and also my publisher has got me working on another book. Dr. Suzuki came through with an interesting article, which, however, had little do with the Desert Fathers. I think I will have a set of proofs sent to you, you might be interested and there might be some points to watch for in the book. I replied to his article, and it made an interesting little dialogue between East and West. I am eager to see the finished book, I think it will have some significance, though it may be perplexing to many readers.

Of all these things I will write again when I have more time. This will suffice to bring you my warm good wishes for the new year, and the assurance of my prayers, in gratitude for your kind and wise help.

To Father Jean Danielou

On April 21, 1960, Merton wrote to Jean Danielou telling him that he was at peace regarding the decision of Rome. He had received, he said, another letter from Cardinal Larraona informing him that nothing had been said about Dr. Zilboorg, whom the Cardinal "airily dismissed . . . with a pleasant Spanish proverb De poeta y de loco tenemos todos un poco [We all have a bit of poetry and a bit of madness in us]. *Merton confesses: "My suspicions overshot the mark." He mentions his contact with Dr. Wygal and the assurance he received from him that he was not neurotic. This letter may be found in its completeness in* The

Hidden Ground of Love, *the only letter to Danielou available at the time of publication of the first volume in the series.*

To the Rev. Father Paul Philippe, O.P.

Archbishop Philippe was secretary of the Vatican's Congregation for Religious. Merton had met him when he visited Gethsemani.

August 6, 1960

I have been thinking for a long time of writing to you, but I have refrained from doing so, knowing how busy you are and not wanting to complicate your already heavy schedule. But now friendship and necessity join together in moving me to write this letter, which I shall try to make as brief as possible.

You know well the desires that for so long a time have dwelt in my heart. You know too that last year I petitioned the Sacred Congregation for an indult of exclaustration, so that I might go to the diocese of Cuernavaca to live under the protection and direction of Reverend Father Dom Gregorio Lemercier, who has done a great deal, and with exemplary generosity, to help me accomplish what seems to him an inspiration of the Holy Spirit, both for the good of my soul and for the glory of God. However, after the very strong representations made by my Superiors to the Sacred Congregation, his Eminence Cardinal Valeri told me that I should stay here and that my presence here was important for souls and for the Church.

This decision, you very well know, I have accepted with a willing spirit, and I accept it fully. I believe that my departure from here could be serious in some ways. I accept living here, if the wisdom of Holy Church indicates to me that this is the will of God. I have no intention of making any direct appeals or of "pushing" my case or of taking any initiative of my own. This letter intends simply to give you an account of my actual state of mind.

Why? Because I know that Dom Gregorio has spoken to you and that he wants me to speak for myself or at least he wants to tell me what has been said by both of you. Now it is impossible for me to write to him. A letter to him or from him would never get through the hands of my Abbot, which seems to me (I say this in parentheses) to be a little arbitrary; and it is this which complicates matters. So be it. In any case I have no direct communication with Dom Gregorio. But I do know indirectly that His Excellency the Bishop of Cuernavaca is actually in Rome. Now if His Excellency were to visit you, he could speak on my behalf and make this or that request on my behalf. He is a bishop; thus he can know (as well as my Superiors) what the will of the Church would be in my case, what would be for the good of souls and of the monastic state.

I want to tell you, therefore, what I think and what I believe I ought to do before God:

1. I think exactly as I thought last year and have thought for more than a dozen years: that I am not where I belong, that I am not truly living as a monk in the full sense of the word, that I am rather a bourgeois monk, respectable, member of a community that is rich, prosperous, active, but hardly contemplative at all, a community that offers a façade for a Catholicism that is worldly enough, a Catholicism that is capitalistic (you will notice that I am not embarrassed to use this word). I feel a falseness in myself, as someone who aids the political and social forces that lead to war and misery, without wanting to do so. I think it would be possible for me to leave this monastery in order to follow a vocation, a more perfect life, one that is more primitive and more solitary: such as the atmosphere of Cuernavaca offers me, in the shadow of a primitive Benedictine monastery. Before God I think that, if it is possible I should take this step, not just for the good of my soul and the good of the Church, but in order to be in a poor country, a country that is not getting involved in war to defend its financial assets, a primitive country, where I would be living among primitive indigenous peoples.

2. But, having articulated the serious situation of my own position, I realize all too well that my departure could have serious effects on souls. I don't have to say this, for my Superiors have already said it very forcefully. Still, I wonder if the effect would be completely bad. For example in the Order: might not this "upset" of monastic souls be perhaps something salutary, since my intent is to find a life more authentic and more monastic? I wonder if my Superiors are too afraid of upsetting the status quo, the mediocre institution such as it is? Would that not be a way of imprisoning souls in mediocrity, with all horizons closed? The longing for solitude—is it a crime or is it not the crown of the monastic vocation? It is true that people can easily deceive themselves, and I could well be deceived myself. That is why I submit myself entirely to the judgment of the Church.

In any case I know my novices (and they know me) and I know that if I were to leave for Mexico, it would be an edification for them; and I think that others in this community would also be edified. Not all of them want solitude. Far from it. Many are perfectly satisfied with the cenobitic life. So much the better for them.

3. It is true that my departure, if it should actually take place, should be kept a top secret. The whole point of my going elsewhere would be that I might be in hiddenness, that I might disappear. There would be the inevitable rumors, but so what? There are always some about me anyway. There actually is one, but that is easily forgotten, as belonging to the past. People like to talk about something else—something new.

The only thing which makes me hesitate a bit is that we actually have a small movement of retreats and dialogues, in which I have taken part, with Protestants, non-Catholic intellectuals, etc. The Holy Father [see letters to Pope John XXIII in *HGL*] is very interested in this movement and has blessed it. But, on the other hand, if this is something I should do, something that God wills, I could do it with more profit in Mexico, although I do not want to give myself to this kind of apostolate down there, but rather to live, in solitude, an authentic monastic life.

In any event, my dear Father, realizing that you understand me well, with my foibles and illusions, I am telling you just what is in my heart. I am not telling you what *I want* to do, whatever that is. I am simply expressing what I think. Pure desires: I desire only what the Church desires. But what I ask myself, most seriously before God, is always this same question: Is it not necessary for me to go elsewhere to find a community more primitive and more purely monastic? Is it not necessary for me to give myself to God in solitude under the direction of a truly enlightened Superior, such as Dom Gregorio? Is it not necessary for me to associate myself with those in the monastic movement who are moving in the right direction, and not with those who have aligned themselves with a bourgeois and worldly mentality? Isn't this in fact the root problem: the scandal of my remaining with the latter group? I simply ask myself these questions. Perhaps His Excellency of Cuernavaca is asking them too. I don't know. The wisdom of God will enlighten you, my dear Father. I want only what the Church asks of me. I ask nothing for myself. If others feel they should ask for me, I am ready to accept all that you think should be arranged for me. I seek only, and in a spirit of detachment, God's holy will. If I must stay here, I can do so without being too unhappy, and without being happy either, and above all without having the conviction that I am truly in the place where my vocation calls me to be. So that is it, Reverend Father. I am happy to be able to speak to you. I ask you to forgive me if all that I have said is about myself. I pray often for you. Please give me your blessing.

August 17, 1960

Since my letter to you of the 6th, which you have probably not had time to consider thoroughly yet, in view of an answer, I have been able to obtain information, indirectly, about what was said in your conversation with my friend Dom Gregorio Lemercier, O.S.B. I learned that the letter of His Eminence Cardinal Valeri to me last fall, denying my application for an exclaustration to the diocese of Cuernavaca, was not absolutely final as I myself had at first thought. Since I now learn that I can, without disobedience, renew the application in spite of this letter which supported my Abbot and Abbot General against me, I feel that I must, in conscience, reopen the case once again.

This morning I have formally consulted, again, my confessor and director on this point. He tells me frankly and without reservations that he believes it to be God's will for me to ask to go and live under the shadow of Dom Gregorio's monastery at Cuernavaca and attempt a new adjustment under his wise direction. (It is not exactly a question of complete eremitical solitude but an adjustment, in view of a more individual, personal, and solitary expansion of my monastic vocation, insofar as Dom Gregorio may help me to work this out.) It is not that my confessor is pushing me to start something radically new, but rather he is most positive that I ought to *leave here*. Cuernavaca is the obvious opportunity. My director further believes that (a) it will be of no purpose for me to try to advance and grow here by struggling to be in all things a perfect "Trappist," which in any case is not possible for me. (b) I cannot really be of much help, as things now are, to others in the community. (c) The compromises which have been offered me here are of no value to me or to the community—except insofar as they "keep me here." The position of my Abbot is that I should be kept here at all costs, because of the reputation of the monastery.

A friend and psychiatrist whom I have also consulted (he knows me very well) assures me that my desires are not in his opinion motivated by neurotic trends but are normal and healthy. He also, after considerable experience with monastic patients, believes that the situation here is not a healthy or honest one at all.

In view of these things and the other points mentioned previously, I believe myself bound in conscience, by my vow of conversion of manners as a Benedictine monk, to ask for an indult that will permit me to extricate myself from this situation and develop more fruitfully and normally in a more favorable situation provided by Dom Gregorio, in the diocese of Cuernavaca. At least I feel that I am bound to *make a trial* of this possibility, and that I should continue to ask permission now that the trial is, it seems to us, rather unreasonably refused by my Superiors, especially since the permission was practically granted by the former secretary, Cardinal Larraona, for whose interest in my case I am deeply grateful.

I intend this letter then to be a renewal of my application of last September 8th (1959) for an exclaustration to Cuernavaca. I make this application trusting that the case is not hopeless and that my Superiors will not once again renew the onslaught which is calculated to overpower all opposition and to silence all hopes.

If for any reason, dear Father, you believe that I am imprudent or unwise in making this petition, or if you believe that I should delay it or make it in some other form, I would be deeply grateful for your advice. But if on the other hand you believe it to be just and reasonable and if you think there is some possibility of success, I confidently place this petition in your hands and beg you in your charity to take care of it.

I write this in the conviction that only in this way can I respond to what I believe to be the inescapable will of God for me—at least insofar as the desire and the petition are concerned. I leave the results entirely in His hands, and beg your prayers that I may have the courage and strength to correspond with every indication of His will and with all His grace.

On August 30, 1960, Archbishop Philippe wrote to Merton discouraging him from attempting to reopen the matter. The following is Merton's own reflection.

MEMORANDUM

September 19, 1960

The request for an exclaustration to Cuernavaca has been renewed. Father Paul Philippe in a personal, unofficial letter, has expressed his own personal opinion that I should not leave Gethsemani and has made a request that I consider this a sufficient answer to the questions raised. But he leaves the question officially open.

Father G. [Gregorio] says that (1) the decision is still up to me and that if I really want an exclaustration I have only to insist and it will be granted. (2) The reasons alleged by Paul P[hilippe] are not convincing or serious. In effect the reasons are the same that have always been alleged, in the last ten years. First that I may be deceiving myself and second that a departure from here would cause too much comment.

What do I think I ought to do?

The reasons of Paul Philippe: I may be deluded. As always, I maintain that I ought, like so many other religious who have come here, to be granted the right to at least *try* the form of life to which I think I am called.

Scandal: there will be comment, yes. Scandal: if I get an exclaustration there may be reasonable cause for scandal. It can be misrepresented. I think I should therefore not ask for an exclaustration but for a transitus to the Benedictine monastery of Cuernavaca. In this way it will be clear that I have not left the religious state but have gone to a more primitive monastery. Far from giving scandal, this ought to have a good effect. At most it would give pharisaical scandal.

What do I think about insisting on the indult?

The question of obedience is delicate.

It is true that the request of PP is not a formal command. He is not speaking officially as my highest Superior but as a friend, giving advice. It is probable that he would grant the indult if I insisted. But he would do so unwillingly. I have to take this unwillingness into consideration, not as a point of obedience but rather of docility or prudence.

If I were not so aware that my pride and self-seeking might be mixed up in my desire for a better life, I would not be so hesitant. In point of fact there has to be some protection against my self-will. If I simply override the desires of my Superior in Rome, I will have no assurance that I have not simply imposed my will arbitrarily on him. If I start another life without any assurance that I have not yielded to caprice, it will be difficult for me to resist the temptations that must surely arise.

If, on the other hand, by humble and patient discussion, I can bring Fr. PP to agree that there is a good reason for my making the change and to approve of it at least to some extent, at least to permit it willingly, then it will be more likely that this is really the will of God.

It is not that we know the will of God for certain, but that we are convinced that this is probably the will of God *if* we follow all the indications of Providence. All the indications have to be followed. If the higher Superior is unwilling to grant the indult, then this seems to me to be an indication that God wills me to delay, to discuss the matter, and that it is not His will for me to insist on getting "what I want." It must not only be "got" by me, it must be "given to" me willingly by those who, after all, represent God in the Church.

I do not feel that I ought to take action which would amount to forcing the Superiors to do what they do not want to do.

It seems to me that this is only a matter of time. Perhaps a lot depends on my own interior dispositions. There has been too much pride and impatience, too much of an uncharitable and negative attitude toward my own monastery, its Superior and his policies. This does not mean that I have to agree with things which I cannot possibly accept in conscience. But it does mean that I have to be careful that I am not just using these as occasions for self-delusion and to support a fictitious idea of my own "rightness." In a word it must be certain that I am seeking a poor and solitary life not in order to justify and glorify myself, but in order to seek pardon for my sins and a genuine gift of myself to God. I *want* this, with all my heart, but there is still danger of delusion.

The monastery that Dom Gregorio Lemercier began in Cuernavaca in 1950 became deeply involved in group therapy and psychoanalysis, and was eventually suppressed by Rome. In July 1968 a brother showed Merton a newspaper photograph of Gregorio Lemercier and his new young bride. Merton was saddened that the monastic experiment that Lemercier had envisioned had not worked.

SEQUEL TO THE CRISIS OF 1959–1960

On August 20, 1965, Merton at last entered into a hermit life on the grounds of Gethsemani. When Ernesto Cardenal visited him in October 1965 as a newly ordained priest, Merton gave him three letters (one to Cardenal himself, a second to the Congregation for Religious, and a third for Pope Paul VI). asking Cardenal to carry them to Rome, but only when Merton gave him word to do so.

On March 17, 1994, Cardenal sent me these three letters, informing me that Merton had never sent him word to take them to Rome. Thus they never reached their intended destination. Cardenal said in his letter to me: "Merton was continually changing his mind as to where he wanted to reside, and in the last years he thought only of coming to Solentiname for a visit of three months or so." The letters are evidence of Merton's lingering desire to go to Latin America. They also suggest the restlessness of spirit which periodically he had to deal with.

To Rev. Father Ernesto Cardenal

This letter was not available when The Courage for Truth *(which contains the Cardenal letters) was published.*

October 22, 1965

It seems to me that the extraordinary interest of so many Christians of Nicaragua in a contemplative foundation must come from the Holy Spirit. Realizing the great need for such a foundation, and also the need for giving the contemplative life a special morality adapted to this situation, you are proceeding with this plan which was first conceived here at Gethsemani, in our conversations, when you were a novice under my direction. I am delighted that you have persevered with your intention and that you have so matured and developed in your understanding of what it involves. God is blessing your project, and has already given you associates, benefactors, and all kinds of support. Everything points to a very successful work, for His glory.

However, you feel that it is necessary for your project to receive guidance and direction from someone experienced in the monastic life. Since you regard me in some sense as an originator of the idea, and since I have always been deeply interested in this project, and further, since I am no longer novice master at Gethsemani and have been relieved of all duties here with the object of advancing further in the life of contemplation and solitude, you have desired that I might be associated with your project and have invited me to join you. Realizing the difficulties that would be involved, you have asked me to give my consent, so that you might proceed to take whatever steps might be necessary to obtain permission from higher Superiors, so that I might be loaned to your project by my Order. I am writing this letter as a formal record of my acceptance and consent, and as a statement of what my role would conceivably be in your project.

I therefore give my full consent to your asking higher Superiors if I might be permitted to leave Gethsemani with an exclaustration, if necessary, or with a simple permission, which would be preferable, to live in your contemplative community and fulfill the functions of Spiritual Father. In this capacity, acting not as Superior but as Spiritual Father in the traditional monastic sense of one giving spiritual guidance, I would be available to the community for direction and would also give conferences and instructions as required. The purpose of my presence would then be to insure that the community, which would follow a mode of life based on the Rule of St. Benedict, would be formed according to authentic monastic traditions and practices. This question of guidance and formation is without doubt crucially important.

It is understood that I would live a strictly monastic life, in solitude, near your community, continuing the hermit life which I have now begun, and that I would not be involved in active apostolic work outside the community, nor in missionary work. I would welcome this opportunity to live a simpler, more solitary life, in a distant country, in the solitude provided by your isolated island [Solentiname] far from the United States and very hidden. I especially think that in responding to the earnest desire of your friends and yourself to offer you this service, I would be fulfilling a function that is demanded by the Church in our time. In fact, your friends and others have repeatedly tried, without success, to obtain an ordinary foundation from Gethsemani. The Father Abbot of Gethsemani has refused more than twenty offers to make foundations in Latin America, including several in Nicaragua and Costa Rica. There is then no hope of obtaining an ordinary Cistercian foundation. Gethsemani has sent no one to Latin America, in spite of the urgent appeal which the Church has made for North American dioceses and religious communities to send ten percent of their clergy or personnel to Latin America in this time of extraordinary need. Surely, if Gethsemani could permit *one* priest to answer this very unusual invitation, it would be only the fulfillment of an obligation.

Because of special circumstances, the Father Abbot of Gethsemani is not disposed to hear of any such project. Hence the permission must be requested from higher Superiors. This letter will signify my own consent and willingness to comply, if they see fit to let me join your community as Spiritual Father. I will write a letter to the Most Rev. Archbishop Paul Philippe, which you can send him with your own request. You may use this letter to show that I am in full accord with your project.

In the meantime, I would appreciate at least one year of full retreat here in my present hermitage, without any responsibilities. I would be ready to come to Nicaragua after September 1966 if permission is granted. In any event, I will write a short directory (rather than a formal "Rule"), which may be of use to you in setting up your community. Since you hope to live by the Rule of St. Benedict, you need no other Rule. But it would be good to have a "directory" that would help apply the Rule of St. Benedict to your own situation. This I will attempt to provide, with God's help. I hope and pray that, if it is His holy will, I may also be privileged to come and serve you personally as Spiritual Father, for I consider that this would be a step toward greater monastic perfection in my own case, since it would be in the ancient monastic tradition of exile from one's own country, and the great solitude of these remote islands would be most conducive to the fulfillment of my vocation. However, the answer rests not with you or with me, but with our higher Superiors. Let us therefore pray that God may guide them and ourselves, and that His holy will may be done in all things.

To the Most Rev. Archbishop Paul Philippe

No one ignores the crucial importance of promoting contemplative life in Latin America today. Further, the Church has urged dioceses and religious houses of the United States to send priests and religious to help in South America. Innumerable requests for foundations have been sent in to Cistercian monasteries of the United States, particularly Gethsemani. It is not possible to say exactly how many such requests have been refused by Gethsemani, but I am sure the refusals number more than twenty, all of them attractive offers of land, etc. At the same time it is understandable that the success of the usual type of Cistercian foundation in Latin America would be problematical. Two foundations made from Spencer are in grave difficulties.

Father Ernesto Cardenal was recently ordained as a secular priest (August 16, 1965) in Nicaragua. He is a former novice of Gethsemani who left for reasons of health. During his novitiate, when he was under my direction, we spoke frequently of the contemplative life in Latin America. He is now beginning a small contemplative foundation, following the Rule of St. Benedict, but not affiliated with any Order, in Nicaragua. Feeling that I am in some way the originator of the idea, and desiring to have the guidance of someone experienced in monastic life, he has approached me and asked if I would consent to accept the charge of Spiritual Father, giving conferences, instruction, and direction while his community is in the process of formation, at least. I have replied that I would certainly consent to undertake this task if I could be loaned by my community to his community, either with a leave of absence or, if Your Excellency thought necessary, an exclaustration. The idea would be for me to continue my monastic life in his community while remaining a member of my own Order canonically. However, as this is a suggestion that my own Superiors would regard as novel and unacceptable, it has been thought well to present it directly to Your Excellency for advice and for some indication of God's will in this regard. It is felt that Your Excellency would be able to see the whole project in better perspective.

Speaking personally, I believe that this step would be a greater perfection in my own monastic vocation. It would fit the traditionally monastic idea of exile from one's own country and people, at the same time providing a life of greater solitude on a small island in the Lake of Nicaragua, and with greater poverty and simplicity. It would also be a response to a call of charity from Catholics who are in serious spiritual need. However, I take no personal initiative in this matter and leave the decision entirely to higher Superiors. I would appreciate hearing directly from Your Excellency about your reactions to this project, and will follow whatever you say.

To His Holiness Pope Paul VI

This letter will be presented to you by a delegation of faithful Catholics from Nicaragua in Central America. These faithful realize in a most urgent manner the great need of the contemplative and monastic life in Latin America today. After repeated, unsuccessful attempts to obtain a foundation from the contemplative monasteries of the United States, especially the Abbey of Gethsemani, they are now beginning to form a contemplative community under the direction of Father Ernesto Cardenal, who was a novice at this monastery under my direction, and who, after leaving Gethsemani for reasons of health, has been ordained as a secular priest and is forming a small community to live a contemplative life and provide a place of retreat for the intellectuals of Nicaragua, for students, writers, and so on.

Since this project was, in part, conceived in conversations with me when Father Cardenal was a novice here, and since I am very interested in the project myself, they have asked me if I would consent to join the community and act as Spiritual Father, giving conferences and direction, and offering guidance that would help the community to understand correctly the Rule of St. Benedict and monastic traditions. The community wishes to follow the Benedictine Rule. I gladly consent to offer this service provided that my Superiors see fit to permit me to be absent from my monastery and continue my monastic life (remaining canonically a member of my own Order) at this new community.

Because this is a very unusual project, and because of the difficulties that present themselves, these petitioners have found it necessary to come to Rome in order to ascertain, from higher Superiors, whether this is not the will of God. It is hoped that higher Superiors will interpret the will of God for all of us in this case. As the situation in Latin America today is so urgent, and as monasteries of the United States have been repeatedly urged to send men to Latin America, it is felt that the Abbey of Gethsemani, which has so far sent no one, could at least spare *one priest* in this very special case, in which the most prominent Catholic intellectuals of an entire nation have joined themselves together to make the petition.

It is felt by all of us that Your Holiness would be in a special position to see, in its full perspective, the meaning of this petition and of the project with which it is concerned. For that reason the matter is being submitted directly to your Holiness at the same time as the secretary of the Sacred Congregation of Religious is being consulted about it. Your Holiness's interest, support and blessing would indeed be most warmly appreciated. Begging the blessing of Your Holiness, I remain your most humbly devoted son in Christ Our Lord.

6. Some "Gethsemani" Letters

Never think that I take the solitary life lightly. I cannot take it lightly. It is the most important thing in my existence and I have to cling to it with all my power.

TO DOM JAMES

To Father Raymond Flanagan

Letters and notes exchanged between Thomas Merton (Fr. Louis) and Fr. Raymond Flanagan, the "other author" at Gethsemani (his books include The Man Who Got Even with God, Burnt-Out Incense, *and others), were discovered in the effects of Fr. Raymond after his death in 1990. Of the twenty-two letters, all but two are from Merton to Fr. Raymond. In most of the letters Merton playfully addresses Fr. Raymond as "Rasputin" and signs his own name "Lousi." Much of what is in the letters is "in-house" material or fairly abstruse discussions of aspects of the contemplative life that would not interest the general reader. The letters I have chosen abound in good-humored confrontation. Unfortunately none of the letters is dated, though the contents at times helps to establish the approximate time. Thus the first letter deals with Merton's book of poems* A Man in the Divided Sea, *published in 1946. So the letter can safely be dated 1946 or 1947.*

Ex toto corde thanks for that long and generous examination of the so-called poems, and for the loan of Mgr. D., whom I shall study right away, so as not to keep it too long.

I don't attempt to *defend* my eccentricities. Frankly, before taking up your points, my feeling about exuberance is that it betrays my weakness. If only I could hit some kind of clean, lapidary simplicity. I think the poem for my Brother is one of the best because it is one of the simplest. I think Clairvaux is one of the worst—merely as *writing* because I am fond of the idea too—because it is too glib. Critics objected to the obvious Hopkinsisms and I agree they are too obvious. I am getting into a rut and this lurid stuff flows out in too great abundance. So I am changing my tune. It may mean getting *obscure* again in order to hit a more monumental structure. But most of this stuff is too lush. I am not going to rush into print so fast either.

The title refers (a) on one level to conversion from no faith to faith and from world to monastery [and] (b) passage through the Red Sea by the contemplative life—a stock image in the Fathers.

Death—another stock image from the "grain of wheat" context. The natural way of knowing God is through creatures, images, species. But by the "dark" light of faith and the gifts (understanding, wisdom) we "die" to that particular way because we travel another way that darkens our vision by the blinding of excessive light—familiar line of talk all the way down from Pseudo-Denys to St. Gregory, St. Bonaventure (even a little in St. Bernard), St. John of the X (don't hit me!), and the rest.

Incidentally, about John X [of the Cross]—I guess you know that he is considered the *safest* ([Jacques] Bossuet said that) of our mystical theologians, because he is the most absolute in forbidding anyone to desire visions, ecstasies, locutions, and indeed any kind of faith experience, so uncompromising is he about the night of faith he insists on. Therefore anyone who follows him and who has a hankering to fly in the air has not read the saint very carefully, if you ask me.

Thanks for those five pages! If they have done these things in the green wood what will they do in the dry—i.e., when the cat falls into your clutches. The "cat" will not be entirely out of that bag until next spring [1948]. It is called *The Seven Storey Mountain*. It is crazy too. So is *Figures for an Apocalypse*.

Pray for me to do what God wants in the matter of poetry. My feeling is that I should write less for a while and get into a *different rut*, at least. Incidentally, some of it was translated into a foreign language—guess which one: Swedish! I felt like telling them "What's the matter, can't you dopes see that it's in Swedish already?" So I guess I am nearly as bad as you with your (congratulations) *Gelijkjki Oop* or whatever the Dutch is for the *Man Who Got Even [with God]*.

I sure pray for you and your work. Incidentally, since we are on the subject—can I persuade you to apply some of that abounding energy and enthusiasm to the study of St. Bernard and his school? You'd do a tremendous amount of good in the community and incidentally you would find them full of themes congenial to you which you have never been able to fully express as yet, at least not in a way that left me entirely sated inside: I mean for instance the insistence on the *dignity of human nature*—I think you have been fighting a windmill in your distrust of St. Bernard's talk on humility, because you never looked any further than the definition about being "vile" in one's own eyes. Actually his doctrine is terrific. You see what he works on consistently all through is this point that our nature preserves *all* that belongs to it, and we must recognize that before we can even start in our ascent to God. We must see God's image there, and it wouldn't be there if our nature had been rotted away. It is the presence of that image in our nature that is the basis of all our *confidence* (tremendously important in St. B!). But at the same time "cupidity" has covered this image with a disguise which makes it *look* rotten. Strip off the self-love, you strip off the rottenness and become your true self. And since your true self is to be exactly like God, you "lose yourself" ("die") in God the way the candlelight dies in the light of the sun—without ceasing to be a separate light. So when he talks about knowing how "vile" we are, he just wants us to recognize the disguise and start peeling it off to get at the true beauty of our nature which he also insists in season and out that we must know. If you are interested, Gilson's *Myst[ical] T[heology] of St. Bern.* will give you all the pointers and you will find plenty in the last sermons on the Canticles—from 80 to 85. They and the *De Diligendo Deo* and the *De Gradibus Hum[ilitatis]* (first xiii chapters) will give you a bird's-eye view of Bernard but Gilson's comments are essential. Forgive my talking like this to someone who knows all the theology you do when I don't know any—but at least I have read St. Bernard a bit; and honestly, Father, you could do a tremendous amount in getting people interested in what is an essentially healthy and simple and powerful spirituality.

n.d. (early 1948)

About style—I don't defend myself. You'll be satisfied, I think, that it is at least vivid when you hit the "7 (Seven) Storey Mountain" which is the "Cat" we have made signs [in sign language] about.

n.d. (probably 1948)

Here are a couple of points at random.

1. Our Founders did not know they were forming a *contemplative Order*. Nothing in the documents says a word about *contemplation*. They wanted the pure, cenobitic, monastic life—in Cassian's terminology & in St. Gregory's this is the *active* life. Do you mean to tell me that running a tractor is *contemplation* while hearing confessions is activity??

2. By a providential accident St. Bernard started a school of mysticism at Clairvaux and in *some* monasteries of the Order they led a contemplative life—proving that it can be done. *But*—they had a slower tempo—more leisurely, longer hours of work if you like—less rushing—*every feast of MM was a whole holiday* for the monks—devoted to reading & prayer —with Sundays this added up to about 100 days a year—almost ⅓. Still—their cloisters were a madhouse. People practiced singing *in the cloister* where the others read—or they washed their clothes or beat the dirt out of their blankets.

3. The big vice of our Order is one of the *most fatal* to contemplation—we are & always have been businessmen. As such we have often been among the *least contemplative* monks in the Church—large-scale farmers & nothing more.

4. The other big vice—too much frantic reading & overwork— overdoing the activities—piling up observances & penances, etc., and neglecting the heart-prayer. We think that if a thing *costs us an effort* it

is *ipso facto* sanctifying & we conclude that sanctity consists in wearing ourselves out & saying a lot of vocal prayers while we are doing it.

5. How many men in the house know what contemplation *is*? Let alone try to arrive at it.

6. Our ascesis of obedience is ideal for arriving at a general sort of detachment but *by itself alone* it is not enough to open the way to contemplation. If the Superior tells you to do things that are per se incompatible with contemplation, obedience will certainly not make you a contemplative—some special grace or a miracle *might*. Obedience by all means, but *directed to contemplation*.

7. Can we be sufficiently solitary? That's the big question. Don't ask me the answer. Solitude is *necessary*. Can we get enough of it? I myself keep to the church & and the cemetery as much as I can & that helps. However—*interior solitude* is *sufficient* & God will not refuse us this grace to arrive at that if we do our part. St. Bernard's cell didn't do him much good—how often was he in it?

8. On the other hand, all the Orders grouse about lack of leisure. The Carthusians kick because they are overburdened with vocal prayers and never have time to get down to "contemplation"—the complaint is universal.

9. *Distinguo*—a tired man is no good for mental prayer in which the activity of the natural faculties predominate, *concedo* [I admit]. But that is not contemplation in the proper sense. At the same time remember, the sick (especially those who get sick enough to go to the infirmary) are seldom up to scratch as far as natural, physical, and mental "tone" is concerned. Weariness and disgust are their lot. But these things don't impede real contemplation, which is a *gift of God*—and we can use them to arrive at it; they can purify us. However, I also willingly concede that we are expected to do a lot of intellectual preparation of our own—reading, meditation on Scripture, Theology, the Fathers—and if you are overworked that is simply out.

10. Real intellectual work is not part of our life, essentially. It is accidental & if someone is singled out to do it—a place has to be made for it in the time of work—I guess nobody would deny that. I.e., you *make* leisure for him. But too much activity in that line is just as bad as excess of manual labor.

11. As a whole the men in this community don't know what to do with themselves if you give them leisure! I think that is one reason why we work on most of the feasts—to keep the fathers from getting into mischief.

12. I don't know the answer. We *can* be contemplatives—we are getting many contemplative vocations in the house—that is evident. What we need is to calm down and not be so steamed up. *Turbaris erga plurima* [Jesus' words to Martha: "You are troubled about many things." Luke 10:41 in the Latin Vulgate]—in fact, *erga omnia* ["about all things"]. That is the motto of Gethsemani at times, I think.

The devil knows it too and he is very interested in keeping us from getting real interior silence, solitude, and peace.

Sed vince in bono malum. ["But overcome evil with good." Rom. 12:21 in the Latin Vulgate.]

(1947?)

About the real question: do we need a different system of contemplation (a different method of disposing ourselves for infused c[ontemplation] that would mean to me: but according to your note it should mean a different method of acquiring it . . .)? (In any case, for all practical purposes it comes to the same.) In all the contemp. orders I know about—I have read the meditations the Carthusians use in their novitiate and a lot of Carmelite stuff—I am convinced that our spiritualities are all very much the same with only very minor differences. The problems are all the same: prayer based on the Presence of God, and kept as simple as possible, constant return to God's presence, use of ejaculations according to individual appeal and not much stress on discursive meditation: on the contrary, imagination drops out and acts get less and less multiple and less frequent. The other ancillary problems are also the same: how to keep united with Superiors, how to be nice to the father who sings so sour in your ear in choir, what to do when you are tired and fed up—it is always the same temptations, the same graces, and the same sort of fruits. I don't see any except accidental differences: viz., the Carthusians have to remind themselves not to get nervous and start roving around out of their cells and we have to remind ourselves about hanging around making a lot of signs . . . The sociability problem is identical everywhere because they all get together in recreation, which is in a sense much more of a burden than our primitive contacts. At least we don't have to make chat with our hair shirts.

(probably 1948)

Evidently I will one day get a dose of the same medicine you have had to take—well, so much the better. It may be a bit grim, but it comes under the heading of love—with a capital L.

When the "cat" comes out, things will really pop around here—although I have soft-pedaled the contemplation angle completely in it.

The Seven Storey Mountain was published officially on October 4, 1948, but copies were available earlier. Father Raymond wrote a long letter of enthusiastic commendation: ". . . You need never care about writing another book! Yes, Frater, you've written a BOOK! *I unhesitatingly say it is more than a minor masterpiece! I am sure it will be a Best Seller . . ."*

October 1948

Man, if those reviewers like the book half as much as you do we'll make a million dollars and all go riding to work in Cadillacs. You sure finished it in record time. I blush to think of what devices you must have used to find time for it . . . Your guess about sales may be correct, as far as signs go. The book clubs that took it were the Catholic B.C., the Thomas More B.C., and the Catholic Literary Foundation in Milwaukee. The latter accounted for 12,000 copies. They turn out to be owned by BRUCE AND CO.! It was on that account that I had to take a straight 10% royalty to allow the publisher to cut down the price to $3.00 stipulated by this outfit. But it will increase sales and I will catch up that way. The second printing is under way, publication date being set for Aug. 12, Feast of St. Clare [even though the official publication date was October 4]. They are trying to get some fancy blurbs from big shots for the jacket, that is why there is no jacket so far.

Bruce and Co. are happy about this, and they are also happy about the fact that the book is published by a non-catholic publisher. They themselves have evidently found plenty of ways of cashing in on it. And I could see they were holding out with *Exile* [*Ends in Glory*], trying to get in *after* the Seven Storey Molehill.

About Pulitzer, well . . . hm. Doesn't seem to me likely that two converts should get a Pulitzer in such rapid succession, let alone the competition the thing would have to meet.

But it has got good backing. It is being handled by one of the best agents in the business, Naomi Burton of Curtis Brown Ltd., and she has got her fingers on everything, already arranged an English edition, etc. And Bob Giroux, who comes into the thing around page 200 and who edited the book for Harcourt, certainly has done a fine job. Only in one or two places does the cutting show. For the rest it is extremely neat and careful. He worked over that huge manuscript for months.

Really he and Naomi are making the book just as much as the author. As far as I can see it is definitely the book God has been wanting me to get off my chest all these years. I was already trying it ten years ago, and He saw to it that I didn't get to first base—although Naomi Burton liked the first trial and that is where we first got together. But doesn't it strike you as significant that God Himself should write the whole of Part III by bringing me here: and that He should get the book published just when Rev. Father needs dough?

Well, it won't make enough dough to build even one wing of a Quonset [hut] monastery, but it may help. That doesn't matter. The important thing is the people or, as the books have it, "souls."

Your best points are about the personal and spiritual angles. You are a shrewd guesser, Rasputin. Still, practically everybody who has read the thing has ended up by telling me in so many words to be sure and stay at Gethsemani. Even the New York Censor told me that, as a sort of a *hors d'oeuvre*. (There was one personality that the N.Y. diocese wanted eliminated from the book, a kid I knew who became a priest and didn't make out so well. Pray for him. He is batting around somewhere with what he imagines is a wife.) I agree with you about the spiritual gluttony angle [see *SSM*, p. 387]. On days of recollection I can't see it that way, but the rest of the time when I am comparatively sober I acknowledge it.

I'll certainly be interested in the reviews—if they come my way. And I am sure there will be plenty of accidental spiritual direction in them!

Well, anyway—the job is finished and I am happy about it and I admit your broadside pepped me up no little. This is one book I am not disgusted with. About that job [of book readings] in the refectory [of *Exile Ends in Glory*], the less said the better. I wonder where I got the idea that that was the way a reasonable being was supposed to talk? I mean my remarks and interpretations—Mother B[erchmans] is fine, herself. She had a head too. Well . . .

Pray for me to keep straight with this mountain on my back now! And thanks, thanks, thanks, thanks. You are some guy, Rasputin.

To Dom James Fox

Dom James was the abbot of Gethsemani from August 1949 to January 1967, having succeeded Dom Frederic Dunne, under whom The Seven Storey Mountain *was written.*

n.d. (probably summer 1966)

In regard to our current "problems." I shall discuss possible psychological causes with Fr. Eudes, but I am sure he will agree that the fault does not lie with the hermitage. The more I think of it, the more I believe that from every point of view it would be wrong for me to return even partially to the community life. First of all for personal reasons which I explained. Second because, whichever way you look at it, this is a step backwards and a step down and if I can avoid that I should. But it seems to me that whatever difficulties I encounter now have to be solved somehow in the context of the solitary life, not by returning to the community. It would really create a very bad impression and discredit the hermit life for others who might want to try it later, if I were to get involved in work in the community now. There is only one way: that I remain in the hermitage and work things out here.

Actually, I feel more and more at home here all the time, and I am perfectly at peace up here; my problems begin when I am with other people. It is true that to some extent I need more normal contacts, but routine work in the community will not provide the kind of contacts that will help me. The kind of contacts that will help me will, I think, be occasional visits or talks with people who do unusual creative work, or are in some way interesting and exceptional people, or come from foreign countries, etc. This will provide challenges and stimulation and perhaps occasions for interesting work.

For my so-called "oral needs" as the psychiatrists say, I can easily take care of them if I have plenty to read and some correspondence and if, for instance, when I go to the doctor, I can get a little time in the library. That is usually sufficient to keep me going in this regard and is not disedifying, I think.

In my own heart I feel very strongly that it would be all wrong for me to turn back. If I ran into the same occasions as a cenobite I would have the same trouble I have had. The hermit life, if I am faithful to it, ought to provide me with graces and ways of guarding against all this in the future. I do not think my failures are a reason for abandoning solitude but for continuing in it with renewed resolution and with greater under- standing, prudence, and reliance on prayer. Never think that I take the solitary life lightly. I cannot take it lightly. It is the most important thing in my existence and I have to cling to it with all my power. If I could not stay in the hermitage, life would not be worth living and I would certainly create far more problems because I would be a burden to myself and to everyone else. As I said before, I rely very much on your prayers, but I am sure that Our Lord will show me the way right here in the hermitage. I am sorry to have caused you so much trouble.

If I get too cooped up in the hermitage it is usually enough if I go for a walk to one of the lakes or climb one of the knobs. This is all I need, and I assume that it is all right to do this.

n.d. (probably summer 1966)

This is an important matter which I have been putting off but I guess I might as well state it frankly and let you decide. It concerns the question of my doctors and where I should go for medical attention. I am frankly convinced that it is not to my interest to change to doctors in Lexington and I would like to say clearly that the non-medical reasons for the change no longer exist.

1. Medically: though I do not have to have an operation soon, the chances of having another delicate back operation sometime are very real. The doctors in Louisville have all my records, know and understand my case perfectly, I have the greatest confidence in them. To change now would not only be bad medical practice but would also be to my disad- vantage, notwithstanding the fact that the doctors in Lexington may be good ones. They too would agree that merely to change at this point would be a bad thing to do. In any case I will not need hospitalization in the near future.

2. Non-medically: the person who created the problem left this area in midsummer. She has no family or relatives in this area and no intention of ever working here. It is true that some of the nurses at St. Joe's in Louisville trained with her, but there are also nurses in Lexington at St. Joe's that trained with her. In any case this does not make any difference as far as I can see. No one knew there was anything special going on between us and there is no reason on earth to think that anyone of them

would think of telling her I was there. Even if this did happen, I think she is concerned enough to protect me and would not want to create talk by coming from a long distance—even if she had time or could do it. She is in any case engaged to [marry] a boy in Chicago. I just frankly think there is no problem anymore. It therefore seems to me quite foolish to change to Lexington for no real reason, when there are strong objective reasons for staying with the Louisville doctors.

I may add that there are no other occult personal reasons for staying with the Louisville doctors. Apart from the medical considerations, I am utterly indifferent where I go. And of course if you decide I should go to Lexington anyway I will gladly do it. I just wanted to make these facts known. Perhaps you might want to talk it over with Fr. Eudes and let me know your decision. Thanks, in Jesu.

n.d. (summer or autumn 1966?)

I think this ought to take care of the essentials, and I presume we agree on the essential obligations of hermits. Also that there may be some room for difference of opinion on accidentals. I also once again repeat my admission that my recent failures have been in the area of essentials not accidentals. I cannot force you to believe the sincerity of this admission. If you don't want to believe it that is your affair, but for my own part I seriously intend to work on the problem. I will follow your suggestion and think more seriously about these essentials. In particular I want to assure you that I will avoid all temptations to smuggle out letters through others or to make illicit phone calls. I hope I can assure you that this source of trouble need bother you no longer. It is needless for me to add that I will not go anywhere (like Loretto) without permission and that I intend to avoid frequenting people's houses when in town (though as a matter of fact I have done this very seldom).

This should take care of the main difficulties we have had to deal with. I hope that now we can continue on a friendly basis as before. The problem here is this: insofar as I am able to believe that you are trying to help me and you are able to believe in my good will and determination, we can get along well. Insofar as you become convinced of bad will and failure of resolve exclusively on my part, I will find myself fearing constraint and (veiled) punitive measures on your part, and we will face each other with a certain distrust. For my part, I assure you of my willingness to stress the positive side in all this. And I will do my best to merit your confidence.

n.d. (probably summer or autumn 1967)

Will you let me make a couple of suggestions, about the future of hermits around here and related topics.

First, there is the question of control by authority. I think we will have to devise some kind of workable system so that you will not be in a position of struggling with suspicions, rumors, half-baked reports, and distorted suggestions that may come to you from various sources. I noticed yesterday that you had a great deal of information that was being slanted this way and that, and your material could easily have taken a form that was completely unreal, though based apparently on "facts." This was due in part to the fact that once you get suspicious, the suspicion really works on you and you spend a lot of time trying to get to the bottom of it, mainly because you don't want anyone to put anything over on you. The point I am making is this: if you are down in your office thinking that the hermits are putting something over on you, life for the hermits will become impossible and there will be a regular detective and spy system working. Perhaps there already is, I don't know. But on that basis, how can we get anywhere? It would be a scandal itself, even though devised to prevent scandals.

Obviously the first thing is openness on the part of the hermit himself. As regards my friend in Louisville, I admit that I have been very reticent, and I felt obliged to be so since the rights of another person and the good of a soul seemed to me to be very deeply involved. I ask you to respect that judgment of my conscience, as the affair is now completely over and there will be no further trouble in that regard. But as for my own affairs I can promise you in the future complete openness as in the past. I assure you that I will not carry on any sinister underground activities of any sort up here, and if you want to check on me and inspect the place, then I think it would be proper and practical to provide for a regular visit once in a while. This might be a routine thing for all the hermits, and would keep you from having undue suspicions. Of course I assume you know I have a hermitage full of books (they have all passed through your office) and many of these, sent to me without any choice or request of mine, are not the most edifying. I try to get rid of them piecemeal as I can, and I assume you trust me in this matter as in others.

With a second hermit about to move in, I think it would be worthwhile to decide now what provision might be expected for checkups on the hermitages, or for reports by the hermits and so on. It would be well to clarify this and then it would make matters simpler. Also if there is something you definitely would regard as scandalous, let us know, we might not imagine it in advance. Or I might not. My imagination is unusual.

However, I would suggest that it would be a good point if ordinary monks did not visit the hermits in their hermitages. I think only Superiors and officers and those who for reason of work etc. go there should be in the hermitages at all. I would suggest this because thinking of the situation here the chief danger seems to proceed not from women but from people of the same sex. (This has no reference to myself, I am not so inclined.)

As to the hermits themselves, my opinion would be that as long as they keep to themselves and mind their own business (and others mind theirs), a relative freedom should be allowed with ample scope for individual differences. I can say that I have had such freedom myself, but I fear that now there might be some confusion about it. If limits are to be imposed let them be definite. But I think in reading, work, and relaxation they should be able to work it out for themselves with spiritual directors and Superiors and real latitude should be permitted, provided, of course, nothing wrong is indulged in. I thought these observations might be of some use. It is very important that we do all this right, and I am willing to contribute anything I can.

To William J. Schickel

William Schickel, then of Loveland, Ohio, had been the designer and liturgical consultant for the renovation of the Abbey Church at Gethsemani. Maurice La-vanoux, editor of Liturgical Arts, *said of Schickel: "[He] has the rare gift of what I call perfect liturgical pitch; rare, I am told among musicians and rarer still among architectural designers."*

August 10, 1967

I just wanted to tell you what a splendid job I think you have done on our Abbey Church, & cloister. I particularly like the interior of the Church—bright, simple, clear-cut, no nonsense, & perfectly in accord with the spirit of our life. Also I am glad to recognize that it is still my Abbey Church, the place of my vows & first Mass—without its ancient defects. I am sure I also voice the opinion of most of those who are, like myself, "rank and file." Thanks very much indeed for your patient & devoted work & for your good ideas. We will have good reason to keep you present in our prayers.

To B.C.

April 28, 1968

You have put me in rather a difficult spot. I must try to say what I am going to say, put it clearly, simply, and honestly, and yet not hurt you.

The question whether or not you have a vocation to Gethsemani is not for me to decide (I am no longer Novice Master). You may, God knows. But I no longer have anything to do with the formation of novices here, I have very little contact with the community, I live as a hermit in the woods, and I am definitely out of the Guru business. Hence, please don't build a vocation to Gethsemani on some special relationship with me, because really that's not the way it is. I don't question that perhaps in some other situation it might be that way, but in the pattern and grace of my own life things have worked out quite differently, and the fact that I may reach people by writing does not imply anything further. I hope you don't take this as a personal rejection, but I just don't have disciples, don't look for disciples, and don't think I could be of any use to disciples.

My suggestion to you is to be a disciple of Christ, not of any man. Jesus told His disciples not to be called Father and Master, and told them not to have a Master on earth. Really that is to be taken seriously. I know that I have vociferously stated in print that Spiritual Masters were needed, and in a way that's true—people, I mean, who have experience and can tell it like it is. But I definitely don't mean anyone should fling himself at anybody else's feet, or even expect a great deal of anything from any human being. God alone is our Master.

The real problem I think is that if you have such an exalted idea of Gethsemani you are bound, just bound to be terribly disillusioned. You don't sound realistic about it.

That having been said, you can certainly interview the vocation director here, or anywhere else. There are some good monasteries out your way, Utah, Colorado, New Mexico, California . . . By all means pray and seek. But don't build on a mud pile like me!

To Vincent Harding

January 16, 1968

Letters as good as the one you wrote New Year's night are hard to reply to: much easier just to dash off an answer to a business letter. Meanwhile after John and June [Yungblut] left, we have been preparing for and then having an abbatial election. That's over and things are getting back to normal.

Also one thing I have done in the meantime is a review of Styron's *Nat Turner*, which strikes me as an affront. The review says why: I don't have a copy to spare at the moment but it is supposed to come in *Katalagete*, so you will see it. Anyway, that's in line with your fine piece on the Afro-American past. Of course I agree with you entirely about that and about the Indians. More and more my work seems to be tending in that same sort of direction, though the new Abbot wants me to concentrate on mystical theology, etc. (He isn't at all aware of what these things mean.) I'll dig around and see if I have some of the other Indian pieces. Eventually they should add up to a book. And also I am very involved in the Cargo Cults and their apocalyptic meaning. It certainly seems to me that white America is right up a blind alley, and under judgment. It is not a situation in which I for one can be comfortable. I don't take happily to wrath.

John—yes, the complete liberal—has probably spoken to you of his idea about a retreat here, Martin King, etc., before a big march this spring. I have been thinking about that and I have another idea. Because our new Abbot is young and doesn't understand what's going on or the import of it, I think it would be too ambiguous to have a retreat more or less overtly hooked up with some public act of that size. He wouldn't be able to cope with the consequences. I think it would be much better to have simply a private and quiet retreat in which the Abbot himself could participate and learn what it is more or less all about by contact with Martin Luther King and you and so on. This would be at some other time and not publicized. Also I think it would be better that way from the retreat point of view itself, to have it unhooked from any other event: and we could just be people in our contemporary predicament.

But anyhow that doesn't have to affect the possibility of a visit of you and Rosemarie. When? Any time, though Lent is bad for me, I want to keep it visitless if possible. Later in the spring? Let's certainly plan something when convenient for you. I'd very much like to have you here for a couple of days.

In any case, to go back to your talk on the Afro-American past: the idea of a history that is lily white is just monstrous. And I am with you in wanting to see it all through the eyes of the black and the red. What myths we have to contend with! The chief of them is of course that this is a peaceful place to live in—for anyone. Newman's saying, "holiness rather than peace," takes on a new meaning in this torn-up place where everyone's idea is to obtain peace by bypassing the holiness of suffering and sacrifice and of love in which conflict is resolved.

To a Gethsemani Brother

November 15 (no year)

I did not attempt to answer your note in the class as the subject is too vast. Normally, a good place to begin would be St. Bernard's book on the love of God. However, many readers are not able to connect with St. Bernard. Still you might give it a try. The chapters you mention in my book are more concerned with love of neighbor, but still they might be of slight use, I don't know.

The whole question of the love of God depends on whether or not you look at Him as an *object*. The more you treat Him as a "thing," the harder it is really to love Him. But there is a difficulty about treating Him as a person, since this very soon gets to be like treating him as an imaginary person, and then sooner or later everything falls through. Hence the answer is *faith*. To love someone we have not only to know him but know him *as he is*. The only way to know God as He is, is through faith.

Love then consists in response. Response to His revelation of Himself, and above all to His revelation of His love. Response to grace, and as one goes on, response to His will, so that in the end one lets go completely and lives for nothing but His will. This is the way of the saints anyway. For us to keep trying requires a lot of patience. So the love that begins with a growth of faith in our case requires in the end lifelong patience and acceptance of God's will in ordinary things, and loss of our "image" of ourselves as amounting to something, etc., etc. Patience I guess is the real test. God bless you and happy feast day tomorrow.

7. *Reflections on Life's Meaning*

To Ray Livingston

Author, among other works, of The Traditional Theory of Language, *Ray Livingston was chair of the Department of English at Macalester College in St. Paul, Minnesota, when he began writing to Merton. He wrote of his interest in the notion of the harmony of the cosmos and its dependence on the spiritual condition of human beings.*

[*Cold War Letter 80*]   June 1962

On looking at your letter again I see you are really asking me whether I would like to see your book, rather than saying that it is being sent. I thought it was on the way and was eagerly awaiting it. Now that I see you may be in danger of giving me up as a lost cause, I hasten to urge you to send it. I have long admired Coomaraswamy, have been in correspondence with his wife [see *HGL*], and even planned a little book of selections from his works which may or may not be published someday. So I am naturally very eager to see your work.

Also I am very anxious to see the article [of Coomaraswamy] on "Measures of Fire" that you mentioned in your letter, and if it is possible to have a copy made, I would be grateful to you.

As to the Patristic sources you ask for: I can only give you some leads, not precise references. But the point you mention, about the harmony of the universe being intimately connected with man's spiritual condition, is tied up with the recapitulation theory of Irenaeus and with the apocatastasis of Origen and the Greek Fathers, but not in the heretical sense of the restoration of all after the last judgment. The classical Scriptural text would be Romans 8:18–27 with commentaries on it. Also see Colossians and Ephesians. By the way, returning to Origen above, I see what I wrote could be misleading. There is an orthodox sense in which

Origen speaks of the restoration of all things in Christ, and a heretical one in which he carries it to the point of emptying hell: though this is held by the Russians and Greeks to some extent. It is an interesting point.

You might find interesting leads in Bouyer's new book *Seat of Wisdom*. And of course there is always Berdyaev . . . His "Sense of Creation" (if that is the English title, I read it in French) is full of wild ideas, but a few good ones also. Have you by the way read Traherne's *Centuries of Meditations*, published recently by Harper's? He has delightful insights on this subject. As to the Scholastics, I would say try St. Bonaventure's *Collationes in Haexemeron*. (In general all the Patristic treatises on the work of the six days would offer interesting material.) I am on and off reading Clement of Alexandria and will try to keep you in mind if I run across more material. Then there is Gregory of Nyssa. A new collection of texts by Danielou and Musurillo should offer a few possibilities.

December 11, 1962

I have thought about you often since you sent the books, and have meant to write. Your fine letter makes it imperative that I write at once, and do not put it off indefinitely. I have a great pile of letters to answer and one of the things that inevitably happens is that some of the best do not get answered. I do not want this to happen to so good a letter as yours.

What wonderful children there are around, and most of them children of my friends! The poem is simply tremendous. One's instinct is at once to say it ought to be published, but perhaps that is a falsified instinct. I think one should be careful of publication (though I am perhaps not, at first sight, the one best qualified to say this convincingly). But I do think the poem is wonderful. And it saddens me to think that there is all this richness in nature, which gets crushed and spoiled by our society as people grow up. How diminished we are as persons, in the apparent greatness of our society. It all hangs together: the death camps, the bomb, the traffic, the things people feed their minds on, the problems of youth, dope, everything.

It is funny, I had entirely forgotten about your question about the relation of man to the universe. But as a matter of fact I preached on that, since it was my turn to give the chapter sermon on the Feast of the Immaculate Conception. Actually, the Chartres school is *full* of this. It is their great theme. Especially the theme of William of Conches: man the microcosm. You will find interesting references that will be of much use to you in Von Simson's book on Gothic architecture (Bollingen Books), which has much to do with the School of Chartres, as the mathematical and musical theories of the Chartres writers were the basis for the principles on which the west front of Chartres Cathedral was built when the school was flourishing. (The main body of the cathedral is a little later, but still shows of course the same basic influences.)

The connection is of course that the cathedral is a cosmos, a sacred world, built on the principles, the "mystique" thought to have entered into creation itself, and found of course in man, the microcosmos. The theme of my sermon in any case was that man is in a way in the universe as an eye in a body, and "if the eye be single the whole body will be lightsome, but if the eye be darkened . . ."

In the *Reader* you will perhaps find that the bit on the "General Dance" will have something to do with this theme, though not as explicitly as I would like.

I am still keeping the books for a little while. The Moralium Dogma Philosophorum I will return soon. It is a kind of anthology of moral texts from Cicero and Seneca. The other, which has very revealing material from William of Conches, especially from his commentary on the *Timaeus*, I am discussing with a friend of mine who is living here and teaching philosophy (Dan Walsh). There is an immense amount of interesting possibilities in the writings of Chartres.

About our tractor: well, I assure you we have more than one now. And many machines of all kinds. Do not worry! I have seen the issue for a long time and for years it has been a problem. It will continue to be. That would require a great deal of discussion to clarify. Opinions are divided around here: some unfortunately do not seem to think that machines in a monastery constitute any kind of problem at all, and hence they do not approach the situation with any special concern or hesitation. This has, shall we say, far-reaching effects. On the other hand I am not exactly of the opinion that a monastery is bound by its very nature to renounce all use of machines. On the contrary, I should think it was in the nature of a monastery to make a wise use of such means of production as are ordinary in the society of the time, a wise use of what the world uses less wisely: if such a thing be possible. I grant of course that certain specific monastic communities could and should devote themselves professionally and with clear purpose to a machineless form of life. But for all this to be intelligible one must reflect more deeply on the whole nature of monasticism itself. I think generalizations are as dangerous here as anywhere else. But I have to some extent abandoned the more intransigent Eric Gill-AKC position of complete hostility to the machine as such.

This requires much more discussion, and perhaps someday you will be down this way and we can talk at leisure.

I will try to find a copy of "Grace's House," a poem I wrote about the drawing done by the four-year-old daughter of another friend of mine. What is this wonderful flowering of art among four-year-old girls?

At the same time I will put in an envelope a few other small things that might be of interest to you. Do not hesitate to send down anything you copy or mimeograph that you think might be useful for novices for their Novice Master. I will send you a copy of the sermon on the Immaculate Conception when it is done.

This brings you all my warmest blessings and prayers for Christmas.

May 11, 1964

Obviously ours is the kind of correspondence which demands that a few months pass between letters (though sometimes one might get inspired to answer at once and even be able to do so!!). For my part I am, as you know, in the stupid position of being regarded as someone important and even as a kind of oracle on some things, and this means I am swamped and practically silenced by piles of letters. I have tried various approaches to this, including that of being "systematic" and sitting down to answer those which "require an answer." This is a curious thing. It means in effect becoming obedient to the illusions of other people about themselves and about society, and entering into a great absurd machinery of nothingness. So I think now I will try to be more outright about it and answer letters that I really think mean something. Like yours. But I bind myself to nothing. It is the binding that is absurd—as in the case of the general agreement, you mention it, to regard the Jews as "the ones who did it."

It is a strange thing: since Pope John brought it up, I realize how much the Fathers of the Church, the "best" of them, ranted against the Jews. Their sermons are read in our refectory often, and how much of it there is! Pope John just took out one phrase in one prayer: but on Good Friday I noticed the rest of that prayer, and the context in which it came!

One is faced with the evident truth that this shocking evasion has been accepted without murmur by the whole Church for centuries and not even the ghastly attempt of Hitler has really awakened the Church to the enormity of it. Someone lent me the Hochhuth play, a terrible piece of work and quite stupid, but there is nevertheless a certain truth in it. There is this official, public way the Church has of being in the world, this embodiment of authority in one figure who answers everything and settles everything and who is therefore *expected* to have an answer for everything . . . We could have been more humble. Pope Paul tried to say we were "to blame" for some things, etc. But you ought to hear how that was understood and nullified by the imperturbables.

I was in the hospital too, and got to read some Blake and some things about Blake in the U. of Louisville library on my way in and out. How few are the people who see. Have you ever read any of John Wild's essays and studies on Platonism? He teaches or used to teach at Northwestern and probably you know and like him. I think he is one of the few who really grasps the meaning of Plato, as against the people like Crossman, who does a liberal hatchet job on P. I am interested in this because I have to do an essay on the tormented subject of freedom: a difficult task because we are in the middle of all the most fatal sophistries about it and one can almost not talk any sense on the point, there are so many anarchies and tyrannies involved in defending "liberty" by throwing everyone in jail, or simply killing people at random.

I want to say how good Claire's poems are. Does she publish them? That is not important perhaps, yet she should. But why doesn't she get together a little book and send them to Laughlin at New Directions? I will give her all kinds of support. I really like them, really respond to them, she is one of the few that has something to say. John Beecher might print them on his press too. Know him?

I have meant to send mimeographed things (forgive this typing) and don't know whether or not I have. Something goes to you now in the mail. Here is a piece of printing the Benedictines of Stanbrook did for me, and I like it.

Best love to you and Claire. I would love to see you both sometime, but not this year, too many are already coming. Later when I am more free.

To Claire Livingston

December 12, 1965

I completely agree with you. I think it is very well put.

At the moment I am trying not to be an authority on everything, so I am becoming silent on a lot of things I spoke of before and not speaking of new ones. I am getting out of anything that savors of politics, and I don't want to start talking about marriage since in any case I am not married and what I know of sexual love goes back to a rather selfish period of my life when I was thinking of getting and not of giving. I am not qualified to speak on this subject, but I recognize your rightness, especially the excellent point about the imaginary woman replacing the concrete flesh-and-blood ones. This is really the key to the whole thing. Do you by any chance know Karl Stern's latest book, *The Flight from Woman*?

Since last summer I have withdrawn from the community to live as a hermit. I am of course still a member of the community and subject to its jurisdiction and rules, but living on my own. It is wonderful, not always easy, but certainly much more real and deep than living in the community. I am learning an enormous amount, and learning to shut up, I think, though I must still write and still have to talk once a week in a conference to novices and students. But I am not involved in "what goes on."

In all of this I feel close to you and Ray. Ray has that sense of the realities which are found only outside the press and rush of the ephemeral. And you do too. I think of you both and pray for you. May God increase the wisdom He is giving you, which is the wisdom of love.

To William Robert Miller

William Robert Miller, managing editor of Fellowship, *had published a couple of articles by Thomas Merton ("The Root of War" and "Red or Dead: The Anatomy of a Cliché"). In 1962 he became managing editor of the* United Church Herald, *a publication of the United Church of Christ. On May 25, 1962, he wrote to*

Merton commending him on a fine article in Jubilee *magazine. He had been brought up, he said, with an almost tacitly anti-Catholic attitude, but recently he had found himself defending the Roman Catholic Church against certain bigoted detractors.*

[*Cold War Letter 81*]   June 1962

Thank you for your kind letter and for the copy of the *United Church Herald* containing your article. I read it eagerly and I agree with you that the evidence of charity in the Japanese death camp on the river Kwai is, like so many other unexpected things in our time, clear evidence of the divine realities which we have so long neglected. We have taken Christianity for granted for hundreds of years and now all of a sudden I think some of us are beginning to wake up to the fact that we have almost forgotten what it means, and that our ideas of God and His ways are far from corresponding to the actuality. I am giving some talks on the Prophets to my novices here and this brings the truth home very forcefully.

We live in prophetic and eschatological times, and by and large everyone is asleep. We realize it dimly, like sleepers who have turned off the alarm clock without quite waking up. It is a time of awful struggle and awful torpor. And we need faith. Moreover, we need to realize how true it is that faith is purely a gift. And that the Holy Spirit is the Giver who, in giving all other gifts, is Himself given by the Father and the Son.

It happens that, as I had rather expected, my writing about peace is now being limited, in fact it has for all practical purposes stopped. I foresaw this and wanted to try to say as much as I could before I would have to stop. I am glad I was able to appear a couple of times in the pages of *Fellowship*.

June 15, 1964

Your book I have not yet seen. I have not been able to undertake reviews lately, as back in the winter I got swamped with reviews and prefaces and had to quit that for a while. So they have not sent me a review copy of it. How is it doing? I would like very much to get a look at it.

My book on peace: this is verboten. I am not able to publish it, and have had to say no to at least three publishers before you came along. It is getting to be a habit. I think, however, that I may possibly get some parts of it into print rewritten and with a new approach (avoiding disputes about ethics of bombs) and this I am trying to do as part of my new book for Farrar, Straus and Giroux [*Seeds of Destruction*]. I hope I will make it, but everything is not clear.

It is getting very hot here and I suppose New York is not terribly pleasant either. But at least here we have the woods and the fresh air and relative silence. I am very grateful for this vocation, I must say. It is a real gift.

February 27, 1965

No need to explain about how it is writing these letters. I know very well how necessary it is to be in the right mood, and to have things come out just so, before a letter that you can mean can be written. That is why it is so easy to sit down and bat out nonsense about business or something allegedly "practical" which is simply an evasion of thought and of communication. But, without claiming to make a lot of sense, I want to answer yours of last December (this is the second December letter I am answering this morning) . . .

The book [*Seeds of Destruction*] has had ambiguous reviews, especially from white liberals [see letter to Martin Marty, *HGL*], though the Catholic clergy has got in behind it (which they do not necessarily do: the fact that one is a priest does not guarantee the support of other priests and some of the most virulent criticism I have had on other books has come from the clergy). I think the best part in the book is about peace, but that has come in for relatively little comment.

I look forward very much to *Patience*. I hope Naomi will send me a copy as soon as there is one. Is there one around yet? Pessimism seems to me to be one of the only reasonable attitudes at the moment. There is a great blind disastrous and complacent stupidity built right into our society here. It is structured so that the truth cannot be seen and cannot be accepted. I used to think that only Communism was as systematically dedicated to a false construction but I think in some ways we have got them beat because we are so much less systematic and there is a kind of virtuosity that gets in there, the concert of phoniness that arises from Madison Avenue (your publisher is now on Park). The Goldwater campaign, the Vietnam thing, the continuation of nothing in the race crisis, and now the heartbreaking madness in the aftermath of Malcom X's murder. (I thought he was rather a good guy and capable of making some sense.) This is a very blind country, and you are right about what is said about love and what is not done. And of course no one has any answers, and an answer that is not in some sense political cannot make anything out of the problem. The blindness is actually, as you say, lack of faith. But the "faith" that people buy is usually illusions. They lack the basic faith in *being* which is the prerequisite for being human. The craftiness and fat dishonest security with which people assume that everything can be manipulated, bought, fixed, tampered with, shot up, drugged, placated, assuaged, destroyed at will, etc., etc., all goes back to a basically cynical distrust of being and a basically paranoid delusion of superior cunning, the capacity to get the better of reality whenever it suits one to do so. This is what has taken the place of faith (in reality) and hence there is nothing but cunning and fear and all of it built on greed. Catholics are still running around saying that the great disaster of our land is too much lust but I agree with Baldwin, maybe there is not enough, or it got into the wrong channels or something. The problem is more likely impotence.

That is why you are right to go at it with myth and symbol. There is no other way, really, and the myth is the only thing they can't monkey with, though they try. I think that you have good insights and good awareness of the trouble and I think that you are going to say more with myth than with political analysis, though that is necessary too. The word "socialism" has become almost meaningless, I think, but perhaps the people who are making sense are some of the ones like Frei in Chile. This I say with all sorts of reservations because I do not read much in the papers and do not really keep track of things. Were you in England? I have much more respect for England now than I did when I was there thirty years ago and she was still highly stuffed. But I wonder if the welfare state is very much of an answer. It certainly does take care of urgent needs (socialized medicine, etc.). And perhaps in the end my politics are on that level: get people medical care, housing, schools, and any way you can, as soon as you can. I think the whole shooting match is going to blow up one of these days, not necessarily nuclear war, but some cataclysmic thing that may be in the works without people being able to stop it, and after that there will be a long era of picking up pieces and trying to get started again. Perhaps neither you nor I will live to see that part of it.

Your intuitions after Europe seem to me right all along the line. But now I have to stop this. When you feel like writing, write again. You know how this kind of thing is. I have half a dozen or a dozen people in this category and they make more sense than a thousand other letters, but the answers are to say the least irregular.

April 10, 1965

Next Wednesday, in the middle of Holy Week, in a Mass which will contain the long reading of the Passion of Jesus, and the reading from Isaiah about the suffering "Servant" who took upon Himself the sorrows of us all, I will offer the Mass for the repose of Jerry's soul. That is about the best I can do for you and for him.

It is natural for you to feel terribly lonely and upset. Death is a terrible thing, and people cover it up with words so as to make it less terrible. But when you come face to face with it, there is nothing you can do or say. It is final. That is why you feel so lost about it. But yet, our faith tells us, it is not final in God's eyes. For man, it is the end. For man in Christ, it is just the beginning. If faith does not give us much comfort sometimes, that is to be expected. Faith is not just there for our comfort. It is there to make us grow, and reach out. You will find help when you get a little stronger and can help others a bit. Meanwhile, you must accept loneliness until our Lord teaches you what to do with it.

I will keep you in my prayers. Have courage. Ask Our Lord to bring you a deep understanding of His sorrow. That is how you will begin to understand your own sorrow.

May 26, 1966

I can't help you much with Joachim of Flora, he is still a great unknown. No recent work has been done on him, as far as I know, and I have seen a little nineteenth-century stuff which is not very interesting. I would say too that the customary presentation of him as a pre-Reformation reformer is a bit askew. He is a great loud old apocalyptic guy who is probably not worth translating except for his tirades against abuses, which are good, but his system is complex, artificial, and—as it turned out—not too prophetic. I doubt if there would be much point in printing the Eternal Gospel right now except that everything is now getting into print, so if everything, why not this also? As to who ought to do it, I haven't the faintest idea.

September 13, 1966

I know what you mean. The problem is that almost everything remains yet to be done. We haven't even started. We are just beginning to collect our thoughts. The Church has spoken in the Vatican Council, but in such a general way that the whole thing can easily evaporate and Catholics can, as usual, go their way without realizing that something momentous has been said. Obviously anyone who has any sense of the real issues will find himself isolated. The thinking of the majority is shaped by mass media dominated by one line of thought; oriented to war and money and with no real concern for man—still less for God, though much lip service is paid to Him when it appears profitable to do so. Or makes people feel that they are very good guys.

So the problem is great. As to non-violence, there ought to be a Catholic training center for this. Someday maybe it will be built up. Hildegard Goss-Mayr, of the FOR in Austria, would be the one to really do something with it. She is my candidate for sainthood in this day (along with Dorothy Day and a few others like that).

Can't write more now, but these lines are at least a token, and an assurance that I am with you and that I keep you in my prayers. Keep me in yours too. As Bob Dylan says, "Everybody must get stoned."

To John Brooks

March 4, 1965

When I observe that your letter was written on January 30th and when I see this date on which I write, and when I consider the question you ask me, it all adds up to a paradox: I certainly don't seem to attend to things in the way a successful man should. Actually, I suppose I have too many other things to do which have no relation one way or the other with "success." In fact, I think I am bound to say that in all sincerity success is something in which I am not personally interested. In entering this monastery I was in fact giving up what chance I may have had for success in what was then my field—university teaching. It is true I remained a writer, but I was perfectly willing to give that up too. I wrote in obedience to my monastic Superiors and with their encouragement and, of course, with a certain amount of interest and élan on my own part. Success came quite by accident. It was not what I was after, and I have never tried to hold on to it. On the contrary, if I thought I was called upon to say something that the public might not like, I nevertheless said it because I thought it was true, or important.

So my "formula for success" actually has no bearing on success itself. My aim in life is to live as I think I was created to live: in truth, in simplicity with all my attention devoted to what is higher and greater than I: the God I serve and the world of man I believe He redeemed. I believe that if I consent to take my rightful place in His plan, everything else will follow from it, and I also believe that I ought to be quite indifferent whether to success or failure, provided I know I am doing what is right.

This may be a formula so monastic that it has no meaning for people in business or professional life, and I certainly do not mean to thrust it upon them. And yet perhaps if they want to give it a little thought they might find it relevant too, in some way. In any case you are perfectly free to make use of this statement, and I certainly do not expect you to use it all: take what suits you, and I hope your book will be—a complete success.

To Mr. Wainwright

July 10, 1965

I have been thinking about your letter and your project, and the best I can do for you is to set down a few random observations on the subject. You see, I do not know you and I do not know what your approach is, and for my own part I have done some autobiographical writing in which moments of truth, if any, may perhaps make their appearance. At the moment, I find myself considering the concept itself.

It comes quite natural to us, doesn't it, to think that "modern man" is a man who faces a "moment of truth" once, several times, often in his life. Your title suggests that to one modern man there is allotted one moment of truth. I don't suppose you mean this to be a hard-and-fast rule. For my own part, I think that life turns out to be a continual series of moments of untruth in which (when the going gets sufficiently ghastly) a moment of truth finally appears in the midst of all the mess. This I suppose reflects the existentialist type of thinking that has become more and more common with me, and which does not by any means prevent me from living a happy sort of life. In any case, I think it is important to face the fact that modern man, whether he likes it or not, leads a life that is low in authenticity. Things are decided for him, foisted on him, and even experienced for him by others. His existence is more and more secondhand, and even his moments of truth tend to be fabricated for him. That is the problem. I would say that as a result of this, the real moments of truth that do obviously occur (since where there is life there is resistance to inauthenticity) appear at first to be quite other than they are. In fact, rather than the dramatic confrontation with "reality" or whatever you want to call the bull, one simply takes a new road without thinking too much about it, and discovers ten miles later that it is new and one has in fact broken through into a whole new region of life. That is the way it generally is with me. I seem to realize only later that a moment of truth was just that.

Often, even the apparent moment of truth, the one that looks like a very momentous bull, has its part in our life even though the bull evaporates. Facing up to something that isn't there is not necessarily a waste of time. But it prepares us for something else later.

I am sorry for these abstract thoughts. To be slightly more concrete, I can say as a Christian, and an existentialist Christian, that I have often experienced the fact that the "moment of truth" in the Christian context is the encounter with the inscrutable word of God, the personal and living interpretation of the word of God when it is lived, when it breaks through by surprise into our own completely contemporary and personal existence. And this means of course that it breaks through conventional religious routines and even seems in some ways quite scandalous in terms of the average and accepted interpretation of what religion ought to be. Hence, those for whom religion constitutes in effect a protection against any real moments of truth are people I cannot understand. I am glad that in our time we have had someone like Pope John, whose life amply demonstrates the validity, I think, of my view of it.

To Robert Menchin

Menchin wrote Merton about a project he was involved in to help people who need to make "career changes." He asked Merton's advice on the topic.

January 15, 1966

Your project sounds interesting, and I will try to contribute what I can in the space of a brief letter. Actually, entering a monastery is something a little different from a "career change." However, it is even more drastic than career changes usually are, normally, so I suppose it can furnish useful data. Since entering the monastery and after being here twenty-four years, I have experimented with a further change, within the monastic life, taking up the life of a hermit while remaining affiliated with the monastic community. This is perhaps more like the change of job in the same general area.

I had always wanted to be a writer. But one had to make a living and so I took up teaching (literature, college level) as a profession that would be favorable for writing. However, the idea of something more fundamental began to grow on me. The idea of a monastic vocation is something distinct from that of a "career." In a sense, you don't pick the monastic life, it picks you. In religious terms, that is expressed by saying that one believes oneself "called" by God to live a monastic life. Translated into ordinary language, this refers to a deep implosion which may even go against the grain of one's conscious inclinations. It entails a fight. There is a considerable amount of doubt and resistance, a great deal of questioning, and at times the whole thing seems absurd. Yet you have to push on with it. There is a sense of one's destiny and identity involved in this struggle.

For me, the monastic vocation even implied that I might have to give up writing, and when I finally decided to enter the Trappist Monastery of Gethsemani (Kentucky) I was reconciled with the idea of not writing anymore unless I was told to do so. As it happened, I was told to continue writing. But for me writing has always remained secondary. What has been important above all has been living in the most meaningful possible way, at least for me. This has meant, again, a lot of conflict, questioning, searching. Entering a monastery is only the beginning of a long road, not the end. People may imagine that the door of the monastery closes behind you and you go into nirvana. Not so. There is a lot of hard work to be done, many decisions to be made, and still many questions to answer. Many in the monastic life reach the point where they feel that they cannot go on, that they have reached a dead end. They then have to leave the monastery and start again (that is a difficult adjustment). For my part, I have never for a moment questioned the vocation to be a monk, but I have had to settle many other questions about ways and means, the where and the how of being a monk. Consequently there has been a great deal of change in me, during the course of my monastic life. I would say that my interests have deepened and broadened as time went on. I have become more and more interested in all different forms of religious and monastic experiences, and it has been my privilege to engage in dialogue with men living according to Hinduism, Zen, Hasidic Judaism, Sufism, and so on. I have also become more deeply concerned with basic issues in the world situation. For me the monastery has not been a mere refuge: it has meant facing responsibility on the deepest level, and it has meant giving an account of myself to others, and being open to them in their problems.

Advice? I would say that there is one basic idea that should be kept in mind in all the changes we make in life, whether of career or anything else. We should decide not in view of better pay, higher rank, "getting ahead," but in view of becoming *more real*, entering more authentically into direct contact with life, living more as a free and mature human person, able to give myself more to others, able to understand myself and the world better. I hope these few notes may be of some use.

8. The Final (Asian) Journey

To Finley Peter Dunne, Jr.

Mr. Dunne was the executive secretary of the Temple of Understanding, a world-wide organization aimed at fostering communication and understanding among the religions of the world. On July 18, 1968, he wrote to Merton inviting his presence at a meeting to be held in October 1968 at Darjeeling. Because of floods in Darjeeling the meeting had to be moved to Calcutta. Merton's talk at Calcutta may be found in AJ, pp. 309-18.

July 23, 1968

I was delighted to receive your letter of July 18th yesterday. The invitation was most acceptable and I hastened to take it up at once with my Abbot. I am glad to say that he granted me permission to accept it, since I am already going to Asia anyway. It just means a slight extension of the trip already planned. Thus I am pleased and honored to accept. I plan to meet with the others in Calcutta on October 21st and I await further information about the time and place and any other practical information. I am already working on my passport and visas, so now I will add an Indian visa—and one for Nepal, since I have been hoping for a long time to see that country and this will give me an occasion to do so. Thus after the meeting I hope to stay in Darjeeling for a little while and perhaps go on to Nepal and Sikkim. But since I am looking forward very much to possible contacts at the meeting, I hope I may also at some time be able to visit centers of Jainism and Buddhism and Hinduism and become better acquainted especially with their monastic forms of life. I hope above all that the Dalai Lama will be there and that I may meet him and perhaps get in contact with Tibetan communities in exile.

One question I would like to get clear on: would I be expected to prepare a paper? I presume you already have a full program. However, I am at your service if you want me to do so. Please let me know one way or the other.

I might mention something of possible interest: the formation of an intermonastic community, with representatives of various traditions, living together and working together for the clarification of common elements in their thought and experience. It may be a utopian plan, but it is worth considering. Of course it would require a lot of preliminary study. I thought, however, I might mention it, as it might come within your field of interest.

I will add no more at present. I just want to thank you again, assure you that I am happy at the thought of participating in the meeting at Darjeeling, and am expecting further details from you.

August 3, 1968

Thanks for your fine letter. I certainly don't want to intrude on your program when others could occupy the time better than I. However, if you do seriously want to consider the possibility of a paper I have the following suggestion. A paper on intermonastic communication, on the need for all religions to develop that which is most deep and the most relevant in them: and also the peculiar problems which this presents in the modern world. I could discuss the apparent inability of so many modern men to grasp anything of a religious dimension, and the implications of this—future implications for Asia, where it has perhaps not developed so far as it has with us. And what the interchange of ideas between different monastic systems, in depth, in terms of a mutual study of traditions, might offer.

As I say, I am not urging this on you, but it is something I can offer if you want to consider it. A treatment of the peculiar question of monastic relevance—if any.

I am glad to hear that there are good chances of meeting the Dalai Lama or others who might help me see some Buddhist monasticism in the Himalaya area. I am really most excited and eager about the chance to see the best of all the different kinds of monasticism in North India and in the rest of S.E. Asia and later Japan. My plans are still flexible and will leave openings for all kinds of possibilities.

I do have one little problem: that of raising some money to pay for the extra leg of my journey. My monastic rules don't allow me much freedom in going around giving talks, especially here. Exceptions are the benevolence of a few generous souls to help out. If you have any other ideas I would be happy to hear them. I am utterly innocent in the methods of getting money from foundations. I can always borrow on a future book.

I really am most happy at the opportunity to be with you all in Darjeeling. Thanks again for the invitation.

August 21, 1968

In Calcutta I hope to meet my old friend Mahanam Brata Bramachari. I think he is still Abbot of his monastic community there. Would there be any objection to his attending the meeting, if he is free and wants to come? I haven't mentioned my coming yet.

I am glad to see my good friend John Wu on the list. I was looking forward to seeing him at least in Taiwan.

As time gets closer, I look forward with eager anticipation to the meeting and I am most happy that it will be possible for me to be there.

October 3, 1968
Santa Barbara, Ca.

I just reached here from Alaska and got your letter, the forms, etc.

My passport visa already has a special notation that I'm okay for Darjeeling but I'll fill out the form anyway just in case.

About the hotel—I'd much prefer a single room. If one can't yet be had I can take care of myself if you'll perhaps reserve me one at the (I believe it's called) Windermere (recommended by a friend).

Many thanks for the check. All is well. After talks in Alaska and here I'm in good shape financially.

Especially many thanks for the information about Lamas and the letter to the Queen of Sikkim. As things now stand, I'll have to change plans and go to Dharmsala right after the meeting to meet the Dalai Lama but will return to that area later, going, I hope, to Sikkim perhaps in late November—or in the New Year (when I am hoping to get to Bhutan).

I'm doing all this in a bit of a rush but I hope all is clear. You may have to fill in some items on the form—you'd know better than I.

More later. Looking forward immensely to the end of the month.

This letter was written at the Redwoods Monastery, Whitehorn, California.

October 10, 1968
Redwoods Monastery
Whitehorn, California

There was a little delay in getting your letter, as I was on the road. However, I have now finished the paper—or partly so, as some of it is still barely in note form. But it is enough to give an idea. You can mimeograph it at your convenience.

I sent you a hasty letter about the permission to go to Darjeeling. I have that on my passport. I hope to return to Darjeeling later in November, as I have Buddhist contacts in the area. Also I mentioned that I prefer to be alone in a room if possible—after years of solitude—and will bunk anywhere this is possible. Could go to the Windermere, as a friend of mine may be there anyhow. Whatever you think best.

In any event I'll look for you at the Oberoi Grand the weekend of the 19th. I hope to see you then.

IV.
Religious Thought
and Dialogue

*It is out of the nothing, the void, of our own self that
we freely create the paradise in which we walk with God.*

TO HERBERT MASON

1. To Herbert Mason

The noted author and translator Herbert Mason, professor of the history of religion at Boston University, is well known for his narrative versions of the epic Gilgamesh, *as well as* The Death of al-Hallaj *and* A Legend of Alexander and the Merchant and the Parrot. *As a youth of twenty-six in 1959, he came under the influence of Louis Massignon, then seventy-six, the distinguished professor emeritus of the Collège de France, a master of the Arabic language and of Muslim studies. They became close friends. It was Mason who interested Merton in Massignon. Merton's concern to bear witness against war and to seek the mystical dimension in various religious traditions coincided with similar interests on the part of Massignon. Mason has also been a close friend of Massignon's son, Dr. Daniel Massignon. In 1982 Mason published his translation of Massignon's greatest work,* The Passion of al-Hallaj.

June 6, 1959

Your paragraph on Prometheus echoes very exactly and sums up what I have been driving at. I am glad P[ère Jean] Danielou gave you the booklet. It is true that there is a certain nobility in fighting for what we already have, because if we fail to do this we do not really have it. But it is best to remember that we already have it and that everything does not depend on the fighting. It is the great mystery of grace. Not grace in the sense of a kind of theological gasoline that you get by performing virtuous actions (that is the sin we commit!), but grace in the fact that God has given Himself completely to us already. Completely. But we have to enter into the darkness of His presence. Not tragic darkness, just ordinariness: but above all what does not appear to be religion.

I tell you frankly that my present struggle with the institutional aspect of religion is enormous and almost overwhelming. It is tempting to ruin the whole thing by dramatizing it as something Promethean, as if truth were something I had to conquer and bring back into the ruins. That would be the most disastrous thing of all. Yet the ruins are really ruins. They are cold and without fire, really. The fire that is there has nothing to do with the external forms which people so carefully preserve. (Perhaps here I exaggerate, through excessive reaction.) The only issue is in a paradox of great humility, a small door through which one goes out, appearing to be nothing: and having become nothing. That is the liberation.

The journey goes with this. No, I have not read Melville for years and years. And the "Landfall" (in *Figures for an Apocalypse*, published in 1948) goes back ten years. The journey is present every day. Better, the voyage. The nothing which happens every day has to be an adventure, and it is. To be Prometheus and to be on a voyage is almost the same thing. It is out of the nothing, the void, of our own self that we freely create the paradise in which we walk with God. This act of creation is— grace. It is all a gift. Grace out of nothingness. The image of a landfall is one of the obvious ones for this daily awakening. I especially like P. Danielou's chapter on *epectasis* [seeking, never fully achieving, yet never ceasing from the seeking] in the book on Gregory of Nyssa (still his best) . . .

I am glad you know P. Danielou—give him my regards, please, and remind him that he owes me a letter.

August 24, 1959

One of the most fascinating things I have had my hands on in a long time is that offprint of Louis Massignon about the Seven Sleepers. It is tremendous, and I want to know more about all those places and things. Especially the dolmen. Is it still there above ground, I mean? Evidently the crypt is still there below, but there were so many things he took for granted, talking to Bretons. And how would you like sometime at your leisure to do into English the [Breton] *Gwerz* for Lax's poetry sheet which is called *Pax*, which pays nothing, inspires no one, and is handed out widely to firstcomers for free, but gets around sometimes, though nowhere important. (I sent you I think a sample.)

Louis Massignon wrote me a letter a long time ago and I was always wanting to answer it. He is a terrific person, from what I know of him, and because of him I have wanted for ten minutes to learn some Oriental languages. Do tell him that I am full of an impassioned interest in the Seven Sleepers and that I send him my good wishes and pray for him. And Frère Charles de Jésus, he should pray for me that I receive some special graces I need, along his own line, a desert line.

Now for your own poem. I am very much impressed with it, especially the last two sections. It ends magnificently, very poignantly: that is one of the aspects of conversion that people do not always treat: you are always supposedly swallowed up by the Church and live happily ever after. When in fact your loneliness begins then, but in a different way, on a higher level of sharp rocks, and of course no one complains because it is right that way. But throwing in the little bit about the girls in first communion dresses heightens it very much. What really *is* this Church? That is the thing.

One thing not too clear, the connection with *Gilgamesh*, but that is because I know nothing of *Gilgamesh*. Why don't you let Laughlin see it? Or let me rather send this copy to New Directions. Laughlin is not in this country at the moment, he is over there somewhere, probably in Germany rather than in France. I can send the poem to [Robert] MacGregor, who ordinarily runs things at ND. If you prefer me not to do this, let me know. Perhaps you want to work some more on parts of the poem? If Massignon knows English well enough to read it, then he will know it enough to read this offprint of mine on Pasternak. I send therefore two copies, one for him and one for you.

P. Danielou's book on History, which I have been reading, steered me toward an interesting Englishman called [Herbert] Butterfield. I strongly recommend his *Christianity and History* [1950], which P. Danielou alludes to in his own book. Perhaps you already know of Butterfield.

Look, if you think about darkness you will naturally get a tired mind. And if you think about it you put a kind of light in its place, that is what makes you tired. When it is dark, it is dark, and you go in the dark as if it were light. *Nox illuminatio mea.* The darkness is our light, and that is all. The light remains, simply, our everyday mind, such as it is, floating on a sea of darkness which we do not have to observe. But it carries us with great power. It is the being carried that is, actually, its light. Float, then. And trust the winds of God, which you do not see either, but they are cool. And tell your Carmelite friend to pray for me because I need it at the moment. Louis Massignon also. I was interested in your paragraph about [François] Mauriac. One book I have liked has been Julien Green's *Journal*—many volumes of it. I have not read the latest, but it is here. I like very much, for theology, people like Fr. [Paul] Evdokimov at the Orthodox seminary there.

September 3, 1959

Your fine letter just came, with the new copy of the poem, which I shall send right along to New Directions, with a few words of explanation. I think they will appreciate it. As I said, they move slowly. But eventually I am sure they will get around to using it, perhaps with something else, in a selection of works by various people. Maybe in one of the ND Anthologies. I am sure they will be interested.

The main purpose of this immediate reply is that I want to say how deeply moved I am at this idea of Louis Massignon's that salvation is coming from the most afflicted and despised. This, of course, is the only idea that makes any sense in our time. It is the key to our time or to any other time. It is the great idea of the Bible, the Prophets, everything. I have been obsessed with it for a long time, and this picture has something to do with it. It is not a very good photograph, lacks all contrast and all light-and-shadow. It is of a statue of the B. Virgin I had done for the novitiate by a sculptor [Jaime Andrade; see *SC*, pp. 107–9, 113–15] in Ecuador. The idea is precisely that of Louis M. The Holy Mother is the Indian woman of the Andes, the representative of all that is most abject, forgotten, despised, and put aside. The artist, who is a bit of a leftist if not a red, caught on to the idea very well, and the face of the Mother is terrific. It has precisely the kind of blindness, the withdrawnness in a great mystery of poverty and darkness and strength. There are barely any eyes at all. It is like a rock, and yet warm and full of life. As for the Child, however—the Christ, the Resurrection to be born from the despised peoples of Mexico and the Andes, He is full of joy and triumph and holds in His hand a completely mythical bit of fruit invented by the sculptor, which is the only lively and ornate thing in the whole work and is very effective: it is salvation.

I wanted you to see this thing, beautifully done in mahogany from the jungles of South America, and carved in the Andes, with the spirit of the Andes and of the peoples who live there. It expresses something with which I am very much concerned, and for which I ask many prayers. It makes me able to tell you that I am in complete solidarity with you and Louis Massignon on this point and that I want badly to go ahead, as God may permit, in somewhat the same directions, but over here.

Your account of *Gilgamesh* is tremendous. I will have to get the epic. I had heard of it, of course, in connection with Genesis. I will be rereading your poem in the light of the summary you send and will write more about it later. I just wanted to get this picture into the mail for you and Massignon. By the way, I want to put something about Hallaj in the book I am writing, and have nothing at hand. Can you lend or send me anything? The book is all about inner experience, intuition, the inmost self that sees in and through our whole being, and not just through intellectual constructions—which too often are a veil between us and experience, deliberately woven to frustrate immediate experience . . .

God bless both you and Louis—thank you for your words on the Pasternak article.

November 14, 1959

It is a long age since I have written to any of you and you must think I have forgotten all my friends. I was in the hospital for eight days in October, nothing serious. But being there was just enough to throw out all my schedule and I still have not caught up with it. Then too, the worst thing was that your poem reached me in the hospital, where I was not able to give it more than a cursory first reading, and then it got lost in the shuffle when I was leaving. Some sisters took it with a pile of things and that is the last I saw of it. But I liked it well, from what I read. I haven't heard anything from New Directions, incidentally, about your other one. They are very much like that, they remain silent for months. The only thing I have gathered at all is that they are slow to publish long poems. I suppose everyone is. They are more civilized and more venturesome in France.

I received Louis Massignon's further brochures on the Seven Sleepers. All that material is really fascinating. I hope he will forgive me for having waited so long to answer him. You will explain, and I will write him a note as soon as I get a chance . . .

How right you are about the exploitation of intuition: it poisons one's whole life. There is no real freedom anywhere because everything has to be "used." Or smeared. One of the functions of our "remnant" is to recognize the supreme value of the useless. That too is certainly part of the message of the Seven Sleepers. They just slept. Yet at the same time, we cannot be consistent about that which has no use, because paradoxically it is the most energetic project of the pragmatist that is the most utterly useless thing on earth. This about the moon, for instance. So I think your book *Requiem* will be very interesting . . .

The face of my Indian Mother of God sends out a quiet darkness that envelops me and all my prayers and all my friends. God bless you again.

Christmas Eve 1959

I am sorry to have let your letter go so long without a reply. As you can well imagine, I have been quite tied up in the past month. The explanation for the disappointment and the rejection of the translation of St. John of the Cross [a book by Rochefort translated by Mason] is that Naomi Burton had to clean up all her business in a big hurry, as she was leaving [the literary agency] Curtis Brown and taking over an editorial job with Doubleday. She would certainly have taken a great deal more trouble with it if she had not been leaving the agency. I am sure indeed that she would have placed it easily, in time. Perhaps she only showed it to one publisher. I know she took much the same attitude toward some small things of mine, so Rochefort must not take the whole thing as a personal defeat. Of course, it is not that. Anyway, you know what trouble one has in this country trying to place manuscripts when the market is glutted with books. It can be very discouraging, especially for someone coming in with a new name. He should by no means be discouraged. I am sure that if you go about it patiently you will be able to place the manuscript in the new year. I suggest you send it to my friend Robert Giroux, at Farrar, Straus, 101 Fifth Avenue. Tell him I suggested this. They publish some Catholic books—and of course my own. He might possibly be interested.

If this fails then there is the whole gamut of Catholic publishers yet to be run. I will look up some addresses. Of course it may be a little inconvenient doing it this way.

This may perhaps cross with a letter of yours in the Christmas mail, I do not know, everything is clogged up now. But I just want to say that your last poem, about the Seven Sleepers and Brittany, moved me very much, and I think it is one of the very finest. It has a great deal in it. Thank you for sending it. I like its dark and austere character.

I have not heard anything from New Directions, but the chances are that they are "afraid of the long poem." I hope to see Laughlin in a few weeks and talking to him will probably be more helpful than anything else. Meanwhile, when I get a few more copies of my own selected poems, I will send one along to you and another to Louis.

The other day I happened to have a chance to see the old Shaker settlement near Lexington [Kentucky]. Only buildings, of course, nobody there since 1910. It was sad and moving. It was once an intense and rather wacky spiritual center, but I think it was very significant. The truth and simplicity of their handiwork remains to bear witness to something tremendously genuine in their spirit. For some reason it made a similar intuitive impression on me to that made by the story of the Sleepers. The spirit of these people was very alive in their building—the one I went into, the only one I could get into, had a marvelous double winding stair coming out in the mysterious pale light of a small dome at the top of the house. The silence, light, and effect were extraordinary. There were some empty rooms at the top of the house, and I went into them to taste the silence—sunlit windows, looking out on the bleak fields and a huge Lebanon cedar, with the wind in it. You would like the place. More of it later . . .

February 6, 1960

Wonderful news—all the more wonderful to me because Catherine Mary saw the light on my birthday, the 31st. Came out of the cave of darkness and sleep and gave that cry and began to swim in the great sea, our mother. I am so happy. God bless all of you. I shall certainly make special mention of her and all of you in my Masses—as I do each day as far as possible. And Louis, I shall remember him, and his eye. I felt his prayer in Jerusalem. I think much of the East, Near and Far. Especially the Far East. That great sea of men. We do not know that the human sea is the wisdom of God in mystery. That of course is the whole meaning of Christianity. And little Catherine Mary gave her cry and plunged into wisdom. She is embraced and washed and held in wisdom. I am so happy for her and for you. And for your dear wife. She too is loved by wisdom.

I have not answered your last letter about France. I should hesitate to tell someone to leave France, even though it might really be the more sensible thing to do, and the more profitable. I do not have the power perhaps to judge straight in such a matter, having been away so long and seeing so clearly what it is to live far from the source and center of our civilization, where everything is peripheral, weak, confused, sham, absurd. Of course there are all these evils also at the center and whatever sham and absurdity are there will always be much worse, because they are the falsity of the center. What can I say? Stay in France if you possibly can. But certainly it will be *easier* here.

What do you mean about De Gaulle? What is happening? I sent him the Christmas book too, incidentally.

This is a hasty note—God bless you all, and remember me please to Louis.

June 1, 1960

It is hopeless for me to try to write you a really good letter. I just delay writing and then write nothing. I have three or four of yours stacked up since Easter waiting for a reply.

First of all, the urgent matters. I have written to Maritain to put in a word for you as translator. But still if you do not want to do the job I see no reason why you should have to. However, it might turn out to be interesting and rewarding. If it does you will not lose anything by trying it out. On the other hand your own creative work is more important and should come first, unless you need money badly or something like that. There are plenty of translators around, though they are not always easy to find right off the bat.

The Rambusches would be very interested in hearing about [Italian painter] Dino Cavallari and I would like to know more about him too. Is there any way of seeing some photos of his work? When is it being shown at the University of Chicago? Would his French friend be interested in coming down this way? I could arrange an exhibit in Louisville for him, at the art center. Could you give me some further information? I would gladly do something about it.

Talking about Louisville, I can very likely get you a job at Bellarmine College there, a very nice and lively little Catholic College that is only ten years old. We are in close touch with them here. It does not have the prestige (relative of course) of St. Louis University, but you might like it, and they could use a good man in English. They seem to want to open up to new ways of looking at things. Why not consider the possibility?

You know I have the greatest respect for every insight of Louis Massignon, and I have no doubt first that he is right about our hope being to unite with the Arabs, and second about his fear that this will not be done and that consequently God will search "Jerusalem with lamps" as the prophet said. It will be a trial by fire. I doubt if America will suffer Communism exactly, unless we are beaten in a war. But God alone knows what is going to happen. We are in a state of blindness and stupor, and what is worse, everybody is beginning to get tough about it, which is fatal. The general feeling here now is that it is about time we crushed the Russians. How frightful, and what consequences that is likely to have!

I have not had any direct contact with the Negro problem in the South, but I was hoping that a Protestant Negro minister who is in the forefront of the non-violent resistance movement would show up here. He may still do so and I would have an opportunity to speak with him. It is a pity that the papers and the police were able to get off their nasty, clever sneer at the non-violent demonstrators in Paris. But those things do not matter. The thing to remember is that in non-violence the important thing is *not* the reaction of the people, the effect on the onlookers, or the use the demonstration can be put to by the papers. That would put non-violence on the same vulgar plane as the other cheap tricks of politicians. It was not the effect on people of Gandhi's fasts that were efficacious, but the fasts themselves. They have their own spiritual effect, quite apart from what people may think, or how they may react.

Louis asked me to pray on some special day, for he intends to begin something to do with Africa. Without any premeditation or planning I picked June 3rd as a day to say Mass for him and only realized much later that this was the Feast of Bl. Charles Lwanga and the Uganda martyrs, precisely the patrons of his work. I shall be very much engaged in this Mass, the day after tomorrow. My heart is very much in Africa. May God open the eyes of the West, instead of letting us blind ourselves more and more. It is terrifying.

Poor Pasternak has died. His story has ended and remains to be understood. There again, the newspapers raised so much dust and smoke that no one could see what it was all about. Our greatest sin and absurdity are in our presumption that we know what we are doing. And because we insist we know . . . It is good to feel the terror and the shame of blindness.

There are various popular biographies of St. Louis Marie de Montfort here but I do not recommend any of them. About him, I go back and forth. Sometimes he strikes me as someone who has thought up a hat that will fit everybody and then goes around making it fit everybody, pressing it down to their ears and beating it on with a club. But the basic idea of his True Devotion [to the Blessed Virgin Mary] is very fine. It is just that I do not think this is the time to shake the exhausted human race with one particular answer, "my" answer, to all problems.

Our Lady certainly has the answer. But a movement is not yet the answer. Nor is a Catholic president for the U.S. an answer to anything.

Did I thank you yet for Bernanos' *Dialogues des Carmelites*? It is a splendid thing, and it is good to have it here in French. I had read it a long time ago in English.

Let us think more about the role of America in all this. I have been feeling rather negative and discouraged, but I realize how little I see and understand. All I know is that I have an overwhelming feeling that we are missing the boat because we have been blinded by money and the love of material things. Yet there is always the blank, innocent, patient, absurd good will. How good is it?—that is the question. I wonder if the answer is not just that we have always rather humbly imagined that we were good because we suspected we might be fools. But now that we are convinced that we are perhaps not fools but very smart people, are we going to commit the sin of deducing goodness from our supposed wisdom? If so . . .

July 5, 1960

Thank you for the several letters, and I am glad you are now in the country. I got your letter, the last one, just on return here from a few days in the hospital for checkups (all right). I am having the people at Bellarmine contact you. They are very interested in the possibility of having you on the faculty there and will, I am sure, be eager to make a place for you and give you encouragement in good directions, rather than just demand that you teach a conventional course with a textbook. It will be for them to work this out with you.

I think it would be fine if you could get down here toward the end of the month or the beginning of August. The only day that is bad for me is the 26th of July, at the moment, and even that is not bad. You can stay a few days at the Abbey and we can find somewhere for you in Louisville if you have to be overnight there. I will of course be somewhat tied up at all times but there will be opportunities for us to speak and work things out while you are here. By this I mean that I won't have whole days to spend but there will be here and there hours and half hours, in bits and pieces, if you know monasteries.

I will write to Louis. I keep him in my prayers and will send him St. Peter Damian's prayer to the Seven Sleepers. Jacques Maritain would like you as a translator, but I told him you might want to give preference to creative work. You *could* do both. More later.

When Mason visited Merton at Gethsemani on August 2–7, 1960, Merton told him about the crisis of wanting to go to Mexico, despite his Superior's opposition. He asked Mason to write three letters on his behalf—letters that were to testify that he was of sound mind. One was to be sent to a bishop in Mexico, a second to the Vatican, and the third to Louis Massignon. Merton apologized for asking him to write the letters. "I'm desperate," he said, "but sane."

January 14, 1961

It is a long time since I have written. Four or five good letters from you, and I have not answered. I am sorry. I have not answered anyone. I heard from Louis too. I can see he is ill. He said Mass for me the last day of the year, and was sitting down for a lot of it, he said. I will write to him.

Louis told a Moslem in Pakistan to write to me, Abdul Aziz. I have two fine letters from him. It looks as though I am being drawn into Louis' Moslem circle after all. The circle of the poor, the outcast. That is good. I like the letters from Abdul Aziz and I have been doing some reading. I read Rumi, and I will read others. In the *Mardis of Dar el Salam* there was a fine article on poverty in Abdallah Ansari. I want to read everything four or five times over. And here is a Moslem poem ["The Moslem's Angel of Death"], but I am afraid that if I sent it to Louis he might think I was prophesying his death.

I liked your *Caritas* article and hope you will do many more such. The *CW* [*Catholic Worker*] is a good place in which to say things . . .

In March and April I have to teach eighteen lectures in mystical theology in the new pastoral course for our young priests, and this is keeping me busy. I want to bring in Hallaj and maybe other Oriental mystics if I have elbowroom. Several times I have fought the temptation to start on Arabic and then Persian, but for me this is nonsense, I think. How is your scholarship coming along? Did you get something?

I was very pleased that Teresa [Chan, a young Chinese student befriended by Mason, who put her in touch with Merton] wrote to me, and I am happy of the news of her parents' conversion. I think more and more of simply being in contact, in friendship, with people of the Orient and of Islam. There is nothing I can do for them, or "do for" anybody. Who are we that we wake up in the morning expecting ourselves to "do something for" somebody or for "the world"? I can only try to be someone for them. This I very much want to be. And the doing part need only be an expression that I am there. This is very much the Foucauld universal brother idea, I think, not big brother either. Nobody's colonial big brother. I think the only thing that will help is being a more or less helpless brother, in Christ. Even a rather silent one, because I cannot write as much as I would like to all the people. Things open out wider and I can say less and less.

I was horrified by the news that Israel had been brought, by France, into circles of the atomic powers, the big brothers, the bastards with power with something to throw. This is very ominous . . .

What you say about people suffering for us and for one another until we can bear it ourselves is very true. And often we put it off rudely, back onto them, without knowing it, and they accept it sweetly. In the end their love becomes so beautiful that we must follow their example for someone else. All blessings for the New Year. Teresa is no burden, on the contrary.

July 31, 1961

You were perfectly right to give me your frank observations on the chant ["Chants to Be Used in Processions around Sites with Furnaces"], and I respect your judgment. I shall certainly reconsider the whole question of its publication, though I think that if a Beat magazine [*Journal for the Protection of All Living Beings*, published by Lawrence Ferlinghetti] in San Francisco wants it, they can have it. They may feel the same way about it that you do. I have to recognize the fact that being here for the last twenty years, and not having gone through the things that people in Europe have gone through, I have in some sense no right to say such things. I am continually coming face to face with the fact that I have lost perspective here, including religious perspective, and that to some extent we monks are out of touch with the real (religious) mystery of our times.

As for the wrestling with the angel of indignation, that too can be ambiguous in my case. In any event, I appreciate your remarks. But what I wrote was not intended as hatred. As I say, I will reconsider the whole question.

I got a telegram from Louis also . . . I am glad the pilgrimage was so great. And I am glad to hear about your article in *Commonweal*. I recently read a rather fine little book by Pierre Van de Meer de Valcheren, a friend of Jacques Maritain and of the very indignant Léon Bloy, who refused to wrestle and just gave in every time. But he again was another case and in other circumstances . . .

August 19, 1961

Well, *The Catholic Worker* snatched the Auschwitz piece ["Chants"] before the Beats in California [Lawrence Ferlinghetti, City Lights Books], and both have printed it before it had been censored, which may land me in trouble. Evidently it is God's will for it to be printed. I still see your point. Maybe there are also other aspects. Anyway, let's pray for peace very hard.

October 1, 1961

I appreciated your remarks on the Cuadra letter ["Letter to Pablo Antonio Cuadra Concerning Giants"]. It won't be published here, at least not without considerable changes . . .

December 1, 1961

I heard about the terrible business, the massacre of defenseless Algerians in Paris. Everything gets more monstrous. Have you heard about the Catholic Peace Movement that is being started? They can tell you more at the *CW* . . .

March 9, 1962

I am going to become a worse and worse correspondent, I am afraid. So you must be prepared to bear with me. Visitors and letters are both more frequent at the moment and they will have to be rationed, otherwise they will cut in on the most important things. And then also this is Lent.

But I owe you so many letters and notes I can hardly remember them all. In all of them you give me perceptive comments on the articles and poems, etc., and for these comments I am very grateful. Fr. Metzger you will by now have seen in *Jubilee*, and it might make a good little leaflet. Have you by any chance got in touch with the FOR [Fellowship of Reconciliation] at Nyack?

"Christian Action [in World Crisis," published in *Blackfriars*, June 1962] will certainly not be published as it stands. It is still in the hands of censors, since months. Target and City [i.e., "Target Equals City"]: I do not agree with your comment on this. [In a letter of February 27,

1962, Mason had written: "Please be careful. Don't print something such as 'Target Equals City'; only your enemies would publish that."] I think the case is quite clear and needs to be stated. It would seem that this is the kind of evidence that needs to be stressed and it is incontrovertible. It shows that the opportunism of military policy overrides everything and that therefore to pretend that conscience has much of a part in it is overoptimistic. On the contrary, Cold War thinking, in which Christians let their minds be shaped (and so easily) by the fantasies of an aggressive policy, purely and simply determines them beforehand to give moral rationalization to justify that policy, however inhuman and unjust. This needs to be clearly shown, as against the cliché of those who confuse passivity with obedience and say that the "leaders know best" and the "government is always right," etc. This is the great danger.

On the other hand I absolutely agree with you on the danger of non-violent and civil-disobedience movements that go ahead irresponsibly. There is a great danger of opportunism and improvisation here too, especially as a lot of them are young and lack perspective. There must be non-violence, and this is one of the only solutions. But precisely it must be real, mature, well-prepared, disciplined non-violence. And for this we are by no means ready. There is every danger that resentment, immature rebelliousness, Beatnik non-conformism, and so on may be taken automatically to be charismatic just because they are opposed to what is obviously stuffy and inert. And cruel.

Unfortunately the opposition, the status quo, is very clever in finding the flaws and the untruths in a non-violence that is not true in depth and solid in charity and understanding. It requires a great deal of spiritual wisdom and formation to do this kind of thing. I am afraid that the little bud of non-violence that is beginning to show itself in this country may be killed by discredit, through the inexperience of its proponents. And through their obvious spiritual eclecticism, immaturity, instability, and so on. Yet on the other hand some of the kids from *The Catholic Worker* were down here and they are in general very solid. Or so I think. Especially Jim Forest seems to me to have considerable possibilities. He is in jail now, and perhaps ought not to be there. I mean he perhaps precipitated things in a way that should not have been done. Yet they have a refreshing hopefulness and energy. This seems to have been lost in the years after the war and is coming back at last, but perhaps too late.

The *Commonweal* [February 9] article was well received, but met with a little opposition. I was perhaps too sweeping. However, an atomic scientist wrote with injured innocence and demanded that I prove that anyone is planning to use nuclear weapons in war. Imagine that, all of a sudden. I would suppose that an atomic scientist would necessarily be literate, and would read the papers and perhaps even magazines, who knows?

On October 31, 1962, Louis Massignon died. A few months before (on June 6, 1962) he had written to Mason: "To remain silent is the main duty for a Trappist. I think Tom could ask now for his Mexican exile?" This statement has special significance, since Massignon had close contacts with the Vatican through Cardinal Montini (later Pope Paul VI). See the letters to Massignon.

November 17, 1962

Thank you for informing me so promptly of the solemn news of Louis' death. I had been thinking of him a lot lately and praying for him. Of course once the Algerian affair was "settled" more or less, or entering a new phase, I suppose it was in the logic of things that this great man should go to his rest. And yet we cannot afford to lose people like him. There are too few, and they are not being replaced. May he pray for us and watch over us and obtain for us the light and the strength to follow in his footsteps. We will understand later his greatness better than we do now.

Next week, on the Feast of the Presentation of Our Lady, a mystery which has ceased to be appreciated or understood, apparently, in the West (and with us it has apparently never really been accepted fully except in a superficial way by "religious congregations"), I shall offer my Mass for Louis, that he may "merit to be presented in the Temple of Heaven" by the merits of Our Lady. It may be the last time that this feast is celebrated as one of major rank in our Order, for it has been reduced to some trivial level.

Thank you also for letting me know where you are. As a correspondent I must necessarily get worse and worse, because it is becoming a real burden. People send all kinds of things I am supposed to read. Manuscripts I am supposed to place for them, books for which I am to write prefaces. I am father and literary agent to half the world all of a sudden. Naturally I cannot do all these things but it takes time just to say so. And of course all the other letters of people with troubles. And the Protestant visitors. You understand.

Yet do not be afraid to write once in a while. I value your letters and rely on you for information and insights that could not come from another. I hope your studies will be really blessed.

April 20, 1965

I fully intended to write to you before Holy Saturday to tell you how moved I was at the news of your intended action with a Buddhist friend or friends in Washington, to march and pray for peace in Vietnam. I would also have wanted to send some sort of appropriate message. Unfortunately I did not have a chance. I was ill in Holy Week, and in any case my correspondence is in such a state that I can no longer even pretend that I am keeping up with it adequately. But I do want to say that I was united with you in prayer on that day especially, but also throughout the holydays.

Certainly/this is the kind of thing that makes sense in the whole huge senseless and sick mess. Louis Massignon was so strong on "*les moyens pauvres*" ["the poorer means"]. (And Fr. Moubarac has recalled that to our minds in the recent bulletin of the Amis de Gandhi.) What is more "poor" and yet more authentic than simply the witness of understanding and fraternal unity between Buddhists and Christians, and only a few at that, on this issue? The Buddhists of Vietnam as far as I can see are the only ones who have anything reasonable to say, and of course what they look for is the right of their own people to determine their own future. If we were not so blinded by our own appetite for brute power, as a nation, we would have no trouble seeing that we are just as much standing in the way of a just and democratic solution as the Communists are, and perhaps more. I am afraid this whole thing is a clear proof of the moral and spiritual blindness of the American establishment. Fortunately there are quite a few people who can take another stand and speak out against the official policy. But what does it do? I don't know, but it must nevertheless be done, and the results are in God's hands.

May God bless your attempts, anyway. Please believe in my deep interest and agreement, even though I have not been able to give signs of awareness before this moment.

August 17, 1967

This summer I have been lecturing here on Sufism. If you run across anything good and new that I may not have heard of (something that is not very generally known, in other words), I hope you will let me know about it.

I have not been writing much in the way of letters, relatively to the amount I receive. It is just not possible to keep up. That is why I have not commented one way or the other on the Arab-Israel war. The situation is extremely painful. I am certainly sorry for the refugees, but at the same time I am in a position where I do not think I can honestly take a public stand which would seem by implication to approve Nasser's policy, which I think stupid as well as ultimately genocidal. I try as far as possible to avoid taking any side at all and to help those who suffer insofar as this is indirectly possible.

2. To Louis Massignon

One of the outstanding Islamic scholars of the twentieth century, Louis Massignon was born July 25, 1883, in Nogent-sur-Marne, an eastern suburb of Paris, of a prominent bourgeois family, his father an outspoken agnostic, his mother a Catholic. Profoundly French, he had a deep appreciation of Islamic culture. Abdallah Laroui, a contemporary Moroccan historian, wrote in 1975: "The work of Louis Massignon is the most honest, the most admirable, the closest to our hearts that Europe's contact with the Arab East has ever produced." Married and the father of three children, he was given permission by Pius XII in 1950 to become a priest of the Melkite rite. He was in touch with Charles de Foucauld, whose life story included a military career, a conversion, a Trappist vocation, and finally a hermit life in the Algerian desert. Massignon was also in close association with the leaders of the Catholic renascence in France—J. K. Huysmans, Teilhard de Chardin, Gabriel Marcel, Georges Bernanos, François Mauriac, Jacques Maritain.

Early Massignon was attracted to the famous ninth-century Sufi mystic of Baghdad, Hallaj, Husayn ibn Mansur al-Hallaj, whose identification of himself with the Divine Reality brought him to martyrdom. Massignon identified with this mystic and his dissertation for the Sorbonne was The Passion of al-Hallaj. It was published in French in 1922 and, in an expanded edition (1975), it is now available in the English translation by Herbert Mason in the Bollingen Series, Princeton University Press. This book revolutionized the way scholars looked at Islam, especially its mystical tradition.

One of Massignon's deep spiritual commitments was to the notion of "substitution mystique," the acceptance and endurance of the sufferings of another, the transfer of suffering through compassion. This notion, called badal by Hallaj, led to the formation by Massignon of a sodality of the Badaliya. One of the members of this sodality was Cardinal Montini of Milan, later Pope Paul VI.

Thomas Merton greatly admired Massignon, who proved to be an important influence in leading him to the study of Sufism. Merton felt humbled before him and looked on him as a kind of spiritual father. Massignon's willingness to speak *out, to take risks, may well have been part of what influenced Merton to do the same in the 1960s. Their correspondence seems to have been fairly extensive. The letters that follow are the only ones that have been located thus far.*

March 18, 1960

How can I begin to write you a letter about the amazing book of the prayers and exhortations of Hallaj [*Akhbar al-Hallaj*, third edition, in Arabic with Massignon's French translation]? I think it is tremendous. In many ways the rude paradoxes are striking in the same way as Zen. But there is the added depth and fire of knowledge of the one God. There is the inexorable force of sanctity. The sense of the Holy, that lays one low: as in Isaias. To read Hallaj makes one lament and beat his breast. Where has it gone, this sense of the sacred, this awareness of the Holy? What has happened to us? How true it is that in the light of such blinding sincerity, our ordinary prayers and protestations of faith are acts of impiety.

Whoever has dared, for centuries, to get up and say the most terrible and important message: *Ne te laisse point duper par Dieu, ni ne désespéré de Lui . . .* etc. (no. 41) ["Do not let yourself be tricked by God, at the same time do not despair of Him"]. Is there no one left to wrestle with the angel, like Jacob and this Hallaj? But of course, where did it lead him? That is the answer.

May the Lord give me the grace to be worthy of such a book, and to read it with a pure and humble heart, as I hope I have been doing. May I have ears to hear this voice, so alien to our comfortable and complacent piety.

When you were in Egypt [Massignon held a professor's chair both in Paris at the Collège de France and in Cairo at the New Egyptian University], did you hear or see anything of the monastery at Scete? I have heard fragments of information about it here and there, and know that it is in some way floundering.

I am sending you a mimeographed study on the early Carmelites [eventually published as "The Primitive Carmelite Ideal," in *Disputed Questions*]. The censors of the Order have been giving me trouble with it: they say that if it is published the monks will want to be hermits, etc., etc. Always this evasion of everything serious and essential, in order to exalt what is peripheral and meaningless. But I hope that with the help of prayer justice will be done.

Often I read your little leaflet on Charles de Foucauld [*Plus qu'un anneau sur le doigt . . .* "More than a ring on the finger"]. It moves me deeply. I am very sad at the lack of seriousness of my life compared with the lives of the men who have really listened to the word of God and kept it. I have not fought Him as I should!

Tomorrow, in my Mass for the Feast of St. Joseph, I will remember you very especially, Louis. I am more and more convinced of the rightness of your spiritual intuition and of the direction in which you travel: the way of mystery and risk, and of fervor.

With warm good wishes and prayers for a holy Easter. God bless you.

In the next two letters Merton refers to the "Seven Sleepers of Ephesus." An early medieval legend speaks of them as Christians in Ephesus who were walled up in a cave where they had taken refuge from the persecution of Decius (249–251). God put them to sleep. Three hundred and nine years later they awoke and found the city Christian. Soon they died and were venerated as saints. Their story is also narrated in the Koran (Sura xviii). Their story meant a great deal to Massignon, who led pilgrimages of Christians and Muslims to a Seven Sleepers shrine in Brittany on their feast (July 27). In a letter of September 3, 1959, he wrote to Merton that when he was at Ephesus itself, in 1951, he saw the place where Mary Magdalen was said to have died. The Seven Sleepers meant to him the mystery of resurrection; and he was struck by the presence at their cave of the burial place of the first witness of the Resurrection.

May 12, 1960

Herbert sent me the absurd reports from the newspapers concerning the demonstrations [for Algerian independence from France] on April 30. One must be prepared to meet with organized incomprehension.

On June 3rd I shall be saying Mass for you and for all your intentions.

Do you know the prayer to the Seven Sleepers composed by St. Peter Damian? If not I'll send it to you.

I like al-Hallaj more and more each day.

God bless you always—in union of prayers, of faith, and of dedication.

On May 19, 1960, Massignon replied to Merton: "We are laughed at for our 'non-violence,' but your approval and your prayer help us. So many thanks for June 3rd: the day of Blessed [now St.] Karoli Lwanga of Uganda . . . There is a wave against non-violence among the Hierarchy of the Church here; the old 'consuetudo' between the 'Established Church' and the Power of the State."

July 20, 1960

For a long time I have practically written no letters because I have been trying to finish a long article and also to read proofs of a new full-length book, along with other duties. Hence I have had to let your letters go, and I am very sorry. However, I have copied out the prayer by St. Peter Damian and I hope it will reach you by the 27th [Feast of the Seven Sleepers]. Though if you are going to Vieux Marché [a tiny Breton village] for the Pardon [the Breton word for "pilgrimage"], it will be too late. I wish I could be there with you, and I envy you. I know you will pray for me. I will remember you in a very special way in my Mass that day.

How is your new plan progressing? I think of it often. These are terrible days for Africa. I do not hear much news, but the little that comes through is very sad. If only we had enough insight to interpret the meaning of these events, and what they tell us about the humanitarianism of which we are so proud. If only we were able to be humble, and to mistrust our powers and our capacities, instead of making gods of ourselves and our progressive methods. How pitiful. But Africa is telling us the truth very plainly, about ourselves. One thing at least: we have the diffidence that makes us withdraw from a situation that our pride has made intolerable. But then we deliver our victims into the hands of those who do not share even this much diffidence with ourselves.

I cannot thank you too much for the latest issue of the *Mardis of Dar el Salam* [regularly published papers that grew out of mutual good will and common interest sessions held at an ecumenical center, called Dar el Salam, which means "the house of peace"]. Is there some way in which I could get all of them, I mean all the back issues? Could you have them sent to me? My [French] publisher, Albin Michel, will take care of the expense and will charge it to me. I think the issue you sent me is full of the most wonderful things and I was above all deeply moved by your own short meditations on the desert and the God of Agar and Ishmael. They are wonderful, and especially the fragments.

Louis, one thing strikes me and moves me most of all. It is the idea of the *"point vierge, ou le désespoir accule le coeur de l'excommunié"* ["the virginal point, the center of the soul, where despair corners the heart of the outsider"]. What a very fine analysis, and how true. We in our turn have to reach that same *"point vierge"* in a kind of despair at the hypocrisy of our own world. It is dawning more and more on me that I have been caught in civilization as in a kind of spider's web, and I am beginning to say "No" louder and louder, though surrounded by the solicitude of those who ask me why I do so. There is no way of explaining it, and perhaps not even time to do so.

Your page on Cheikh Baye is one of the most inspiring things I have read for a long time. More and more I see the meaning of the Seven Sleepers, the excluded ones, who in the *"point vierge"* of complete passivity and "death" wait like seeds of light and of resurrection because in their sleep they hope. I think the prayers of Peter Damian are very fine. We sleep with our mouths in the dust, the dust of Europe and America in our throats.

In the fall I hope to send you the new book. It contains a long piece of mine on solitude ["Notes for a Philosophy of Solitude" in *Disputed Questions*], which I think will interest you. Under separate cover I am sending translations of four poems of César Vallejo, the Peruvian half-Indian poet, who died twenty years ago. The last one especially speaks of the *"point vierge."* You will see. All blessings to you, Louis. I keep you in my masses and prayers.

While Herbert Mason was visiting Merton in August 1960, he wrote to Louis Massignon, telling him that from their talks he believed—from Merton's own statements—that it was important for him to leave the monastery. He wrote: "Merton believes, as you do, that the really apocalyptic thing about our times is not that communists are killing people, but that Christians are killing people— and he humbly feels that the 'identity' his books have created tends to become used to justify the military practices of Christians—who let him do their contemplating for them. He must thus get away in order that they can stand alone. And this is true: we must lose 'one light' in order to find it ourselves." Mason also enclosed a copy of the letter that Merton had sent to Archbishop Paul Philippe at the Vatican (see pp. 221–25).

September 4, 1960

As you know, Herbert has been here. He was telling me that you were going to Moscow, etc., and I did not write to you. I hope your trip was not too wearisome, but very fruitful. I have read the fascinating book on St. Francis and Mohammed [by Fr. Giulio Bassetti-Sani, published in Montreal in French]. It is very clear, very original. We need books like this and I found some magnificent sentences from the Koran.

I have received the *Mardis* and I enjoyed them—there is a richness from which I am going to profit.

Herbert will tell you about his visits and our conversations. I scarcely know if we are even in the region of the possible. I know what I want before God. But I also know that the obstacles are formidable. I am continually being told that I should absolutely drop the whole matter. One can always hope and pray. In any event God is master of His graces and of our whole life. We only do what we can to serve Him with our whole hearts. He can do all and will do the rest.

Pray then for me and for my intentions. Whatever my desert is, I must remain in it. You will have received the little book, the deluxe edition of this subject [*The Solitary Life*].

October 29, 1960

Several times news has reached me of your continued sickness. Herbert sends me your messages. I have been wanting to write to you. I have not had time to write anything adequate. Today at least I can tell you that Herbert's message reached me and I, with the monks, am praying for your "Isaac" whom God asked of you and whom you surrendered to Him. [The reference is to Massignon's eldest son, Yves, who died at the age of twenty.]

Louis, in the presence of the darkness, the cloud of falsity and pretense, of confusion, of evasion, of desecration, one grows more and more to distrust words, to distrust even human communication itself. There grows in my heart a need to express something inexpressible, and I do not dare to find out what it might possibly be. So I can only fall back on half-articulate utterances. Forgive the lack of meaning.

First I struggle in my heart with the mystery and the need of peace, peace for the world. As a priest and a monk I must be a man of peace.

I tell myself that there must be some truth in that idea. But in fact we are surrounded by and committed to a climate of violence. This is to me a terrible problem. Pray that I may be worthy to face it before the Lord of mercy and of peace. I am sending you under separate cover a little thing I did about the poor, mostly a translation from the Italian of Don Mazzolari. Are we in this country worthy to face the mystery of the poor? We do not seem to know about it.

I am studying reverently Gandhi's two volumes on non-violence. Maybe someday I can make suitable selections and publish them here with an introduction [*Gandhi on Non-Violence*, published in 1964]. I think I am bound in conscience at least to try to do something of this sort, certainly I feel that I must align myself with les Amis de Gandhi [the Friends of Gandhi, an organization founded by Massignon in the 1930s, even before he met Gandhi. After World War II, les Amis de Gandhi and the Badaliya were joined together].

I think of the Moslems. The other day I happened to be in a museum, in Cincinnati, where they have many fine Persian things. I was utterly stunned by the magnificent tomb cover of a Moslem saint, Imam Riza, once seen by thousands of pilgrims, now ignored by tourists. It had on it a wonderful Sufi poem, translated for those who were interested. This encounter had a deep effect on me, as also my seeing everywhere faces of saints, angels, liberated ones from France, Catalonia, Persia, India, Cambodia. All of them innocent, silent, enigmatic, smiling in their humble understanding and acceptance of their position: they are at home everywhere, and we who think we are at home are, among them, aliens.

Let us be united in our prayers. This I say not as a formula, but in desperate poverty and need. With everyone else who is in need, who is an exile, a captive, who hungers for truth and cannot find truth, let us pray and mourn in our hearts and cry out to God, the God of Abraham, the God also of Agar and Ishmael. May He give you strength in your sufferings and may His angels stand guard over you at all times. May the Holy Mother of God console you. May the Savior of the world bless you.

November 6, 1960

On the 22nd of November I shall offer the holy sacrifice of the Mass for your intentions, especially those that concern Africa. On the 25th I will offer it again for all the Friends of Gandhi and for all those who are non-violent. I want with all my heart and with tears to be in union with all those who use the poor, humble, non-violent, truly Christian way to peace. Pray also for my intentions and ask them to do the same. Would there be some possibility of my being enrolled among the Friends of Gandhi and participating, even in some small way, in what they do? I am now reading Gandhi. He is someone I must write about; the others are "meat-eaters." May the God of mercy bless you.

November 22, 1960

Today I am offering Mass for you and all your intentions, as I wrote to you before. And I am also fasting for peace and for Christian-Moslem understanding.

I was happy yesterday to preach a sermon for the Presentation of Our Lady in the Temple.

Thank you for referring Abdul Aziz [see *HGL*] to me. I have written to him and sent him some books. He seems very interesting. Who is he?

Louis, I hope you are well, or not too sick. I am united with you in all your deep concerns. We must be passionately devoted to all the desires of God for men and for peace and justice among men. Let us love and serve Him with all our being! Let us be united in prayer always.

Louis Massignon died on October 31, 1962.

3. To Leslie Dewart

*We confront a basic inconsistency in clerical and often
ecclesial thought . . . : a great "respect for life" when it
comes to contraception and a great unconcern for it when
it comes to the bomb, tests, etc.*

TO LESLIE DEWART

*Leslie Dewart, who taught at St. Michael's College in the University of Toronto,
discussed a book of his with Merton*—Christianity and Revolution: The Lesson
of Cuba *(published in 1963 by Herder and Herder). The book studies the relationship between a major historical event (the Castro overthrow of the Batista
government) and a major social institution (the Roman Catholic Church). Other
Dewart works attempt to bridge the gap between the human experience of the
world and the human experience of faith-realities, such as* The Future of Belief:
Theism in a World Come of Age *(Herder and Herder, 1966),* The Foundations
of Belief *(Herder and Herder, 1969),* Religion Language and Truth *(Herder and
Herder, 1970). Dewart, now retired from teaching, resides in Toronto.*

[*Cold War Letter 103*]   September 1962
    Thanks for your letters and for the articles, which are excellent. First
I read the one in *Liberation*, which is very gentle and understanding,
and I think it says a lot. It touches on a very central problem. The whole
issue today depends, in great measure, in the last resort, on the American
mentality. And that mentality is involved in deep illusions, most of all
about itself. These illusions are nevertheless part and parcel of its goodness. It seems to be an immensely complex problem. The problem of
Christian hopes, after centuries of frustration and deviation, suddenly
finding an unexpected, secular fulfillment and a new, seemingly secular
direction. The illusion of America as the earthly paradise, in which everyone recovers original goodness: which becomes in fact a curious idea that
prosperity itself justifies everything, is a sign of goodness, is a carte
blanche to continue to be prosperous in any way feasible: and this leads
to the horror that we now see: because we are prosperous, because we
are successful, because we have all this amazing "know-how" (without
real intelligence or moral wisdom, without even a really deep scientific
spirit), we are entitled to defend ourselves by any means whatever, with-

out any limitation, and all the more so because what we are defending is our illusion of innocence . . .

In a word, I am perfectly agreed that there is an opportunity for the realization of a fully universal Christianity, just as at the end of the Roman world there was not only the opportunity but even in some sense a relatively universal realization of Catholicism, but how relative? . . .

We are running off some more copies of "Peace in the PCE" [Post-Christian Era] and I will send a couple. I don't think I ever sent you [the first edition of] the Cold War Letters. There will be a new, enlarged edition of that too, and I will try to remember to send them to you. What I would much rather know is: do they have any interesting texts of the XII century school of Chartres that are not available in Migne and other common sources? I am especially interested in William of Conches, and would like to get a copy of something of his, anything, for we have nothing. Microfilm, photocopy, anything. As you see, I have a medieval mentality.

I am returning your article and the letters of the bishops, which are most gratifying. Archbishop Flahiff of course I know about, through Dan Walsh. Maybe I will send him a copy of the peace book, though now he will probably be completely tied up in the Council. That Council! Such hopes and such fears! But the Holy Spirit really is in command there, though He may not be at the Pentagon. So there I can dare to hope without limitations. And without necessarily expecting to see clearly the object of my hopes realized.

All blessings, and with every best wish. Keep in touch, keep writing, as my Beat friends say, keep turning on the peace.

April 27, 1963

First of all, about my pessimism and your optimism. The only difference is that you are a little more ready to see *temporal* hopes than I am. My attitude on this has certainly been modified by *Pacem in Terris*. A very fine document indeed. I certainly did note the phrase you mentioned immediately, and applied it where it was meant to be applied. There is no question at all that this is a statement that the Church is happy with us *anawim* and that she wants a remnant like us to keep in there. I have no intention of doing anything else. The fact that we are a minority, the fact that the majority is made up of stuffed and stupefied conformists, the fact that theologians and co. will soon have digested the encyclical and found it to be something quite different to what we fellows thought . . . etc. This does not bother me, or raise any doubt in my mind as to what we ought to do. But I just hesitate to make any kind of prognostic on the results. Frankly, I am rather indifferent to the results as such, I mean as the "anticipated fruit" of my gallant efforts. I think we must all be perfectly ready to make all kinds of efforts and even get destroyed into the bargain, without particularly worrying about any fruit that we can anticipate. The Lord has His ideas and they will not fail to bring forth the fruit He wants, which is also what we want. We should be exercised about a limited political issue? Yet of course, in another perspective, since we do live in a political world, and we have to see this side of it too, I am certainly happy that [Lester B.] Pearson got in [as Canadian Prime Minister]. That is the right estimate, isn't it? I don't know too much about your lineup there, but I assumed that [John G.] Diefenbaker is the one we don't want. Good for Canada.

I mention the above points not as an ascetic sermon fit for novices, but as one of the most basic tenets on which genuine non-violence is based. Without indifference to immediate fruits, non-violence is powerless. And I would tend to think that it does not matter whether we can continue to keep the world in a "Christian Era" or not. Certainly we should try, it is absurd to throw out the last hope of order that does remain, as far as I can see: a society based on rational norms, natural law, and all that Catholic philosophy sees, teaches, and calls for. If this goes, then we are really in the soup. But on the other hand, it has to such a great extent already gone. Not beyond recall, of course. But the situation is as precarious as it ever can be. We have to go ahead with our principles and our faith anyway.

Now what is my predicament about publishing on peace? The higher Superiors of the Order, specifically the General—a very autocratic Gaullist type, Legion of Honor and all that—has decreed that my writing about the "controversial topic" of war and peace is decidedly harmful to the image of our contemplative Order in the eyes of the populace. Imagine that, now. It "falsifies the message of the contemplative life," he says. Anyway he has forbidden it absolutely, forbidden the book, refused to allow any more writing on this subject even to be censored. *C'est net* [It's clear-cut]. On these grounds, he can logically argue that *Pacem in Terris* changes nothing. At least with his logic he can. However, I wrote to him rather a cheeky letter saying it was a good thing the Pope did not have to be approved by the censors of our Order, etc., etc., and asking if I could revise the book in the light of the encyclical and submit it for censorship. He might possibly permit this, I don't know. I will let you know.

Now to the subject of your book.

Certainly I see no possibility that I will be allowed to write anything with a political slant to it. I will indeed have to be very careful of writing about it in a way that assumes I have heard the news, because, you see, the popular image of the contemplative is that he never pays any attention to the wicked world and its affairs, and if it were ever thought that one took the slightest interest in the news, why this would ruin the old image, you see. And heaven knows, what matters is to preserve not peace or anything like that, only the image. The Old Testament suggests rather rueful reflections on this theme, I fear. Something about first two commandments.

What has actually been happening is that, without writing about war and peace, I have been getting off statements of one sort and another that have a general relevance to the situation (I hope) and somehow they get printed more or less while I am not looking, in forms that traditionally require no censorship. However, I do not know how long this can last either. It is possible that I may run into more difficulties. Hence it is very hard to promise anything, except that I will read the ms. and do what I can.

I certainly agree that a postface of the kind you suggest ought to be possible, but on the other hand it is very unlikely at the moment. Let us wait and see what happens about the "Peace" book, before I plan anything more definite. But in any event I want to read the ms.

Actually I think this is a crucially important subject for the Church at the present moment. It is ironical that the fate of the Church in the Western Hemisphere seems to be mixed up with the idiocies that pass as policy in Washington. It is terribly important to do two things.

a) Prove that the Church is not committed to follow the Pentagon or the State Department anywhere, least of all in Latin American affairs.

b) Show that the Church has something very definite and very relevant of her own to say about the human dimensions of the Latin American question.

And then keep the way wide open for something to be done about it. Actually, it seems to me that instead of all this screaming about the horrors of Castro Communism, there have been opportunities for the Church to do quite a lot, and they have perhaps not been understood. But the ambiguity is that under Communism our position is not as cushy as it is here. It seems to me that we have to get down to cases and be willing to work under the realities of Communist oppression as they are, really, and not as we dream them up to be in our self-glorifying fantasies. They are hard and bitter and difficult realities, but if they are accepted, a great deal can be done with them by God's grace. I think the Pope realizes this very well, and has learned a lot about it from the Bishops who came to the Council from behind the Iron Curtain, and that now the Church is following the realism of Wyszinsky, and not the melodrama of Mindszenty. (Though I don't mean to suggest Mindszenty did not suffer but his story could have been different and more rational, and less of a batch of grist from the American mass media.)

So that's it. I think the same problems confront me in trying to write for *Coexistence*, but at least I would like to do what I can, and am interested in exploring the territory.

I think George Lawler has got a real good thing under way, in *Continuum*.

Finally, there is one aspect of my own work that we have to consider for the future. When I go underground, as far as publishing may be concerned, there is still the very important field of personal action and contact, and mimeographed material, discussions of various kinds, and moral support. I am of course absolutely committed to what is clearly God's will, in its peculiar difficulties for me: namely, to do what He obviously asks of any Christian at such a time, to work and pray and fight for peace and order first and foremost, as an integral part of my vocation, without which the whole concept of my vocation becomes farcical, and contemplation would be meaningless. But to do this within the limits set forcibly by uncomprehending officials, or well-meaning types who cannot see the importance of the issue. In other words, reconciling obedience to men and obedience to God: until such a point that they come in direct conflict. And then I am going to need some pretty good advice.

May 10, 1963

Your manuscript has arrived and I am about halfway through it. The book is terrific. You are very clear, convincing, and as far as I can see quite fair. I think it is a very important study of the Cuba affair, and in many ways it is more important even than Zahn's study of Germany [*German Catholics and Hitler's War*, Sheed and Ward, 1962].

At the same time, I have received a letter from the Abbot General of the Order, categorically refusing me permission to publish *Peace in the PCE* and ordering me to drop all thought of doing so, with or without comments on the encyclical. His reasons: I am a contemplative monk and my business is silence and solitude. Besides that, though the encyclical says that war cannot be an instrument of justice, etc., nevertheless this does not deprive a nation of the right to acquire nuclear weapons and arm with them for its self-defense, and I am being very rash, etc., etc., in saying so. And finally I am just incompetent anyhow and my opinions are of no value since I don't know what I am talking about in the first place.

This is of course exactly what I was expecting, and there is little I can do about it—that is to say, about the book. It is simply an indication that the book goes onto the shelf. Those who have read it in mimeograph have enjoyed it. That is enough for that. I do, however, still have a Christian conscience, and I have read the encyclical, and I am aware that the Pope wants Catholics to work for peace. So I will have to do what I can, short of publication on this precise subject.

This brings up the question of your book. There is absolutely no point whatever in my even trying to get an epilogue through the censors. The first thing they will want to know is "what kind of book is this?" Then they may even want to see it, and, if they do, you know what they will say. The mere title is enough to disqualify all such participation on my part, the way things are. There is nothing I can do about this, it is hopeless to try to argue with the Abbot General on this point. His mind is closed, and there is no communication. He is convinced that I am nothing but a rabid pacifist with wild ideas, and that I have to be silenced on this point. In other words I am right in the middle of the problem which your book raises so cogently. There are moments when obedience completely blocks valid social action and Christian witness in society. This is extremely grave. I do not think that at this precise moment I have reached the point of frank contradiction, because there are still other things I can do. But it is serious.

Here is what I suggest. The thought came to me as I read a rather mixed-up paragraph of yours (a very rare one, I assure you, you are very clear most of the time). It is the one at the bottom of p. 61, about the Church getting into a "dark night" of temptation. Your wording is confused and I think you have not thought it out thoroughly. What I might do is this: write you a long letter, developing this idea in my own words, and making other comments. And then if you find anything in the letter that is of use to you, you could simply quote it as from a personal letter. I know this is not much to offer but it is at least something. The epilogue is out.

Is Fromm the best man for a preface? I doubt it. I wish you could get some Latin American Bishop! The trouble is they are not too well known around here, but the mere fact that a Bishop spoke would be of immense value. Unfortunately I don't know them personally but surely one or the other would back you up.

Is there no one else, a Catholic thinker or writer (there must be Catholic thinkers around, come now!) who would be good for this job?

I am completely with you on your diagnosis. The Catholic laity and some of the clergy are capable of a great deal of generosity and dedication until they run into the kind of bind we are all in over Communism. Then they stop dead. This is because they are too negative, passive, confused. We are shouting all day and all night about the revival of Catholic life, but it is mostly peripheral. When it gets down to cases, we are not Christians but anti-Communists. That is to say, we have really nothing positive of our own to offer, only a negation of what somebody else is doing. And what they are doing is to a great extent a negation of what our society is doing. Psychologically this adds up to a situation in which war would logically seem inevitable . . .

The situation regarding authority and so on is very complex. It is not by any means that a lot of conservative Superiors are standing in the way of enlightened subjects. The whole concept and practice of religious obedience has stultified the clergy and the religious, so that they are incapable of any creative action, and equipped only to run in one familiar organizational groove. The way we are now, the Church is simply incapable of genuine adaptation. In a word, if the Council doesn't continue waking up the Bishops and Superiors, we are going to be in a bad way.

This is not conclusive, and it is all from the top of my head. More of the old pessimism, and I don't mean it to be as bad as it probably sounds. I am just wondering. Where do we look for something genuinely positive? The encyclical is beautiful, but God knows it is nothing new. As I. F. Stone pointed out, it goes back to Marcus Aurelius.

Are we really so identified with a rotten and crumbling edifice that we are bound to collapse with it?

There is where I stop. I think that if the thing collapses, and it must, a great deal of what we have called "Christianity" will go with it, and if we are around to rub the dust out of our eyes we will finally see that it wasn't Christianity at all. Who will deliver us from the body of this death?

The following is the letter Merton suggested Dewart might quote from in his book.

n.d. (between May 10 and June 28, 1963)

Your manuscript on the Cuban revolution and on the ambivalence, hesitations, and withdrawal of the Cuban Church is a very perceptive and exciting political meditation and there is good reason for us to meditate politically when the moral and spiritual crisis of man at the end of an era of his history comes out in political conflict. I believe that the great religious temptation of our time, the apocalyptic temptation, will be (and already is) in the realm of politics.

What do I mean by apocalyptic? I mean quite simply "final" and decisive as a manifestation of the secret of God in history and of the Christian capacity—or failure—to act according to His love. We are in the time of "the end"—not that everything necessarily has to blow up tomorrow. But we have certainly passed a point of no return and we live now in a world of fantastic perspectives, most of them, as I say, apocalyptic. To none of them are we yet adjusted. Your text is a good beginning. It shows the way we must attempt to seek some kind of clarity and understanding in the events of our time which ought to be supremely relevant to the Church insofar as these events all have Christian or "post-Christian" implications, either for us or against us. *In these events we, and the Christian centuries, are now, at this very moment, being judged.*

This, first of all, has to be made clear and its implications to some extent grasped. I do not mean that we are to be saved merely in politics. Yet we must face the fact that we may be lost there.

What happened in Cuba? A failure of the Church in the realm of politics. That is to say, a failure to meet a new situation with a creative understanding that would have helped the Cuban revolution to be what it was first intended to be—a means of instituting an equitable, honest, and progressive social order in that community. A means of taking a forward step that would have helped the liberation and progress of all the Latin American countries. In a word, the Church in Cuba had a chance to help put into effect her own social teaching and she missed the chance, partly through her own fault, and partly through circumstances utterly beyond her control. Where the Church did fail was not in good intentions but in genuine political insight and in the ability to make a serious, long-range, creative evaluation of the possibilities of the revolution . . .

This would not be so bad if the Church were not really interested in politics. In actual fact, especially in the last two centuries, but certainly since Constantine and Charlemagne, the Church in the sense of the hierarchy and the powerful among the laity has been deeply involved in politics: so much so that issues that seem on the surface to be purely issues of faith turn out, on the most superficial examination, to be political in their source and in their import, or at least inextricably involved in political action, or even, more frankly, *in the struggle for political power*. In actual fact, then, while we have been going along in a comfortable feeling of apolitical insouciance, convinced that we were far above the things of this wicked world, and citizens of a purely heavenly city, we have in reality been very much engaged in the world and its struggles for power, and our attitudes of seeming disengagement have enabled us to commit ourselves rather more deeply than we might have otherwise done to positions that were not always very Christian. In a word, by telling ourselves that we were not of this world we have actually made it easier for ourselves to be worldly in a manner that is very often not only uncharitable but also very ineffectual as well.

Thus it has happened that insensibly the faith of Christians has been habitually used and manipulated in the power struggle. Without anybody thinking too much about it or being willing to admit the fact, the involvement of interior faith and the exterior struggle for power has at times become so deep as to amount to a real alienation of faith and spirit, a state in which the Christian, without knowing it, mobilizes what for better or for worse seems to be his "faith" and his spiritual "conscience," in what is really, beneath the surface, part of a very human and perhaps even demonic power struggle that has nothing remotely to do with God or things of God: indeed may even be completely against the Law of God. But if necessary, God is called perfunctorily to justify these unchristian positions.

This has resulted in the following situation. Large masses of Christians, whole "Churches," if we may so designate Christian blocs in given nations, for instance the "Church" in the U.S., become masses in the strict sense, faceless collectivities with a rudimentary and almost vestigial interior faith, and an external, almost fanatical loyalty to certain symbolic positions, shibboleth-type positions, which identify one as a "Catholic." Anti-birth control, use of state school buses, prayers in public schools, clean movies, and anti-Communism. These, together with blind attachment to the Holy See and devotion to Mary, tend at times to become for us the real signs and manifestations of our Catholic faith. About the rest, well, maybe we have heard about it or maybe we haven't. We have heard about the Cross: it comes into our lives when we get sick, or when we are fired, or when we bow to authority and do our duty, when we obey, when we obey civil authority, when we follow along with the properly designated side in our power struggle, when we give our life for the properly designated side, when we consent to the sacrifice of the whole human race for the sake of the prestige of the side that has been defined as sacred by our sacred press.

From this arises the helplessness of "the Church" in certain situations to face the realities of our time with an authentic position of her own.

Certainly that position is defined beautifully in abstract and universal terms in Papal Encyclicals. But in fact this position rarely gets reduced to practice in time to meet the demands of a critical situation.

We are very good at coming out with declarations and resolutions, usually a little late. When it has become quite evident that a situation is unjust, and when it is clear that the "safer" liberal elements have recognized the injustice, some Bishops or some Catholic association will produce a declaration deploring the injustice. And indeed some attempt may be made to tackle it. But on the whole the Church is too cautious, too inert, and too slow to have a really creative influence in social affairs. She never leads. She always follows, often with rather pathetic attempts to scramble onto the back of somebody else's bandwagon. One gets the feeling that she is not so much concerned with burning social questions as with showing the masses she is really on their side—while at the same time not antagonizing those in power, unless they are Communists.

In one word: the Church is involved in the political life of the world but not as a creative or constructive force. When a showdown comes she tends to become reactionary because she is too often committed to the status quo.

The Cuban hierarchy could, by all means, approve of land reform in Cuba because this fitted in with the papal doctrine on social justice, and rightly. But this approval could hardly be more than theoretical and verbal because the hierarchy, for many reasons which you bring out very persuasively, could not lead Catholics to take a new position, a radically different and independent position of their own that was in between the two extremes, Russia and America. But if she had done this she might have saved Castro from falling into the arms of Moscow for good and all. Of course the complications in such a case are almost endless. For one thing, the laity have no way of working out original solutions because they are supposed to follow the hierarchy even in politics, and the hierarchy is usually, almost inevitably, committed to positions that are so full of compromise, so inert, so safe as to be meaningless.

And why? Because of "souls." But here is one of the great weaknesses of the Church today. We seem to be incapable of thinking of the Church's work for the salvation of souls except in terms of her *power over* souls— that is to say, except in terms of control.

Hence an appalling vicious circle. We believe that in the Church is our salvation. But how can the Church save men if she does not get to them before anybody else? How does the Church save men if she does not begin to control them from the cradle on? If I do or say or think anything that tends to weaken this all-important control, I am sinning against the faith, endangering my soul and the souls of thousands, millions, whole nations. Thus it becomes necessary *first of all, before anything else* (since faith is after all the *initium salutis*), to accept and defend certain pragmatic positions which guarantee, or seem to guarantee, this control, this access to "souls," this power over souls . . . But of course is it the power to teach, rule, and sanctify which God gave His Church? Well, is it? Have we perhaps lost our true perspective on the teaching, ruling, and sanctifying power of the Church? Have we secularized that perspective? Have we secularized it so completely that defense of the faith means defense of certain very worldly compromises and *deals* made by the hierarchy in the worldwide struggle for power? What happens, in that event, is that in order to safeguard and defend the faith, indeed my immortal soul, I have to accept certain undeclared assumptions implicit in a political policy, and I have to accept them as if they were of faith. In other words the real test of my Catholicity comes to be not my belief in God, or in Christ and His teachings, His Church and her Sacraments, so much as my commitment to extremely pragmatic and often very short-sighted views which have been dreamed up in chanceries and sacristies. I have to go along with policies that are often so inert, so blind, so stupid that they utterly stifle the true life of the Church and make it *impossible* for the most clear-sighted and courageous of her members to do anything that will further the real manifestation of the truth and charity of Christ in the world. Thus it is that at a time when the Popes have pleaded for creative social action, for a really living apostolate, for social justice, for international collaboration, for peace, etc., the Catholic press comes out everywhere with enthusiastic editorials about all these things in the abstract, while in the concrete everybody who tries to do anything really serious about them is blocked, silenced, and forbidden to act. All the energy of the best-intentioned and most zealous Christians then blow off in symbolic and image-making inanities, in campaigns and movements which mobilize the great religious publicity machine and involve everybody in senseless, futile, and exhausting collective rituals which, in the end, produce nothing. And behind all this spurious Pentecostal wind one can hear, if he listens a little carefully, the hideous merriment of demons.

We are living in a condition of endemic self-contradiction and frustration which is extremely dangerous, because each new move, each new spasm that goes through the Body of the Church makes us momentarily hope and imagine that we have not stifled the Holy Spirit: but then we discover, once again, or are in danger of discovering that we really have. (His voice, after all, is not easy to silence.) Then a new and more violent spasm becomes necessary, lest we hear Him and live.

Each new spasm aggravates all the problems we are trying to solve, both our own and those of the "world" we are meant to save. Each new self-contradiction, each new retreat from truth, each new abandonment of a position that was, for a moment, almost conquered, each new retreat into the old after proclaiming our advance into the new, leaves us more and more discredited in the eyes of a world that has *long since ceased to be interested in our inner contradictions*. Sure, a great Pope like John XXIII could get a marvelous and friendly press all over the place: but it was because he was a nice guy. As to the Church, its beliefs and its "renewal," the world couldn't care less.

Take the race question in the U.S. We are now in the middle of a real American revolution, just as real as the one in 1776, and perhaps destined to have an even more decisive importance. This too is a "microcosmic" situation, another apocalyptic sign like the Cuban revolution. What has the Church done? She has made token and symbolic gestures of good will and justice. She has integrated schools and colleges in many areas. She has been *less* prejudiced than most of the other sectors of white society, and she has roundly condemned racial injustice on paper. She has shown good will and motherly concern. Apart from that, she has taken a safe position, neither too much of this nor too much of that, and has carefully avoided signs of haste in getting anywhere. Whatever may be the merits of the various arguments for a more radical approach, it is certain that the Church has striven, as much as possible, to avoid every kind of risk, anything that might compromise her stable and quasi-respectable status in the South. In other words, she has made sure that the Catholic did not fall back into the same gehenna as the Negro, and did not become, with him and the Jew, bottom man on the totem pole. To guarantee this, it was necessary that no priest be seen on a freedom ride, that Catholics as Catholics should be kept out of anything messy (jails, sit-ins, etc.), and that the Church remain in the background. While of course retaining its influence over souls.

But what is happening is that there is extraordinary life surging up in the Negro community all over the U.S. In some of its forms this life is magnificently and explicitly Christian (Martin Luther King and his nonviolent movement). But in other places the movement is anything but Christian, and reflects disillusionment and disgust with Christian values and claims, whether Catholic or Protestant. It is not very hard to detect the irrationality, the fanaticism, and the potential cataclysmic violence contained in the new Negro racism. But it is not enough to detect this and deplore it, and then withdraw into a defensive, truculent, or even repressive position, using violence and hate against violence and hate. Yet this is the risk we run if we refuse to see to what extent our own vagueness, indecisiveness, and lack of creative initiative has engendered Negro violence.

What has happened is that the Church, in order to retain its respectability in the South, has risked losing the Negro entirely, not only in America but perhaps even to some extent in Africa. In other words, where there is life, where there is a real movement indicating the course of history (and Pope John somewhere said that we have to listen to the voice of history because it is the voice of God), where this voice is heard Catholics don't listen, because, with all the good will in the world they *cannot* listen. We cannot listen, because, after centuries of Holy Roman Empires and the rest, we cannot look upon history otherwise than as a force sustaining the Church's power to reach and *control* souls. The sin, hidden but real, is in this concept of the *absolute need for external control* over souls in order to save them.

And with that sin is another: our compassion for man has too much in it of secret contempt. We do not believe in man, we do not accept the fact that he is in the image of God, and we are pretty slow to attach any real importance to the fact that he may also be the temple of the Holy Spirit and a member of the living and omnipotent Christ. We therefore do not really believe in freedom and in the inexhaustible fecundity of the Spirit . . .

That being the case, the best I can do is get out the sackcloth and ashes and go into solitude and pray that God may save us from our damned consistency.

Thank you for your book, Leslie, and for your courage. I hope you will be heard.

June 28, 1963

This appendix is great, and really packs a wallop. I think we really should do what we can to get it through, if not into the book, then perhaps in *Continuum*. But you are right that a little circumspection is called for on my part.

Certainly as it stands this appendix would mean a pile of trouble for me. At the same time I think that by a little judicious work we can not only reduce the undesirable reaction, but build up the power of the piece and make it more telling.

1. I think my name should not appear in the title. This will be a big help right away. I suggest something like "Post-Christian World? Notes on a Controversy" or even "Echoes of a Controversy." That is corny, but it gives something of the idea that is desirable: to make it quite clear that this was purely a private exchange of views. Perhaps controversy is too strong a word (as regards the contemplative image that so exercises my higher Superiors). Discussion?

2. There is from my point of view a distinct disadvantage in long quotes from my letters. The first long one might well stand, but as we go on I think it would be wise to break them up. I have marked the pages where I think this is called for. Here, instead of simply quoting me at length, you would have to break the quote at the points indicated and continue in your own words, doubtless summing up briefly what is omitted from the quote and perhaps profitably adding insights of your own. This I think would in the long run improve the text as a whole, lighten it and liven it up.

3. I have gone through the quotes from my last letter and tried to cut out little phrases or expressions that might be needlessly offensive. One thing that bothers me about the "power" section is that I do sound a little like a clerical Paul Blanshard, and that is not an advantage. Perhaps some suggestion should be made that I am deeply aware of the problem the Church faces when confronted with the menace of Totalism: and that in actual fact, the Totalitarian state, or even the Affluent Mass society *does* get complete control over the person before he has begun to function

even as a fully conscious being. There is every reason to think the Church's fears are justified in this realm, but they do take a secularized form, a sort of counter-totalism in some respects. I think, by the way, that your summation of the sin of secularization (within the clerical frameworks) is very well put and I agree completely. I also agree with your existential approach. My term "post-Christian" was purely and simply for those who are content to describe and define situations from the outside, in terms of conformity with a preconceived or pre-announced standard. Neither the world nor we of the Church are presently doing a good job of measuring up to announced standards. As to the essential need of the world and of the Church being definable *only* in Christian terms, I fully agree: but I still tend to think they are more Apocalyptic than Teilhardian. May I be wrong. Pope John was certainly a great and unexpected blessing, and in the light of his pontificate I am willing to revise a lot of my pessimism in that other aspect of the discussion which we have really left.

Sorry to impose more work and revisions, but with these I think we can get by and my head will be relatively safe. I don't want to get myself completely silenced.

August 11, 1963

The decision of the publisher to keep the appendix out of the book may perhaps in the long run be a good one. I think it will be more likely to be read as a magazine article, to tell the truth, and it was a little different from the rest of the book. For my part I am not worried about the change.

About the misgivings in your earlier letter, I suppose you have already forgotten them. Certainly this question of dissent is always delicate, if we want to make our dissent effective. There is necessarily a danger of overemphasis when one tries to say that others have gone wrong and that their orientation must be corrected. That is the risk implied by dissent itself, and let's hope that most of our peers are still mature enough to understand the fact. At the same time I suppose one must remember the people who will be easily and unnecessarily shocked because they are in an insecure position. I presume it is better not to frighten them without sufficient reason, yet one does not always succeed in this. There are some who go into a flurry whenever the things they are accustomed to are treated with even a minimum of sarcasm, let alone subjected to outright attack. That cannot be helped. We have to keep moving.

I am glad about the test-ban treaty, and though it is not much, it is still something and we cannot afford to be ungrateful for even such things as this. What you say about China and Goldwater is no surprise. This was to be foreseen, and I suppose now the relaxation of tensions with Russia will be bought at the same price of a hate campaign based on fear of Red China. If Mao gets his bomb, and I don't doubt that he will, the whole thing will begin over again. But one can never say what may come out of it. I am no more optimistic than I have ever been, and I think we simply have to be ready for anything. Chances of a reasonable and positive attitude toward China do not seem to be very great.

Paul Peachey, secretary of the Church Peace Mission, is trying to get a group of Protestant and Catholic peace people down here from October 4th to 7th to talk about peace and think about problems connected with it. I have suggested your name to him, along with that of George Lawler and a couple of others, as Catholic possibilities. I hope you can possibly fit this in. He will probably get in touch with you himself about it, and he is the one who is making the plans. Hope you can come. He has an alternative date later in October. Weekends are not good times for us here. Big retreats.

April 24, 1964

Thanks for your two letters. I note with my habitual and unreformed malaise that the long one is dated February 20th. As to the second one, I did not have a copy of *Peace in the PCE* to send your priest friend [William H. Dubay], so I sent him Cold War Letters instead. Actually some of the letters, not all, are being published in a book [*Seeds of Destruction*] together with the piece I did last summer on the race question and I was going to add the essays on nuclear war that I had previously been allowed to publish, but I found that I was not allowed to republish them. That puts me momentarily in difficulties with the publisher. Again.

George Lawler says that you and I and he are now becoming known as a sinister and red-tinted triumvirate, and that *Commonweal* or someone is being accused of following the "Merton-Lawler-Dewart-line." Well, well. It is nice to know that one is a triumvirate. What precisely is our line? I have momentarily lost my instructions from Moscow, or perhaps I have misplaced my bifocals. It is nice to be at the same time silenced and to have a "line."

I read your good article on academic freedom, which I thought was very reasonable and moderate, but direct. Thanks for your remark on "The Monk in the Diaspora." I forgot which version you read: the one that was in *Commonweal* or the one including the review of Rahner. In any event the review part has been somewhat rewritten and is being published in *Ramparts*. I agree about the inadequacy of the term "diaspora." It really shows a sad lack of imagination. And there is no correspondence between it and the situation of the Church, say, in East Germany. I was rather scathingly criticized by a Benedictine and could not really see why until it dawned on me that he had read "diaspora" as "ghetto." Such is the poverty of all these clichés.

The new *Cross Currents* has not yet reached me but I look forward to your article, which sounds very lively. Also I agree with you in thinking it most important to get to that basic idea of Greek epistemology and its influence on Christian thought. It just occurred to me that the weakness of Luther (who is often pretty strong really, as long as he stays with the

Bible) is due to the fact that he had entirely assimilated the body-spirit split. And that reminds me that I wish I understood Buddhist epistemology better, because one of the things about Zen is that it has no split at all. I am thinking of doing an article that will consider spiritual freedom, "liberation" from the viewpoint of Zen, of Lutheranism and the primitive monastic documents of Christianity. Might be interesting. What I mean about Luther is that his *fide sola* is ambiguous mostly because it means "by interior and spiritual graces" alone. Graces not his term, but you know what I mean. What happens inside is what justifies, what happens to and with the body is in the realm of sin, or at best irrelevant.

I am glad you liked the "Message to Poets" [published later in *Raids on the Unspeakable*]. Actually there are a lot of interesting young poets floating around in Latin America with a sense of mission and purpose, and of course a feeling that there is no hope of comprehension from anyone in this country except a few Beats. What do you think, by the way, of the new Brazilian business? It looks very bad to me. Just what is needed to strengthen Maoist-type Communism in Brazil. If people would pay attention to utterly obvious lessons. All I run into are comments that now we are getting somewhere in Brazil, now the Communists have been routed and so on. I have completely given up hope for the political sanity of the United States, except for a handful of people like I. F. Stone and those who read that sort of thing [*I. F. Stone's Weekly*]. What can they ever do? Your book spelled it out clearly enough and no one much was able to recognize the fact. Their only response is to imagine that there is another red plot afoot. Haven't they heard about Russia? Do they still imagine that Russia is Marxist? And that Russian society has ideals which seriously conflict with those of the U.S.?

The Lutheran ecumenist Max Lackmann was here. A very good person and interesting to talk to. There was a lot of discussion of his plan for bringing the Evangelicals into the Church in such a way they keep all they have that is characteristically theirs and does not conflict with the faith. But in the discussion that this raised, I found everybody talking about things that are actually of little or no importance, though naturally they become important when this project is pushed forward in any way. It made me wonder about the whole ecumenical business. Hopeful, certainly. But there is so much in it of the same time-wasting and hairsplitting concern with trivialities. We are condemned to take every little gnat seriously, however, and to strain at each one for seven years before we can swallow it, or rather before we give up trying, swallow a few camels, and then go on to the next gnat.

In a day or two I hope I can put a few things in an envelope and send them along to you. I wrote a thing on mercy which you might like. It is supposed to be in a commemorative volume for Albert Schweitzer that is being put out abroad. I have done a little book of selections from Gandhi with a long introduction. That too may have possibilities.

Now I must close. Since we are triumvirs we must continue in close touch or we will all forget the "line" and that will never do, will it? I find, as a matter of fact, that I have already forgotten it again. Rather I did not remember it. And I am tempted to think that I have never even known what it was in the first place. Can this be possible?

Seriously, however, getting back to real plots: there was a very good article in *Commentary* about Oswald some time ago. I wonder if that thing will ever be unraveled. I am perfectly convinced that it was a very dirty deal and that some important people were mixed up in it.

June 10, 1964

I have read your piece on "Kennedy and the Cuba Crisis." It seems to me to be basically fair and reasonable, yet at the same time I am not sure that it is something you ought to feel obligated to publish. I would say that you could publish it if you wanted to, but I would be inclined to let it go unless you felt there were some compelling reason. I do not feel that there is one, from reading it. It seems to me that everyone more or less knows, or can guess, that in this affair Kennedy got the wind up and played fast and lose with some of the rules, and everyone let him get away with it. This much is accepted even by those who don't admit it is something to be sorry for. To say that he actually set the thing up in cold blood is another matter. And I don't think you quite say that. So what it comes back to is that things turned out the way they did, and somehow or other he let them get that way, and in my opinion God alone can now tell exactly what developed, step by step. It would be a case where, I would be inclined to think, we ought to leave the judgment to God, and I don't think the proving of a few more details that might be regrettable will add much. This only a suggestion. I thought the article was good and a tight piece of reasoning, in fact very interesting and well done.

Archbishop [Thomas] Roberts came through here. I don't know if I mentioned this yet. The brief visit I had with him impressed me greatly, because he struck me as a man that has acquired none of the pomposity or official front (however chummy and democratic) that Bishops usually acquire, and it is good to meet a Bishop who can feel free to speak exactly what he thinks. This one does.

The Cold War Letters are not yet published, and only a few of them are to be published, in *Seeds of Destruction*, this fall. I'll see you get a copy, but remind me if Christmas comes and you still haven't received one. Actually the book has been held up and might be put off until spring. I am now rewriting about a third of it. The earlier stuff on the bomb which had been permitted is now no longer licit and I have to do it all over, writing about peace without treating the question of the bomb. I suppose the next thing I can do is write about marriage without referring to sexual love.

September 23, 1964

Thanks for the letter. It was good to hear from you again, and I was interested in the Cuba trip . . .

I passed your English-Gregorian texts to our choirmaster, who is a little cool toward Gregorian with English as I am myself. But I am not as cool as he is because I am no professional, and as far as I am concerned I think people ought to try out everything feasible and see what happens. The texts look all right but not inspiring to me.

Actually, however, this liturgy thing has, at least in monasteries, become so much of a professional specialty that I am not one of those that can afford initiatives and declarations. I go along with it, and enjoy what is offered, but I cannot do the offering (of new texts and ideas) though people have pestered me a little to write hymns and whatnot. I don't intend to touch any of it because I think it is all extremely fluid (as it ought to be) and the flowing is usually a mile ahead of me, as I cannot keep up with the required information, attend conferences, and so on. It would be naive of me to try to contribute anything worthwhile. I have a rather silly article on liturgy coming out in the *Critic* in December, but that is only a gesture of good will.

Yes, I heard about the book Lawler is doing with Archbishop Roberts and some others [*Contraception and Holiness*, Herder and Herder, 1964], I did not know that you were in it. Actually the theological importance of the question is tremendous because it is radically the same as the question of the bomb. And we confront a basic inconsistency in clerical and often ecclesial thought about it, a great "respect for life" when it comes to contraception and a great unconcern for it when it comes to the bomb, tests, etc. And in the middle, a purely academic sort of concern for feeding all those starving people. Sure, they ought to eat, nice. But then what? If we are going to forbid all forms of birth control, then we take upon ourselves, or rather openly recognize, that we have to put everything else aside and see that all the people that get born are going to be able to live a decent human life. We are not too worried about that, though, except in big resounding and vague declarations.

I certainly hope the book goes well. It will be a riotous discussion.

April 12, 1968 (Good Friday)

I have very much enjoyed your article in the Winter *Continuum* on "Metaphysics and the Presence of God." It is clear and good, states the problem very correctly, and is the same sort of thing I have been coming to myself, through Zen. It ties up neatly what was still not for me a compact package in *The Future of Belief*.

Wondering about the whole question of metaphysics being a dirty word: certainly this is quite right about Thomist textbook metaphysics. On the other hand, Maritain's "metaphysical intuition of being" really seems to me to coincide with an intuition of what you call presence— i.e., a revelation in "being" (as object of consciousness) of that which cannot be an object of consciousness and is also more real than "being." Buddhism goes further than that with Sunyata (Void). You might look into the Japanese philosopher Kitaro Nishida—though he is a bit old hat now. Probably his best work has not been translated however.

Just wanted to tell you this. Happy Easter. Let's keep in touch (though I am sure we are both wildly busy).

4. Other Letters on Religious Thought

[Charity] is the best formula I can think of for Christian unity, and I have a strong suspicion that it has something to do with the Gospels.
TO MRS. LEONARD

To Mrs. Leonard

Thomas Merton had sent Paul Tillich a copy of the limited edition of his book Prometheus, *published by Victor Hammer. Tillich's secretary, Mrs. Leonard, acknowledged the gift. This initiated the two letters that follow.*

June 20, 1959

Thank you for your kind letter telling me that Dr. Tillich had read and enjoyed *Prometheus*. I was glad to think that he had been able to read it at leisure, in the peace of his summer vacation. I am sending him another book of mine which he might like—*Thoughts in Solitude*. It might go well on the sands of East Hampton. The book is rather limited in scope, but it says things I want to say. And of course I hope you will read it, too, if you feel so inclined . . .

Thank you for saying you had liked *The Silent Life*. That, too, says many of the things I want to say. Since you liked this book, I am taking the liberty of sending you another little one, not available in most stores or libraries, *Monastic Peace*. You might find passages there, also, that would appeal to you.

I do have a great respect and admiration for Dr. Tillich's work, but I have not read as much of it as I would like, and have not seen any of his recent books. We are not very well posted on recent publications here. I have just been busy with the publication of a book on Religious Art, and I understand Dr. Tillich has written something on the subject. I would like very much to know his views, though it is too late to comment on them in my own book. Is there anything you could send me, perhaps an offprint of an article, or something like that? I would return it as promptly as possible. I need not add that if Dr. Tillich would want to sign his name on some recent book of his and give it to me, I would be greatly pleased and proud of such a "possession."

For some time past the thought has been growing on me more and more that since Christianity is simple life in Christ, a life that we all share, then the more we can be conscious of that sharing and rejoice in it together, the more we will be Christians and the more we will be one in Him. And I do feel that what we all have in common is so much greater and more important than what we do not have in common, at least dogmatically and juridically. There is One Christ on earth when Christians really will to be one in mind and heart, in Him. The institutional differences are there, and they are unfortunate, but they are not stronger than charity. That is the best formula I can think of for Christian unity, and I have a strong suspicion that it has something to do with the Gospels. The rest follows from this, and must, if anything is to follow at all.

July 7, 1959

The two books of Dr. Tillich arrived yesterday morning with the autobiography of Albert Schweitzer, and I am deeply grateful to you, particularly for the personal gift of the latter. I have begun the *Dynamics of Faith* and find it very congenial and practical. Meanwhile I have misplaced the letter in which you referred to two other books of Dr. Tillich, one of which he would sign and send to me. I remember that one of the books you named was the *New Being*, which I have read and enjoyed. The other was new to me. Therefore, if you remember what the other one was, that would be very welcome. That or any other book of Dr. Tillich, besides the two you sent. I know I shall like the *Theology of Culture*. It is refreshing to hear, in Dr. Tillich, a really contemporary voice, speaking freely on deep matters that are spiritual and not just abstruse or intellectual. After all, our concept of faith must be such that it allows us to give ourselves freely and wholly to Christ, as men of our time.

The conference on art was extremely interesting to me and I am in fundamental agreement with all he said about religious styles. Our tastes are the same, and when my book on art finally comes out, it will be saying much the same thing: that for an expression of the sacred in art we must not turn to realism but to expressionism like that of the Byzantines. I note that Russian philosophers of religious art speak of "spiritual realism" in the ikon. It is a good concept, which pushes a little further what Dr. Tillich and I are both trying to get at. Perhaps I can slip in a quote from the lecture into my book. I enjoyed the sentence about one apple of Cézanne having more of ultimate reality in it than a Jesus by Hofmann, and may be able to insert this somewhere. Proofs have not yet come. I hope the book will be ready early next year and promise Dr. Tillich a copy now. Please don't hesitate to remind me if I somehow fail to come through, I often get mixed up when I have to wait several months to carry out something.

I was interested and touched at your final paragraph about the monastic books and your friend who is thinking of a solitary life. What a deep and complex problem it is! I assure you that I have no easy solutions. Of course in our day it is further complicated by the fact that anyone with a grain of humanity left naturally wants to get away, for a time, from the inordinate pressures of our world, when all they want is a little peace *in* ordinary life. As a Novice Master here I have to cope with the problem of men who mistakenly come here seeking the *natural* balance that is more and more lacking outside. But our life, alas, presupposes such balance. And we find it less and less in our candidates. The real solitary vocation (Trappists are not solitaries) is a rare thing, and presupposes not flight but the acceptance of the highest responsibility and the most delicate and difficult freedom. I am convinced that this is necessary in the Church, so that some may be and remain entirely outside and above all social forms. Of course the risk is great. If I can be of any help to your friend, please do not hesitate to let me know. I will, in any case, keep you all in my prayers. Please pray for me too.

To Mr. McCallister

October 29, 1961

Thank you for your very kind letter and the invitation to the conference at Pleasant Hill next Saturday, November 4th. I regret that it will be impossible for me to be present, much as I should really like to be there. As you may know, I am hoping someday to do a picture book on the Shakers, and the experience of being present at the conference would be invaluable. On the other hand I rarely leave the monastery, and I would probably not be given permission to attend a conference like this in view of the fact that we are not supposed to speak before an audience outside the monastery. I debated whether to ask permission to be there without speaking, but decided against this also as I have an aunt from New Zealand visiting me that day and this will be our only occasion for a quiet conversation for many years.

On the other hand I am delighted that you will be over on Monday with the Andrewses [see *HGL*] and look forward very eagerly to this visit. I suggest that the best time to get here would be sometime about noon. I can arrange for your party to have lunch here if you let me know, but our facilities are such that the guesthouses for ladies and gentlemen are separate. You would probably prefer to have lunch on the way over. I shall be expecting you any time after twelve, November 6th . . .

I want to take this opportunity to say that I am very pleased at the efforts being made to restore the Pleasant Hill Shaker village. The Shakers and their spirituality seem to me to be extremely significant, as an authentic American form of the Monastic Life, with a utopian and eschatalogical cast. The superb and simple products of their craftsmanship are

not only eloquent in themselves, but they also speak for the genuine
spiritual vitality of the Shakers, and testify to the validity of their ideal.
I believe that much is to be done in the study of the Shaker spirituality
in the light of Western and Near Eastern mystical traditions, and also in
the light of Jungian depth psychology. Doctrines which were certainly
heterodox from a traditional Christian viewpoint may then assume a special significance in the history of our time. I cannot help feeling that the
Shaker movement is something of a mystery that withholds from us, still,
a deep significance which may even throw some light on our present
predicament in the world. I think this can be said for all the utopian
movements of the nineteenth century, but is especially true of the Shakers. I have as yet no way of substantiating this intuition. Perhaps someday
research scholarship may help us to see more clearly into the problem.
At any rate, it seems to me that the Pleasant Hill community center can
stand as a witness to the vital spiritual forces that were at work in American
history of a century ago. Certainly these honest and noble people manifested a sincere desire to seek the highest truth by the means that they
thought most adequate for the purpose. They felt that it was necessary
to dedicate their lives completely to their ideal, and they did so without
reserve. At a time like the present when we are witnessing the moral
disintegration of our society under the pressure of enormous and perhaps
demonic forces of the mind, we can ill afford to neglect the simplicity
and dedication to truth of these good, sincere people who lived up to
their belief.

These few words contain the substance of what I would probably try
to say if I were to participate in a symposium. If you wish to quote them,
I hope you will feel free to do so. Meanwhile, I extend to you and to Mr.
and Mrs. Andrews, and to all who are to be present next Saturday, my
very best wishes.

To John Whitman Sears

*John Whitman Sears, a licensed psychologist now retired, sent Merton some
material he was writing on war and peace. Merton sent him, along with the
following letter, a copy of his dialogue with Dr. Suzuki, called "Wisdom in Emptiness" (published by New Directions in* Prose and Poetry, *#17). Dr. Sears found
the article bewildering and asked Merton, in a letter of September 5, 1962,
whether the doctrine of original sin was related to neurotic or psychotic disorders.*

[*Cold War Letter 89*]   June 23, 1962
Thanks for your papers on "The Arms Race as a Chain Reaction." I
think it has a lot of very good things in it and completely agree. I think
you have hit the nail on the head, as also Fromm and others have. It is
a question of insanity.

We are just not big enough to handle all the ironies and contradictions we have brought upon ourselves (innocently enough, I suppose) by developing too fast. Yet looking at it on another level as a spiritual problem, it really becomes apocalyptic. I know men are seriously asking themselves now whether this sort of thing has happened somewhere before, and whether on other planets somewhere there have been races which have reached a point of development where they ended by destroying themselves.

Reading as I do the obscure writings of the fourth-, fifth-, sixth-century Church Fathers, I find that in the light of all this the doctrine of original sin is not as absurd as it sometimes sounds in a blatantly puritanical context. It has subtleties which even a Zen man appreciates, and so I send you an offprint of a dialogue with D. T. Suzuki on this subject. I think you may be interested.

November 12, 1962

I hope you haven't given up waiting for an answer. The fact that I waited so long is a sign that I took your letter seriously enough to give it a little thought. But perhaps not yet enough. But I will at least make an attempt because I believe in the importance not so much of abstract notions as of living human dialogue. I have come to see that perhaps the most fruitful things we can do today are in the realm not of "proving" this or that, or of "convincing" anyone, but simply of communicating more or less validly with someone else on a level of genuine interest and in a matter of importance.

It seems to me that the best I can offer you is a sort of introduction to an unfamiliar territory. For some reason I assumed this kind of thinking is familiar to all analysts because it happens to be familiar to some . . .

The concept of original sin belongs to a different order than psychology. It is not a matter of subjective experience, conscious or unconscious. It is something ontological and objective. That is to say, it claims to be this. I suppose inevitably it gets to be connected with a sort of Platonic metaphysic, and that is in a way unfortunate. Certainly Augustine is a Platonist and his concept of original sin is affected by this, very strongly. In fact there are resonances in his treatment of original sin which I myself cannot accept, and which are wrongly stressed and of course exploited wrongly by sick minds. This would be, for instance, the concept that human *nature* is itself vitiated by original sin. (Nature here not in the sense of psychological temperament, but as the human essence, man in his radical being.) If human nature is affected by original sin, then man is less man, he is not himself. I do not hold this. Man's nature has not been wounded by original sin. And a man who is in original sin, or any other sin, can be perfectly well adjusted psychologically. Sin is not neurosis, though the two can get mixed up with each other. But one of the cardinal mistakes of the religious people who have opposed psychiatry is that they supposed that what psychiatrists were after was sin, and that sin had to be attacked by something else than psychiatry. However, just to complicate things, it seems that, de facto, with us sin and neurotic drives do tend to interfere with each other and to become inextricably mixed up.

Sin, however, is a conscious and deliberate disloyalty to ethical truth and rectitude, while neurosis is an unconscious and indeliberate disloyalty to truth, dictated perhaps by a false conscience and a distorted sense of sin (in some cases). Does this make sense?

Where original sin causes a problem is that it is not conscious, nor deliberate, nor even an act. It is a condition in which people are conceived to be born. Here we are not in the realm of science at all, but very close to that of myth (if you will permit me to hold that a myth can somehow express a reality conceived to be objective, yet invisible and inexplicable). Hence the need to explain it in a parable, like that of the Prodigal Son: and here your own explanation, based on alienation, etc., is basically correct. The only thing I would add to it is another dimension. The experience of alienation, pardon and return, reintegration, etc., is a symbol of a deeper metaphysical reality which is below the level of feeling or moral action.

Hence the Church uses the rite of baptism to "reconcile" with God the person who through no fault of his own is in "original sin."

Here is where Buddhism and Christianity get together in my dialogue with Suzuki. Our basic agreement is on the point that man, no matter how well balanced, healthy, integrated, and sane, is still alienated from his "true self." He may be perfectly integrated in his society, his family, etc. But he is still like a displaced person, an exile, with regard to the true spiritual country in which we really belong. That is to say, according to the Buddhists, that he has a basically deceptive and illusory view of life, and according to Christians, that he does not "see God," does not have access to the ultimate meaning of life and is not in accord fully and deeply with the supernatural love that brought him into existence. He is not "united with God."

Hence in both religions there tend to be degrees of perfection, an ascent to enlightenment, to union, and to fulfillment in self-transcendence. Baptism obviously does not do all this, it just puts one on the road, which must then be traveled. A spiritual road of inner discipline, development, working toward a breakthrough into a different mode of being, and a transformation of one's whole attitude toward life, indeed of one's whole being itself.

That is what Suzuki and I were "dialoguing" about: the different aspects of this inner struggle toward a spiritual breakthrough, and the nature of that breakthrough.

On the other hand, in the realm of everyday experience and in the struggle with the obstacles one meets in ordinary life, there are really profound analogies with this spiritual struggle. As a matter of fact, the sphere of both struggles are the same, and insofar as psychology is inevitably involved, the same type of experiences are gone through. Hence your analogy is perfectly valid, except for one thing: you are applying it on one level, and not as an analogy.

Perhaps I could send you another book of mine, *The New Man*, which deals with this: but it might confuse you. It is a mix-up of theology and liturgy. Perhaps it would be better if I sent you the *Merton Reader*, which is just out and with which I am happy, as it gathers together all sorts of diverse bits of writing that might add up to some kind of a clear picture in the end.

To Jerome D. Frank

Psychiatrist, director of clinical services, Johns Hopkins Hospital, author of numerous articles, many dealing with group psychotherapy. One of his articles, "Breaking the Thought Barrier: Psychological Challenges of the Nuclear Age," was published in Breakthrough to Peace.

February 7, 1963

Breakthrough [to Peace] has not been doing as well as the publisher would have liked, but it has done better than I myself expected. Of course some of the reviews made special mention of your own essay, for which I am grateful. Have you been publishing other articles of that kind, of which offprints are available? Please do not forget me.

You mentioned in one of your letters that though our philosophies of life might differ in many points, there was still a fundamental agreement. I wonder if perhaps the agreement might not involve more of philosophy itself than a scientist would think. For me, life and philosophy have to be to a great extent the same thing, and what matters most is the living of it, rather than the formulation. I think one of the difficulties presented by formal and organized religions is that they have come to give the impression that what matters most is the formulation. Of course the reason why this is so is that for centuries people have been slaughtering each other for formulas. I do not believe that I could hold to a religion on that kind of basis.

To Father David Kirk

David Kirk, active in the peace movement, had joined the Company of St. Paul, a secular institute. When he first wrote to Merton, he was a student at the Beda College in Rome, a seminary for late vocations. He hoped to return to the United States and commit himself wholly to the work of social justice.

April 2, 1963

Thanks for your wonderful letters. Do not get discouraged if I do not reply right away. They mean much to me. I have greater and greater admiration for Patriarch Maximos, ever since the article in *Jubilee* last year. Do keep me posted about the Thabor foundation and so on . . .

Perhaps out of a deep suspiciousness and human lack of faith (lack of readiness to accept good signs on the part of the human element in the Church) I have been slow and diffident in my optimism. But really the things Cardinal Bea has been doing, and statements of Hans Küng, and above all that great Maximos: these have all lifted up my heart a bit. Do tell Patriarch Maximos how much I thank God for his great statements and my deep filial veneration for him. I hope to meet him someday.

Yet at the same time it is going to be slow and frustrating and I do not think we can promise ourselves to see the full dawning of the light to come in our own day. It is good to see the first light, however, and it has a special beauty, which the pre-dawn always has. But the refusals to comprehend, the rigidities, the evasions, the patient, continual perversions of reality are all there to contend with. Here in the monastery there have been so many really good subjects, really promising, who have had to leave for one reason or another because the life in the end turned into a stupid and deadly negation. It is so easy to say "No" to life, and we have been accustomed to that for centuries, because life has been identified with risk.

I am happy to hear of all the possibilities you suggest. It is true there should be many more Catholic members in the FOR, and the American Pax ought to be more alive, and less a deliberately inactive group, though I don't know too much about it. Don't hear much of anything, and I don't suppose there is anything to hear.

Here I am still in a quiet way working with individuals and groups who come in, and Josef Smolik, the Protestant theologian from Czechoslovakia, was here and we had a good talk. I have a lot of good contacts with the Protestant seminary faculties in this area. Of course, John Heidbrink has been down, and Paul Peachey of the Church Peace Mission was here, and wants to organize a retreat of ministers and priests interested in the peace movement. Douglas Steere was here. I will also send you sometime a contribution I made to a seminar in a Quaker publication, with Fromm [*War Within Man*], etc. When I get copies. Remind me.

I wonder what turn the measures dealing with religious Orders will take in the Council. I am hoping to write a letter to [Archbishop] Paul Philippe about it. It would be tragic if in that area they bogged down in the usual formalities and rigidities. I don't think they will, now, but certainly that is the kind of "reform" a lot of people still want. What is badly, urgently wanted is *life* and not this frozen, living death formula for "perfection" in which all vital development is forcibly crushed and negated from the very start. The first commandment in religious Orders seems to be "thou shalt not grow." Enter the novitiate, return to the mental age of six, and stay there. If you have never left that stage, then all the better: the novitiate has been taken care of in advance. I suppose it is the same in seminaries. Except that one must have the relative maturity necessary to be a sharp operator. Did you read [J. F. Powers'] *Morte d'Urban?*

Some mimeo stuff is on its way under separate cover. Keep writing conscience matter. You ought to know Fr. Bruno James in Naples, Collegio Newman, Via dell Duomo. Get him to drop by there sometime. He knows people at the Beda. Is a bit way out, and probably not *persona grata* round the place.

January 5, 1964

You have probably given me up completely as a correspondent. If I have not answered your very good letters it is for obvious reasons. There is a saturation point in my work, etc., and I often reach it. I did last fall after being in the hospital and have barely caught up since then. I no longer seriously try to answer all letters. It is just not possible to do this and give myself to the more important tasks. But that does not mean I am not immensely interested in everything you say. I think you are one of the few people who are really in contact with what is most alive in the Church. And I include Patriarch Maximos under that category of "most alive."

There is such a terrific effort to be made to break through the crust that has gathered on the Church, especially Rome, in two thousand years. When a little effort has been made, a tiny bit taken off the crust, then there is a huge noise in all the press, universal acclamations, and a great cloud of dust, under cover of which the Curia people (and their like) busily restore what was done to the crust and we are back where we were before.

It seems to me there is a most awful problem in this rootedness of the Church in permitted social structures and traditions, and the inevitability with which even in the best of moods and intentions we all fall back into a bland bourgeois stupor of self-congratulation and inertia. Even a lot of the activity has a character of inertia about it, it is so crude and so futile.

I have no answers, except that we have got to stop first of all our sin of handing down categorical answers to everything, in terms of absolutes, right from the word go. We have got to have (institutionally) the humility to accept a lot of unverified possibilities as points of orientation in a period of uncertainty and crisis. The crisis comes in large part from our own ossification in absolutes. And our own instinct to throw ourselves headlong from one absolute into another, wanting everything to be immediately final. There is a lot of good going on in the liturgy for instance, but with a kind of desperation, a lust for liturgical bliss, in all finality, at once, forever.

What I do think has to be done is an enormous job on everybody's concept of the Church. This has barely even begun (all acclamations notwithstanding). I have read that Hochhuth play about Pius XII. It is a bad play, and all that, but he is intent and probably right in his attack on the awful papal image which Pius permitted and encouraged and which is as a matter of fact the approved pattern, accepted by most Bishops (not Maximos, I know!!). But it is an abomination of desolation, this absurd, rigid, bedecked, petticoated, pseudo-mystical father image. How can we live and breathe with this kind of nonsense? If only they would change their fool costume it would already be something, a beginning. The way our monastic Superiors are attached to the idiot pomp of baroque pontificalia too. Won't give up!

The news about the Dutch Cistercian on Carmel is exciting. It is of course top secret in the Order. Please keep me posted. I want always to be in contact with you about this kind of thing, because I am still convinced that it is very important to emphasize the solitary consummation of the monastic call, not imprisoning it forever in a rigid cenobitic framework. Keep well, work hard, may the Holy Spirit enlighten all your works and ways.

December 24, 1966

Tomorrow is Christmas. Probably Christ is more likely to be born where you are, though He is not particular, even here it is possible, since He is born all over the place. But more especially, I think, in Harlem. That's where the real wilderness is, I think.

To Mrs. Lytton

November 21, 1963

I am afraid your question catches me off base: it is so long since I have dealt directly with these problems, since here we do not have parish work. The best things that have come my way have all been quite theological and not at all useful on the more practical level. Of course the theological level is important, and often neglected.

Probably one of the most practical books I can recommend is Erich Fromm's *The Art of Loving*, which is published by Harper's. This is sensible and good. Dr. Fromm is an analyst and a friend of mine, but I don't think you will find him sticky or unpractical. Try this, anyway. It ought to be of some help, though I don't think it gets into intimate details. But it concerns the psychological problem involved in sexual love.

If you want my opinion on the subject, I think that we live in a society which *makes* a problem out of love and marriage, whether one likes it or not. There is so much nonsense, explicit or otherwise, about sex: there is a myth of sex, it is glamorized, and impossible ideals are proposed, people get the idea that marriage is a failure unless one attains to utterly hopeless ideals of perfect adjustment, and so on. One has to face the fact that sex is both intoxicating and disconcerting, that it takes a person out of himself and leaves him in confusion. It is beautiful but it is also in some ways ugly. It is full of consolation and bliss, but it also arouses the power to hate. Love and hate go together, and sex is full of ambivalence. The real thing then is to learn to give oneself maturely, without futile idealization, accepting the unsatisfactory realities and the transient intoxications. The intoxication lasts a few seconds, the painful responsibilities are years long. I think it is terribly important to be realistic and religious about all this. By the way, there is a book ostensibly for nuns, etc., but which besides virginity also treats married love quite sensibly: it is Dietrich von Hildebrand's *In Defense of Purity*. As you would not have picked that in a thousand years, I might as well mention it, as married people would not realize it also concerned them.

The great thing in marriage is not an impossible ideal of fulfillment and exaltation but a mature rational Christian acceptance of the responsibilities and risks of human love. There is no harm in discussing all this frankly with your children, with the idea that you might learn on both sides from a frank exchange. Easy for me to suggest this, I suppose. It might be worth trying.

To Mrs. Nunn

January 10, 1964

Of course a lot of water has gone under the bridge in the years (almost twenty) since I wrote *The Seven Storey Mountain*. I would have said many things differently today. Including that statement about becoming a "saint." Obviously, this is not, and I never meant to say that it was, a matter of mere will. Far from it. Only the grace of God in Christ Jesus can free us from sin and evil and reconcile us to God, bringing us to perfect union with His will. But on the other hand since grace is freely offered, if we accept it can be said in some sense to be "put up to us." But it is still not simple, and as one goes on one realizes how absurd and equivocal it is to think of oneself "becoming a saint." What does that *mean*? Certainly not becoming able to think of oneself as a saint. If it is a question of arriving, I was never further. Yet I never trusted more in the mercy of God, and really it is He that matters, not I, not "becoming a saint."

Spiritual gluttony, etc. This means hungering for spiritual experiences, virtues, and so on just as one hungers on a lower level for food.

In the experience that shakes us so mightily in the Spirit, I would say that this powerful impact is due to a great extent to our own selfhood and self-awareness. We are always close to ourselves and in some sense the grace of God tends to "destroy" the self that we are. Too much exaltation can leave us exhausted, but then if we become more humble and selfless we can "take it better." The thing to seek is the humblest and lowest place, and let Him do the exalting in His own way.

I think that deep experience of God should normally be the common thing for Christians. Surely that is familiar in your Methodist tradition. On the other hand, I think too much attention to spiritual experience and concentration on it is not helpful. I mean, it is too bad to get everyone thinking that they have to have great experiences, and to look for these things in themselves. This makes them look at themselves when they should abandon themselves in faith and submit to God without trying to see or understand except what He shows them, in regard to this kind of thing. Of course we must all try to see and live our Christian faith and taste in our hearts the gift of Redemption in Jesus.

The title *Seven Storey Mountain* is based on Dante's "Purgatory." Besides St. Theresa I suggest you read some of the other mystics. One of the best is Julian of Norwich (a woman) published by Harper's recently. Evelyn Underhill has good things on mysticism, in fact there are numerous good books on the subject today . . .

To Mrs. D.

February 26, 1965

Believe me, I sympathize with your difficulty. It is, of course, characteristic of our time and hence you can at least comfort yourself with the thought that in facing it, according to God's will, in all its dimensions, you will not go wrong even though you may not find a quick and easy solution.

First of all, since you are married, it is not just an individual matter. Though it is true that your first obligation is to God and to conscience, I would take care not to interpret this in too absolute a way because your marriage enters very intimately into this. Hence you should, as far as possible, work the thing out with your husband, by which I mean that you should not just come to some personal decision without him and hand him your decision as an accomplished fact to be taken or left.

Second, I am not so sure that it is utterly impossible to be a Catholic wife of a Baptist seminary professor. It used to be. But perhaps with a certain amount of daring it could be done today. Someone I advised in the South, a wife of an Episcopalian minister, came over and is living with her family and everything is going fine, even though she came over while living in a very small Southern town. Now they are in a city.

In any case, I think you should go slow and do everything you can not to push this thing to a point where it means breaking up your marriage. If it were a question of waiting to come into the Catholic Church, then perhaps it would be better to wait. The Lord understands our difficulties with the human blocks and obstacles that we have built up over the years, and what comes first is true Christian love, rather than open identification with this or that institution, even though it be the Catholic Church. Certainly the consolation and strength of the Sacraments would be of immense help to you, but let us realize that when we cannot approach the Sacraments God gives grace without them. He is not bound by any system, however good and holy.

In substance then, trust Him, approach Him with confidence and simplicity in prayer, and talk it out with your husband insofar as that is possible. Our Lord will show you the rest of what you need to know and will give you strength to do what is necessary—even if that is only a matter of patient waiting.

To Lord Northbourne

Lord Northbourne describes himself as "thoroughly involved in the affairs of a hereditary landowner and farmer," with five children and eleven grandchildren. He was seventy years of age when he wrote Merton. The address he gives is Northbourne Court, Deal, Kent. He had sent Merton a copy of his book Religion in the Modern World *at the suggestion of Marco Pallis. Merton in turn sent him a copy of his analysis of Vatican II's Constitution on the Church in the Modern World* (Gaudium et Spes). *Called "The Church and the 'Godless' World," this essay became Part I of Merton's* Redeeming the Time *(published in England by Burns and Oates in 1966). Though the two men were not in complete agreement about the meaning of religion, God, and the world for a contemporary Christian, Merton does his best to find points of accord between them where he can.*

Easter 1965

I have just finished reading your book *Religion in the Modern World.* Since I did not want to send you a mere formal note of thanks, but wanted also to share my impressions with you, I have delayed writing about it until now.

After a careful reading, spread out over some time (I have read the book a bit at a time), I believe that your book is exceptionally good. Certainly I am most grateful for the opportunity to read it, and needless to say I am very glad that Marco Pallis suggested that you send it to me. Not only is the book interesting, but I have found it quite salutary and helpful in my own case. It has helped me to organize my ideas at a time when we in the Catholic Church, and in the monastic Orders, are being pulled this way and that. Traditions of great importance and vitality are being questioned along with more trivial customs, and I do not think that those who are doing the questioning are always distinguished for their wisdom or even their information. I could not agree more fully with your principles and with your application of them. In particular, I am grateful for your last chapter. For one thing it clears up a doubt that had persisted in my mind, about the thinking of the Schuon-Guenon "school" (if one can use such a term) [an association of Sufi masters with whom Marco

Pallis was associated], as well as about the rather slapdash ecumenism that is springing up in some quarters. It is most important first of all to understand deeply and live one's own tradition, not confusing it with what is foreign to it, if one is to seriously appreciate other traditions and distinguish in them what is close to one's own and what is, perhaps, irreconcilable with one's own. The great danger at the moment is a huge muddling and confusing of the spiritual traditions that still survive. As you so well point out, this would be crowning the devil's work.

The great problem that faces me in this regard is twofold. The Council has determined to confront the modern world in some way to decide what ought to be its attitude, and where it ought to stand. Now I must say in this area I am very disturbed by both those who are termed conservative and some who are called liberal in the Council, and out of it too. I am afraid that on both sides too superficial a view of "the world" is being taken—whether that view be optimistic or pessimistic. I don't think that the implications of the technological revolution have even begun to be grasped by either side. Then there is the unfortunate fact that Catholic tradition has become in many way ambiguous and confused. Not in itself, but in the way in which it is regarded by Catholics. Since people have got into the unfortunate habit of thinking of tradition as a specialized department of theology, and since spiritual disciplines have undergone considerable shrinking and drying out by being too legalized, and since the traditional styles of life, worship, and so on have become, for us, merely courtly and baroque to such a great extent, the question of renewal does become urgent.

Here is where we run into the greatest difficulties and confusions, especially in America. Personally I can see the wisdom of simply trying to purify and preserve the ancient medieval and earlier traditions which we have in monasticism, and which can easily be recovered. Thanks to the work of Solesmes and other monasteries, the material we need is all at hand. Unfortunately it becomes clear that in America at least, and even to some extent in Europe, this will no longer get through to the new generations. And the misfortune is that they seem happy with the most appalling trivialities and the silliest of innovations. In my own work I do my best to keep the novices in touch with monastic sources and convey to them something of the real spirit of monastic discipline and interior prayer. I find that they respond to this, and that the sense of living tradition is not totally dead. But on the other hand, if one is to get into polemics and start battling for tradition and for right interpretations, one tends oneself to lose the spirit of tradition. And of course perspective and the sense of value disappear along with one's real spirit. If one must choose, I suppose it is best to try oneself to live one's tradition and obey the Holy Spirit within one's tradition as completely as possible, and not worry about results.

More and more I become aware of the gravity of the present situation, not only in matters of tradition and discipline and the spiritual life but even as regarding man and his civilization. The forces that have been at work to bring us to this critical point have now apparently completely escaped our control (if they ever were under it) and I do not see how we can avoid a very great disaster, by which I do not mean a sudden extermination of the whole race by H-bombs, but nevertheless a general collapse into anarchy and sickness together. In a certain sense, the profound alterations in the world and in man that have resulted from the last hundred years of "progress" are already a disaster, and the effects will be unavoidable. In such a situation, to speak with bland optimism of the future of man and of the Church blessing a new technological paradise becomes not only absurd but blasphemous. Yet at the same time, this technological society still has to be redeemed and sanctified in some way, not simply cursed and abhorred.

The great problem underlying it also, as you so well see, is idolatry. And here the great question is: can the society we have now constructed possibly be anything else than idolatrous? I suppose one must still hope and believe that it can. But in practice I cannot feel too sanguine about it. In any case, I think we have our hands full seeking and helping the victims of this society, and we cannot yet begin to "save" and spiritualize the society itself. I am certainly not one of those who, with Teilhard de Chardin, see the whole thing in rosy and messianic colors.

In any case I am very grateful for your important and thoughtful book, and I am sure you can see that I am in the deepest possible sympathy with your views. It is not possible for me, and doubtless for you, to get into lengthy correspondence about these things, yet they are so important that I do hope we will be able to share at times ideas and suggestions that might be profitable. I will try to send you some books and writings of my own that you might like. In the book of poems I shall send there is a long letter which you might find interesting, together with a prose poem, "Hagia Sophia." I should be most interested in your own writings or statements that might come out from time to time.

February 23, 1966

Thank you for your kind letter and for the copy of your lecture, which I read with great interest, finding it clear, objective, and firm. Many thanks also for the first copy of *Tomorrow* in the attractive new format (I very much like the design on the cover). I like this magazine and will be happy to receive it. Last evening I read your article on "Flowers," which I enjoyed very much. The purely utilitarian explanation of the attractiveness of flowers is always annoying, it is so superficial.

I have written a commentary on the Council's Constitution on the Church in the Modern World. This was done not because I particularly wanted to do it, but because it was needed and asked for by [the London publisher] Burns and Oates. I am very much afraid that the job is unsatisfactory in many ways. At least I am not at all satisfied with it. The basic purpose of the Constitution is one that I obviously agree with: the maintaining of reasonable communication between the Church and the world of modern technology. If communication breaks down entirely, and there is no hope of exchanging ideas, then the situation becomes impossible. However, the naive optimism with which some of the Council Fathers seem to have wanted a Church entirely identified with the modern scientific mentality is equally impossible. I have said this in the end as conclusively as I could, with respect to one issue in particular. But in any case if I can get some copies made of the text I will send you one. There might be a few points of interest in it. I am of course very much concerned with one issue which is symptomatic of all the rest: nuclear warfare. It is true that one should not focus on one issue so as to distract attention from the entire scene in all its gravity. I think I have touched on a few other things as well, but have certainly not done a complete job, and have tried to be conciliatory in some ways. In a word, I am not satisfied with it and perhaps few others will be.

Meanwhile, as I do have a copy of this meditation on "events" ["Events and Pseudo-Events," published in *Faith and Violence*, 1968] I am sending it along. I hope I am not burdening you with too many things but obviously I realize that you will not feel obligated to read them, and will do so only if you are really interested.

August 30, 1966

I am really very grateful for your thoughtful letter [on Merton's "The Church and the 'Godless World' "], and of course you know that I am basically in agreement with you, temperamentally and by taste and background, when it comes to appreciating the values of the ancient cultural and spiritual traditions which today are not only in many ways threatened but even to some extent undermined. As you know, too, that in writing my book on the Constitution on the Church in the [Modern] World, I was not so much trying to clarify a personal philosophy as to interpret what the Council was trying to say, and do so objectively. I have come to the conclusion that the effort was unsatisfactory and have decided not to publish this material in book form in the U.S.A. With this in mind I will take up the points you raise, not with the intention of "answering" arguments but simply of clarifying my own position—if possible. And it is not easy.

First there was a deliberately permitted ambiguity in the title of the book. There is much discussion now of what it means to be "godless" and one of the ambiguities about it is that certain Christian values have in fact been smuggled over to the "godless" side at times. But this too is ambiguous insofar as they tend to become merely "humanitarian" and so on. But behind the whole question is the fact that the Church has had to admit the futility of an embattled, negative, ghetto-like resistance to everything modern, a "stance," as they say, which was rather unfortunate in the 19th and early 20th century, not because it was conservative but because it was also quite arbitrary, narrow, uncomprehending, and tended to preserve not necessarily the best of the Catholic tradition but a kind of baroque absolutism in theology, worship, and so on. Now, since the Church obviously has to outgrow this, and since in doing so it has to become for better or for worse "contemporary," there has been an inevitable reaction, with an insistence on "openness" and so on which I think is necessary though I do not accept without reservation some of the naive optimism about "the world" that goes along with this. The general idea is that man has to be understood in his actual present situation, and not with reference to some situation which we would prefer to have him in.

The situation of man today is one of dreadful crisis. We are in full revolution, but it is not the simple, straightforward old-fashioned political revolution. It is a far-reaching, uncontrolled, and largely unconscious revolution pervading every sphere of his existence and often developing new critical tendencies before anyone realizes what is happening. Now, I think that the Constitution, though it does vaguely recognize this, does not say enough to underline the real seriousness of the situation, and it does, as you say, tend to accept the surface optimism of some secular outlooks on progress without much hesitation. It does seem to say that if we just go along with technology we will have a happier and better world. This is by no means guaranteed. On the other hand I do not feel, as some do, that the Constitution should simply have admitted frankly that the future promises little more than apocalyptic horror. Though this possibility is very real and was perhaps not brought out very clearly. In other words I think the attitude taken by the Council is basically reasonable, and it seems to be this:

Much as we appreciate the great value of ancient and traditional cultures, the coming of the industrial and technological revolution has undermined them and in fact doomed them. Everywhere in the world these cultures have now been more or less affected—corrupted—by modern Western man and his rather unfortunate systems. It is simply not possible to return to the cultural stability and harmony of these ancient structures. But it is hoped that one can maintain some sort of continuity and preserve at least some of their living reality in a new kind of society. For my part I am frankly dubious: I foresee a rather pitiful bastardized culture, vulgarized, uniform, and full of elements of parody and caricature, and perhaps frightening new developments of its own which may be in a certain way "interesting" and even exciting. And terrible. The Council assumes that we just go on peacefully progressing and reasonably negotiating obstacles, making life more and more "human."

I certainly think that we need a much "better" world than the one we have at this moment, and I make no bones about insisting that this means feeding, clothing, housing, and educating a lot of people who are living the most dreadful destitution. Remember that in South America, Africa, Asia, we are no longer comparing the ancient tribal cultures with modern culture but the rural and urban slum culture of destitution and degradation that has ruined and succeeded the old cultures. This *must* be dealt with, and in facing the fact the Church has simply done her plain duty: and a great deal more needs to be done on the spot. It is a well-known fact that if in South America the people who call themselves Catholics would get down and work and do something about the situation, it could be immensely improved. Hence I see nothing wrong with the Council demanding work for a "better world" in this sense. It is not a question of comfort, but of the basic necessities of life and decency. In this respect, "humanism" is a matter of simple respect for man as man, and Christian humanism is based on the belief in the Incarnation and on a relationship to others which supposed that "whatsoever you do to the least of my brethren you do it to me" (i.e., to Christ). Here I have no difficulty. Except of course in the way in which some of this might be interpreted or applied. Literacy is not a cure-all, and there are plenty of absurd modern social myths. Nevertheless, there are realities that must be faced in the terms of our actual possibilities, and return to the ancient cultures is simply not possible. Though we should certainly try to see that their values are preserved insofar as they can be.

Since the purpose of this Constitution was that of giving largely practical directives for the way in which Catholics should participate in the work of trying to help man through his present crisis, the "first things" were simply stated in a few obvious broad principles in the places where this was most relevant: beginning of the Constitution, beginning of various sections, and so on. It must be remembered that the Constitution is part of a whole, and the work of the Council fills a volume of nearly eight hundred pages in the edition I have. The "first things" are treated much more extensively in places like the Constitution on the Church and on Revelation. But in practice, with man in a position literally to destroy himself and his culture, I do not think that concern about saving him temporarily and giving him a chance to set his house in order is merely secondary.

It is for this reason that I cannot take a merely conservative position, though I see a great deal wrong and suspect about the progressive view and I do not find myself always able to speak its language. But I wonder if the traditional spiritual language of charity and mercy does not in fact demand to be put into action in these social forms in our new situation. But of course here we are in a realm where I cannot completely speak. I am not an economist or a politician.

In any case I really appreciate your letter. Doubtless it was my own fault if the book was not clear and gave the impression that this was just a matter of the "social gospel" over again. It is much more complex a problem than that.

Stated in the baldest terms, in my own situation, I meet the problems daily in this form: I can completely turn my back on the whole "world" and simply try to devote myself to meditation and contemplation, silence, withdrawal, renunciation, and so on. I spent at least twelve years of my monastic life with no further object than this. At the end of that time I began to see that this was insufficient and indeed deceptive. It was unreal. It could indeed create in me the impression that I was putting first things first and striving for sanctity. But I also learned in many ways that it was false and that the whole thing rested on a rather imaginary basis. I still devote most of my time to meditation, contemplation, reading—in fact I now give much more of my time to these things since I am living in solitude: but also I read a great deal more about what is happening and the common problems of the world I live in, not so much on the level of newspapers (I do not get the paper) or of magazines, still less radio or TV (I have barely seen TV once or twice in my life). But I do feel that if I am not in some way able to identify myself with my contemporaries and if I isolate myself so entirely from them that I imagine that I am a different kind of being, I am simply perpetrating a kind of religious fraud. I quite simply believe that I have to hear the voice of God mostly in the Bible and other writings, but in the crisis of this age, and I have to commit myself to a certain level of responsibility: in my case being a writer I have to be able to speak out and say certain things that may need saying, to the best of my knowledge and according to my conscience and to what seems to be the inspiration of the Holy Spirit. I realize the enormous difficulty of this, and have no illusion that it is easy to be a prophet, or that I must necessarily try to be one. But there are things I think I must say. In the case of the book about the Council Constitution, however, I am, I think, quite aware that what I was saying did not need to be said, at least by me, and I have decided that there is no point in having the book published here. It is not the kind of thing I am supposed to be doing.

In the long run, I think that is what you were trying to tell me in your letter, and I quite agree.

Thus you see that in the end we do meet, though I think there are genuine accidental differences in our viewpoint. I think you are simply more straightforwardly conservative than I am and that for you the conservative position does not present the difficulties that it does for me. You are fortunate, because your position is thus much simpler than mine can be, and it is easier for you to be quite definite on every point where I might have to hesitate and qualify. In fact there are many points that are to me uncertain, and I cannot say what I think about them.

June 4, 1967

To begin with, I am more and more convinced that *Redeeming the Time* is a superficial and inadequate book. I do, of course, believe still in the urgency of social change in places like South America, where, frankly, too many people are living in appalling conditions, brought on in many cases by "progress." In any event, this book is not being published anywhere else.

What really prompted me to write you today: I am reading a curious book called *Evolution and Christian Hope* by one Ernst Benz. Curious is not the word for parts of it. He has a chapter which justifies technological progress by the Bible and by ideas like God the potter framing his creatures on a potter's wheel. And he finds in Catholic medieval tradition (where the Victorines for instance speak of the "arts" in terms like Marco Pallis) warrant for the idea that "technology is a means of overcoming original sin." I thought that gem of modern thought should be shared with you. Fantastic, isn't it? Really, you are so very right. That is what we are facing now. I do not suggest that you read this book, it would shock you. But that particular chapter is so funny, in its own bizarre way, that you might dip into it there if the book ever comes your way. But I do not suppose it will, and do not encourage you to go looking for it.

I just thought I would send you these few badly typed lines as a sign of life and a reminder that I do very much appreciate all that you have to say, and that I am very aware of the ambiguities of the current Catholic position. I am frankly quite alienated from much of the thinking going on in my Church, on both sides, both conservative and "progressive."

To Mrs. Mycock

April 2, 1965

Your supposition that if I wrote that book (*The Seven Storey Mountain*) again today I would speak differently of Anglicans was both charitable and correct. My thought at the time of writing was hardly matured and I just said what came to mind, as people so often do, and more often did in those days. It is, unfortunately, so easy and so usual simply to compare the dark side of someone else's Church with the bright side of one's own. Thank heaven we are getting over that now, I hope.

Needless to say, I regret having offended you, and as to the injustice I may have done to Anglicans, there are, I hope, ways in which I have since been gradually repairing it.

As to the effect my book may have had on anyone's hopes of an "ultimate reunion of Christianity," all I can say is that we are all up against a huge accumulation of injustices, faux pas, errors, cruelties, iniquities, on every hand, and there can be no hope of reunion unless these are seen for what they are, admitted, accepted, understood, painfully atoned for, replaced by the opposites. Reunion is not something that will painlessly happen. It depends on us, and even to some extent on you, not to say me. The best we can do at this moment is to be prepared to understand and tolerate a great deal that is utterly regrettable, and try as far as possible not to add more to the accumulation. At the moment, I can hope for your forgiveness, and assure you of my own contrition and of my prayers.

To Richard Bass

April 5, 1965

I am happy to say a word to your fellow members of the Guild of St. Paul in your Parish: you leave me in the wide-open prairies as far as the choice of subject goes. So if the following does not fit . . .

One thing that affects us all, converts or cradle Catholics, most deeply at the present time, and is probably going to affect us more acutely in the near future, is that we are now going through some rapid and perhaps rather fundamental changes. I know that one of the things that helped bring me into the Catholic Church was the consciousness that the "vernacular" worship of the churches I had attended elsewhere was not the last word in religion as far as I was concerned. Hence it may seem strange that I am one of the few people in the monastery here that is still interested in retaining Latin for the monastic choir, and still very fond of Gregorian chant. I mention this only in passing, not to say that a convert is necessarily a "conservative" (I am certainly considered pretty radical by a lot of people) but to show that we have perspectives and a sense of values that can contribute something to the present discussions.

One thing that converts have is that they have had to accept the Church with a rather clear view of some of her shortcomings, culturally, etc., and they have learned that these things do not matter. When cradle Catholics suddenly become panicky about these shortcomings, there is surely no need for the panic to affect us. But we can work peacefully and calmly to make things better where we can.

In a word, what it comes down to is gratitude to the Lord, who has called us into His true Church, and a real love and devotion to the Church, to whom we owe everything. We can have this, and still not go in for foolish and servile routines of "triumphalism" in an effort to make out that there is never anything left to be desired. The Church is Christ, often a wounded and bleeding Christ, surely more often bleeding than glorious, in this age of history. Let us be very careful and faithful about avoiding everything that makes the wounds of division bleed more. I think that is going to be a very crucial point to keep in mind in the next few years. And let us meanwhile all pray for one another that we may be faithful and strong.

To Gabrielle Mueller

May 10, 1965

You seem to think that if I don't answer all the letters that come here it is because I just can't be bothered. Let's face the fact that if I tried to answer them I would scarcely have time to do anything else and my reasons for being here would no longer exist. I don't have the time or the right to try this.

I suppose I should not have been surprised that the Protestants out there are still putting out that kind of material against Catholics. Indeed, I have had a lot of meetings and discussions with Southern Baptists from the seminary in Louisville, and always got along very well with them. I thought the animosity was dying down. I find it quite possible to get across to them what the Church thinks about relics, etc., and also that this is of minimal importance anyway. Not that they accept it, but they see we are not totally nuts. They can begin to comprehend it as a social phenomenon that happened, so it happened.

The only thing I have to say about this material is that any set of arguments that is drawn up for purely intramural discussion, in order to convince those who are already convinced anyway, without any reference to what the other side is really thinking, is just a waste of time and a self-deception. That goes for Catholic arguments against Protestants as well as Protestant arguments against Catholics. This all adds up to absolutely zero and anyone who wants to waste his time with it has only himself to blame. Life is too short for that.

The only advice I can give you is to seek God with sincere faith and concentrate on the essentials: His redemptive and merciful love to all men, His goodness to you in particular, the indications of His will for you as shown in your own life, the grace of Baptism you have received, by which Christ dwells in your heart, and the fact that you have received the Holy Spirit, the Spirit of Love, which helps you to understand and love others in spite of their faults and limitations, in spite of the harm they may do to you. These are the realities of the Christian life and the Church will fit into this pattern if you seek first the Kingdom of God and can stand on your own feet. If you are dominated by what other people think, then obviously you will find it tough to live among a majority of non-Catholics. My honest opinion is that this business of trying to get people to cross the line from one Church into another is a sign that one no longer is really in touch with what the Holy Spirit is trying to tell the faithful in this age. I personally never encourage Protestants to become Catholics even when they seem to want to. I only go along with it when they are firmly convinced that they must themselves make the change. I have never, never tried to persuade any Protestant that his religion was an error. I hope I shall never do so. It seems to me to be simply a matter of common decency and respect for another person's conscience. There I stand.

To Dolores

November 16, 1966

It was very good to hear news from you after all these years, and to read your letter. How much time has gone by: and I can see that life in New York has not become simpler. You are right to be guided by compassion and humaneness. The big movements get lost in their smoke and nothing comes out of them but perhaps confusion and greater inhumanity: the individual contacts and gestures are the most telling and the most fruitful. So every little thing can be of great consequence. The question of addicts is frightfully urgent and will be more so.

I guess the Church is going to go over some bumps, and if the institution gets a bit shaken, I think I will be secretly glad. It needs to be. But the Holy Spirit will not sleep and neither will redemptive love. May they both wake and act in us always.

To Robert Walker Hovda

Robert Hovda of the Liturgical Conference in Washington, D.C., wrote to ask Merton to write some samples of petitions to be used in the Prayer of the Faithful in the new liturgy. He told Merton that they urgently needed sample petitions in "honest-to-God ENGLISH."

September 30, 1965

I have taken a stab at some petitions for the Prayer of the Faithful, as you suggested. I don't know whether anybody could pray them in that form, and I don't yet have in my ear any echo of what the prayer is supposed to sound like. But anyway these samples might give someone else an idea to go on. I think it would be great if people could make up their own prayers at the time of worship, but obviously there has to be some kind of decent form.

If you want some more, I will keep the project in mind. This is just a first attempt, and obviously I haven't had time to think about it. I have been busy with other work—like all the people you have asked.

Naturally, I would be very interested to hear how the project progresses.

In the samples you sent, I think the difficult one for Jewish believers ["For Jewish believers, and the manifest oneness of the people of God, let us pray to the Lord"] is not clear and may be a bit too sweeping, I mean from the Jewish point of view. I like the mark of Cain one ["For the unity of all the faithful, that the mark of Cain may no longer be upon us, let us pray to the Lord"] but maybe that would do better in a petition about the oppressed races.

One more suggestion for the prayer of the faithful: "For Tom Merton, the poor bastard, let us pray to the Lord" . . .

To Mr. Omloo

October 12, 1965

I might as well say quite bluntly that we live in an age which, from the point of view of religious faith, is a very difficult and confusing one. The religious reality of our time, as I see it, cannot be understood unless we take into account that it must, for some reason or other, be a period marked apparently by the "absence" of God. If then you are wondering why it is difficult for you to know how to approach the question of God, the answer is that it is difficult for everyone, and for some people it is simply impossible. I would say quite frankly that those who have the clearest and surest answers are probably the ones who are in some sense the least fortunate. Those of us who have chosen to seek God in the desert of the contemplative life have ample experience of the emptiness of so many slogans, proofs, declarations, and so on that are made about Him. On the other hand I must say that we also have learned in some measure to experience the great paradox that when He is "absent" He is in a way most "present." It seems to me that instead of stressing the fact that the existence of God can be rationally proved, scientifically, etc., etc.—which may be true but which is also very ambiguous—it is more helpful today to stress the existential approach to Him in "darkness" and in "dread." It is by the sense of what the world is without Him, and in His absence, that we come paradoxically to experience the radical presence in the very ground of our being. However, this awareness of God is not something that one can turn on like a light. On the contrary, it is a gift and is subject to some very exacting demands, one of which is the ability to be able to get along without "seeing clearly." This is something which many people can hardly do anymore. If you do not know what it is all about, but if you desire to understand it perhaps in some other way of your own, I think that if you will be patient, and continue to seek honestly some answer, you will find something unexpectedly in good time. But meanwhile, be patient with the enigma of life. We are not called upon to have answers to everything, and in giving up this futile expectation of being able to account for everything, we may find it easier in fact to come to terms with a life that is moving toward death and does not seem to acquire any sense. There is indeed a sense, but it remains for us to discover it personally and existentially. Official answers are not enough, as I am sure you agree. However, there is a religious tradition which does retain some relevance. You can find examples of this wisdom in the words of men like Jacques Maritain, for example. But in general religion has not learned the language of science, and I am afraid that I myself do not speak the language.

To Susie

November 1, 1965

I will try to answer your question in a few words. It seems to me that the law of love is written by nature itself in the heart of man. The command to love God and our fellow man does not come to us out of the blue somewhere. It is implied in our very being. For me, the experience of love is rooted first of all in a deep sense of the value of *being*. I think that if we once realize what it means that we *are*, and that we have received the gift of life, whereas we need not have come into being at all, and if we see that this is a pure gift of God who is Himself pure Being, then we begin to see that in making us "be" He has given us a participation in His own being, and called us also to be His own children. But it is by the additional gift of grace that He makes us aware of ourselves as His sons in Christ. It seems to me that if we learn to experience the meaning of these gifts in our own lives, there is no further problem about loving God and other men who share the same gifts and the same finalities. The reasons are not to be sought outside ourselves: if we learn to listen to our own hearts, and keep those hearts true in the faith of the Church, we will hear the answers.

To Rita

November 14, 1965

Thanks for your long letter. It was a good idea to write and express your feelings exactly as they are. The real notion of the Church depends on the possibility of frank exchange and a genuine quest for truth. For my part, in a day or two I will be at the anniversary of my baptism again (almost thirty years now) and the vivid memory of these days keeps alive in me gratitude for my faith and for the Church.

It is certainly true that when I joined the Catholic Church I was myself fed up with the superficial hymn-singing vernacular worship that I had grown up with, and deeply attracted to the austere, traditional Latin liturgy of Roman Catholicism. I was even more attracted to it in the monastery and I grew up in it as a monk, so that now when I see even the monks discarding Gregorian and Latin I realize that it is a great loss, for monks at least ought to be able to keep alive this ancient tradition so valid in itself.

But at the same time, Rita, I have been able to swallow my own reactions and have come to see how much real value and grace comes to the new generation from the changes. There is no question that their hearts are really in all this and that there will be a true deepening of faith. Hence I am willing to sacrifice my own feelings and enter into the spirit of the new, and I must admit that this sacrifice has been a grace for me too. After all, the heart of our religion is love and sacrifice of ourselves for the good of others. Naturally when we cannot see it as a good for anyone, then the sacrifice becomes impossible. And here is where the great temptation lies. And it is an awfully hard thing. Do not think I reprove you and condemn your ideas. I know too well how difficult a position is yours.

So be patient and have courage and realize the difficulty you are in. There is *no substitute* for the Sacraments of Holy Church when you can easily get to them. I pray that it may not become too hard for you.

In a time of crisis like this there will be many conflicts of opinions on every level, religion, politics, and everywhere. Whatever may happen let us remember that persons are more important than opinions and that what counts is the immortal soul, not this or that idea concerning what ought to be done, for example, in Vietnam. Let us always give the other side the benefit of the doubt and credit others with good will even when they seem to be heading in a very wrong direction.

For my part, though I tend to go along with the modern views and on some points am probably what you would call very radical, I still want above all to try to be a bridge builder for everybody and to keep communication open between the extremists at both ends. That is an awful task, and I don't expect to get anywhere. But let us all try to keep the lines of communication open, especially among fellow Catholics. So much depends on it.

To Mr. J. H. Richards

June 26, 1966

I have your long and interesting letter, and I will not attempt to answer it in all its details. I find I have rather a hard time keeping up with letters in the hermit life and it gets more and more difficult to write anything much and frankly I just cannot summon up much interest in putting forth arguments for Christianity. I will therefore not attempt to do this, and doubtless that is not what you want anyway.

Psychologically, since all the so-called "great religions" seek to marshal the deepest inner resources of man they have certain essential things in common, and their experiences are certainly very much alike. When you get on the metaphysical level the problem becomes immensely complicated because there just has not been enough work done in collating the different concepts and in trying to see where and where not they may correspond. And finally when it gets to be a strictly religious or even theological affair the whole thing is a thousand times worse. In a word, on the level of conceptual formulation and doctrine there will always be the utmost confusion. On the level of experience there need be little or none at all. Peace and tranquility for a Buddhist and for a Christian are pretty much alike as long as they are on the same psychic level.

The essential difference of approach between these two disciplines is, I think, this: The Buddhist gets into the metaphysical ground of being and is there liberated from accidentals and from contingencies, and the Christian regards Christ as the revelation of the hidden God beyond all being. Insofar as the Christian may also take a mystical and metaphysical approach he may tend to rejoin the Buddhist in his cultivation of an inner awareness of the "original self" and through this an awareness of God. Where the problem now comes is: Is the Christian *adding* something to the pure Void or is he just seeing the Void in a fuller and more inexplicable way? The Void as pure revelation? "He who sees me sees the Father." Eckhart may help you in this sort of thing, or John of the Cross. I don't know what to suggest except that you work it out for yourself as you go along. Perhaps the key is to see it in a slightly less purely intellectual way than the Buddhists usually do, and see the Void also as love and gift. Only it is not for you to say what you are going to see. In the end it is God who knows Himself in us whichever way you look at it, and we are not terribly important. In fact we are in the way. Yet we are not, and there is no point in saying we ought not to be there when in fact we are.

I would be interested in knowing what kind of meditation they teach in the monasteries of Burma. My acquaintance is mostly with Japanese Buddhism. If you can send me anything on Burmese Buddhism, especially meditation, I would be very grateful. I can in turn send you some of the things we put out here, but I do not know if they would interest you much. I wish you all the best in your solitary and meditative life.

Mr. Donn

September 23, 1966

I have received your book and the copy of *Israel's Anchorage* which you so kindly sent. I hope to read these with interest because I certainly agree with you that we must look to God's word for light by which to understand our action in history. I also agree that the Bible teaches us to regard the place of Israel in history as absolutely central, from the religious point of view. The Prophets have taught us that Israel is a great sign of the fidelity of God to His promises and His revealed plan for mankind.

It is in this spirit that I hope to read your book with profit as well as interest. In my daily recitation of the Psalms I find myself deeply united with your people, which I regard also as my own in a special way: we are traveling together in the desert.

To Katharine Champney

November 10, 1966

You ask a very relevant question which I probably cannot answer. If I assure you that I am only thinking as I go along, improvising maybe, you will understand that I am not really claiming to know much more about it all than you do and am certainly not in a position to clear up "problems" religious or otherwise with a wave of the hand. All I can say is that I think I am looking at it from a vantage point which is not yours and not that of your religious friends either. Whether I can make that comprehensible or not I don't know. But let me say at the outset: there are many reasons why I think the whole question of whether or not one is a believer has become an impossible one to handle—and whether or not it matters. Of course, in the abstract, it matters, it is crucial, it is *the* question, etc., etc. (at least I know the choice is presented that way). But in the concrete, historically, there has been so much noise and confusion and the whole thing has become so impossibly obscure (what with all the fighting and nonsense there has been) that, to my mind, anyone who has never had serious doubts has something the matter with him. You *should* doubt. When your friends say they think you are a believer they are paying you the compliment of saying you respect the truth enough to be honest about it, and if you can't see something you don't say you see it.

Now that is precisely it. That is precisely what I do too. Believing is not only *not seeing* but it is also a staunch refusal to say you see what you don't see. I was a non-believer until the day it dawned on me that the absolute void of nothingness in which I could not possibly see anything or hear anything was also the absolute fullness of everything. This was not so much a religious insight as a metaphysical or Zen-like one, and the religious implications followed later, without changing the essentially negative view (since there cannot possibly be an adequate idea of God). To put it crudely, your "unnamed something" without ceasing to be pure Nothing suddenly ran over me like a truck. The trouble with saying this is that it may just confuse things more: so let me make it clear that I am not suggesting that *you* have to wake up one morning feeling that way. I am just saying that this is the way it is metaphysically (being is structured like this) and some people may have a special capacity for realizing it, which maybe I have, being a poet, a person able to cope with religious myth, familiar with religious and literary traditions, etc., etc., etc. But that doesn't mean anything, and it does not change the fact that if you don't see it, it doesn't matter.

"Alone." But I am utterly alone in the Void. God is not an "object" I am "with" and it is useless to listen to "hear him"—just as useless as trying to see the eyes you see with. You just see, and everything falls into place. Again, if you don't, it doesn't matter. You obviously have some other way of getting at it. Your formulation "un-named something that at once binds us together . . ." is the same as the "ground of my-our-being." It is a philosophical rather than religious insight, okay.

Now, you will be irritated with me and think I have got away with the dirty trick I promised I would not play: that I have insidiously robbed you of your unbelief. That I have elevated you in spite of yourself to the cozy level of the believers. No, I have not. You are an unbeliever. The only thing is that I am also: but in a different way. You will come back at me, and of course if you read some of my (early) books you will point out that I have given evidence of a whole superstructure of religious idea, meditations, experiences, and so on. What people don't seem to notice is that in the same breath as I say all these things I also say "but that is not it."

So the position where I am is different from yours only in this: that I am perfectly happy with traditional religious concepts, I can use them, I see how far they go, and—I also see that they really go nowhere. No matter what you say, no matter what you experience, no matter how often you "hear" God, etc., etc., it is all zero. It is nothing. It is misleading. It is a bum steer, except for those who understand it in the right way. In the end we all get back more or or less to where you are in the first place, "un-named something . . ." Of course there is Christ. But "He emptied Himself taking the form of a servant . . . the death of the Cross . . ." This is the same reduction of the whole thing to zero, to unnamed something, you don't know what it is, you have no control over it, you can't call out and be answered at will, you have no right to expect an answer anyway ("you" now means me too). In a word, the fact that I am a believer does not give me in any way the kind of advantage you assume: that I am entitled to voices and consolations which are denied you.

All I am entitled to is my own particular direction, which is a straight line into the void and the wilderness without having to look over my shoulder and see whether anyone else is coming along. I know plenty of people are coming along: people like you, who are in the same wilderness, but who can't quite understand it in the same way. And honestly, I don't think it matters. The "consolations of religion" are something that in your concrete case, you are just as well without—if they are going to mislead you into thinking you have got something when you have them.

That is my quarrel with religious people. They are selling answers and consolations. They are in the reassurance business. I give you no reassurance whatever except that I know your void and I am in it, but I have a different way of understanding myself in it. It is not that much more delightful. But it does to me make a great deal of sense—for me. I will say this, that it is to me after all reassuring to be able to run into Zen people and Moslem masters and so on and realize we understand each other perfectly. And I hasten to say that you don't have to feel all that alone either. Incidentally, in an earlier and less chastened version of that article I said that really I felt much more at home with unbelievers than with believers. In a sense I do. But I can't that easily evade the embarrassment that Church people cause in me perpetually.

So, friend Katharine, I am not Father Merton inside the warm Church calling you to come and sit by the fire of positive thinking or something. I am out in the cold with you because (forgive the flip saying) God is where He isn't. And maybe that's where the Church is too (when all the miters are off and the vestments are hung up in the closet). I won't run on anymore, but I think I have said enough to make clear that I think the whole business of faith and the message of faith is in process of finding a whole new language—or of shutting up altogether. Hence the answer to your question: if God does not speak to you it is not your fault and it is not His fault, it is the fault of the whole mentality that creates the impression that He has to be constantly speaking to people. Those who are the loudest to affirm they hear Him are people not to be trusted. But nevertheless, there is a way of understanding that non-hearing is hearing. Maybe it is all too subtle.

To John Hunt

John Hunt was senior editor of The Saturday Evening Post. *In December 1966 he invited Merton to write an article on monasticism for the "Speaking Out" column. As the following letter indicates, Merton had other ideas. The article was never written.*

December 18, 1966

Thanks for your letter of the 13th. All right, I am still open to all kinds of suggestions and even have one of my own. It could be seen as a variant of the other one, and even comes close to that other suggestion on the love of God. Let's see how I can put it in a few words.

Say an article "Speaking Out for the Inside." An attempt to make people realize that life can have an interior dimension of depth and awareness which is systematically blocked by our habitual way of life, all concentrated on externals. The poverty of a life fragmented and dispersed in "things" and built on a superficial idea of the self and its relation to what is outside and around it. Importance of freedom from the routines and illusions which keep us subject to things, dependent on what is outside us. The need to open up an inner freedom and vision, which is found in relatedness to something in us which we *don't really know*. This is not just the psychological unconscious. It is much more than that. Tillich called it the ground of our being. Traditionally it is called "God," but images and ideas of the deity do not comprehend it. What is it? (Something about the God-is-dead pitch would come in here.)

The real inner life and freedom of man begin when this inner dimension opens up and man lives in communion with the unknown within him. On the basis of this he can also be in communion with the same unknown in others. How describe it? Impossible to describe it. Is it real? People like William James "scientifically" verified its reality at least as a fact of experience in many lives. The appetite for Zen, etc., reflects a need for this. What is Zen? What about LSD? What can one do? And with some observations on the tragic effects of *neglect* on this: possibly our society will be wrecked because it is completely taken up with externals and has no grasp on this inner dimension of life.

That is rather tough, and it will demand a lot of your readers. But I am willing to tackle something like this, and don't promise to write down to anyone. My suggestion is: frankly admit the toughness and unpalatableness of the subject and treat it as it is. Some may be hit hard, most will remain indifferent.

To Marie Byles

Merton is writing to a scholar in Japanese religions who wrote him from Cheltenham, New South Wales, Australia.

January 9, 1967

Your kind letter of October 20th took a good long time to reach me via India, and I only got it a couple of days ago. Thanks for your favorable remarks about my Gandhi book.

I have not read anything about Tenko San, but what you say of him sounds interesting and I shall look forward to learning more when your book appears.

You ask about the Catholic idea of holy obedience. What you are really interested in is evidently the ancient ascetic idea of obedience which goes back to the Gospels, the Sermon on the Mount, and so on, is exemplified by the saints, and is analogous to the perfect obedience, docility, and so forth found in other religious ideals. The idea is fundamentally the same: to become free from the need to assert one's ego, to be liberated from the desire to dominate others, to renounce selfish demands, and so on. Ultimately the idea is that if you renounce your own will you will be guided directly by God and moved by Him in everything. Hence in the Rule of St. Benedict it is said that the monk will obey not only his Abbot but also all his brethren insofar as this does not conflict with obedience to the Abbot and to God. The real purpose of obedience is to obey God and give one's will to Him.

This idea of obedience is somewhat ambiguous in the later legalistic context that it got into, when the religious Orders got highly organized and became big impersonal structures run by bureaucracies. The ascetic idea was pressed into the service of a different kind of ideal, and "blind obedience" was stressed as an ideal since it meant the subject simply submitted to authority and became a cog in a machine. This of course has led to a perverse idea of obedience (ultimately Eichmann is the exemplification of all that it can lead to) and in fact has brought great discredit upon the authentic notion of obedience. So at present people are confused, struggling with these ambiguities. I think that what is needed is certainly a return to the pure Gospel idea, as far as possible, in a new context. How far this can be done is another matter. The confusions remain our big problem in the Catholic Church today, I am afraid. As long as the notion of obedience is implicated in an impersonal power system it will be corrupted by the very things it is supposed to liberate us from—worldliness, selfishness, ambition, and so on.

Are there still copies available of your book on Gautama the Buddha? I might be able to do a short review for the magazine of our Order if I could have one. I do not promise, but in any case I would like to read the book. I am sending you my own book on Chuang Tzu.

To Maseo Abe

Merton writes to a Zen scholar in Kyoto, Japan.

May 12, 1967

Just after I had sent you my last letter, the copies of *Japanese Religion* arrived here. I read your articles with the greatest interest, and I ought to have written my comments when everything was fresh in my mind, but I was not able to do so at that time. Now, I suppose that, ironically, this may cross with a letter from you. But in any case I would like to jot down a few impressions.

1. In discussing Christianity you take Barth as more or less normative. That is not unreasonable, since Barth is an uncompromisingly Biblical theologian and certainly takes a characteristically "Christian" stand upon the revealed Christian message of salvation. In other words Barth is clear-cut: indeed uncompromising. But precisely because he is so clear-cut, it seems to me that he makes dialogue between Christianity and non-Christian religions very difficult, since he himself is hostile to such dialogue. Or at any rate his teaching sharply divides the Christian revelation against any other form of religion. You are perhaps right in tackling the problem of communication at its difficult point, and not where it is easy. But I feel that at this precise point there is not much hope of real progress. One remains blocked.

2. I agree with those who suggested an approach that would favor a consideration of Christian mystical experience as a meeting ground. Obviously, since Daisetz Suzuki studied Eckhart in this light and understood him so well, and since the other Rhenish mystics, the Flemish mystics, St. John of the Cross, etc., offer rich material, the dialogue here would be worthwhile. However, it is true that the mystics are not regarded as

characteristically Christian, and the dialogue would be held ambiguous by "the Churches" except perhaps the Catholic Church, which is friendly to mysticism, and certain scholars among Protestants.

3. I think that one ought also to consider the level of *ontology* (though some would hold there is no such thing). I think the dialogue between Christianity and Buddhism will be most fruitful on the plane not of abstract metaphysical systems but on the plane of what I would call metaphysical experience—that is to say, the basic intuition of being the direct grasp of the ground of reality, which is essential to a true and lived metaphysics. I repeat that I am not concerned with purely abstract metaphysical systems. The basic metaphysical intuition is close to the kind of religious intuition which opens out into mysticism. On this level I think we come very close to what Buddhism is saying. On this level Zen seems to me something very close to home, very alive, very helpful, indeed necessary. In Christian metaphysical-and-mystical experience there is something very close to Zen.

4. Furthermore, I believe that exploration of this area would also open up a possibility of understanding with those modern atomic physicists who seem to be developing quite new insights into the structure of matter: men like Bohr and Heisenberg. I am not a scientist, so I am not qualified to judge in this area, but I find it most challenging.

5. Finally, there is another area that would be very interesting to investigate—namely, the Islamic mysticism and metaphysics of the Sufis, as a bridge between East and West. I am at present reading a most revealing book by a Japanese scholar, Toshihiko Izutsu, comparing the Sufi mystic Ibn Arabi with Taoists. The first volume only, on Ibn Arabi, is available, I believe. Others will follow which will show the resemblances. This is very important. If you do not know it already I recommend it to you, and it is easily accessible to you, being published by Keio University. Now, you may have received my new book, *Mystics and Zen Masters*. It is very sketchy and imperfect, but it may perhaps have some useful material in it. If you do not know the treatise on the "Cloud of Unknowing" I think the remarks in my book will indicate that it would interest you. A friend of mine [William Johnston] has written a study of it with some reference to Zen [*The Mysticism of the Cloud of Unknowing*, 1967]. It ought to appear soon. I wrote a preface to it. I will send you a copy of the book if and when I get one.

I cannot prolong this letter, though there are many more things I would like to share with you. I hope your health is better, and I look forward to hearing from you when you have a moment. I wish it were possible for me to travel. I would dearly love to come to Japan and meet those who are keeping alive the best traditions of Zen in its most serious and basic aspect. I am unable to be enthusiastic about the superficial and popular Zen craze which passes for Zen in this country.

To a Priest

May 20, 1967

Sorry to have let your poignant letter go without answer for so long. I should have got right down to it then and there, but you know how it is. So many immediate demands, and I hate to answer a letter like that from the top of my head.

Of course now we all have very much the same problem. There is so much that is sick and false in our institutions. Submission is canonized and all opposition is suspect. There is a machinery that grinds everyone to powder. Then, as you say, the effect is that when we finally open our mouths we are so wrought up that we explode, and that, too, is held against us. From my own experience, I would suggest several things:

1. No point in direct confrontation when it is hopeless. You don't have any obligation to speak out if it just means you will have your face kicked in—except in an extreme case. In the ordinary routine struggles, silence is preferable, and then go ahead and do what you have to do without asking. Just do it, and let them figure it out afterwards.

2. Things are never quite as hopeless as they appear to us in our moments of crisis. Unexpectedly a good Bishop appears or someone open-minded is on the scene when needed and things just clear up, at least to some extent. Or you get support. If you have been patient, and stuck to your principles without making a federal case out of them, your turn will come.

3. In things like the wrestling with censors, I have always stood up for my rights and for my work. Often decisions against me have been reversed when I least expected. (A censor declared that *The Seven Storey Mountain* should be put on the shelf for twenty years. Fortunately it had already been accepted by the publisher . . .)

4. Seek some company with like-minded people and work together with them. That gives a better understanding of problems.

5. In ordinary conversation with people who are suffering, the best thing is to be quite frank about abuses and injustices and not to defend what is moribund and indefensible. Try to be as realistic about it as possible, and help as much as you can, without raising hopes of an impossible solution.

If you are frank in expressing your contrary opinion and yet accept obedience when it is imposed, they will soon come to respect you and will not use you as a stooge, should they be tempted to do so.

To Tim Scimeca

July 11, 1967

Thanks for your letter. I wish I were able to write an adequate reply, but it is just not possible, I have too much work and cannot handle correspondence properly.

Problems about the Bible often arise from our expecting the wrong things from it. It is not a manual of the spiritual life but a very mysterious record of events which are not always explained or explainable. A lot of it seems to me irrelevant, in my bad moments, especially in the Old Testament, and that is perfectly normal, I guess.

As to your problem about Christ: it comes from imposing on the Bible the demands of a non-Biblical Christology, and expanding nature. I have no explanation of how He was able to feel such dereliction, but the fact that He did so does not trouble me because it reminds me that He shared a lot of my own kind of feelings and was therefore closer to me: is closer. Each one has to work those things out in his own life, I guess. The Bible does not pretend to explain everything, and we have to be content to let a lot go without being able to figure it out logically. That does not mean there are not other, deeper ways of understanding, which are granted in response to prayer and patience, I suppose.

To Richard Rousseau

Merton was invited to a meeting with Cardinal Koenig, Archbishop of Vienna, who was head of the Vatican Secretariat for Non-believers. The meeting was to be held in Fairfield, Massachusetts.

August 6, 1967

I have taken up the question of possible meeting with Cardinal Koenig, have been through the mill with my Abbot, the decision is final and it turns out (as I expected) to be "No." I do not know if he is writing to you about it, giving his reasons. All that I can add is that I am sure there are plenty of other Superiors in the Order who would have said "Yes" and that these are not all renegades.

It might conceivably have been possible for me to join you in a state of apostasy or temporary flight, or perhaps having made my way to Fairfield at the point of a gun. However, as I am getting on in years and have become addicted to relative inertia, I can only send my apologies instead. What it amounts to is, as I interpret the message, a firm determination on the part of my Superiors to see that I am confined to writing and that I do not also get involved in more direct contacts. Whether or not this is in accord with the spirit of Vatican II is something I will not attempt to surmise here. I will go along as best I can with old-fashioned obedience and the stoicism appropriate to one in a period of change when the machinery of change grinds a bit rustily.

Seriously, I wish you a happy and fruitful session with the Cardinal [Koenig] and trust you will convey to him my very sincere regrets.

To Aly Abdel Ghani

Aly Abdel Ghani, employee of the Banque de Port-Saïd in Alexandria, Egypt, wrote to Merton to tell him of the pleasure he derived from reading The Seven Storey Mountain. *He chided Merton for withdrawing from the world. He said, "So I hope, Father, that you will be more useful to humanity, try to speak, to write, to keep us out of misery and wars, perhaps God helps you and makes people hear your voice."*

October 31, 1967

Thank you for your kind letter. I understand your reaction to the idea of total isolation, and I assure you that my isolation is not so absolute that I do not have some contact with others. Sometimes I am able to meet with others and discuss religious or human problems, and occasionally I correspond or at least answer letters. I have friends and contacts in many parts of the world. In a way my retirement permits this, since if I were engaged in an active life here I would be taken up with so many material responsibilities that I would have time only for my immediate surroundings. But of course it is true that my contacts with the outside world are limited.

I am very familiar with the traditions of Sufism, and have of course read much of the Holy Qur'an. I have read Avicenna, or some of his writing, and very much like others, such as Ibn-Arabi, Ibn-Abbad (of Morocco), the Persian Rumi, etc. I wish I knew Arabic, as I could read more in the original. Some of the Sufi masters did live alone at least for certain periods of time. The practice of at least temporary retreat is held in honor in Sufism.

Though I am not always able to answer letters or to reply in full, I appreciate your kindness and assure you of a common interest and concern about the deepest realities of life: they all concern the salvation of man and man's total obedience to God. In this we can deeply agree. May He bless us all and teach us His Holy Way.

To Dick

March 28, 1968

Some time ago I did a study on the question of "the Humanity of Christ" in Christian mysticism. It is a standard problem. Obviously as long as there is a subject-object relationship and a conceptual and imaginary representation of Christ as object of knowledge, you get a devotional and affective relationship, not the kind of "emptiness" of a Zen experience. Hence two kinds of Christian mysticism, one centered in a religious eros and a deeply personal union with Christ and another in a totally different dimension which is more like Zen. If this second is to be Christian there must be "Christ" in it, but here it is about the same sort of thing as Buddha in Zen. It is not so much Buddha as object, but Buddha as subject. This is true of Christianity too, it is not Christ that we see but Christ who sees in us: this is based on a theology of the Spirit, of transformation and awakening which is very like Zen. But of course as soon as you break it down again into a doctrinal explanation, it gets back into the subject-object formulation. But that isn't the last word on it.

I haven't time to write more . . . You'd find some light on this in the writings of St. John of the Cross . . .

To Water A. Weisskopf, Roosevelt University

April 4, 1968

Thank you for your warm letter and for the offprints. I am most happy to be in contact with you and to find in your thought such clear expression of things which have preoccupied me for some time. To my mind, the really hopeful thing today—perhaps the only hopeful thing— is that some men like yourself with *scientific* training are stating the urgent need for a restoration of balance, a dialectical, holistic recovery of man's entire self as a part of nature and as a contemplative as well as active being: *homo faber* and *homo sapiens, homo ludens* and *homo contemplans,* above all *homo amans.* And not just man the mechanic, the moneymaker, and the warmonger. The essay of yours that struck me the most was the excellent one on "Repression and the Dialectics of Industrial Civilization." Indeed it struck me so forcibly that while reading it I was possessed by the idea—or the temptation—of editing a collection of essays along these lines by various people. Let me share with you this idea.

You may or may not realize that in the current renewal of religion in the Catholic Church, in ecumenism and so on, there is a radically "secular" orientation which has much that is good and necessary about it, and which is by no means a simple phenomenon. But in many minds, especially in America, this means an exaggerated emphasis precisely on the technological, the sociological, the economic, and a very aggressive, almost bitter repudiation of the "interior," the contemplative dimensions of existence. This of course has a basis in history: a truncated and short-sighted kind of "contemplative life" has been de facto what has been encouraged, against a background of a sort of ecclesiastical politics, in convents and monasteries. Thus unfortunately the contemplative and spiritual side of Catholicism has been associated too intimately with the conservative, authoritarian, repressive and hierarchical element in the

Church. A purification is called for. But in the process, I am afraid these people will simply rush to the other extreme, into a kind of naive activism which is, in reality, a somewhat guilty compensation for being so late in catching up with the modern scientific world. Well, the point of my book would be this: to assemble essays by people all or most of whom would be non-Catholic or non-Christian, or at least not obviously associated with the Church—men of science, analysts, anthropologists, etc., who would say, as you have said, that we are repressing a most vital element in our lives in order to promote a meaningless economic development, and in the end this may prove suicidal. Many names spring to mind. I am sure Fromm would be interested. Mircea Eliade, too. I have friends in Japan and a Vietnamese Buddhist who would probably participate. Then there is a very interesting Persian psychoanalyst, Reza Arasteh, and another Persian scholar. One could assemble a collection of most unusual interest. Perhaps you might know a few people who would otherwise not occur to me and who would fit into such a project. They would not necessarily have to write anything new. For instance, your essay on "Repression" could fit in. But perhaps you are already using that in your own book. The material would have to be articles that had never appeared in book form.

Now to return to your letter.

I think you have been remarkably perceptive in asking whether the Marcusian tie-up between eros and technological society is not really a blind alley. Personally, I agree with you that one must hope for a dialectical working out of the tensions between the forces of technology and those of love within the situation that we have for better or for worse. I certainly do not feel that it is realistic to say that technological culture must be destroyed and an aesthetic and contemplative one substituted for it. Some of the things I have written (in fact quite a few of them) take such a negative view of the technical society that I have been accused of being Manichaean. I'll send you a book with the essay "Rain and the Rhinoceros," which has led most people to believe that I live in the woods out of misanthropy and disgust with the "wicked world."

Actually, I would say that my viewpoint is neither the one nor the other. It is basically *eschatological*—but this must be explained in a fully Christian sense. Eschatology as I understand it is not simply an "end of the world" belief, but, in the light of the New Testament, a belief in the decisive and critical breakthrough in man's destiny. We are on the verge of this breakthrough, in fact it has begun. But we still do not know what form it will take, on the surface of history. Still less can we really *plan* it to come out according to some limited set of ideas. Whatever is happening, is happening both with us and without us, in us and beyond us. Our errors and our luck, our good and evil acts, our honesty and our lies, our love and hate, all our injustices and failures enter into the picture. None of it can be repudiated because it is all there. Your idea that the effort to repudiate part of it that we don't like only gets us "in deeper" is exactly what I mean by "judgment" in the religious sense. But my "eschatology" says that underlying all of it, in the deepest depths that we cannot possibly see, lies an ultimate ground in which all contradictories are united and all come out "right." For a Christian this ultimate ground is personal— that is to say, it is a ground of freedom and love, not a simple mechanism or process. But since we are all in potentially *conscious* contact with this deep ground (which of course exceeds all conscious *grasp*) we must try to "listen" to what comes out of it and respond to the imperatives of its freedom. In doing so, we may not be able to direct the course of history according to some preconceived plan, but we will be in harmony with the dynamics of life and history even though we may not fully realize that we are so.

The important thing then is to restore this dimension of existence. My own ostensible repudiation of "worldly life" is not a program. It is simply an assertion that I find that life tedious and stupid, and in fact a waste of time, and that I prefer to live in a way that I find more fruitful. Of course I can waste time and become inauthentic here too, but some- how—there is this at least to say for it—it is never boring. I am afraid that the routines of social existence just bore me to extinction.

Nevertheless, there are all sorts of good things happening in the "social" framework, things that do break through the cadres of routine and no nonsense. One of them is this "Forum" which enables us to exchange ideas like this. I do hope we can keep in touch, and above all I hope you will think about the proposed collection of essays on this subject. It could be very important, and this is the time for it. Do please let me know if you have any ideas on it. Meanwhile I will send some offprints and tear sheets with this letter, and a book under separate cover.

To Eugene Setiore

January 16, 1968

Many thanks for the buttons and all the other cultural symbols and above all for the letter. In answer to the latter: yes, there is a complex problem of communication and it has many aspects. Usually I get through better to "worldly" people (hippies, etc.) than to believers. But I am myself developing in a direction quite other than that of most Catholic writers at the moment. Hence when people see me speeding by in the "wrong direction" it does not seem a bit disconcerting. However, let me give a brief and partial attempt at an illustration of what is involved.

In the myths of some primitive cultures, notably some of the North American Indian cultures, you find a double stratum: on one hand an esoteric mythology which tends to explain the normal levels of culture and existence. On this esoteric level, man is represented as well endowed with cultural means for assuring his survival, his meaning, and his sal- vation. Civilization is presented as good, holy, sacred. Then there is also an esoteric level in which man is represented in his existential nakedness, helplessness, loneliness, and in which the ambiguities and shortcomings of his culture are emphasized. The chaotic, the evil, and the mendacious in cultural establishments are made clear. But then other, deeper initiations are proposed and man discovers his helplessness in order to transcend it with the help of the spirits and gods. In so doing he transcends the limits of his present culture, renews himself, and in so doing renews his culture.

At the present time, Catholics are sloughing off a decayed remnant of "Catholic culture" or cultural Catholicism in which a formal "unworldliness" is nothing better than an obsolete convention. To do this they must turn to the "secular world," etc., etc. But in the secular world there are others who confront the insufficiency of the secular and technological culture itself and other problems that go with this. And what they are tending toward is not merely renewal but even revolution. In any case they profoundly question the cultural system which others take for granted as a kind of sacred and perfect structure, an image of definitive achievement, a place where man has finally arrived (of course where he also begins to move on).

Without going any further into this, my task lies on the esoteric side of things, and what I have to say is largely eschatological. Naturally it grates on the ears of those who find cultural patterns are assuring and in some sense definitive. I don't accuse you of doing that, because like most people you are caught in between the two. What is necessary is not that one or the other prevail, but that both remain in dialogue. (Primitive cultures preserved their balance precisely by this kind of dialogue.)

To Agnes Smith

April 28, 1968

I got your letter, and believe me, I understand. I feel very close to you because recently I have been doing some work on the Indians in the Northwest—working on the Ghost Dance movement back fifty or sixty years ago. I think I have some idea of the suffering and bewilderment of your people out there.

You ask for answers: the big thing is to recognize the questions. Before we can find the cure we have to know the sickness. There are so many people running around with their "answers," trying to impose them on everybody. That is part of the sickness. The sickness is in history. The sickness is in this country itself, in the injustices committed against the Negro, the Indian, against the wildlife of the country, the beautiful nature God made. Yet the white man did not fully realize what he was doing. There is at work in man an awful force for destruction. Man is a self-destructive being, and when he tries to make himself happy he still destroys himself. Drink is one of the ways. Drink hit the Indian so hard

340 / THOMAS MERTON

because he was not used to it like the white man. The sickness of the white man has affected the Indian disastrously.

Just as the Negro had been injured in his sense of his own worth, so too with the Indian. You Indian people have to recover a real sense of your own value, and not see yourself through the eyes of the white man. You must see yourselves as God made you, not as the white man transformed and degraded you. You have to believe in yourselves again as really fine people, even though in the white man's world you have a hard time and are pushed down to the bottom of the ladder. This is not your fault, it is the white man's sin.

In my opinion Martin Luther King has a message and an example for the Indian as well as for everybody else. He understood better than anyone that the whole country is sick, and that the oppressed people must not remain just passive. They must resist with dignity and love, realizing they have a mission and a power to help redeem the country by love that is also firm resistance and working for rights. Unfortunately the violent way can bring great harm, and the worst people for violence are the whites themselves.

You say you have a sense of bearing the sufferings of others. We all do. There is great sin in this country, and some people have to bear it. It is Christ who alone can give us strength to do this well, with love. We cannot afford to be just passive and negative. We have to try to make things better, by love, by awareness, by helping people to remedy their lot. I wish I knew definitely what needs to be done in each case. But these are the general principles. God bless you.

And all the hopes that seem to founder in the shadows
*   of the cross*
Wake from a momentary sepulchre, and they are blinded
*   by their freedom!*

FROM *Figures for an Apocalypse*

Sit finis scribendi, non finis legendi.

Acknowledgments

The publication of this final volume of the Merton letters offers me the opportunity of expressing my gratitude to Robert Giroux, James Laughlin, and Mrs. Frank O'Callaghan III, the trustees of the Merton Legacy Trust, for giving me the happy opportunity of overseeing the publication of the Merton letters. I want also to express my appreciation to Anne McCormick, secretary of the Trust, for her always gracious way of expediting communication with the Trust, as well as for her friendship and encouragement. I owe a big word of thanks to Dr. Herbert Mason, who not only made his own letters from Merton available to me but was also chiefly instrumental in enabling me to obtain the fascinating letters of Merton to Louis Massignon. He also gave his generous help in interpreting the background of these letters. I am indebted to Louis Massignon's son, Dr. Daniel Massignon, who at great inconvenience to himself located Merton's letters to his father. I am grateful to Ms. Evelyn Douglas, who transcribed the very interesting correspondence between Fr. Louis and Fr. Raymond. I express also my thanks to Sr. Sienna Cameron, S.S.J., for her typing of much of this manuscript, and to Sr. Bernadine Frieda, S.S.J., and Sr. Veronica Frieda, S.S.J., for their help in compiling the index of this volume.

It is most appropriate that I express my gratitude, too, to my colleagues in the editing of the letters, namely, Dr. Robert Daggy, Brother Patrick Hart, and Dr. Christine Bochen, not only for their able editing of Volumes II, III, and IV, but also for their help, advice, and encouragement in my editing of Volume V.

Finally, and perhaps most of all, I want to pay tribute to Robert Giroux, who over these twelve years has brought care, loving attention, and rich insight to the editing of these five volumes of Merton letters. His guidance has been a crucial factor in bringing this work to its completion and I cannot thank him enough for the generous support and direction he has given me as editor. It is indeed an honor to have him as a friend.

It only remains to send this volume on its way with the hope that it will help many readers to understand more clearly how Thomas Merton through his writings remains a bold and courageous witness to freedom.

Index